HISTORICAL PERSPECTIVES
ON BUSINESS ENTERPRISE
SERIES

Mansel G. Blackford and K. Austin Kerr

Editors

HISTORICAL PERSPECTIVES ON BUSINESS ENTERPRISE SERIES
Mansel G. Blackford and K. Austin Kerr
Editors

Henry E. Huntington and the Creation of Southern California
William B. Friedricks

*Eagle-Picher Industries: Strategies for Survival
in the Industrial Marketplace, 1840–1980*
Douglas Knerr

*Daniel Willard and Progressive Management
on the Baltimore & Ohio Railroad*
David M. Vrooman

MAKING
IRON AND
STEEL

Independent Mills in Pittsburgh, 1820–1920

John N. Ingham

OHIO STATE UNIVERSITY PRESS • *Columbus*

Library of Congress Cataloging-in-Publication Data

Ingham, John N.
    Making iron and steel : independent mills in Pittsburgh, 1820–1920
/ John N. Ingham.
        p.   cm.   —(Historical perspectives on business enterprise
series)
    ISBN: 978-0-8142-5330-4
    1. Iron industry and trade—Pennsylvania—Pittsburgh—History.
2. Steel industry and trade—Pennsylvania—Pittsburgh—History.
I. Title. II. Series
HD9518.P57I54   1991
338.4'76691'0974886—dc20   91–11199
                                                           CIP

The paper in this book meets the guidelines for permanence and
durability of the Committee on Production Guidelines for Book
Longevity of the Council on Library Resources. ∞

9 8 7 6 5 4 3 2 1

for Lynne

CONTENTS

PREFACE

WHEN I first began studying the steel industry as a graduate student a quarter of a century ago, one thing was clear to me: the industry was indisputably "big business." Certainly some, like Carnegie and U.S. Steel, were far bigger than others, but even "Little Steel" companies like Jones and Laughlin (where I had worked in the mill one long, hot summer in the mid-1960s) were massive affairs. What one found, I was convinced, were steel firms that were big, bigger, and biggest, but none, or at least few of those that I was dealing with, could really be considered "small business." Small businesses, after all, were "mom and pop" convenience stores or, if they were in the manufacturing segment, were tiny affairs producing for a local market with a small work force and rudimentary plant and technology.

Over the years, I gradually—very gradually—evolved a new perspective on the industry. It became more and more clear to me that many of these large firms, with their intimidating plant structures, were small businesses in virtually every practical respect. As such, although they were hardly corner store affairs, they diverged radically from the principal outlines of big business developed by Alfred D. Chandler, Jr., and others. Viewing them as small, or at least smaller, businesses allowed me to see these iron and steel firms in a new light, opened up a perspective on American business that is just beginning to be studied in some detail, and particularly created a fundamentally different image of the steel industry than that which has dominated the literature. This book, then, looks at a different type of steel manufacturer than we usually encounter in the pages of academic accounts. He is neither the swashbuckling robber baron entrepreneur of the ilk of Andrew Carnegie or Charles Schwab nor the cool, calculating professional manager and bureaucrat found in the pages of Chandler. The iron and steel men encountered here (there were no women running Pittsburgh mills) were independent businessmen whose mills generally were not absorbed into larger consolidations. Producing specialized goods for niche markets, they seldom developed the intricate organizational hierarchies characteristic of the largest steel firms and generally took a very different approach to labor relations. They remained masters of the mill well into the twentieth century.

When someone works on a project as long as I have, he or she comes to depend on many people for his growth and development. First of all, I owe my principal intellectual debt to Samuel P. Hays of the University of Pittsburgh, who served as my adviser in graduate school and has provided leadership by example for me since that time. Similarly, David Montgomery, in whose course in labor history at the University of Pittsburgh I first encountered the iron and steel industry, was a source of inspiration. Edward J. Davies, formerly a graduate student at Pitt and presently at the University of Utah, has provided insight into business relationships and elites for me, read this entire manuscript in a much earlier form, and been a strong source of encouragement. Similarly, Don Davis of the University of Ottawa has provided me with the benefit of his trenchant but judicious criticism and has often served as a lone Canadian voice expressing an understanding of what I was trying to do in my writings. Michael Wayne, my colleague at the University of Toronto, did not always understand much about the steel industry but was also a source of encouragement and friendship during discouraging times.

Bruce Leslie of State University of New York at Brockport, Laurel McDowell of the University of Toronto, W. Edward Muller of the University of Pittsburgh, Naomi Lamoreaux of Brown University, and W. Burton Folsom of Murray State University read all or part of various drafts of the manuscript and provided powerful criticism and much-needed encouragement. Austin Kerr and Mansel Blackford, both of Ohio State University, as editors of this series were unfailing in their encouragement of my work, and both made a number of extremely helpful suggestions. I am also highly indebted to an anonymous reader at OSU Press, who read the manuscript with great sensitivity and acumen, making a number of critical suggestions that I endeavored to follow as far as I was able. Alex Holzman, acquisitions editor at OSU Press, was a model of professionalism mixed with compassion when besieged with my requests for more time to make changes in the manuscript. I would also like to thank the staff of the manuscript department, Baker Library, Graduate School of Business, Harvard University; Frank Zabrosky and David L. Rosenberg at the Archives for an Industrial Society, Hillman Library, University of Pittsburgh; and the staffs of the Pennsylvania Room and Science and Technology Room at the Carnegie Public Library of Pittsburgh. I am also thankful to the Social Science Research Council of Canada, which provided research grants at critical junctures of the research and writing of this manuscript.

Finally, I would like to thank two people who have provided me with the kind of friendship and support so necessary to continue working many years on a project. Bruce Leslie was my friend and colleague when we were both at Brockport and has remained a close and dear friend ever since. I value his friendship and unflagging support more than I can adequately express. Similarly, my wife, Lynne, my best friend and closest colleague, has always been there with support, love, and encouragement when I have needed it most. Heartfelt thanks to both of you.

Introduction

SMALL business has always been with us and in America's early days was considered the quintessential business form. Throughout much of the twentieth century, however, small business has been regarded by scholars, if considered at all, as somewhat of a poor relation—that branch of the business family that has remained poor, unsophisticated, and vaguely disreputable. When in 1980 Glenn Porter assembled his impressive three-volume *Encyclopedia of American Economic History: Studies of the Principal Movements and Ideas*, there was no room for a chapter on small business. Although there was a segment on big business by Alfred Chandler, Jr., and one on mergers by Leslie Hannah, small business received only an incidental and passing mention in the chapter "Competition" by Alfred S. Eichner and Davis R. B. Ross. Even there, the discussion of small business was rather disparaging and dismissive: "Outside the oligopolistic core, the pattern of cooperative and independent behavior has changed little from what it was during the heyday of nineteenth century atomistic competition. Time horizons remained short, with the emphasis on earning the largest possible returns for the individuals directly involved in the management of the ownership and management of the firms."[1] In other words, in terms of the highest standards of business management, small business was hopelessly archaic.

In the late 1970s and 1980s, however, small business captured the attention of a growing number of historians and social scientists. Writing about, and urging the support of, small business in itself became a virtual cottage industry, which has resulted in a new appreciation of the economic, political, and cultural importance of small business. In the next few pages I plan to survey the historiographic traditions concerning large and small business in American life, relate those developments to recent studies of manufacturing and the iron and steel industry, and develop the approach to be utilized in this study.

Historians and economists have recognized the existence of a dual economy in America from the late nineteenth century onward. This economy was composed of center or core firms on one hand and peripheral firms on the other. In the early years of this emerging awareness, the approach was primarily moralistic. In the early twentieth century, politicians and writers, alarmed at the rise of massive new core business units, warned of their threat to traditional American values and institutions. Small business, to most of these commentators, was the heart of the real America and had to be preserved at all costs. In reaction to that view, a number of years later an entrepreneurial school emerged, headed by the historian Allan Nevins, which stressed the contributions of men like Andrew Carnegie and John D. Rockefeller to the creation of a new corporate economy that brought prosperity and power to America. In this account, small business was a nostalgic but retrograde business form. Neither of these groups of writers expended much effort analyzing small business.

These early studies pursued a largely moralistic approach to the question of large and small business. To the first group, big business was evil and foreign and small business was American. To the second, small business was anachronistic and large units were progressive and efficient. After World War II, however, a group of social scientists and historians began developing more sophisticated frameworks within which to view the operation of the American business system. In 1955, the economist Harold Vatter attempted to clarify the relationship of large and small business in American life, claiming that the two sets of firms were fundamentally different from one another, with large businesses' forming an oligopolistic core, and smaller firms' operating on the periphery of that core.[2] The former firms were capital-intensive, took advantage of economies of scale, and used techniques of professional management to control their giant enterprises. The smaller firms, on the other hand, were largely labor-intensive, were run in a personal manner by owner-entrepreneurs, and had no scale advantages.

These ideas were further refined over the next several years by other economists. John Kenneth Galbraith in the mid-1960s published *The Rise of the New Industrial State*, which postulated clearly the existence of two separate economic sectors. On one hand were capital-intensive center firms that benefited from economies of scale and were technologically sophisticated. Located primarily in the manufacturing sector, these firms formed the most progressive and important core of the American economy, while the peripheral firms, labor-intensive companies that engaged in little technological innovation and did not enjoy the benefits of economies of scale, operated primarily in the service and sales sectors of the economy. There was a strong underlying bias in the writings of Galbraith and others: the center firms were progressive and their development was inevitable—all part of a continuing process of modernization. Small business, on the other hand, was a relic of a premodern, anachronistic past.[3]

The historian who has done the most to enhance our understanding of the evolution of the American business system is Alfred D. Chandler, Jr. Positing a powerful new conceptual framework that has come to dominate American business and economic history, he shifted emphasis from individuals to institutions, and from entrepreneurship to management techniques. His work dovetailed nicely with that of Galbraith and others. Like them, he was concerned mostly with the emergence of large oligopolistic enterprises, but he clearly demonstrated how that system came about historically, how it had evolved from a nation of small, locally oriented businesses. Chandler's vision has captivated an entire generation of historians. Although Chandler's brilliant work was sensitive to the survival of small business in many sectors of the economy, his magisterial *The Visible Hand* nonetheless was quite legitimately concerned with large, vertically and horizontally integrated, multiunit, diversified business enterprises.[4]

Chandler's preoccupation with the large firm, with big business, is understandable. First of all, like most historians, Chandler was concerned primarily with the phenomenon of change. He therefore isolated precisely those elements that in his view represented the "dynamic factors in American business history."[5] These factors created what Chandler calls modern business enterprise, characterized by "many distinct operating units and . . . managed by a hierarchy of salaried executives."[6] The single-unit business; the business managed by an owner-operator; the concern that had only a local or regional market, had relatively few employees, and did little long-range planning, were of less importance to Chandler. They were traditional American business firms, ones that ceased to have much significance for the American economy after 1900.[7]

No one can deny the fundamental importance of the large firm in American life. Nor can anyone protest the tremendous insight into the functioning of that big business system that Chandler's works have provided. But it is important also to recognize that he has analyzed just one aspect of the system. He has brilliantly told part of the story, but it is necessary to broaden the outlook to include the role played in the American business system by those smaller, peripheral firms.[8] We must also recognize that Chandler, with his intense, microscopic analysis of large-scale management systems, has failed to view business within its broader operating framework. This was not simply an oversight but was clearly set out by him in the introduction to *The Visible Hand*, where he declared it was not his intention to deal with the impact of profound business changes on the labor forces, or on "existing political and social arrangements."[9] He quite rightly justified this exclusion by pointing out that each subject would require at least a volume of its own to do it justice.[10] That may well be the case, but the fact remains that Chandler's studies do leave us with a very incomplete view of the American business system during these years. We must understand better not only the relationship of smaller business units to the emerging system but also the relationship of the system to labor, and the political, social, and cultural universe in which it was set. We must, perforce, restore a more holistic approach to the study of business in America while remaining sensitive to the remarkable insights Chandler has given us into one aspect of that system.

Let us first of all, examine the theoretical and empirical universe of the role and position of small business in the economic system. The bias in the literature on American business in the past has favored bigness and greatness. The dominant assumption was that massive, large-scale multiunit enterprises serving a national market were without question the most efficient and effective. Chandler has argued that the move toward the creation of larger units by integrating mass production and volume distribution brought about a reduction in the cost per unit of output and resulted, a priori, in "large works operating at minimum efficient scale" that had significant cost advantages over smaller firms that used more labor-intensive technologies.[11] This assumption, however, was never tested empirically by Chandler but has been accepted as axiomatic by most economic historians and nearly all historians of American business. In recent years, though, this bias has been challenged by a number of theoretical studies of business.

George J. Stigler, writing in 1958, clearly articulated an important concept regarding economies of scale and optimal firm size. Rejecting the idea that bigness is automatically correlated positively with efficiency, Stigler instead postulated what he called the survival technique. In simplest terms, Stigler asserted that the most efficient firm, the optimum-size firm, was the firm that survived best and longest in its particular market. As he noted, the "fundamental postulate [of the survivor technique] is that the competition of different sizes of firms sifts out the more efficient enterprises."[12] For some industries and markets, particularly those serving a national market and producing goods amenable to high throughput and the technological innovations that went along with it, the giant firm was certainly most efficient. In other industries and markets, however, it was often the smaller, less bureaucratic firms that survived best. As Stigler noted: "An efficient size firm, on this argument, is one that meets any and all problems the entrepreneur actually faces: strained labor relations, rapid innovation, government regulation, unstable foreign markets, and what not."[13]

Stigler applied his analysis to the American steel industry in the period from 1930 to 1950. He found that the very smallest firms, those with less than 0.5 percent of industry capacity (374,000 tons or less in 1930, and 484,000 tons or less in 1951) tended to decline as a result of the diseconomies of small scale over this period. At the same time, however, he found that the very largest firm in the industry (U.S. Steel) also declined because of diseconomies of multiplant operation beyond a certain scale. The most efficient plants were those that held between 0.75 and 10 percent of industry size. He concluded, "there is customarily a fairly wide range of optimum size," rather than a single standard of bigness equated to efficiency.[14]

Leonard W. Weiss later refined Stigler's analysis by introducing what he called the minimum efficient scale (MES) of operations. His focus was on defining the smallest unit of size that could still operate efficiently, and he had little interest in the diseconomies of large-scale operations.[15] As a result, although Weiss's estimates of optimal minimum size gave a somewhat greater emphasis to the concept of bigness, one is nonetheless struck with the variability of firm size over time. Minimum efficient plant size, which stood at 1.5 million tons in the late 1920s, escalated rapidly in the early 1930s with the adoption of continuous strip mills, which needed higher production and greater throughput to be efficient. This increase, however, was not unitary, and the MES began dropping in the late 1930s and declined steadily until the end of World War II, by which time it had slumped to 1 million tons. After that time, it began expanding, reaching 2.25 million tons in the 1950s, which allowed some mills of that size to accommodate the new oxygen-process furnaces then being introduced.[16] The most important point for our purposes, however, is that minimum efficient size did not simply augment in a unitary fashion but fluctuated over time according to technological and market demands.

These insights have been further enhanced in recent years, and, most importantly, scholars have extended their analysis to the late nineteenth century, making them more germane to this study. One of the most important of these investigations was that of John A. James in 1983.[17] James attempted to use quantitative analysis of American industry in the late nineteenth century in order to test Chandler's assumption that labor-saving technological innovations were crucial to the development of large firms. In other words, "did biased technical change, by increasing capital intensity, increase optimal firm size" in specific industries in the late nineteenth century?[18] James's analysis exhibited quite a variation from industry to industry in the increase of efficient firm size, with iron rolling mills showing a significant advance in that size over time. He concluded that iron rolling mills "would have been a tight natural oligopoly since the industry could have supported four firms of efficient size."[19] James's conclusion, then, gave credence to Chandler's hypothesis but indicated that it was fulfilled most fully in distilling, flour and meal, and pig iron, and just partially so in iron rolling.[20]

The most important alternative to the model developed by Chandler and others has come from Jeremy Atack. In several articles published during the late 1970s and 1980s, Atack brought a new level of complexity and sophistication to the analysis of the problem.[21] Focusing on the period from 1820 to 1870, Atack found two seemingly contrary tendencies. On the one hand, he discovered that larger firms emerged in a wide variety of industries during this time. In 1850, no more than nineteen establishments had sales of $1 million in 1860 dollars. By 1870, seventy-eight firms had sales of this magnitude, reflecting the rise of a national market and increased plant size to service that market. Further, these firms emerged in a wider variety of industries than before. In 1850, million-dollar firms were confined to just seven industries (none of which was in the iron industry), whereas by 1870, twenty-six industries had million-dollar firms (including iron). These were, as he notes, "prototypes of Chandler's modern business enterprise" and were represented strongly in the iron industry, where average plant size increased twenty-eight-fold to nearly $100,000 by 1870.[22]

All of this, however, was rather deceptive. As Atack comments: "Despite the emergence of more large firms in a wider range of economic activities and growth at the top, most businesses remained small." Even in the iron industry, where the average plant size grew more rapidly, smaller firms continued to survive and prosper at an impressive rate.[23] "This," Atack says, "has tended to be neglected in our preoccupation with the emergence of the large."[24] The implications of Atack's findings are manifold, but an important conclusion was that small firms were complementary to large firms rather than direct competitors. Of course, it might be argued (and indeed has been) that Atack viewed these firms and industries before the great industrial explosion of the late nineteenth century. As Chandler and others have pointed out, the turning point for most American industries came in the 1880s, when truly large firms began emerging.

In another study, Atack looked briefly at the period from 1870 to 1900 and did indeed find that average plant size increased significantly during this time. He discovered, "The ratio of the actual number of establishments in an industry to the minimum number of optimal 1870 plants declined with each decade from 1870."[25] At the same time, however, he noted that most of these industries by 1900 failed to exhibit a radically different structure than they had in 1870. He took that fact as evidence of an absence of "dramatic technological change forcing a break with historical evolutionary patterns."[26]

These works by economists have generally been focused on the aggregate level. However important their findings to our understanding of the operation of the broader business system, to a historian they are somewhat unsatisfying and incomplete. Our comprehension of small business and its relation to larger units and to the broader social and political system has been more crucially formed by microlevel analysis of individual industries and firms by historians. Many of the early studies of small business in America focused on the retail and wholesale sector of the economy. Some of the most important early work in this area was done by Lewis Atherton. In a series of studies, he stressed the importance of rural shopkeepers and country stores to the development of America's marketing system. Other scholars picked up on this theme, expanding it to include the role of these individuals in providing credit and business information for their localities.[27]

Less attention has been paid to the importance of small business in the manufacturing sector. Two very significant works in the mid-1950s, however, gave clear evidence of the continuing significance of small manufacturing endeavors. In 1955, Martha Taber analyzed the development of a series of small firms in the Connecticut

Valley's cutlery industry. Unlike many other industries, cutlery was never dominated by the large oligopolistic core firms. Instead, the industry remained the domain of small enterprises from the 1830s through World War II.[28] Similarly, in 1956 Theodore Marburg published a history of the Smith & Griggs Company. Smith & Griggs was a small firm in the brass fabricating industry that had survived and prospered over the years by developing specialty products that were marketed to distinctive niches in the economy, thus avoiding direct competition with mass production core firms until around World War I. After that time, however, Smith & Griggs was increasingly drawn into that competitive arena and, as a result of that and the Great Depression, went out of business in 1936.[29]

One of the most important works dealing with smaller manufacturing concerns came out a decade later when James Soltow published his path-breaking study of small metal fabricating and machine-making companies in New England from 1890 to 1957, precisely that period when big business was presumed supreme. In his work, Soltow demonstrated clearly the relationship between large and small firms in a single industry. Whereas one could dismiss the cutlery industry as a surviving aberration on the American business scene, and one could similarly view Marburg's study of Smith and Griggs as demonstrating the long-term inability of small firms to compete effectively in the twentieth-century economy, the same could not be said for the metal fabricating and machine-making industries.[30]

Soltow's findings were of great significance in refining our understanding of small business, especially of smaller manufacturing establishments, and its relationship to the broader business system. He pointed out that the entrepreneurs in these establishments were a far cry from what Chandler found in large business units. In the latter, as Chandler put it, structure followed strategy, whereas in small business just the opposite was true. Further, these owner-entrepreneurs remained closely involved with the direction of their firms, functioning in practice as if they were still partnerships or single proprietorships. The retention of older management characteristics did not mean these firms were shortsighted or solely profit-oriented, or at least no more so than larger institutions. The most important aspect of Soltow's findings, however, dealt with the relationship of these smaller firms to the market. Earlier studies had been acutely aware of the fact that small business could not take advantage of economies of scale but had generally assumed this shortcoming doomed them to extinction. Soltow, taking a cue from

Stigler, asked how they were able to survive. His findings were of fundamental importance.

Soltow's small businessmen succeeded and survived by employing two important strategies. One was to specialize in a particular product: to find a market niche that giant firms could not successfully exploit with the advantages of scale. These were sometimes local markets and sometimes markets for products that used specialized processes that involved custom work and nonstandardized design. In this way, small metal fabricators did not have to engage in direct head-to-head competition with giant enterprises. They also succeeded by doing something different, by engaging in what is termed product differentiation, which "had to be based on special services to customers, reputation and reliability, and personal sales representation."[31]

These findings on small business in the manufacturing sector by Soltow have been followed by a number of other significant studies. One of the most important of the historical studies was done as part of the Philadelphia Social History Project. Bruce Laurie and Mark Schmitz conducted an innovative analysis of the creation of Philadelphia's industrial base during the period from 1850 to 1880.[32] Using a simple classification system whereby they divided Philadelphia's firms into artisan shops, sweatshops, manufactures (none of which used inanimate power sources), and factories (which did), their study showed a sharp increase in factory employment during the years under study. Although this seemed to give credence to the idea of large business predominance, a closer analysis indicated otherwise. As Laurie and Schmitz argue, "Traditional and transitional forms of production existed along with factories as late as 1880."[33] Further, they found that in very few cases were there increasing returns to scale, noting, "Rather than scale economies, therefore, the results are more consistent with diseconomies, so that proportional increases in inputs did not lead to an equivalent expansion in output. . . . Such results would indicate that . . . size was actually a deterrent to efficiency."[34] They believed, however, that these diseconomies were the result of the newness of large industrial ventures and that "mid-century entrepreneurs presiding over large enterprises were pioneers of a sort, feeling and sometimes stumbling their way through uncharted terrain."[35] The implication was that once they had the hang of it, once Chandler's vaunted professional managers got their hands on these sprawling and diffuse complexes, they would achieve the economies of scale assumed to accompany large size. That assumption, however, was untested.[36]

The most revealing and important microstudy of nineteenth-century industrialism is that of Philadelphia's textile industry by Philip Scranton.[37] Scranton objected to the textile paradigm that he believed has dominated discussion of the development of that industry in the United States. This paradigm, which has focused almost exclusively on the industry in New England, and most particularly on the massive complex of mills at Lowell, Massachusetts, has established a linear model of industrial development. According to this paradigm, "primitive early forms were superseded by a more modern corporate system, whose competition eradicated its predecessors."[38] "Meanwhile," Scranton laments, "the closely held corporation . . . the unincorporated proprietorship have gone largely unexamined, much less analyzed."[39]

To remedy that situation, Scranton developed a sophisticated and highly nuanced study of textile manufacture in Philadelphia. Using what he calls an accumulation matrix, he analyzed a broad range of social and economic factors that "together constitute the total situation for production and profit faced by entrepreneurs."[40] What Scranton found using this methodology was a production system in Philadelphia textiles that differed in practically every respect from the textile paradigm derived from the Lowell experience. Rather than focusing on technology to achieve volume production and high-speed throughput, Philadelphia textile mills instead stressed flexible output and a more specialized market response. Practically none of them became a vertically or horizontally integrated operation, as each continued to specialize in one phase of production. Yet this was not, as Scranton pointed out, "a fading system, for expansion after mid-century showed no displacement of disintegrated relationships by integrated firms."[41] These were, in Stigler's terms, survivors, firms that achieved some sort of optimum size to enable them to compete in their chosen markets.

Scranton's study is a vitally important one for understanding the evolution of American industry in the nineteenth century. Yet there are still some gaps. Despite the influence of Lowell on our understanding of the development of the textile industry, we have long been aware of other models in that industry. The tiny textile mill, located in an isolated mill village to take advantage of a fall line for waterpower, has long been a part of American industrial folklore and has recently come in for its share of sophisticated analysis.[42] The iron and steel industry, on the other hand, has long been viewed in a largely linear and unitary fashion. According to this model—the Andrew Carnegie archetype—early iron firms were small, labor-intensive, and dependent on highly skilled labor. Their capital needs were small, their markets local, and their technology crude. Then, with the development of the Bessemer converter, steel rapidly displaced iron. Under the guidance of such a crafty and audacious entrepreneur as Andrew Carnegie, the minimum size of plant needed to compete in the steel industry escalated rapidly, so that by 1900 the massive, vertically integrated, technologically advanced, and capital-intensive steel firm totally dominated the industry. At that point, Wall Street financiers and professional managers came on the scene to create a huge, horizontally integrated steel firm, the largest corporation in the world, one that controlled some 60 percent of American iron and steel production. If any small-scale iron and steel firms still survived, they were anachronisms, a dying remnant of an older economic and social order.[43]

A number of studies of the industry, however, indicate that this was not the case. Mansel G. Blackford in 1982 published his analysis of a small steel firm in Columbus, Ohio, one that was able to survive handily for over a century by using many of the market techniques outlined by Soltow.[44] A year later, Amos Loveday, Jr., brought out his study of the cut nail industry, an industry that had been rendered technologically obsolete by the invention of the wire nail and the large mass production plants that went along with it. Although this was a study of ultimate business failure due to an unwillingness and inability to innovate, it was nonetheless an important and sensitive analysis of business strategies and market techniques in an industry segment.[45]

One of the aspects of greatest value of the microstudies, however, is that they were not simply concerned with the relationship of small business to the market. Most of the studies discussed also dealt, to some extent, with the nature of labor relationships in a small manufacturing concern. Soltow characterized labor relations in small metal working firms as largely paternalistic, "stressing the importance of personal relationships and fostering what [the firms] called 'a family atmosphere.' "[46] These findings were echoed by David Brody, whose earlier work had greatly clarified our understanding of labor relations in the giant steel firms. In 1980, he analyzed the nature of the phenomenon in smaller firms.[47] Brody's general focus was on the benefits that accrued to small manufacturers who did not have to recruit and administer large numbers of workers. He theorized that that advantage may have helped the smaller firm survive longer than many expected. Brody's study, however, was more suggestive than conclusive.

A particularly important analysis of the steel industry, one that greatly amplifies our understanding of the process of labor relations for small firms, is that of Michael Santos.[48] In his study, Santos sensitively evoked a pattern of labor relations at an independent Pittsburgh iron mill that differed in myriad ways from the situation at the steel giants. There was, to be sure, a strong dose of paternalism in its relations, along with a certain degree of personalism. But there were significant differences from the classic view of paternalism.[49] The Byers firm was unionized throughout this period, a condition absent from account of most other small firms, and since it was a relatively large operation, face-to-face personalism between owner and worker was muted. The result was a very complex and nuanced labor/management situation.

Another area of concern, and one in which even less work has been done, is the relation of small business to the community. The whole question of the control of cities by economic elites is a thorny one, tied to strongly held political and ideological beliefs. Marxists have posited the idea that with the emergence of industrial capitalism the older landed aristocracy was displaced by a new industrial bourgeoise. Cities, like the rest of society, were passing through programmed stages from feudalism to capitalism and, ultimately, to state socialism. Liberal or classical analysis of the situation has generally posited a similar transition from traditional to modern modes. The problem has come when that untested axiom has been subjected to empirical verification. In general, the proof of the axiom has simply rested on its assertion. Virtually every bit of quantitative evidence concerning the nature of the economic elite in most Western countries that have undergone industrialization has failed to substantiate the hypothesis.[50] Nonetheless, general treatments of American urban society in the late nineteenth and early twentieth centuries continue to insist on the emergence of a new, more aggressive, and dynamic group of business leaders—robber barons, if you will—whose giant firms and cutthroat methods submerged the older mercantile elite in their wake.

The issue has been addressed most directly in recent years in Britain. There, it has long been patently obvious that the older landed aristocracy, let alone the mercantile and banking elite, had enormous staying power, even after one of the most complete industrial transformations in modern history. This has usually been explained as a form of British exceptionalism: that is, Britain is held to be anomalous in relation to normal patterns of development. Attempts were made to show that capitalism emerged too early in Britain, causing the industrial bourgeoise to be too weak to overturn the feudal aristocracy completely. This has resulted in a prolonged debate on the topic in Britain, but the key point that all commentators agree on is that in Britain there has been a "persistence of traditional cultural forms and ideological legitimations; a powerful traditional or aristocratically based element within the elite or ruling class."[51]

The problem is more complex in American cities, particularly new industrial cities like Pittsburgh. After all, Pittsburgh had no titled aristocracy, not even a particularly large or powerful landed establishment. In the early years there was, of course, a mercantile elite, which was joined in the early nineteenth century, when the city was still quite small, by an industrial elite of iron and glass manufacturers. Thus, Pittsburgh came of age as an industrial city, one controlled by an industrial elite. Yet this was an industrial elite, as we shall see, composed mostly of small- to medium-size business owners. Their companies would be overwhelmed (at least figuratively) in the late nineteenth century by the rise of massive new business consolidations. When historians speak of modern business, they are referring mostly to those giant concerns that came on the scene after 1880. Older and smaller iron rolling mills were, by definition, engaging in traditional means of production. Similarly, when historians speak of the control of American society by a plutocracy or an industrial bourgeosie in the late nineteenth century, it is the owners and managers of these large new firms to whom they are referring. In the American, and particularly Pittsburgh, context, the older aristocracy were those men and families who ran the smaller iron and steel mills, the great bulk of which were founded before the Civil War. The question on the Pittsburgh scene, then, is the extent to which they were replaced by the factotums of large national industrial corporations like U.S. Steel.

One of the problems for the historian who enters the area of community political power is that it is a virtual mine field of conflicting theories put forward by sociologists and political scientists. David C. Hammack, however, has done much to give his colleagues some insight and direction in this area.[52] The leading controversy about community power theory, according to Hammack, "has to do with the relation between power and the social order and, ultimately, with the impact of economic development and the increasing scale of most urban communities on the distribution of power."[53]

In this controversy, four main positions have been developed: the stratificationist,[54] which holds that the distribution of power always follows the distribution of wealth (which is always skewed in favor of the rich); the pluralist,[55] which holds that power is the product of efficient organization and thus is divided among a number of groups in society according to their ability to organize; a multivariate approach,[56] which also believes the distribution of power varies according to a number of factors—political, ideological, cultural, economic, and so forth. Finally, the skeptical position[57] holds that we do not know enough to construct any theory of community power. Historians' debates over the nature of political power in America's cities have followed a similar configuration.

As Hammack has pointed out, the most influential theorist of community power for an early generation of historians has been James Bryce. In *The American Commonwealth*, Bryce posited the existence of two elites in American cities: the new industrial capitalists, and the best men, the older, established social and cultural elite. According to Bryce, the industrialists sought to rule in their own self-interest, whereas the best men tried to act in the broader community interest. It was between these two groups that most conflict occurred. The people were seldom involved.[58] Also, despite the rise of industrialism and the massive economic power accruing to the new industrialists, Bryce thought the older elite would retain control of their communities and would absorb the new industrialists through the universities and marriage.

Other historians, however, have adopted an approach informed by Marxist theory and describe a situation of elite decline and demise during the late nineteenth and early twentieth centuries. Frederick C. Jaher demonstrated how older social elites lost power in New York, Boston, Philadelphia, and Charleston, and Stow Persons argued for a general decline in American gentility after the Civil War.[59] The key factors in elite decline, according to them, were the increasing size and complexity of the city and its institutions, which made it impossible for the older elite to continue to dominate as they had in the past.

Not all recent historians have been convinced of these arguments. Edward Pessen, Michael Katz, and Michael Frisch all postulated a continuing elite control in the various cities they studied.[60] Their findings have at least implicitly followed the ideas of Moisei Ostrogorski, who saw little distinction between the best men and the industrial capitalists and asserted that a broadly united capitalist elite ruled America's cities in the late nineteenth and early twentieth centuries.[61] This ability to rule, however, was based on the fact that the elite limited its influence to those issues that affected it most directly and that political leaders served as effective mediators between the capitalists and the mass of voters, balancing the real needs of the two groups in a manner that preserved the economic health and political stability of the community.[62]

Despite the multiplicity of theories concerning the nature of power, a generally accepted picture of the nature of political power in America's cities at the turn of the century has emerged among historians in recent years. Most agree that a small, well-to-do mercantile elite ruled these cities in the years prior to the late nineteenth century. Although there is some debate about the method of rule, most believe this elite remained fairly sensitive to the felt needs of the masses of citizens. This sensitivity rested on a number of factors, including the spatial configuration of the walking city, whereby workers and the elite lived in close proximity; the nature of the workplace, which was characterized by much shared authority; and a basic homogeneity in ethnic and religious backgrounds. As the cities grew and industrialized, becoming more heterogeneous and complex in the years after the Civil War, the older elite began to lose touch with the masses of citizens. As a result, two competing forces emerged to challenge the elite for control of the cities. The first were the masses of unskilled immigrant workers who poured into the cities during these years; the second, the industrial robber barons who possessed great wealth and enormous economic power.[63] The older, informal system of deference politics gave way to new political machines whose power was based on the combination of immigrant votes and money from large economic interests.

The resultant political machines that emerged have been the source of much controversy among historians, but most recent interpretations stress the extent to which they acted as engines of accommodation between business groups and immigrant voters. On one hand, one of the functions of the machine was to organize the political domain, to form links with various private interest groups involved in city building, and to centralize political power in order to enhance development. This power to obtain quick action on a number of measures made the machine popular with many of the large business groups in the city. At the same time, in order to remain in power, the machine had to respond to the real needs of the city's working-class voters, thereby supplying them with a plethora of city services that might not otherwise have been forthcoming.[64]

Next came the great Progressive reform movement around the turn of the century. In an older analysis, reformers were selfless, high-minded individuals bent on saving the common people from the evil plundering of immigrant machine politicians and the special interests who paid graft to these officials in order to receive benefits from the government.[65] Later historians, however, have been more critical of that reform group. There have also continued to be major differences of opinion among those who view reformers as representatives of the new middle class, others who see them as members of older elite groups attempting to recapture their power, and some who see them as members of the largest and most powerful of the new industrial enterprises.

The most sophisticated analysis of political power in Pittsburgh during this period is that of Samuel P. Hays. During the 1890s, according to Hays, the largest business interests (manufacturers, downtown merchants, central-city bankers, and managers of public property), along with what he calls the urban upper class and various professionals, such as educational administrators, public health doctors, civil engineers, and architects, successfully pushed for the "integration and centralization of decision-making" and the exclusion of working-class groups from public office.[66] Hays's analysis, however, has left room for a number of alternative interpretations of his evidence. Most have judged his findings to indicate that the largest corporations, specifically U.S. Steel, Westinghouse, and the like, became the dominant forces on the local scene, but so many different groups were included as part of the reform coalition that others have taken this as proof of continued middle-class or older upper-class influence.

Despite this, there is a very general sense of agreement among historians and social scientists that economic elites increased their participation in voluntary civic organizations and in this way retained at least some of their former influence. The degree of influence varies according to the ideological and theoretical perspective of the investigator, and also according to the size of the city, the number and types of industries within that city, and the extent to which the city's economy was dominated by branch plants of national corporations. Generally, smaller communities have retained elite domination longer than larger ones, cities with heavy industry and large immigrant populations have eroded elite control more quickly, and cities with a large number of absentee-controlled branch plants have followed a similar pattern.[67]

Although there is at least some consensus that economic elites of one kind or another have continued to play some influence in the affairs of the city, just what that influence has been, on what issues it is exerted and how, and precisely who these elites were are still matters of debate. A key point, however, concerns the whole distinction between large and small, and independent and absentee-controlled businesses. The role of smaller business firms and executives in broader community affairs has been particularly neglected or obscured in the debate over whether the people or the interests have controlled community affairs. Studies of community power have generally tended to ignore the role of small business, while students of small business itself have tended to disregard their role in the community.

James Soltow touched on the subject briefly in his work but believed his small manufacturers could spare little time from the management of their enterprises to become involved in municipal political or civic affairs.[68] Mansel Blackford also dealt with the issue in his study of Buckeye Steel, wherein we saw the company's continuing involvement with the city of Columbus.[69] Since, however, it was just one firm, and its involvement was somewhat idiosyncratic, it is a little difficult to draw any broader inferences from it. The most suggestive work in this regard, however, has been done by Hammack,[70] who noted how proprietors of smaller businesses in the period after 1870 were often able to use municipal government to their own purposes. That conclusion was echoed by Carl Harris's findings on Birmingham, Alabama. In Birmingham, like Pittsburgh a major steel center, the large steel concerns, owned by absentee capitalists, were able to secure the services they needed and to block those to which they were opposed. Nonetheless, smaller retail and manufacturing firms were also able to obtain virtually all the items they needed from the government, although, unlike the largest steel concerns, they had to absorb most of the cost of these services themselves.[71]

Our examination of Pittsburgh's independent iron and steel manufacturers provides a remarkably cogent test for this question of power in industrial cities and the distinction between large, absentee-controlled corporations and smaller, locally dominated firms. These iron and steel makers were indisputably members of Pittsburgh's older upper class, and most were not involved with the largest, mostly absentee-owned corporations on the Pittsburgh scene. Further, they displayed a great deal of political and social activity during these years. The argument to be developed here is that although all of the groups Hays mentioned were involved in urban reform, it was the members of the older upper class, especially those whose families were in the iron and steel industry, who had the greatest influence on the direction of that reform. Just as they became niche marketers on the economic scene, they found a useful niche in the political, social, and cultural world of Pittsburgh that allowed them to exercise power far beyond their numbers. Their influence derived from their ability to become power brokers in the city—men (and women) who were able to act as mediators between the large national economic interests of such significance in the city and a myriad local interest groups. It also rested on a continuing tradition of muted paternalism by which that upper-class group put itself forward as the guardians of public weal in the city. As a result, I will argue, the older upper class in Pittsburgh was able to retain far greater power and influence on the urban scene than appears to have been the case in Boston, Philadelphia, or New York.

Previous studies of small business have been enormously suggestive, but more remains to be done. Most pressing is the need to integrate far more fully than in the past the study of small business and its leaders into the economic, social, political, and cultural framework of the city, state, and nation. Too often our understanding of business affairs has lacked a rooting in the local environment in which they are based. When this is done, our comprehension of the role and importance of smaller business enterprises is greatly enhanced. It is hoped that the present study of smaller independent iron and steel manufacturers in Pittsburgh will provide some of that needed framework.

Pittsburgh in the late nineteenth century was "America's Birmingham," the center of this country's iron and steel industry, and as early as 1850 had a larger proportion of its population employed in heavy manufacturing than any other American city. Production of metal products made up a significant share of the city's production.[72] By the 1870s, Pittsburgh had become the nation's leading steel center and the first integrated steel mills were being built in the region. Thirty years later, the Pittsburgh region produced 30 percent of the nation's steel and the city's leading manufacturers were power brokers of the industry on a national level. Throughout most of the twentieth century, metal manufacturing accounted for between 70 and 75 percent of the city's manufacturing output.[73]

Pittsburgh, then, was America's preeminent heavy industry city and one in which large-batch mass production industries held undue influence. It was also a big business city in the most fundamental way, one that, at least on the surface, saw its affairs dominated by America's largest industrial corporations. Yet, it was the leaders of the smaller independent iron and steel companies who made up the greatest number, and most important members, of that city's social upper class. Further, this same group tended to dominate the boards of directors of the major manufacturing and banking institutions in the city.[74] Evolving into a powerful and cohesive social and economic force, these manufacturers were also able to translate that influence to the political and cultural spheres. These iron and steel manufacturers played a major role in organizing the Republican party in the city and from that time enjoyed a position of overwhelming political power. When their influence over normal political parties and channels was challenged at several points in the twentieth century, they were able to develop new instruments of control. Through their influence over, and control of, civic organizations, Pittsburgh's social elite played an inordinant role in municipal reform in the early twentieth century, and in the great Pittsburgh Renaissance after World War II.[75]

We shall examine the many layers and textures of Pittsburgh's most important industry in the following chapters. We shall develop what might be called a new social history of the entrepreneur in this way. Just as early political and social history tended to focus on great men to the exclusion of the common working men, women, blacks, and ethnic groups, so American business and economic history has been obsessively concerned with bigness and greatness in its analysis. In the process, the vast majority of business leaders—the average or "common" entrepreneurs—have been ignored. The result has been the creation of a curiously skewed and false picture of American industry in the nineteenth century. As Philip Scranton has so cogently commented: "Manufacturers outside the main line of development seem peculiar, anachronistic, and doomed, and workers become ciphers. Culture, family and religion are viewed through a filter that merely assesses their acquiescence, resistance, or indifference to the inevitable."[76]

Many of the iron and steel manufacturers in this study—in fact, most—eschewed the large-batch high-throughput production techniques that would have enabled them to compete in an undifferentiated national market like iron and steel rails. It is important to recognize that this was a business decision made by these individuals, not some failure of will or lack of insight. Aware of the high mortality rate among the firms that attempted that large-scale approach, they willingly and realistically pursued an alternate path. Finding profitable market niches, they did not compete directly with the likes of Andrew Carnegie, nor were they absorbed by U.S. Steel and the other consolidations at the turn of the century. Instead, they continued to conduct their businesses in a profitable manner for decades after the turn of the century. This was a dense, highly textured social and economic world these iron and steel men created, one in which economics, society, and politics were highly integrated. It shall be the purpose of *Making Iron and Steel* to unravel that world.

1

Forging an Aristocracy: Pittsburgh to 1870

To the unknowing eye the mill seemed only a formless mass
of corrugated iron shed, some roofless and open to the brassy
sky, some dark and mysterious in their walls and roofs of
blackened metal. A fearful shattering noise roared up from
the rolling mill at the eastern end of the meandering string
of buildings, and at the far western end there was teeming
activity, centering around piles of different sorts of masonry
brick and blocks, plunging teams, shouting drivers and
laborers, and the ear-splitting hisses of a dinkey-engine which
was hitched to a flat loaded with castings. . . . the Old Man's
glance went back, almost as if for assurance, to the row of
stacks blackening the summer sky with their eructations.
These were the old puddling furnaces which antedated
everything else in the mill. They were the core of the Scott
Iron Works.

Marcia Davenport, *The Valley of Decision*

PITTSBURGH was a "new" city of the nineteenth century. A raw
wilderness in 1750, it was still a small and rude settlement by the
end of the American Revolution in 1783. It was so inconsequential
that a visiting congressman, Arthur Lee, predicted, "This place, I
believe, will never be considerable."[1] Shortly after Lee's visit, however, Pittsburgh began growing more rapidly. According to the census of 1790, there were 376 inhabitants in the town, including some
thirty-six mechanics. This latter statistic is important, since it indicates that the formerly transient population of traders and spec-
ulators was being replaced by those who planned to make their
permanent livelihood there. And this new economic orientation was
to include new modes of handicraft industry.

By the end of the War of 1812, Pittsburgh had become the largest city in the West, with over five thousand inhabitants. As the service center for a relatively large hinterland, Pittsburgh's mercantile community had gained a good deal of prominence and represented the most powerful influence in the small city. Men like Joseph McClurg and James O'Hara, the city's wealthiest merchants, not only successfully ran wholesale and retailing operations but also provided capital to start some of the city's earliest industrial ventures. O'Hara built a glass factory, a brewery, and a shipyard, and McClurg opened the city's first iron foundry. As Richard Wade notes, "In 1809, when a public meeting created a committee to explore the possibility of organizing a society for the encouragement of manufacturing, almost all of its members were merchants."[2] This practice of mercantile capital's making possible the expansion of industrial enterprises in the new and raw frontier was widespread. Glenn Porter and Harold Livesay noted, "the contributions of these specialized merchants to the process of economic growth were absolutely essential. . . ."[3]

Pittsburgh by 1820 had a population of seventy-five hundred and was in the process of developing a culturally distinct and highly cohesive upper-class group. This group came from Northern Ireland, belonged to the Presbyterian church, and created thriving mercantile empires in the city during its early years.[4] One study, which analyzed the family founders of Allegheny County, in which Pittsburgh was located, indicated that about two-thirds of the twenty-five were self-made, but criteria for this category were quite imprecise. About half were born in America, and, most significantly for the cultural stamp of Pittsburgh, 71 percent of the self-made group and 25 percent of the old upper-class group was Scots-Irish, and about half of those for whom information was available were members of the Presbyterian church.[5] This mercantile aristocracy, as was true in most other cities in the early nineteenth century, dominated the political, social, and cultural environment, as well as the economic.

By the 1820s, however, industrial concerns were beginning to overshadow the commercial, and, by the same token, industrialists were assuming increasingly important roles in the city. Iron manufacture by this time had become an important Pittsburgh concern. The first iron foundry, as we have seen, was started in Pittsburgh in 1804 by Joseph McClurg. As with most foundries, it was a small operation servicing a largely local market, making mostly hollow ware: pans, pots, kettles, stoves, grates, andirons, and the like.[6] By the end of the War of 1812, four other air foundries had been established in the city. Producing iron castings, one of the largest made just four hundred tons annually.[7] There were, in addition, three nail factories, which each year made about two hundred tons of cut and wrought iron nails.[8] A most important development also occurred at this time when Christopher Cowan, an immigrant from Northern Ireland, built the first rolling mill in the city in 1811–12. The next great advance was in 1818, when the first rolling mill with its own puddling furnaces, the Union Mill, was established.[9] By the mid-1820s, Pittsburgh had been established as a major supplier of finished iron goods to the great expanding frontier region to the west.

By 1826, in addition to eight foundries that employed 106 workers and produced a total of 2,126 tons of cast metal, there were six rolling mills in the city. With a total of 181 hands working in these mills, they produced 4,900 tons of iron annually.[10] Christopher Cowan's rolling mill was still in operation, making about 500 tons of bar iron yearly. The Union Mill was by this time the largest in the city, employing 100 hands and producing 1,500 tons of iron. Grant's Hill Iron Works, erected in 1821 and capable of producing 600 tons of iron with 30 hands, was one of the newer operations. These mills, however, had little impact on the later history of Pittsburgh's iron industry. The Union Mill was dismantled in 1829, and a short time after, the old Cowan mill ceased to operate, as did the Grant's Hill works. Several of the men involved in these ventures, such as William H. Hays, William S. Robinson, and William Beltzhoover, nonetheless became part of an emerging local aristocracy in the city, and it was already clear to most people that Pittsburgh's future was in iron.

This transformation from a mercantile to a manufacturing center might have spelled a vast upheaval in Pittsburgh's economic, social, and political leadership, except for two important factors. One was the cultural homogeneity of the mercantile and industrial groups: both were Scots-Irish Presbyterian. The second was the iron industrialist's great need for capital, a demand the young mercantile aristocracy was willing and able to provide. The process by which this financing of early iron operations was accomplished, however, is open to a certain amount of conjecture.

This concern for the acquisition of capital has been addressed by a number of students of the antebellum iron and steel industry. The issue was first analyzed by Louis Hunter with regard to the emerging iron industry in Pittsburgh. Hunter's pioneering work noted the great importance of mercantile capital for the birth and later expansion of the city's iron industry.[11] Yet Hunter believed that in many instances the intersectoral linkages between merchants and iron manufacturing were incomplete. The lack of the corporate form in Pittsburgh industry was, in his opinion, a deterrent to investment. Hunter calculated that the capital investment for an average rolling mill in Pittsburgh in 1857 was $156,190, about the same as for a textile mill, but well above the $55,000 needed for a glass factory, the other major manufacturing enterprise in antebellum Pittsburgh.

In addition, the iron manufacturer needed enormous amounts of liquid short-term capital with which to meet current costs of plant operation and to carry sufficient inventories. These, Hunter believed, were inadequately met by mercantile and banking capital in the antebellum period. As he concluded, "Financial problems were the most harassing, if not the most serious, problems which the Pittsburgh iron manufacturers had to contend with in the period prior to 1860. . . . [These conditions] made the business of the iron manufacturer uncertain and difficult."[12]

Arthur C. Bining, writing a couple of years later, recognized the problem of the scarcity of capital for Pittsburgh iron manufacturers but pointed out that the profits to be made from iron mills were quite considerable. This, he reasoned, made the mills increasingly attractive to mercantile capital. Bining, however, had little evidence to back up this assertion.[13] It was not until the early 1970s that historians again addressed this question. Glenn Porter and Harold Livesay presented a far more complex and sophisticated view of the situation in the iron industry, although most of their attention was focused on rail mills, which engaged in large-scale production and were often vertically integrated. In their analysis of the iron industry, Livesay and Porter, like Hunter, noted that fixed capital requirements comprised a minority of the iron manufacturer's total financial needs. More than anything else, the rail manufacturer needed liquid capital.[14]

These short-term (generally six months in duration) capital needs Livesay and Porter claim were fulfilled in significant measure by iron and hardware merchants who discounted the manufacturer's own bills, or the railway securities in which the owners of the rail mills were paid, and also provided advances against future sales.[15] The merchants also sometimes extended credit on receivables and were often involved in partnerships and joint-stock iron firms.[16]

Additionally, private banks, which often evolved out of mercantile operations, did a great deal to meet the financial needs of the iron manufacturers during these years, while public banks and insurance companies also discounted notes to the manufacturers, thereby furnishing short-term finance. There were, according to Porter and Livesay, a number of reasons why merchants involved themselves in financing iron operations. They, first of all, possessed the necessary temperament and risk-taking skills, along with the requisite liquid capital and access to information resources such as the R. G. Dun & Co. reports.[17] Also, through their investments merchants had the potential to achieve a position as a more or less privileged supplier or marketing agent.

The nature of the evidence accumulated in this chapter is somewhat inconclusive on this issue, since company records for the vast majority of these firms are simply not available. A couple of points, however, do need to be made. First, although Porter and Livesay raise important issues and provide extraordinary documentation for their assertions, it is important to remember they are dealing with only the rail mill segment of the industry. The rail firms were far more likely to be joint-stock companies or corporations than Pittsburgh's iron and steel mills, thereby making it easier for them to acquire capital. Also, the magnitude of their orders was larger and the number of customers relatively limited, giving some sense, at least in the short run, of the size or number of orders to be expected. This made longer-term planning and financing a bit easier than for the Pittsburgh iron mills, which sold mostly merchant bar iron or hardware in a widely scattered market.

It is quite clear from the evidence available that a variety of wealthy Pittsburghers, men who had accumulated large fortunes in mercantile, transportation, mining, and other endeavors, were providing a good deal of backing to the Pittsburgh iron and steel mills. Those who were in the iron and steel trade in some way obviously had expectations of mercantile benefits from their association, but for most, I suspect, it was the potential of massive profits that attracted them. Perusal of the R. G. Dun & Co. reports indicates that these iron firms grew rapidly, that profits were generally quite high, and, rather surprisingly, that the failure rate was remarkably low. In most instances, a firm failed because of the lack of financial acumen of a workingman-turned-capitalist. This was just the sort of situation that a wealthy merchant, with his business training, was confident he could transform into a profitable operation. It seemed an ideal situation. The worker-capitalist would provide the technical expertise for iron or steel making, a scarce commodity, and the merchant would provide the capital, another dear item in those times. In most instances it worked quite well, and by the outbreak of the Civil War Pittsburgh had developed a strong and well-articulated local upper class, composed of a mix of mercantile and industrial capital.

The Iron Barons

Most important for the development of the city's iron industry in the early years were Juniata Iron Works, Sligo Rolling Mill, and Pine Creek Rolling Mill (later known as Etna Iron). These three firms formed the basis of a strong and continuing set of independent iron firms in the city. Combined, the three mills produced about half of the iron made in Pittsburgh in 1826 and employed 130 workers.[18] Two of these mills, the Juniata and the Sligo, were founded by families which had recently come to Pittsburgh from the Juniata region of central Pennsylvania and had been "local notables" in that area for over a generation. They were able to transfer that prestige to Pittsburgh quite readily to meld with the emerging local upper class.

The Juniata Mill had been built in 1824 by Dr. Peter Shoenberger, whose family dominated iron production in Pittsburgh throughout most of the antebellum period. Their mill was located on the Allegheny River just northeast of the downtown core. Peter Shoenberger's father, George, had immigrated from Germany in the eighteenth century and in 1804 built the Juniata Forge in Huntington County. In 1815, Peter took over the business and two years later constructed a blast furnace in Blair County. In large measure, his Pittsburgh mill was considered simply an adjunct to the Juniata County operations. There were no furnace or puddling operations in Pittsburgh, and the Shoenbergers had to transport iron blooms made in central Pennsylvania to Pittsburgh by Conestoga wagon. In 1825, Juniata produced eight hundred tons of rolled iron in this manner.[19]

The Sligo Rolling Mill was established in 1825 by John Lyon and Robert T. Stewart, both of whom had also been engaged in iron production in the Juniata region, and this mill was also a branch of their operations in the latter area. They, too, transported all the iron blooms by wagon to Pittsburgh, conducting only rolling operations in the western city. Their Pittsburgh works were capable of producing nine hundred tons of rolled iron annually. Both Lyon and Stewart became integral parts of Pittsburgh's upper class in the decades to come.[20]

Pine Creek Rolling Mill was built in 1824 a few miles from Pittsburgh proper. In 1826 it was owned by M. B. Belknap, a leading

engineer and mechanic in the region, who also served as superintendent of the Juniata Iron Works. The Pine Creek Mill was sold in 1829
to Henry S. Spang and his son Charles, iron mill operators from
Juniata County, whose family ran it under the name Etna Iron as an
independent operation for over one hundred years, until it went out
of business in the late 1930s.[21]

There are several significant points to be made about this rudimentary iron industry in Pittsburgh in the 1820s. First, the mills
were remarkably disintegrated. Not only did they not make their
own pig iron but none even puddled their own blooms. The blooms,
in several cases, were hauled in from hundreds of miles away or
purchased from other operations. Nor did these men have much
access to local Pittsburgh capital during this early period. Iron making was a risky venture, and some mills went bankrupt, so Pittsburgh merchants in this early period were generally wary of investing. As a result, many of the earliest mills were built with outside
capital and manned by entrepreneurs who came to Pittsburgh from
elsewhere.[22] They nonetheless rapidly became part of the emerging
Pittsburgh establishment. Although the Shoenbergers were later to
move to Cincinnati and maintain only a marginal presence in Pittsburgh, they were an important cog in the developing upper class, as
were the Lyon, Spang, and Stewart families.[23] The young city, however, was just on the edge of a great transformation that took place
over the next thirty years.

By 1850, the city of Pittsburgh had 46,601 inhabitants, with another 21,262 in Allegheny City, which at that time was a separate
city across the Allegheny River. Pittsburgh had become a large, mature urban area, and its economy and society reflected that maturity.
Pittsburgh's iron industry grew rapidly during the 1830s and 1840s
and was barely ruffled by the Panic of 1837 or a devastating fire in
1845. In 1836, the year before the panic, there were nine rolling
mills in operation in Pittsburgh and Allegheny, along with eighteen
foundries. Twenty years later, there were twenty-five rolling mills.
No pig iron was as yet produced in the city, meaning that there were
no truly integrated iron operations wherein furnace, puddling, and
rolling mill operations were all combined at one site. This began to
change in 1859 when Graff, Bennett and Company "blew in" the
first blast furnace in Allegheny County. Designed to use coke from
the Connellsville region, the furnace was a success and led to Pittsburgh's becoming the largest aggregate producer of pig iron in the
country by the 1880s. That development, however, was still in the

future. The antebellum iron rolling mills of Pittsburgh remained relatively small and disintegrated, although most by then had their own puddling facilities.[24]

It is not clear just when the first puddling operations were established in the city, but by 1843 puddled iron was listed in market reports from Pittsburgh. According to Louis Hunter, however, Pittsburgh's puddled iron was inferior to the charcoal iron imported from Juniata, in terms of both price and quality.[25] Pittsburgh rolling mills in 1857 produced 67,100 tons of bar iron; 33,488 tons of nails, spikes, and rivets; 10,850 tons of blister, plow, spring, and cast steel; 5,637 tons of sheet iron; 3,212 tons of boiler iron; plus a couple of thousand tons of miscellaneous products.[26]

In these rolling mills in Pittsburgh and Allegheny during the 1850s, Louis Hunter counted 113 owners, of whom he was able to trace biographical information on sixty-eight individuals. He found that some important changes had taken place between 1826 and 1856. In the earlier period, the most successful iron manufacturers in Pittsburgh were men and families who transferred their experience from elsewhere. Only a few local merchants had ventured into iron manufacture. By 1856, however, 60 percent of the iron men were also involved in mercantile professions. Only nine had been engaged in iron manufacture elsewhere. Another nine were mechanics or workmen who had achieved entrepreneurial status. The remaining nine came from a variety of occupations, including workers in glass manufacture and foundry operations, a steamboat captain, an attorney, a railroad contractor, and a man engaged in the grain and milling business.[27]

Tracing these same individuals through the R. G. Dun & Co. reports, several biographical collections for Pittsburgh, and, finally, the various social directories of the city, a number of other characteristics become clear. The Shoenberger, Lyon, and Spang families from the 1826 group continued as powerful influences on the Pittsburgh rolling mill scene. In addition, the Graff family had become vitally interested in the operation of three rolling mills in the city and would in 1859 construct the first blast furnace. With the exception of B. F. Jones and James Laughlin, the Graffs were perhaps the most dynamic individuals in Pittsburgh's midcentury iron industry. Of even greater significance was the fact that the Graffs were, like the Shoenbergers, of German descent. If there was a strong cultural continuity between the older mercantile elite and the newer iron manufacturers, it is also true that iron making introduced, in the person of the Shoenbergers, Graffs, and several others, a new ethnic and cultural dimension to Pittsburgh's upper class.

Henry Graff was born in Westmoreland County and began his business career in 1822, when he opened a retail store in that area. In the early 1830s he began a large grain-processing concern with his brother; a few years later he went to Pittsburgh, where he became involved with a large canal transportation company. In 1845, Graff entered the iron business for the first time as a partner in Sable Rolling Mill with the Zug family.[28] After eight years, Graff sold out to his partners, at the same time also disposing of his canal business. Then with his four sons (John, Matthew, Thomas, and Christopher) Henry expanded his iron interests. After Henry died in 1855, John Graff took over the Clinton Rolling Mill, subsequently taking in James I. Bennett as a partner. The two of them later built Pittsburgh's first blast furnace near their rolling mills. Thomas Graff organized Graff, Hugus & Co., stove manufacturers. Matthew Graff became a partner in Graff & Woods, an iron rolling mill, and Christopher Graff joined with William H. Everson in Pennsylvania Iron Works. William Graff, another son, ran William Graff & Co., an iron commission house, which gave the Graff family an informally integrated iron empire that ranged from the manufacturing of pig iron to the selling of finished products. None of these operations, however, was formally integrated under one corporate style, and it is impossible to know how completely their activities were coordinated.[29] James Bennett had also been a commission merchant in Pittsburgh before becoming a partner in the Clinton and Millvale rolling mills with the Graffs.[30]

The Painters were another important German family on the iron scene in Pittsburgh in the 1840s and 1850s. Jacob Painter, like Henry Graff, was the son of German immigrants who had been born in Westmoreland County and moved to Pittsburgh in 1827. He engaged in the commercial trade there, with the successful firm of Painter and Meyer. Sometime during this period Painter also became involved with the Lorenz, Sterling Iron Company in running blast furnaces on the Allegheny River, some distance from Pittsburgh. Having entered the iron industry near the raw material stage, Painter soon decided to get involved in the production of finished iron products. In 1854 he joined Christopher Zug and John Lindsay in running the Sable Mill. As part of the deal, Painter sold Zug his interest in the blast furnace firm, thereby allowing Sable Iron also to undertake an informal, and somewhat geographically distant, integrated operation. Painter later dropped out of that partnership, which ran two mills and the blast furnace operation, to start the Pittsburgh Iron Works in the late 1850s. At that time, Painter's sons (Augustus, Park, and Jacob, Jr.) joined him in the latter concern. It became one of the largest mills in the city, for a long time ranking behind only American Iron (Jones and Laughlin) and Andrew Carnegie's Union Mills.[31]

A number of mills were also started by members of Scots-Irish and English families during these years. Henry Lloyd and George Black ran the Kensington Rolling Mill. Lloyd was a native of Huntington County who went to Pittsburgh in the 1830s. After working for a number of years in D. Leech & Co., one of the oldest and largest transportation companies on the Pennsylvania Canal, in 1854 he became a partner in the Kensington Iron Mill, which had been built in 1828. His partner at Kensington was George Black, who had also been involved with D. Leech & Co. Black had run his own packet line on the Ohio River between Pittsburgh and Cincinnati. According to R. G. Dun & Co., Black was the wealthier of the two men, with a fortune estimated at about $100,000, whereas Lloyd owned just $10,000 to $15,000.[32] Black remained with the firm until the 1870s, but the Lloyds stayed with the concern until the 1890s.

John W. Chalfant joined the Spang family in running the venerable Etna Rolling Mill. Chalfant was a member of an old Westmoreland County family who went to work in the Sable Rolling Mill after he graduated from Jefferson College in 1850. In 1856 he purchased an interest in the Etna mill; he maintained his connection with the venture until he died in 1898. The Etna mill in 1858 was still one of the soundest in the city, and R. G. Dun & Co. called it "well conducted, safe and sound."[33]

Another important antebellum mill was Vesuvius Iron, which had been built in 1846 by members of a number of Pittsburgh's oldest and most prominent mercantile families. Perhaps the most eminent of that group was James O'Hara, son of Gen. James O'Hara, the city's most important early industrialist and a large real estate owner in his own right. O'Hara left after two years and was replaced by Robert Dalzell, who was one of the wealthiest men in Pittsburgh, having made his fortune in the grocery trade. Neither O'Hara nor Dalzell knew anything about iron manufacture, so they allied with James Lewis and George Lewis, Jr., sons of George Lewis. The elder Lewis was widely known as the "Welshman who rolled the first bar of iron in America." He had come to America in 1816 and taken charge of Pittsburgh's Union Rolling Mill in 1823. Later he superintended the Sligo Works and the Juniata Mill. The two Lewis boys were also practically trained iron men, so the Vesuvius mill had a well-balanced combination of mercantile capital and iron-making expertise. As a result, it was a highly successful venture in the 1850s, which R. G. Dun & Co. gave its highest credit rating, calling it a "safe, cautious house."[34]

In the later 1840s and early 1850s a number of new mills sprang up in Pittsburgh. Among those were Eagle Rolling Mill,[35] Pennsylvania Iron Company,[36] McKeesport Rolling Mill,[37] Glendon Mill,[38] and Birmingham Rolling Mill.[39] The best known iron firm in Pittsburgh in the 1850s, and arguably the most important, was the American Iron Works, owned and operated by the firm of Jones and Laughlins. The American works were begun in 1850, when a group of mechanics started a small rolling mill on the south side of the Monongahela River. Led by Benjamin and Francis Lauth, immigrant ironworkers and mechanical geniuses who perfected a cold-rolling technique for iron that gave it a smooth, hard exterior surface, it was an early example of worker capitalism. But the firm was also desperately short of cash during its early years and in 1853 sought additional capital in the city's mercantile community. The Lauths attracted the interest of Benjamin F. Jones and Samuel Kier, freight commission merchants who ran the Mechanic's Line of Packets between Pittsburgh and Philadelphia. Jones and Kier invested a total of $12,700 in the business and became equal partners with the Lauths.

At the point when Kier and Jones joined American Iron it was a feeble operation with just two heating and four puddling furnaces and a daily capacity for only seven tons of iron. The entrance of the dynamic Jones into the firm transformed American Iron almost overnight. Jones was born in Claysville, Pennsylvania; when he was nineteen, he moved to Pittsburgh, where he began working for Kier's Mechanic's Line. A year later, Jones became manager of the concern. By the mid-1850s, however, the completion of the Pennsylvania Railroad into Pittsburgh had made the packet service outmoded, so Kier and Jones began seeking other business opportunities. As a result, they were receptive to the Lauths' entreaties. Kier never became an active partner in the iron manufacturing firm, and in 1856 he traded his one-quarter interest to Jones for the latter's share in their iron commission business.

Since Kier was the major source of financial backing for the struggling iron firm, Jones had to find additional avenues of capital. For this he turned to another merchant, James Laughlin. Laughlin was an Irish immigrant who had amassed a huge fortune as a meatpacker and commission merchant in partnership with his brother, Alexander. James Laughlin also married into one of Pittsburgh's oldest and most prestigious families, the Irwins. James and Alexander began investing in blast furnaces in the late 1840s and early 1850s and also opened iron commission houses in Pittsburgh and Indiana. Serving as a selling agent for the American Iron Works, James Laughlin had advanced the firm some $8,000 by 1855. In the same year he put an additional $40,000 into the business. Laughlin ultimately invested about $150,000 in the rapidly expanding iron mill but took no role in its management, allowing Jones a free hand in that area.

Backed by the vast resources of James Laughlin, Jones transformed American Iron into a giant of the antebellum iron trade, rapidly expanding the operations of the rolling mill, giving it the capacity for one hundred tons of iron daily by the outbreak of the Civil War. At first, the American mill purchased its pig iron from furnaces owned by the Laughlin family near Youngstown, Ohio. In 1861, however, Jones became the second Pittsburgh iron maker to construct a blast furnace in the city, erecting the Eliza Furnace directly across the Monongahela River from the American works. Somewhat earlier, in 1856, Jones also established a warehousing and jobbing outlet in Chicago, so that by the time of the Civil War, American Iron was one of the few iron firms to become vertically integrated from blast furnaces to the selling of finished iron products. A number of others, however, as we have seen, were vertically integrated in a more informal manner, owning these agencies through partnerships with other individuals. Nonetheless, outside the rail mills, American Iron stood, as Porter and Livesay have commented, as "one of the few unintegrated antebellum iron firms that succeeded in adopting the integrated, high-volume structure."[40]

Analysis of American Iron in the 1850s raises some important questions about the nature of business development in the nineteenth century and the relation of the iron industry in Pittsburgh to those developments. Porter and Livesay, in their pioneering study of the relationship between merchants and manufacturers during this period, focus on the development of the vertically integrated rail mill as the most important element in the antebellum iron industry. It was, to them, a wholly new and different kind of business.[41] It was new and different because it used the corporate form of organization, employed professional managers, established bureaucratic systems patterned on those of the railroads (which often had an ownership interest in these mills), had a separation of ownership and management, and, as a result, developed strict procedures for accountability. Also, "the backward integration of rolling mills (to ownership of blast furnaces) marked the beginning of the gradual removal of middlemen from the iron trade."[42]

Porter and Livesay leave an impression that is somewhat misleading: "In the last third of the nineteenth century, integrated firms, in control of their own raw materials and run by professional managers, dominated the industry."[43] They may have dominated the industry in terms of their ability to produce large quantities of goods and attract media attention, but in other respects they remained somewhat exotic creatures. On the eve of the Civil War, the only integrated iron firms in America were rail firms, mostly created by railroad companies. There were just eight of them in the United States, and none in Pittsburgh. Yet Pittsburgh was by this point the iron manufacturing center of the country. In that respect, Porter and Livesay have distorted the reality of the iron industry in nineteenth-century America. The typical firm, both before and after the Civil War, was not an integrated behemoth producing iron or steel rails. Those always remained an atypical segment of a large and varied industry. It is all well and good to posit a preference for largeness, bureaucracy, and professional management, but if one wishes to understand the generic nature of the iron business in the nineteenth century, especially in Pittsburgh, it is necessary to look at other, smaller, and less integrated institutions.

It is of utmost importance that the reader understand precisely the kind of manufacturing endeavors in which these merchant-capitalists were becoming involved. On the one hand, iron manufacturing was a quintessentially industrial operation, one that must have forced the merchants to stretch their mind-set and capabilities in dealing with its operations. On the other hand, the vast majority of these iron firms were not iron rail mills, with their special and unique demands (which Livesay and Porter analyzed), nor were they Bessemer steel operations. These iron mills had a psychology all their own that must be understood.

The Psychology of Iron Making

David Brody's seminal *Steelworkers in America: The Non-Union Era*, published in 1960, begins with the brilliant chapter "Psychology and Method of Steelmaking." Taking his cue from Andrew Carnegie, Brody stressed the fanatical drive for economy that characterized steel making in the late nineteenth century. Although Brody was fully aware of early traditions of iron puddling, and how they differed from those of Bessemer steel manufacture, his focus was on the latter process. Brody's preoccupation with Bessemer steel was quite proper but has, unfortunately, tended to leave a mistaken impression of the nineteenth-century iron and steel industry with most readers.[44]

There has been increasing recognition in recent years of the importance of the manufacture of wrought iron and its difference from Bessemer steel. Whereas most earlier treatments had, like Brody's, tended to dismiss iron making as a dying trade not worthy of analysis, a number of commentators in the last several years have stressed the continuing importance of iron traditions. These works, however, have all focused almost exclusively on the skilled iron worker, the nature of his work, and the struggle for control of the workplace between him and his boss. Much less attention has been paid to the owner-entrepreneur in this environment. It is this individual who will be our primary concern in this chapter.

Our focus is on the processes of puddling and iron rolling. The first stage of iron and steel production is the blast furnace, wherein raw iron ore and fuel are burned to create a substance known as pig iron (or cast iron if used in iron castings). Most iron puddling and rolling mills were not integrated units in the nineteenth century and did not produce their own pig iron, so only incidental consideration will be given to that stage. The principal production process in which we are interested is called puddling. In this highly complex and labor-intensive process, a reverbatory furnace was used. It was slow, demanded considerable skill to determine the precise state of the iron as it was being manipulated, and involved a good deal of heat and heavy labor. It was a production process relatively impervious to technological development and resultant economies.[45]

More than anything else, perhaps, wrought iron production required patience from both the worker and the mill owner. If Bessemer steel production was typified by speed of production and economies of scale, iron puddling was just the opposite. It was a process characterized by work complexity and small-batch production, and not much could be done about either. By its very nature, then, puddled iron manufacture was the antithesis of Bessemer steel production. Since the raw materials of iron production varied in their chemical composition, it was necessary for each batch of iron to be manipulated manually. To do so, just enough heat was applied to make the iron sufficiently malleable for an iron puddler and his helper to refine it to the proper point. This process, of course, was imperfect and depended on the unique skill of the iron worker, who had to make a whole series of decisions about the small batch of iron as the heat progressed. Since each batch was manipulated by hand, the scale of production was limited to the physical strength of the worker. The U.S. Bureau of Labor noted these physical restrictions even in the early twentieth century: "Five hundred and fifty pounds is as much as is charged in a majority of mills and in none is the charge over 600 pounds. . . . Puddling is very hard work, and the average man can not charge over 550 pounds and make five heats a day."[46]

Thus, the owner had to be patient. As David Montgomery has noted, the manager's brain was often under the workman's cap, so the owner was largely a captive of the speed and decision-making expertise of his skilled workmen.[47] Therefore, speed, a key component of continuous processing techniques and of economizing moves, was simply not possible in iron puddling. Although iron mill owners continually experimented with mechanical puddling devices, they met with little success. The owner was also dependent on the physical strength of the workmen. However much the mill owner might want to move toward large-batch production to meet surging demand, it was simply not possible. True, he could add puddling furnaces and hire more puddlers and helpers to run those machines, but that was merely a linear expansion. It did not achieve the kinds of economies of scale Carnegie and others achieved with Bessemer steel production. For example, Pittsburgh Forge and Iron Company in 1875, a moderate-size operation capable of producing twenty-three thousand tons of wrought iron annually, had fifteen puddling furnaces manned by 30 puddlers and an equal number of helpers.[48] Ten years later, American Iron Works, the largest iron (as opposed to Bessemer steel) operation in the city, had a capacity for seventy thousand tons of wrought iron from seventy-six puddling furnaces manned by 158 puddlers and an equal number of helpers.[49] Expansion of wrought iron production was arithmetic, not geometric, and there was little efficiency or economy of scale to be gained by an increase of production.

Nor did these iron masters have much sense of what their costs of production were anyhow. Most used what was called the lump system of accounting. This was, in fact, one of the factors that caused Andrew Carnegie, who never considered himself an innovator, to begin pushing so early for the adoption of the Bessemer process. As he noted in his *Autobiography:* "As I became acquainted with the manufacture of iron I was greatly surprised to find that the cost of each of the various processes was unknown. Inquiries made of the leading manufacturers of Pittsburgh proved this. It was a lump business, and until stock was taken and the books balanced at the end of the year, the manufacturers were in total ignorance of results."[50] Iron puddling, for both the worker and the owner, was an inexact science, one in which traditions and folkways carried more weight than did any modern management methods or accounting techniques.

The next stage of production was only slightly more amenable to technological change and large-batch methods, at least in the early years. Conventional wisdom among historians has long given great importance to the three-high rolling mill, developed by John Fritz in 1857. This was indeed a marvelous device and did much to bring about high-speed, large-batch continuous processing in some rolling mills. But it was used only in the iron rail mills, an important minority sector of the industry. Not until the 1880s and the invention of an automatic rising and falling table could the three-high mill even be used successfully for Bessemer steel rails. Carnegie's Edgar Thomson mill did not create an integrated production line for Bessemer rails and the three-high mill until 1888. By this time, all rail mills, whether iron or steel, used the three-high mill. For the bulk of iron rolling mills, the transformation to any kind of continuous processing came much later, if at all.

It made little sense to look for techniques to increase the speed and efficiency of the roll train if the puddling process remained slow, small-scale, and uncertain. Each puddling furnace produced paltry units of some 150 to 180 pounds, and the first stage of the rolling process was to build up the small pieces of metal into larger ones. The puddled iron, after having been cooled, was first reheated by a heater, who built the small pieces up into larger units. The next stage was to send the iron to a rougher, who used a process similar to the kneading of bread to increase the strength of the iron and make it more compact. These bars of iron were then cut and laid out to cool in piles of five to seven bars each.

At that point they were again reheated in a furnace and put into a roller to be final rolled. This was an arduous and difficult process, requiring a great deal of skill and patience. The rollers transformed these bars into their desired shape by repeatedly passing them through the rolls, reducing the bar a little each time. On each pass, the worker made minute adjustments, adjustments based on his skill and knowledge rather than any standardized practice. One prominent engineer wrote, "Conditions of varying work, percentages of slag, and irregularity of the same irons, not to mention the possible overheating of piles, complicate the relation between the chemical composition and the physical properties of [wrought iron.]"[51]

Despite the presence of large, power-driven machines in the rolling mill, the work performed there, as in the puddling mill, was largely hand work, requiring a great deal of skill and patience. Even though the mill owner often did not personally have this skill (although it was traditional for men of old iron families to spend an apprenticeship in the mills, often working as a helper at the puddling furnace, and a good number even became rollers before moving on to management), he was fully aware of the necessity for time and patience in making a good product. Therefore, the majority of wrought iron manufacturers, unlike their colleagues in steel production, were content to settle for time-honored, traditional ways of doing business. As was noted in a metallurgy text as late as the 1920s: "The manufacture of wrought iron is easily carried on in small quantities at a time and there has, therefore, never been the . . . incentive for employing elaborate machinery in its production. . . ."[52] If Carnegie and other Bessemer steelmakers were itching to economize and substitute machines for hand labor, this drive was far more muted in the wrought iron mills.

Crucible Steel Production

Pittsburgh was "Iron City" throughout most of the nineteenth century, as production of that metal dominated the economy and culture of the young city. What is less often recognized is that Pittsburgh was also the hub of steel production from the 1850s onward. Prior to Carnegie's erection of a Bessemer works at the Edgar Thomson plant in the mid-1870s, however, steel was produced by the blister or crucible process. Wrought iron is converted to steel by carburization, that is, by the adding of carbon to iron. In early nineteenth-century Pittsburgh, the only process for making steel was by use of a cementation furnace to create what is called blister steel. Iron, when red-hot, absorbs carbon very slowly, so in the cementation process small strips of iron were wrapped in carbon and allowed to absorb the carbon for several days. Then the piece was hammered to squeeze out the slag and heated and cooled several more times. It was a very laborious and costly process but produced a high grade of steel. Just prior to the Civil War, cementation was replaced by the crucible process, in which wrought iron was melted in a crucible (or Huntsman furnace) with carbon, a faster and less expensive process that still produced a very high-grade steel.[53]

Crucible production was vastly different in every respect from Bessemer steel making and in many ways resembled the same kind of production culture as the puddling mills. Like iron puddling, crucible steel production was a slow, arduous process requiring a good deal of patience. Although American crucible steel makers, unlike the English, did learn to carburize and melt their steel in one operation, it was a process that was relatively impervious to mechanization, continuous process, and other economizing methods.[54]

Like puddling, crucible steel making was more an art than a science, one that made extensive demands on the abilities of the skilled workman operating the furnace and on the patience of the owner of the mill, who had to weigh his desires for greater production with the need for high-quality tool steel. To a large extent, quality and speed were antithetical, and American crucible steel makers, although they were more innovative in this respect than their British counterparts, nonetheless remained aware of the need to maintain a balance between productivity and quality.[55]

As in puddling mills, rule of thumb procedures, rather than chemistry or modern management methods, predominated. Detailed recipes for making steel from different grades of iron were kept, and much of the knowledge and expertise for determining just when the proper cooking point had been reached lay in the head and hands of the skilled workman. Nearly every aspect of the process was an art, from making clay crucibles to tending the furnace, where the melter had to decide just when the steel was sufficiently killed.[56] If a mistake was made at that stage, the whole batch had to be scrapped and the long, arduous process started over again. Next, the ingot was poured and cooled; it was then sent to the rolling mill, where, similar to iron, it was shaped into its final product.

The scale of production at these crucible mills was far lower than even at the iron rolling mills. In 1874, Hussey, Wells & Co. and Black Diamond Steel were by far the largest and most productive crucible operations in Pittsburgh and among the largest in the country. Hussey, Wells made just 13,000 tons of fine tool steel annually, and Black Diamond produced 12,000 tons. Other large crucible mills in the city, such as Sheffield Steel and LaBelle Steel, produced only about half that much. Nor did these crucible mills experience much growth. LaBelle managed to increase its production to 10,000 tons by 1884 and only reached 15,000 tons in 1894 by installing two 15-

ton open hearth furnaces. Hussey, Wells increased its production to
15,500 tons in 1884 and 25,000 tons in 1894 only by the addition of
open hearth works to the plant. The same was true of other crucible
steel producers.

Crucible production itself was almost completely impervious to
demands for increased production, faster throughput, and economizing. Nor did the crucible mills become integrated operations. Although many had their own finishing mills, where they manufactured agricultural implements and fine tools, virtually none made
pig iron or owned coal and coke fields. They remained basically
small-scale independently owned and managed operations until the
turn of the century. In this respect, and in virtually every social
aspect, as shall be demonstrated, the crucible steel makers were
nearly identical to the wrought iron manufacturers. Both groups
differed dramatically in workplace experience, social background,
and temperament from the makers of Bessemer steel.

In 1831, there were fourteen blister-steel furnaces in the United
States, capable of producing a total of just 1,600 tons annually. To
that point, no blister steel had been produced in Pittsburgh, but
within two decades that city became the center of the American
crucible steel industry.[57] The first blister steel in Pittsburgh was
produced by the Shoenberger family, owners of Juniata Rolling Mill,
in 1833. They successfully made what was evidently a fairly low-
grade steel and in 1840–41 first attempted to erect a crucible works,
bringing over an Englishman to superintend the operations. That
facility was abandoned after about a year. During the 1840s a
number of other Pittsburgh firms (Jones & Quigg; Singer, Hartman;
and Coleman, Hailman) made blister or cast steel in the city. In
1852, the firm of McKelvey and Blair pioneered in the production of
cast steel, but the operation also ceased after two years. That plant
was then bought and run by Hussey, Wells & Co. During this same
period, Singer, Nimick & Co. and Isaac Jones's Pittsburgh Steel
Works also began producing cast steel.[58] By 1850, the Iron City was
producing 76,749 tons of iron, compared to just 10,850 tons of blister and cast steel.[59] Beginning in 1860, however, Pittsburgh firms
commenced a revolution in crucible steel production.

The most important firm in bringing about this revolution was
Hussey, Wells & Co. The key individuals in this operation were
Curtis G. Hussey, Thomas M. Howe, and Calvin Wells. Born on a
farm near York, Pennsylvania, Hussey became one of Pittsburgh's
most dynamic and innovative antebellum business leaders. Beginning as a physician, Hussey soon purchased a number of general

stores throughout the western territory. Before long, Hussey found he was devoting all his time to the management of these stores, so he abandoned his medical practice. In the 1830s, like James Laughlin, Hussey began dealing in pork and soon moved the center of his operations to Pittsburgh. In 1842, hearing of rich copper deposits in the Lake Superior region, Hussey began investing in mines there. Soon, he organized the Boston and Pittsburgh Copper Co., which opened the fabulously successful Cliff Mine in the Lake Superior region. In 1859, Hussey joined with Thomas M. Howe to found C. G. Hussey & Co. copper manufacturers, one of the earliest enterprises of its type west of the Alleghenies. By the time of the Civil War, Hussey was perhaps Pittsburgh's first millionaire, or even multimillionaire. With his great wealth and innovative personality, Hussey looked for investments in Pittsburgh's burgeoning ferrous metals industry. Disdaining the established route of iron manufacture, he instead took a chance on a daring new steel-making procedure.

In 1859, Hussey, Howe, and Wells bought the old steel plant of Blair & Co., which had been developed by Thomas S. Blair to make crucible steel by the direct process. Hussey spent a good deal of time and money perfecting the process and made Pittsburgh's first crucible steelworks a successful operation. Thomas M. Howe probably ranked second only to his partner Hussey among Pittsburgh's businessmen in the 1850s. Member of an old New England family, Howe was born in Vermont and moved to Pittsburgh in 1828. He began his career as a clerk in the dry goods store of Mason and McDonough, and in 1830 he became a partner in the hardware store of Leavit & Co. Nine years later, Howe turned his attention to banking, becoming cashier of Exchange National Bank. By 1851, he had become the bank's president and also founded the Pittsburgh Chamber of Commerce, serving as its president until his death in 1877. A leading Whig, Howe was elected to Congress in 1850 and helped found the Republican party in Pittsburgh a few years later. Wells, a native of New York, was also a member of an old New England family but, unlike his two partners, had little wealth or eminence in 1859. He had moved to Pittsburgh as a young man, attended Western University for a time, and then gone to work in Hussey's copper mill. Two years later, he became a partner in Hussey's pork packing business. In 1859, Wells was given primary responsibility for erecting the furnaces at Hussey, Wells, and he was the active manager of the plant during its early years of operation. He remained there until the early 1870s.[60]

The second major crucible steel operation in Pittsburgh was

Black Diamond Steel, founded by James Park, Jr., and David E. Park. Unlike the founders of Hussey, Wells, the Park brothers were both born and bred in Pittsburgh. In other respects, however, they resembled their crucible colleagues. They were the sons of the elder James Park, who, like so many Pittsburghers, moved to the city from the north of Ireland, arriving in 1812. Their father ran a successful china and metal store and became one of the leading merchants of the city. As young men, David and James, Jr., joined their father's firm and made it one of the largest and most prosperous in the city. In 1858, they began to explore new business opportunities. First, like Hussey and Howe, the Park brothers built a copper rolling mill and also became involved in Lake Superior copper mining and a Pittsburgh cotton mill. Having accumulated some $300,000 between them by 1859, James and David Park decided to embark on the manufacture of steel. They organized the Black Diamond Works and built a mill in 1862 just north of Andrew Carnegie's Union Iron on the banks of the Allegheny River.

As superintendent of the mill, the Parks, who had no expertise in these matters, chose Thomas Shoenberger Blair, inventor of the direct process and former owner of the Hussey, Wells mill. Blair was also a relative of the Shoenberger family of Juniata Iron and had worked as a manager at Juniata for a number of years. After one year at Black Diamond, he returned to the Shoenberger mill. Despite some preliminary failures with Blair's direct process, Black Diamond succeeded in producing a high-quality product and became one of Pittsburgh's premier steel producers in the days before Bessemer.[61]

The third great crucible steel firm was Sheffield Steel Works, which had been making a relatively low-quality cast steel for a number of years after it was built by John F. Singer and Samuel Hartman. Little is known of Hartman, but Singer was a member of a prominent Pittsburgh family of German origin. He was the son of George Singer, a native of Greensburg, Pennsylvania, who in 1833 moved to Pittsburgh, where he had a furniture business. John F. Singer worked at various commercial ventures for a time before founding Sheffield Steel in 1848. When Hartman left the struggling firm in 1859, William H. Singer and George Singer, Jr., became partners, along with several members of the Nimick family. William H. Singer had worked at the Shoenberger's Juniata works and then became senior partner in the Sheffield mill. He was also involved in a number of major steel ventures, including Carnegie Steel,[62] in the 1880s.

While the Singers were the active managers of Sheffield Steel throughout its history, the Nimicks were mercantile men who provided much needed financing. Alexander Nimick and William K. Nimick were sons of William Nimick, a wholesale grocer in Pittsburgh. Both were born in the city and entered the commission trade at an early age. In 1845, Alexander and William founded a forwarding and commission business of their own; later they also set up an iron commission firm. The latter business became enormously successful, being worth $200,000 by 1855. As a result the Nimicks, like a number of iron and steel merchants, began looking for a stable source of supply of steel products. This prompted them to invest in Sheffield Steel and created yet another example of informal vertical integration during this time. They also became financial backers of the Park brothers in Black Diamond Steel in 1862. Alexander Nimick was president of Western Insurance Company, and William organized Pittsburgh Trust, which later became the First National Bank of Pittsburgh. They later also took over the venerable Sligo Rolling Mill.[63] Sheffield Steel never became a mass producer but was regarded as second only to Black Diamond in the production of high-quality tool steel.

The last of the major crucible concerns was Crescent Steel, built in 1867 by Reuben Miller III, George H. Barr, and Charles Parkin. Reuben Miller was from an old Pennsylvania family; his grandfather was one of the earliest cut nail manufacturers in Pittsburgh. His father owned a tobacco factory and an iron foundry and later opened the Washington Works, makers of steam engines and machinery. Reuben Miller worked in his father's machine firm and foundry and at age twenty-eight organized Crescent Steel, which he ran for thirty-four years. Charles Parkin was a native of England who was often known as the father of crucible steel making in America. In 1859 he immigrated to the United States to work as superintendent of the hammer shops at Hussey, Wells, where he remained until he joined Crescent Steel. William Metcalf was from an old New England family, and his father, Orlando Metcalf, was a prominent attorney in early Pittsburgh. Metcalf was trained at Rensselaer Polytechnic College in Troy, New York, and worked for several years in Pittsburgh's foundries. For a year he was managing director of Crescent Steel, which became one of the most successful crucible steel operations in the city.[64]

There were a number of other steelworks (Wayne Iron and Steel,[65] Pittsburgh Steel Works,[66] Fort Pitt Iron and Steel,[67] and LaBelle Steel[68]) in Pittsburgh during the 1850s and 1860s, but they either went through such a succession of owners or made such small amounts of steel that it is not necessary to consider them in detail at this point. One of the key elements that all of these firms demonstrate is that, first of all, merchants tended to predominate in the crucible steel firms just as they did in the iron rolling mills. The proportion of merchants was around 60 percent in both groups. Also, the steel firms remained quite small, and formally disintegrated, although a couple did have connections with selling houses and one was allied with a blast furnace (Fort Pitt Iron and Steel). The crucible firms, even more than the iron rolling mills, served small, specialized, diversified markets. They never competed, or generally wished to compete, in the highly competitive rail and railroad products markets.

Conclusion: A Cohesive Mercantile and Metal Aristocracy

By 1860, Pittsburgh and Allegheny combined had a population of over seventy thousand, and although mercantile pursuits still predominated, 20 percent of the work force was engaged in industry, and iron and steel manufacturing had become the city's major business. A transformation of this magnitude in the economic base of a city could quite legitimately be presumed to create a similar circulation of elites whereby the older mercantile elite was replaced by new men who exploited their skills and daring to create these new industrial enterprises. This was not the case in Pittsburgh. By this time a highly integrated, rather than bifurcated, local aristocracy had been created, one with its feet in both the mercantile and industrial camps. A number of studies substantiate this conclusion.

Michael Holt, in his analysis of the rise of the Republican party in Pittsburgh in the 1850s, extracted 149 men from the 1850 census who owned real property worth more than twenty-five thousand dollars. He found that half of them lived near one another in stately old mansions on or near Penn Avenue in the Fourth Ward. A majority (57 percent) were Presbyterian, and most of these were members of the First or Third Presbyterian church. A large minority (41 percent) were Episcopalian and attended Trinity Church. Even at this relatively early stage in Pittsburgh's history, 70 percent were native born, and of the foreign born, 83 percent were from Northern Ireland and 10 percent from Germany. The Scots-Irish foreign born had lived in the community for some time by 1850 and had achieved a great deal of social and economic success.[69]

Like Porter and Livesay, Holt found that merchants and manufacturers among this group had mutual rather than antagonistic interests and provided several examples of merchants who had invested in manufacturing endeavors to prove his point.[70] These economic
ties were abetted by strong social connections. Many of the men
went to the same churches and lived in identical neighborhoods.
They also joined forces to support similar charities and hospitals,
went to fancy dress balls together, attended the same teas and parties, and intermarried extensively. By the mid-nineteenth century,
according to Holt, Pittsburgh had developed a strong, tightly knit
local aristocracy that evidently managed to integrate the older mercantile elite with a newer manufacturing group.[71]

A couple of other studies substantiate Holt's findings. Harold
Twiss studied forty-five directors of downtown Pittsburgh banks in
1850.[72] He found that 47 percent of them were engaged in mercantile pursuits, and 33 percent were involved in manufacturing or mining. He discovered about the same percentage of Presbyterians, Episcopalians, and native-born individuals as Holt. One important
finding by Twiss was that nearly two-thirds of these men got their
start in family businesses, indicating that few were self-made. Of
those who entered family enterprises, 38 percent were in mercantile
concerns and 25 percent in manufacturing, giving credence to the
idea that mercantile ventures, which required less start-up capital,
were still relatively more open to "new men." All in all, Twiss's
bankers seem to represent the same sort of old family aristocracy
that Holt found. They were a privileged group whose eminence and
position on bank boards derived at least as much from their old
family status as from their own business accomplishments.

James C. Holmberg has also studied Pittsburgh's elite during the
1850s.[73] Through an analysis of the manuscript census schedules
and specific newspaper mentions for Allegheny County between
1850 and 1880, Holmberg examined the phenomenon of community
leadership. From this he isolated a large group of 4,356 leaders of
various kinds. The group most germane to our interest is the one he
termed the entrepreneurial elite. He found this group to be exceptionally homogeneous in social and cultural characteristics, extremely cohesive in its leadership activities, and nearly un-
challenged and highly pervasive in its economic prominence.
Pittsburgh had developed, in other words, a highly cohesive urban
aristocracy by the time of the Civil War. An integral part of this now-
settled upper class was the city's iron and steel manufacturers.

The present study bears that out. Of the forty families involved in the iron and steel industry in the 1850s and 1860s, the vast majority appear to be indisputably upper class. This is a difficult point to prove, since most indices of class status do not appear until the twentieth century. By that time, of course, families (such as the Shoenbergers) might have left Pittsburgh for elsewhere or the family line might have ended. Nonetheless, fully 78 percent of those families were listed in the Pittsburgh *Social Directory* of 1904, the most selective of the published society books. A nearly identical number, and virtually the same families, were listed in the Pittsburgh *Social Register* of 1908. Because of the fact that these directories measure prestige in the twentieth century, and we wish to know the status of families in the midnineteenth century, I have developed a schema to illustrate the relationship. Pittsburgh families are grouped into Core, Non-Core, Marginal, and Elite family groups, according to the incidence of their membership in prestigious social clubs—the Duquesne, the Pittsburgh, the Allegheny Country Club, and the Pittsburgh Golf Club, among others—and the degree to which they have intermarried with one another. This allows us to create, I believe, a more realistic and sensitive barometer of class status, one that is far more restrictive than either of the published directories. Even by these more rigid criteria the antebellum iron and steel elite in Pittsburgh appear to be indisputably upper class.

Sixty percent were members of the Core Upper Class; 23 percent were Non-Core upper class. That 83 percent in the Core and Non-Core groups is roughly comparable to the percentages (and the actual families) listed in the *Social Directory* and *Social Register* in the twentieth century. Another 13 percent were marginal members of the upper class, and 5 percent were outside the upper class, often because they moved out of the city, or in some other way disappeared from consideration.[74] And this upper-class status of Pittsburgh's iron and steel manufacturers persisted throughout the nineteenth century (see table 2.2 in chapter 2).

By the time of the Civil War, Pittsburgh's iron and steel manufacturers almost without exception ran disintegrated operations, selling merchant bar iron to regional and local markets. Only a few were servicing a national market, and just a couple of plants were making rails (American Iron, Kensington Rolling Mill, and Wayne Iron and Steel), the latter two producing only very small quantities. Only American Iron was truly competitive in the vast railway market. Many men who had made their fortunes in mercantile concerns had become members of these iron and steel companies, and some ran iron commission firms that gave a few of the companies an informally integrated arrangement. Then, too, a small number of firms had their own blast furnaces, but only a couple of those were in Pittsburgh itself to provide the actual physical integration that American Iron Works and Graff, Bennett & Co. enjoyed.

Pittsburgh by the mid-1870s, however, was on the verge of a vast transformation, as Bessemer steel and the Carnegie mills were about to revolutionize much in the industry nationally and locally. Important as these transformations were, there has nonetheless been a tendency to overstate their effect on the iron and steel industry in Pittsburgh and, in turn, their impact on the social and cultural structure of the city's upper class. The young city had developed a strong and cohesive upper class by the time of the Civil War. It was homogeneous, had a high degree of value integration, and included a number of powerful institutions to help knit it together. If our interest is the national Bessemer steel rail industry, our focus would quite properly be on Carnegie and his competitors. If, however, one wishes to understand, as we do, what was going on in an industrial city like Pittsburgh, then we must understand the nature of local business—those smaller independent iron and steel manufacturers—and its relationship to the large national-market firms. The pre–Civil War iron and steel makers were vitally important cogs in that upper class, and the succeeding chapters will demonstrate their powerful resilience in the face of a massive economic, social, and cultural challenge.

2

Clash of the Titans: Carnegie and the Challenge of the Old Iron Masters

> By all means make your first approach to Pittsburg [*sic*] in the
> night time, and you will behold a spectacle which has not a
> parallel on this continent. Darkness gives the city and its
> surroundings a picturesqueness which they lack wholly by
> daylight. . . . Around the city's edge, and on the sides of the
> hills which encircle it like a gloomy amphitheater, their
> outlines rising dark against the sky, through numberless
> apertures, fiery lights stream forth, looking angrily and
> fiercely up toward the heavens, while over all settles a heavy
> pall of smoke. It is as though one had reached the outer edge
> of the infernal regions, and saw before him the great furnace
> of Pandemonium with all the lids lifted.
>
> William Glazier, "The Great Furnace of America"

IF Pittsburgh's mercantile aristocracy was confronted by a sizable
challenge with the emergence of the iron industry during the antebellum years, it faced an unbelievably awesome encounter with the
rise of Andrew Carnegie and the Bessemer steel industry in the years
after the war. The stable, contented, almost smug Presbyterian local
elite watched massive steel mills rise from dusty fields and observed
the emergence of new men who commanded these enterprises—
men who were sometimes from divergent social, economic, and
cultural origins but who also brought radically new ideas about the
way business should be conducted in the city. This new group, most
dramatically presented in the person of Andrew Carnegie, bid fair to
be a plutocracy in the young industrial city, one that would supplant
the older mercantile and small industry iron and steel elite. Within
this context, then, a class war of enormous proportions ensued during the last years of the nineteenth century.

That class war had its origins in Braddock's Field, about twelve miles from downtown Pittsburgh on the Monongahela River. There, in 1875, Andrew Carnegie was building a massive Bessemer steel complex, one larger, more integrated, and more complete than existed anywhere in the world. Since the nation was caught in the grip of its first modern depression, most sensible businessmen were cutting back, waiting out the hard times before expanding their operations. Not the impetuous Carnegie. Like Henry Clay Frick, his future partner, Carnegie viewed hard times as ideal for expansion, since costs were so much lower. Nonetheless, the depression caused him much trouble, as several of his business associates were bankrupted and Carnegie's own resources were stretched to the limit. All of this was characteristic of the man and his technique. It was a method that would frustrate, awe, and alienate many members of the older Pittsburgh aristocracy.

But what a wonder Carnegie constructed at Braddock's Field! Soon to be known as the Edgar Thomson Works (significantly and not coincidentally named for the president of the Pennsylvania Railroad), it was a technological and organizational marvel of the modern world. Located at the junction of three railroads (the Pennsylvania, the Baltimore & Ohio, and the Pittsburgh & Lake Erie), it was a sprawling series of buildings, switchyards, engines, sheds, and smokestacks. The crowning glory of the mill was a wonder of the industrial world: a screaming, belching series of Bessemer converters, capable of making steel in vast quantities. This new company was a model of modern integration. Although in the first few years it relied on the output of Carnegie's nearby Lucy and Isabella furnaces for pig iron, it soon had its own massive stacks. As the plant's designer, Alexander Holley, commented: "Coke and pig iron are delivered to the stockyard with equal facility. The finishing end of the rail-mill is accommodated on both sides by low-level-wide-gauge railways."[1] The pig iron went from the blast furnace to the Jones Mixer, which facilitated the flow to the Bessemer converter. The steel ingots were then cooled and carried on rollers to the massive rail mill. There they were put through continual passes in John Fritz's three-high mill, until finished steel rails rolled out the other end.

When the Edgar Thomson Works reached its production peak later in the century, it was capable of producing three thousand tons of steel rails daily, as much as a typical Pittsburgh puddling mill of the 1830s could produce in an entire year.[2] This greatly increased velocity of flow through the works placed increased demands on the managers. As a result, Carnegie hired William P. Shinn, formerly a railroad accountant, to install railroad accounting techniques in his new steel plant. Establishing what is known as the voucher system of accounting, Shinn and Carnegie revolutionized manufacturing practice and the traditions of accountability in American business. Carnegie's dictum had always been "Watch the costs, and the profits will take care of themselves,"[3] and his accounting system, a revolutionary change from traditional lump accounting techniques in the iron industry, allowed him to fulfill his ideals. Carnegie used Shinn's cost sheets to give him control over the entire operation, even from New York City, where he had already moved by this time. All of this was an enormous departure from the hovering, personal, idiosyncratic rule-of-thumb methods practiced by most Pittsburgh iron masters.

As a result, Carnegie and his massive steel complexes have naturally dominated our view of the late nineteenth-century iron and steel industry. He was, after all, the most dynamic element on the Pittsburgh industrial scene. And his techniques of mass production, high throughput, accountability, control, and professional bureaucratic management came to characterize large-scale American industries increasingly in the twentieth century. Carnegie was a harbinger of what Chandler has called "the managerial revolution in American business."[4] Yet, the unspoken assumption seems to be that the rest of the iron and steel industry, especially in Pittsburgh, the very cockpit of America's industrial transformation, either followed suit or, more likely, was bludgeoned to death by the massively efficient Carnegie mills. Nothing could be further from the truth, and it is the intention of the next few chapters to develop the authentic history of the iron and steel industry in Pittsburgh during the late nineteenth century.

Three interconnected events of great significance occurred in the iron and steel industry in the last half of the nineteenth century. First was the replacement of iron by steel as the principal product of the industry. Second was the enormous transformation in the size and productivity of the average mill and the industry generally. Third was the movement of the center of the industry from the eastern seaboard states, especially eastern Pennsylvania, to the west, particularly to Pittsburgh and surrounding Allegheny County.

Until the 1860s, as noted in chapter 1, iron was the primary metal used in American industry. What little steel was produced in America was either blister, cast, or crucible in origin; was produced in small quantities; and was either terribly expensive or of low quality. In 1864 the Bessemer process for producing steel was introduced into the United States, and a few years after that came the Siemans-Martin or open hearth process. Steel output nationwide soared from just 19,000 tons in 1865 to a staggering 10 million tons by 1900. By that time Carnegie Steel alone produced more steel than the entire industry of Great Britain.

One result of the change to steel production was a vast increase in the average size of a firm in the industry, which, in turn, went hand in hand with sharply increased production, technological improvements, substitution of machinery-driven equipment for manual labor, concentration of ownership, and other elements characteristic of a modern industrial economy. Pig iron production jumped from 2,854,000 net tons in 1872 to 10,307,000 tons in 1890, a four-fold increase (see table 2.1). Semifinished iron and steel products increased from a gross tonnage of 1,210,000 in 1870 to 6,023,000 tons in 1890.[5] More significant, however, was the increase in average firm size. In 1870 the average firm was capitalized at $210,000. Just ten years later average capitalization had increased to $360,000, and by 1890 it had risen to $805,000.[6] The typical firm producing rolled iron and steel in 1869 had an annual product of 3,000 tons and employed 119 workers. By 1879 the average company marketed 7,000 tons of semifinished metal with a work force of 220. Ten years after that, the typical firm had 332 workers to produce an output of 14,000 tons. This meant that productivity in rolling mills rose from 25.2 tons per worker to 42.1 tons during this twenty-year period, the result of increased use of technology and power plus rationalization of the means of production.

Yet this increased productivity was not accomplished uniformly in the United States. Pennsylvania was the most important producer of iron and steel between 1870 and 1900, accounting for 42.4 percent of the pig iron produced in 1875 and 54 percent in 1885. Within Pennsylvania itself there was a distinct westward shift of the industry. In 1872 the four eastern districts of Pennsylvania (Lehigh,

TABLE 2.1
Iron and Steel Production in the United States: 1870–1900

Year	Pig Iron Production (1,000s of Tons)	Semifinished Iron and Steel (1,000s of Tons)	Mean Firm Size		
			Capital ($)	Output (tons)	Workers (No.)
1870–72	2,854	1,210	210,000	3,000	119
1890	10,307	6,023	805,000	14,000	332

Schuylkill, and Upper and Lower Susquehanna) accounted for 68 percent of the state's pig iron production. By 1882, this had declined to 58 percent, and by 1890 to just 44 percent, even though the east's actual output more than doubled during this time. Proximity to bituminous coal deposits in the Connellsville region, along with relatively easy access to a veritable mountain of iron ore that was discovered in the 1840s in Michigan, gave Pittsburgh locational advantages that its entrepreneurs were able to exploit.

Just as the scale of industry changed nationally in the late nineteenth century, so was it transformed in Pennsylvania and Pittsburgh. In 1860, when the industry was still heavily concentrated in the eastern part of the state, there were sixty-seven blast furnaces employing 4,734 men in the eastern districts, compared to fifty-eight furnaces with just 2,800 workers in the west. The situation of rolling mills was almost the exact opposite. Although there were sixty-one mills in eastern Pennsylvania, as opposed to only twenty-six in the west, the mills in the western Pennsylvania area were already larger, employing 4,808 men (an average of 185 per mill), compared to 5,269 (an average of 86 per mill) in the east.

Although Pittsburgh increasingly dominated semifinished wrought iron production in the state, with larger, somewhat more integrated, and more efficient mills, the real key to its rise lay in steel production. Accounting for just 8.7 percent of the nation's steel production in 1875, Pittsburgh had enlarged its share to 21.6 percent by 1883, and to 30.2 percent by 1890, by which time it was the undisputed leader of steel production in America. Despite this massive increase in steel manufacture, iron production did not just wither away during this time. In fact, the volume of iron produced nationally continued to rise until 1886, and rolled steel products, excluding steel rails, did not surpass rolled iron until even later. Because of its malleability and it noncorrosive quality, iron was still superior to steel for many uses, and the puddling furnace did not reach its zenith of production until 1887. In addition, many producers combined iron and steel production and did not begin to phase out their iron puddling operations until late in the 1880s or 1890s. Not until 1892, in fact, did Carnegie Steel and Jones & Laughlin decide to close down their puddling furnaces—the symbolic end of the era of iron in America. During the balance of that decade, rolled iron products experienced a precipitous decline.[7] Pittsburgh and Allegheny County, as indicated by stocks of unsold pig iron, were never hit as drastically by this decline in demand for iron products as other areas of the nation. Better equipped generally to find markets, the mills in Pittsburgh were more prosperous in both good and bad times than those in other areas of the state or the nation as a whole. In 1880, unsold pig iron in Pennsylvania amounted to 7.8 percent of total production in the state, but just 1.1 percent of the Allegheny County pig iron stock was not sold. In 1890, with 4 percent of the statewide production of pig iron unsold, only 1 percent in Allegheny County remained so.[8] The mill owners in Pittsburgh, as will be made evident in chapter 3, were better able to survive the transition from iron to steel, and much of their story is one of successful adaptation, survival, and profitability.

By 1870, Pittsburgh had emerged as a major American city. With its twin city of Allegheny across the river, population by that time stood at 137,000, an increase of nearly 75 percent over 1860. Then, during the 1870s, the number of inhabitants increased to over 235,000. With the single exception of the 1840s, those two decades witnessed the greatest percentage increases in the city's history. By 1890, the population of Pittsburgh and Allegheny had surged to 344,204. Although Pittsburgh's population increase was less than for the previous two decades, it was still quite impressive.[9] The vast expansion of the city's industrial base, particularly its iron and steel industry, which supplied 40 percent of the nation's steel by 1900, provided the economic incentive for these heady population increases. At the same time, large percentage of these new inhabitants of Pittsburgh were significantly different from earlier residents.

Pittsburgh had always had a large number of immigrants among its populace. In the early years, many Scots-Irish newcomers had swelled Pittsburgh's population, giving the city its distinctive cultural stamp. Then, in the 1840s, large numbers of Catholic Irish poured into Pittsburgh, so that by 1850 more than 10,000 Irish immigrants lived in the city, comprising 21.4 percent of the residents.[10] Another large group by 1850 was the Germans, with 13.2 percent of the city's population.[11] During the three decades after the Civil War, however not only did the number of immigrants soar but many of them were from new and different regions. Of the 340,000 inhabitants of Greater Pittsburgh in 1890, nearly 100,000 (28.9 percent) were immigrants. Additionally, another 40 percent of the population were children of immigrants, making nearly two-thirds of the population of fairly recent immigrant origin. Most of the immigrants flocked to Pittsburgh to man the city's burgeoning industries, especially its iron and steel mills. As a result, the city's working class became a mosaic of nationalities. As Francis Couvares has noted, it was "made up of Croats, Serbs, Slovenes, Slovaks, Lithuanians, Bohemians, Romanians, Poles, Ukrainians, Russians, and others," who were later joined by "Italians and southern Blacks in the mills and neighborhoods of Pittsburgh."[12] By 1900, these groups had largely replaced the older immigrants in these environs. Perhaps the most graphic representation of this transformation is shown in the composition of the Carnegie Steel plants of U.S. Steel in Allegheny County in 1907. Just 24.5 percent of the workers were defined as "American Born–White." Fully 76 percent were foreign born, 55.7 percent of Slavic birth.[13]

Thus, Pittsburgh's antebellum aristocracy faced a dual challenge in the late nineteenth century: the rise of the massive Bessemer steel mills, most of which were run by men from outside Pittsburgh's older upper-class community, and a population base from which potential aspirants for business leadership might be drawn that had also altered dramatically. Pittsburgh was the textbook-perfect industrial city. Its population had increased dramatically over a short period of time, vast numbers of immigrants from divergent cultural sources had made up the vast majority of the new inhabitants of the city, and a profound change in its economic base had opened the potential for new men to rise to the top. This made the prospect of a revolution in the city's upper class from an older mercantile and small-industry group to a new industrial plutocracy a very real possibility. Yet, Pittsburgh's iron and steel makers in the 1870s and 1880s reflected little of this transformation of Pittsburgh's economic and population base.

In 1874, there were thirty-eight iron and steel plants in Pittsburgh, not including the still uncompleted Edgar Thomson mill. Thirty of these were iron puddling and rolling mills; the rest were crucible and blister steel operations. There was as yet no Bessemer steel produced in Pittsburgh. The largest of the iron puddling mills (Jones & Laughlin's American Iron Works) had seventy-five puddling furnaces and produced 50,000 tons of iron annually. The smallest of the iron mills produced just 4,000 tons yearly. Mean annual production in these mills was 14,600 tons. Median annual production was 11,500 tons, indicating little variation in the productive capacity of most of the mills. The eight steel operations were even smaller, averaging only 8,000 tons per year, with a median production of only 6,500 tons. There were just three mills making iron rails, with only one, Jones & Laughlin, a significant producer of the product.[14] (See table 2.2 for slightly altered statistics on the social class origins of Pittsburgh's iron and steel manufacturers.[15])

The social and cultural characteristics of these iron and steel

TABLE 2.2
Mills and Mill Owners by Social Class: 1850–1900

Year	Mills (No.)	Families (No.)	Blue Book (%)	Social Directory (%)	Social Register (%)	Core	Non-Core	Marginal	Elite
1850	24	40	98	73	78	60	9	5	2
1870	39	44	98	66	66	52	25	14	9
1880	49	93	94	54	63	34	32	14	19
1890	58	102	84	50	56	28	26	13	32
Totals	69	146	89	45	56	27	27	16	30

manufacturers had also changed little since the late 1850s. Of the thirty-nine families who controlled these various mills (again, not including the Carnegie operations) in 1874, thirty-one (80 percent) were pre–Civil War iron and steel manufacturers in Pittsburgh. Of the new families, four were members of other antebellum Pittsburgh upper-class families (10 percent). Therefore, outside the Carnegie mills, just 10 percent of the iron and steel entrepreneurs in Pittsburgh were new men from outside the city's upper-class social framework. On the other hand, in the Carnegie mills, none of the listed officers in 1874 was a member of Pittsburgh's pre–Civil War aristocracy (although, a couple, such as David Stewart and David McCandless, who were not listed in the AISI *Directory*, probably were upper class).

Considering the entire group (including the Carnegie men) in terms of social prestige, a familiar pattern emerges. As in chapter 1, to determine their social status, the entrepreneur's listings were checked in a number of sources. They were, first of all, traced in the 1887 *Pittsburgh Blue Book*, a listing of eminent, but not necessarily upper-class, Pittsburghers. Next, the Pittsburgh *Social Directory* of 1904, the single most select published social listing, was consulted. Then they were checked in the 1908 Pittsburgh *Social Register*, a national, but somewhat less selective, ranking of persons of upper-class status. Since many of these individuals and families had either died or left Pittsburgh by the early twentieth century, however, it was also necessary to develop a status ranking system that took into account membership in social clubs, marriages with other upper-class individuals, and other indices of social prestige. This was accomplished through the use of Core upper-class, Non-Core upper-class, Marginal upper-class, and Elite (non-upper-class) family groupings.[16]

Ninety-five percent of the iron and steel families, as one might expect, were listed in the 1887 *Blue Book*, an elite rather than upper-class register. In the two instances of families not listed in the *Blue Book*, both had left Pittsburgh by the time it was published. Thus, for all practical purposes, the *Blue Book* listed all iron and steel families. The other two directories, however, revealed a very different picture. Just 41 percent of the iron and steel families were listed in the 1904 *Social Directory*, and 76 percent were listed in the 1908 *Social Register*. Fifty percent of them were among the Core upper-class families, roughly comparable to the listings in the prestigious *Social Directory*, and another 29 percent were Non-Core upper class. Those two family groups together were nearly identical to the families listed in the 1908 *Social Register*.

Of the thirty-one pre–Civil War iron and steel manufacturing families who were still active in the industry in Pittsburgh in 1874, 58 percent were Core upper-class families and 26 percent were Non-Core, making 84 percent solid members of Pittsburgh's upper class. Of the other eleven families, five had been business elites in Pittsburgh prior to the war, and 40 percent of them were Core families, with another 40 percent Non-Core. Of the other six families, three were in the Carnegie mills and three were not. None of the Carnegie families ever became Core upper class in the city, although two (including the Carnegies) became Non-Core upper class. One of the other new families (the Olivers) became Core upper class; two were never part of the upper class. The pattern is quite clear. Despite the great linear expansion and change in the Pittsburgh iron and steel industry by 1874, it had changed little in the composition of its iron and steel makers since the prewar period. Most of the families involved had been in the industry in the antebellum years, and another large group had been prewar elites in other business ventures. About three-quarters of these families in 1874 were indisputably part of Pittsburgh's upper class, and most had acquired this status because of eminence in the city in the years before the Civil War. They were already part of an established aristocracy.

Ten years later, despite the tremendous explosion of Bessemer steel production in Pittsburgh, matters had not changed a great deal as far as the makeup of its iron and steel manufacturers is concerned. There were by then forty-nine mills in the city and environs. Of these, thirteen were new concerns, since three of the establishments from 1874 had gone out of business. That, by the way, represents a failure rate of just 8 percent during that decade. Of these forty-nine mills, thirty-two, nearly two-thirds of the total, still made only puddled iron. The other fifteen mills used a variety of steel and iron processes. In total there were twelve crucible steel operations in the city, four plants with Bessemer converters, and nine with open hearth operations.[17] The largest iron puddling operation produced about 50 percent more iron annually than it did in 1874, and many of the other iron mills increased their production proportionately. Mean annual production in iron mills was 20,000 tons in 1884, compared with 14,000 tons ten years earlier. The median annual production was 15,000 tons, up from about 11,000 in 1874. Two mills produced between 3,000 and 4,000 tons annually, about the same as the smallest mills in 1874.

There were, by 1884, ninety-two families involved in these mills. Since two of the families from 1874 were no longer in the industry, it means that fifty-three new families had entered iron and steel manufacturing in the city during the decade. Of the forty families who remained in the industry, the great majority, of course, had also been involved in Pittsburgh's iron and steel industry prior to the Civil War. But what about the large number of new individuals? Do we see with them the emergence of a vastly new and different industrial elite?

A rather surprising number of these new men were members of families who had been prominent in Pittsburgh economic and social activities prior to the Civil War. Twenty-five of the fifty-three fell into that category, making 47 percent of the total. Therefore, about sixty of the ninety-two individuals involved in Pittsburgh's iron and steel industry in 1884 were from families who were part of the city's pre–Civil War aristocracy. Of the new additions in 1884 were members of such eminent Pittsburgh families as Otis H. Childs, Theodore Wood Friend, Joshua Rhodes, James and John Irwin, William G. Johnston, a number of members of the Scully family, and James K. Verner, among others. In addition, thirteen of the fifty-three new families (25 percent) were members of families who had achieved eminence outside Pittsburgh in the antebellum period. This especially included a number of the families involved with National Tube, who were part of the Boston establishment.

Thus, of the fifty-three new families drawn into the expanding iron and steel industry, nearly three-quarters had established economic and social roots. Yet, the social ranking of this group of fifty-three ranged below that of the early iron and steel families. Although 91 percent were listed in the 1887 *Blue Book* and 40 percent in the 1904 *Social Directory*, about the same as in the older group, only 51 percent were listed in the 1908 *Social Register*. The dichotomy becomes more pronounced when we categorize them according to my family schema. In the new group of families, just 19 percent were Core upper class, and 38 percent were Non-Core. Another 17 percent were Marginal upper class, and fully 26 percent never attained upper-class status. Thus, in the newer group, about 55 percent were solidly upper class, compared to nearly 80 percent of the 1874 group of families. Similarly, 26 percent were clearly not members of the upper class, compared to just 10 percent of the former group.

By 1894, the transformation of the nation's iron and steel industry was nearing completion. Iron puddling plants were being dismantled, steel was recognized as the undisputed king of Pittsburgh, and open hearth furnaces were challenging Bessemer converters for supremacy in steel making. By that time, there were a total of fifty-

eight iron and steel mills in the Pittsburgh area. Three of the firms
from 1884 had gone out of business, and twelve new firms had been
added to the group, about half of which were outside Pittsburgh
itself in the various river valleys. Seven of these new firms were,
indeed, steel plants, but few had the kind of productive capacity one
usually associates with that process in the latter part of the century.
Although one had the capacity to produce 150,000 tons of steel
annually and another 120,000 tons, several were quite small. Thus,
although the average annual production of the new steel mills was
about 55,000 tons, the median production was just 19,000 tons.
There were, on the other hand, sixteen mills in Pittsburgh that still
made only puddled iron. The largest produced 100,000 tons a year,
and the smallest 9,000. Mean annual production was 32,000 tons,
not much above what it had been in 1884, and median annual production was 24,500, indicating that most mills were about the same
general size. Although iron puddling was a dying industry nationally, it was to continue in Pittsburgh for a remarkably long time.
Crucible steel production, although always small-scale, was also
holding its own, with twelve plants in the area. Eight plants made
Bessemer steel in Pittsburgh, and twenty-one were making open
hearth steel, the production process of the future for the steel
industry.

The turnover among iron and steel families by the mid-1890s had
been stunning. Whereas just two families had left the industry in the
previous decade, a staggering thirty-six families left between 1884
and 1894. Another forty-seven families entered the industry for the
first time, and fifty-four families continued from the previous period. Of the fifty-four continuing families, however, twenty-eight (52
percent) were members of pre–Civil War iron and steel families.
Another sixteen (30 percent) were members of other Pittsburgh pre–
Civil War elite families, and one other was from a pre–Civil War
elite family from outside Pittsburgh. This produced a total of 83
percent of the families continuing in the industry in the 1890s who
traced their elite status to antebellum times, a remarkable record of
continuity in turbulent times in a rapidly changing industry and
city.

Of the thirty-six families who left the industry between 1884 and
1894, twenty were members of pre–Civil War elite families. But
only two (Lewis and Moorhead) were members of antebellum Pittsburgh iron and steel families, and another eight (22 percent) were
elites in other Pittsburgh industries prior to the war. The largest
number of this elite group, however (10 or 28 percent), were from

pre–Civil War elite families from outside Pittsburgh. Almost without exception, these were families who moved to Pittsburgh in the late 1870s and early 1880s with nationally oriented firms (such as National Tube or Braddock Wire), stayed a few years, and moved on. By far the largest single group among the families who left were the new men of 1884 (44 percent). They, not the older elites, were the most transient and vulnerable to economic change.

In terms of social status, the iron and steel masters in 1894 exhibited some familiar characteristics. Those who were descended from pre–Civil War economic elites, as we have noted previously, were overwhelmingly upper class. Most were listed in the 1904 *Social Directory* and 1908 *Social Register*, and the great majority (57 percent) were Core upper-class families. Virtually all of the rest were Non-Core. Those families who had left the industry by 1894 were of uniformly lower social status than those who remained. Just 22 percent were listed in the *Social Directory* and 44 percent in the *Social Register*. Eleven percent were Core families and another 31 percent were Non-Core, making a total of about 40 to 45 percent who were quite firmly in Pittsburgh's upper class. The majority, however, were not.

What of the new men who had entered the industry by 1894? They were, indeed, from less prestigious backgrounds than was true in earlier years. Just 21 percent of the new group were listed in the *Social Directory*, along with 29 percent in the *Social Register*. Additionally, a tiny 4 percent ever became Core upper-class families, and 19 percent became Non-Core. That made less than a quarter who achieved upper-class status in Pittsburgh. They were new men— outsiders—and largely remained that way.

If we draw back at this point and take a longer-range view of all the families involved in the iron and steel industry in Pittsburgh over the half-century from the 1840s to the 1890s, we can recognize some clear patterns. Of the 141 families involved at one time or another in iron and steel, 84 percent were listed in the 1887 *Blue Book*, as one would expect. In terms of social status, just 34 percent were listed in the 1904 Pittsburgh *Social Directory* and 54 percent in the 1908 Pittsburgh *Social Register*. That would indicate that about 50 to 55 percent of the families were considered upper class on the Pittsburgh scene. This is borne out by examining the families according to my family groupings. Twenty-three percent were Core upper class and 28 percent were Non-Core, yielding a total of 51 percent who were undeniably upper class. Another 16 percent were Marginal upper-class families, and about one-third (most of whom entered the industry in the 1880s and 1890s) were quite clearly never part of Pittsburgh's upper-class structure.

Pittsburgh's pre–Civil War iron and steel families, then, had a remarkable record of survival in a rapidly changing, profoundly dynamic industry and city in the late nineteenth century. Despite the rapid pace of technological and organizational change and the large numbers of new men and families who were drawn into the industry as a result, these older Pittsburgh upper-class families survived remarkably well, and, as George Stigler has commented,[18] survival is simply the market determining those firms that have achieved the optimum size, technology, and market strategy. How did they do it?

To understand better how they managed to survive in this turbulent environment, it is perhaps instructive to see first of all how not to do it. A number of these older iron and steel families attempted to compete head-on with Andrew Carnegie in Bessemer steel and steel rail production, and these attempts were, in most instances, dismal failures, which helped create an image of incompetence and failure of these older iron and steel families. Partially as a result of these failures, the older families looked for smaller, more specialized markets and for technological innovations that allowed them to survive and compete, but not to overextend either their capital or their abilities. In the balance of this chapter we shall look at the direct challenges to Carnegie and consider their alternative market responses in chapter 3.

The Challenge of the Old Iron Masters

About a mile below Carnegie's massive Edgar Thomson plant at Braddock, ground was broken for a huge Bessemer steel enterprise in 1879. An enormous complex, it was to have a rail mill, two Universal mills, a sixteen-inch bar train, and a muck train all contained within one 684-foot-long building. On land adjoining this complex were a large converting works and blooming mill. The plant, when completed, was scheduled to produce fifty thousand tons of steel rails and thirty thousand tons of structural steel products annually. If not as large and proficient as the Edgar Thomson mills, it would nonetheless provide Carnegie with his first really serious competition locally and was built practically on his doorstep. The construction of these works by Pittsburgh Bessemer Steel, capitalized at $250,000, was the most dramatic incident in the iron and steel industry of the early 1880s. And the mills were owned and operated by several members of old pre–Civil War Pittsburgh iron and steel families, along with a couple of important outsiders.

An exceptionally complex series of events and passions came into play in creating this new venture in the first place, and in deciding its ultimate fate in the final instance. Superficially, at least, the immediate genesis of the works was the shortage of Bessemer steel ingots used for merchant steel. A deeper reason was a long-simmering hatred and lust for revenge against Andrew Carnegie held by at least one of the original members of the new firm. Although most American iron and steel men had harbored a deep antipathy toward the use of Bessemer steel for anything but rails since the 1860s, these attitudes began to change in the 1870s. They found, first of all, that Bessemer steel could be used successfully for a number of products: buggy springs, railroad car axles, stovepipes, and even plowshares. Further, Bessemer ingots could be melted in crucible pots and made into higher-quality crucible steel for an even greater variety of uses. So, many of Pittsburgh's crucible and blister steel makers had become dependent on a steady supply of Bessemer steel ingots. Since the Edgar Thomson Works was so phenomenally productive, and the rail market during the 1870s had been terribly depressed, the steel makers had little problem securing their ingots from Carnegie at reasonable prices.

By 1879, however, a number of important developments had taken place. Carnegie had made improvements in his rail mill at the Thomson Works, allowing him to roll a greater number of rails daily. At the same time, the market for rails improved greatly, so that Carnegie was able to sell every rail he could manufacture during this time. As a result, the Edgar Thomson Works no longer had any excess steel ingots to sell to the Pittsburgh manufacturers. Desperate for a new source of semifinished ingots, several of these manufacturers formed a syndicate for building their own Bessemer steel converting plant. At that point, the plant was simply being designed to make a relatively small number of ingots that could then be rolled and shaped into a variety of finished products by the participating firms at their own mills. The firms involved in the syndicate at this point were Singer, Nimick & Co.; Hussey, Wells, & Co.; and Black Diamond Steel, which were joined by Solar Iron and Steel and Crescent Steel a short time later.[19]

The shortage of Bessemer ingots was the immediate cause for forming the syndicate, and if the object had simply remained supplying relatively small amounts of merchant steel to its members, the venture would neither have attained the significance it has nor failed. But the original plans for a fairly small-scale Bessemer merchant steel works were soon superseded by a grander design to compete head-on with Andrew Carnegie in the steel rail market. The change came about initially in tying the fortunes of this project to the plans of Andrew Kloman, an embittered former Carnegie partner. Kloman, who had done a great deal to develop the early Carnegie iron mills, had become overextended during the depression of the 1870s and was unceremoniously cut adrift by Carnegie. As a result, Kloman thirsted for revenge for several years, and the venture at Homestead was to be the instrument of his vengeance.

In 1878, Kloman leased the old Superior Mill in Allegheny City to begin making structural steel for bridge purposes on a small scale. He was given backing in this venture by the prominent Core upper-class Pittsburgh steel man Curtis Grubb Hussey. R. G. Dun & Co. was very sympathetic to the undertaking and to his situation, calling Kloman a "good mechanic—capable and very industrious and good . . . a very honest man."[20] Kloman, like the other steel makers, made his finished products with merchant steel ingots purchased from Carnegie. In 1879, Kloman's one-year lease on the Superior plant was up, and rather than sign a new one, he decided to build a mill of his own. In early 1879 Kloman bought a small tract of land in Homestead and began erecting a large building to contain a twenty-one-inch rail mill, two universal mills, a sixteen-inch bar train, and a muck train.[21]

Within a few months, however, the merchant steel manufacturers mentioned previously joined Kloman in a new and greatly expanded venture. The consortium organized and incorporated the Pittsburgh Bessemer Steel Company on October 21, 1879.[22] The completed mill was no longer to be simply a small Bessemer producer making merchant steel ingots for the subscribing steel mills. It was to produce rails—lots of them—and compete directly with Carnegie's Edgar Thomson Works. The new mill was in many respects admirably suited for this task. James H. Bridge commented that the plant "was unsurpassed not only in the completeness and efficiency of the works but in the rapidity of construction. While the Edgar Thomson plant was three years in the building . . . the Homestead works were put into operation fifteen months after the land was bought."[23] This statement, however, has been challenged by later historians and will be dealt with in greater detail later.

Andrew Kloman supervised the construction of his own mill and that of the adjoining converting plant while the Mackintosh &

Hemphill firm had the contract for supplying engines for the concern. Before Kloman could complete the task, however, he died in December 1880.[24] At that point the Pittsburgh Bessemer Company purchased his unfinished rail mill, proceeding to carry out Kloman's contracts for rails. By September 1881, the mill was turning out two hundred tons of rails a day and had orders booked for fifteen thousand tons at profitable prices.[25]

When the Bessemer plant opened in 1881, the firm's officers were joined by a new man, William Clark. Clark had been chosen to take Kloman's place as general superintendent of the mill and was a relative newcomer on the Pittsburgh scene. Also, unlike his eminent colleagues in the venture, Clark was of working-class social origin. Born in England in 1831, he immigrated to Pittsburgh with his parents in 1842. His father was a skilled iron worker, and a few years later young Clark found work in the city's iron mills, soon becoming a skilled iron roller. Clark worked for several years in mills in other parts of the country and in 1860 established a foundry in St. Louis. This venture was followed shortly afterward by ownership of a mill in Cincinnati, and in 1862 by the organization of the Enterprise Iron Works in Youngstown. In 1869 Clark returned to Pittsburgh to join the Sable Iron Works; a short time later he set up Solar Iron Works in partnership with his son. A recognized expert in iron and steel manufacture and rolling mill practice, Clark introduced the use of the flat billet in rolling ingot strips and was also the first to produce steel hoops for barrels. He also patented a cambering machine for manufacturing rails. With his great technical expertise, Clark seemed to be the logical person to head the new Pittsburgh Bessemer Works.

The appointment of Clark to head the works, however, was a fateful decision in many respects. It demonstrated a crucial shortcoming of these older families with respect to innovations such as the Bessemer process. Although they certainly showed great courage and foresight in their willingness to engage in a venture of this magnitude, their past experience in iron and steel production had not equipped them with the requisite expertise. They were iron puddling and rolling men or crucible steel producers. Although they had a great deal of capital and were willing to risk it on this undertaking, they needed a man like Kloman or Clark to provide the special expertise demanded by Bessemer steel making. Thus, they hitched their wagon first to Andrew Kloman's star and then to William Clark's. Kloman suffered an untimely death just as the plant was due to open. Clark, who was recruited in haste to take his place, carried with him attitudes toward labor that ultimately helped bring about the demise of the new venture.

Despite the presence of Clark, the impending war with Carnegie was in many respects a class war, a valiant, though ultimately unsuccessful action fought by a group of old family aristocrats against someone they viewed as an interloper and an outsider. They had watched Carnegie's Edgar Thomson Works overwhelm the older iron and steel firms in the city: firms like Jones & Laughlin, which had once been the largest and most dominant in the trade, now were small and relatively insignificant compared to Carnegie's giant. This upset what many assumed was the natural and proper order of things. Pittsburgh Bessemer Steel was their chance to even the score.

Pittsburgh Bessemer Steel in 1880–81 seemingly was on top of the world. With what appears to be excellent capital backing, the owners had just completed construction of one of the best and most efficient steel plants in the country. Peter Temin, however, in his analysis of the failure of Pittsburgh Bessemer Steel, put forward three reasons for its collapse: the firm's labor policy and the strike that resulted from it, the decision to make rails rather than billets, and, third, and to Temin most important, the fact that because the firm's owners refused to pay full royalties to the Bessemer Steel Association as a way of saving money, they were denied use of many of Alexander Holley's patents for steel plants. It was, according to R. W. Hunt, the only Bessemer plant in the United States that was "outside his [Holley's] patents." As a result, Hunt said, "I think my fellow Bessemer managers will unite with me in deciding it far below the standard of a Holley plant."[26] Thus, despite the praise heaped on the Homestead works by many of its contemporaries, it was apparently a less efficient operation than Carnegie's, and that aided its undoing. It was a case of penny wise and pound foolish on the part of its aristocratic owners. They saved some cash outlay in terms of royalties, but that saving may have cost them in terms of profit for every steel rail rolled in the plant. None of this, however, was clear in 1882.

Pittsburgh Bessemer Steel faced two other major obstacles to success in 1882: a sharp depression and serious labor troubles. After the long depression of the 1870s, economic indicators had been positive for several years. Then, without the traditional commercial crisis or panic that usually accompanied depressions, trade fell off drastically and stock prices began a gradual decline from 1882 to 1886. An undramatic and largely unnoticed depression, it had a severe impact on the iron and steel trade. Prices for iron and steel declined steadily, and business failures abounded.[27] When the price of rails was high, as it was when Pittsburgh Bessemer Steel was being organized in 1879, a few more dollars of cost per ton made little difference. By 1882–83, when the price of steel rails had declined greatly, it had a devastating impact, especially since Carnegie's Edgar Thomson Works could still produce rails at a profit.

Pittsburgh Bessemer Steel might still have ridden out the depression, just as Carnegie did, but for the labor disturbances. William Clark, as was so often the case with workingmen who climbed up from the shop floor to possess their own plants, was rabidly antiunion. He had dealt harshly with the union at his own Solar Iron Works and was proud of the strikebreaker label that his workmen had hung on him. When Clark took over management of the Pittsburgh Bessemer mills from Kloman, he found to his disgust that lodges of the Amalgamated Association of Iron and Steel Workers were deeply embedded in various departments. Further, groups of skilled workers, organized by the Amalgamated, made a series of minor demands on Clark from the moment the plant opened. Caught at a critical time, Clark acceded to these demands but vowed that he would get revenge. Details of Clark's union attitudes, along with those of other Pittsburgh iron and steel manufacturers, are given in detail in chapter 4. At this point, it is sufficient to comment that a strike soon commenced in the plant, and it played a role in bringing about the firm's demise.

It also brought an end to Clark, who submitted his resignation as superintendent when the other owners refused to comply with his antiunion demands any longer. The owners of Pittsburgh Bessemer Steel, however, found that they could no longer operate their mill profitably in the disorganized iron and steel trade of the time and on August 21 shut down the works for lack of orders. After lying idle for a few weeks, the plant was reopened in mid-September. The owners of the firm by this time were fed up with the situation. Weary of continual labor dispute, discouraged by constantly falling rail prices, and fearful of the loss of their huge investment in the steel plant, the syndicate approached Carnegie with an offer to sell. Carnegie, who had been expecting this, readily agreed and made a generous proposal. He offered to buy at face value all shares in the company, giving them the option of payment in cash or in stock in Carnegie Brothers Ltd. Park, Hussey, and Miller, detesting any association with Carnegie and hungry for cash for their order-starved mills, took the cash settlement. Only William H. Singer took the offer of stock.

He became a partner in the Carnegie enterprises, patiently enduring the scorn of his fellow iron masters for associating with the hated Carnegie, and watched his $50,000 worth of stock in the Carnegie enterprises rise in value to $8 million.[28]

In October 1883, the Homestead mills became part of the Carnegie empire. Carnegie immediately announced that the plant would no longer make rails but would instead concentrate on structural shapes. He also announced he was spending $4 million on the plant to bring in those Holley innovations to which it had been denied in the past. By 1887, Homestead's two 4-ton converters were able to produce a staggering total of 19,572 tons of ingots in one month and set a record of 915 tons in one day. This was glaring evidence of the great improvements in the operations made by Carnegie after he took over.[29]

Although Pittsburgh Bessemer Steel was certainly a failure as a business enterprise, it did represent a valiant attempt by the older Pittsburgh iron and steel manufacturers to overtake Carnegie. Their failure gave Carnegie a large and technologically advanced steel mill for his enterprises but also saddled him with a tradition of labor unrest that would bedevil him for years and would ultimately explode in the great Homestead lockout of 1892. This whole episode is generally seen as the working out of some sort of Horatio Alger drama. Carnegie, the new man, was not the captive of hidebound antilabor traditions. His more flexible response to labor was yet another reflection of his genius for innovation. Just as he was willing to replace outmoded machinery with little remorse, so he was willing to pay a higher scale and grant his workers the eight-hour day. The Homestead episode of the early 1880s often appears to accent dramatically in the particular what many argued in the abstract—that innovations must be brought forward by new men who are not captive of conservative social and economic attitudes.

There is, perhaps, some truth to that in the case of Pittsburgh Bessemer Steel, but the reality is far more complex than appears on the surface. Certainly it seems that the older iron and steel men were out of their element with large-batch Bessemer steel production and rail making. This was neither a technology nor a market in which they had any experience or confidence. That fact forced them to depend on men like Kloman and Clark for technical assistance. With Clark, however, they got a rabid antiunion man whose reactions to unions and strikes were far different from their own.[30] The older Pittsburgh steel men may have been guilty of a lack of de-

cisiveness at a critical point and an unwillingness to spend a bit
more money to acquire some critical patients but cannot be faulted
for conservatism in their willingness to be flexible and innovative in
either plant equipment or labor relations. The labor troubles at
Homestead were precipitated by Clark, a man from outside the old
family network. A new man, Clark brought to his position an extraordinarily inflexible attitude toward unions. It is apparent that the
other partners, all from prestigious Pittsburgh families, did not
share this attitude. Unlike Clark, they had long tolerated the Amalgamated in their mills. Why, then, did they not step in to overrule
Clark at an earlier point in the dispute, when it might have saved
the situation for them? It seems that having lost the technical genius of Andrew Kloman so suddenly, they could ill afford losing the
undoubted expertise of Clark. In order to finish the plant and get it
into operation, they desperately needed the contribution of Clark,
and for that they would have to tolerate his eccentricities on the
labor issue. Only when it was too late did they realize that it was not
worth it. If they did not replace Clark's policy with a conciliatory
one toward the union, the infant plant would go under. This threat
was compounded by the unexpected depression in the rail trade.

In summary, it was not their conservatism that doomed the
owners of Pittsburgh Bessemer Steel. They were willing to invest a
great deal of money in the venture, to install the latest and most
innovative machinery, and ultimately to be very flexible and accommodating toward the union and their workers. In this respect they
differed little from Carnegie. The main difference, of course, lay in
the trust they bestowed on William Clark. But Clark, like Carnegie,
was a new man, an outsider. His prejudice was not the result of class
privilege, but quite the reverse. Clark was a skilled iron worker who
through diligence and thrift had become a powerful and respected
mill owner. He simply could not understand the attitudes of the mill
workers who did not share his drive and ambition. In this respect he
resembled such militantly antiunion steel executives of the twentieth century as Tom Girdler. In the end, the old-family manufacturers displayed poor business sense in backing Clark. But one
must remember that Clark was a highly regarded expert in steel
mill practice, and these skills were extraordinarily scarce in late
nineteenth-century America. Having suddenly lost the services of
one of these experts, Kloman, could they just as suddenly jettison
the services of another? It did not seem to make sense. Homestead
was clearly a mistake for these old Pittsburgh iron masters, but the

failure cannot be traced to their social origins. They were innovative and flexible in their response; they simply backed the wrong man, one from outside the upper-class milieu.

One must admit, however, that the lesson should have been clear to these families. Large-batch Bessemer steel making and rail rolling were not for them. Most apparently understood that lesson very clearly, but not all. As a result, in the late 1880s they mounted yet another challenge to Carnegie's dominance of the Bessemer steel trade. The second attempt by the older Pittsburgh steel masters to compete with Carnegie occurred in 1886 with the founding of the Duquesne Steel Company. A Bessemer steel company intending to make steel rails, the plant was erected at Duquesne, which lay about halfway between Homestead and McKeesport on the Monongahela River. Duquesne Steel was organized with capital of $350,000 and the steel plant began to be built in the summer of 1886. It is not clear from available evidence exactly what happened during this period, but before work had progressed very far, disagreements broke out among the original partners and construction was suspended. Part of the problem at this point was the need for more capital to complete the work, but other problems evidently were festering. In any event, in March 1888, nearly eighteen months after it was begun, the enterprise was reorganized as the Allegheny Bessemer Steel Company with capital of $700,000.

A rather curious amalgam of men tried to run Duquesne Steel before it was reorganized. The first president was George Boulton, a native of Bedford County, Pennsylvania, and a close friend of Andrew Carnegie, who had been allied with him in a number of ventures. In 1865, for example, Boulton joined with Carnegie, David Stewart, and others in organizing the Columbia Oil Company to develop the oil lands of Venango County. In 1885 Boulton returned to Pittsburgh from the oil regions to organize Acme Gas, which became the principal supplier of natural gas to Carnegie's Edgar Thomson Works and also supplied several other Pittsburgh steel companies. At the same time, Boulton helped organize and became president of Duquesne Steel, designed to compete directly with Carnegie.[31] Robert B. Brown was vice president of Duquesne Steel in 1886. Born in Pittsburgh and educated at the University of Pittsburgh and Sheffield Scientific School at Yale, he became president of Union Bank in Pittsburgh while still a very young man. In 1885 Brown joined with Boulton in founding Acme Gas, and the two men then cooperated in organizing Duquesne Steel in the following year.[32] The general manager of the concern was Charles Hamline

Read, the son of the Reverend James Logan Reed, and a descendent of two of Philadelphia's oldest and most prestigious families. Charles H. Read was an iron and steel merchant in Pittsburgh for many years before turning to the manufacturing end of the business.[33] This was a curious group of men to challenge Carnegie. Boulton was an old friend and business associate. Brown, at least by extension, was also a business ally of Carnegie. Read was from an old upper-class family but never part of Pittsburgh's upper-class establishment.

The reorganization of the firm in 1888, however, radically changed its social profile. The new owners and managers, significantly, were from families who had been involved just a few years before in the ill-fated Pittsburgh Bessemer Steel Works: Edward L. Clark, son of William Clark, and William G. Park, son of James Park, Jr.[34] Edward L. Clark had taken over the family's Solar Iron Works after his father died in 1884 and ran it with his brother until his own death in 1893. In 1888 Edward Clark made a massive investment (amounting to some $540,000 if all the capital stock was paid in) in Allegheny Bessemer Steel and was named president of the firm until late 1889 or early 1890. William G. Park, along with other members of his family, was originally only a minor investor in Allegheny Bessemer Steel. As problems mounted, however, the Park family increased their commitment until William Park was the largest single owner in the firm. The works manager at Allegheny Bessemer was Francis H. Treat, a native of New York, who had become an expert in steel plant management with Joliet Steel and Illinois Steel.[35]

The new owners resumed construction of the works in 1888. They hired C. Ansler, consulting engineer of Mackintosh, Hemphill, to superintend building of the works. Ansler set out to make it the best, most technologically advanced plant in the industry, sparing neither money nor effort in the process. The buildings themselves were extraordinarily well built. They contained a converting and blooming house, a rail mill, and a finishing plant. In the converting house were two seven-ton Bessemer converters with an annual capacity of 220,000 tons. Most important and revolutionary, however, was a new process developed for running the steel ingots directly from the soaking pits, without further heating, through the rollers that pressed them into billets and rails. Known as the continuous process, this was an unheard-of innovation in the American iron and steel industry, although it had been practiced in England for some time. What it did was to dispense with the time-consuming and expensive practice of reheating the ingots. This, together with a myriad of other labor-saving devices, made the Allegheny Bessemer plant by far the most modern and efficient in the industry and represents one of the most important innovations in the trade. It was also a quantum leap into the future in terms of continuous processing and the degree of speed and managerial and organizational change that accompanied that phenomenon.

All of these innovations, however, cost money, far more money than the partners had originally intended to spend. It was at this time that William G. Park advanced massive amounts of capital (up to $500,000) to the concern, making him the dominant partner. By the time construction was completed, the Allegheny Bessemer owners had a gem of a plant, the very best in the industry. Operations were commenced in February 1889, and the rail mill was started a month later. Most important, they were now ready to compete head-on with Andrew Carnegie. And, according to Herbert Casson, they were determined to "beat Carnegie this time."[36] Surely they would not repeat the mistakes they had made at Homestead. Just as surely they did.

One reason for the old steel masters' downfall at Homestead had been labor unrest, and they were quickly plagued with the same problems at Duquesne. Shortly after the Duquesne mill went into operation, Carnegie's rival Homestead plant was crippled by a strike called by the Amalgamated. Common sense dictated that this would provide a golden opportunity for the new steel firm. All they needed to do was make peace with the union in their new plant, accede to their demands—anything—just keep the mill running at this critical juncture while Carnegie was incapacitated. Later, when matters had stabilized, they could deal with the union from a position of strength. This, of course, had been Carnegie's policy for years, and it had succeeded brilliantly for him. F. H. Treat, the works manager, however, decided to support Carnegie in his stand against the union and posted "NO UNION MEN ARE ALLOWED IN THE WORKS" signs. The Amalgamated, naturally, fought back, and the Allegheny Bessemer plant was soon embroiled in unending labor conflict. William Park, again not daring to discredit his mill manager, did not order the offending signs removed.

Even more important to the future of the company, Carnegie was beating them in the marketplace. Knowing that the labor costs at the Duquesne plant were about half those at his own mills and aware that the continuous process saved the further expense of reheating, Carnegie used his influence to keep Duquesne out of the rail pool that divided up the nation's rail business. Also, before the first rail was even rolled at Duquesne, Carnegie sent a circular to the railroads, warning them that rails made by the continuous process, that is, going directly from the soaking pits to the rollers, would be defective because of a lack of homogeneity. Carnegie, of course, knew that this claim was false, and after he took over the Duquesne works he retained the continuous process with never another word said about its defects. Later, when one of Carnegie's partners was asked whether he considered this a legitimate form of competition, he replied that under ordinary circumstances, he would not have thought it legitimate, but the competition set up by the Duquesne people was also not legitimate, because of the direct rolling process.[37] Carnegie, the industry's great price-cutter and innovator, justified his attack on Duquesne on the grounds that they could make rails cheaper than he because they possessed a technological process that Carnegie did not have. The duplicity of Carnegie at this juncture was stupendous; little wonder that Carnegie and his mills were so despised by the older Pittsburgh steel men.

The troubles at the Duquesne mill mounted. Murphy's law took effect: everything that could go wrong did go wrong. Shut out of the rail pool, ostracized by the railroads, Duquesne had difficulty obtaining sufficient orders to keep the mill operating. Desperate, they took even the most undesirable orders, at prices so low they lost money on every ton. Labor troubles of a minor variety nagged at them incessantly, and, despite the fact that the mill was the most modern in existence, it did not perform well. Although Francis Treat would later be a highly successful mill superintendent at other plants, Duquesne was evidently a painful learning experience for him. Large quantities of defective rails piled up in the company's yards; labor costs, which should have been the lowest in the industry, were high; and the cost of processing pig iron into rails in 1889 was $8.14 a ton.

The Duquesne plant was losing masses of money during the summer and fall of 1889. As a result, the stockholders were called on for additional capital. First, $100,000 was requested, then another $200,000. The other stockholders refused, and William G. Park had to pay the entire amount. Henry Clay Frick, newly appointed chairman of Carnegie, Phipps Ltd., watched all of this with great interest and anticipation. Sounding out Park, Frick found him receptive to selling. In fall 1889, Frick offered Park $600,000 for the plant. Since the works had cost at least twice that much, Park and the other stockholders refused the offer. Frick, however, declined to increase the bid, simply sitting back to bide his time.

Over the next nine months, Park made valiant efforts to make a success of the mill. By August 1890, the output of the rail mill was 16,814 tons for the month, indicating that it was finally running close to capacity. The output of raw steel was over 20,000 tons, and 17,000 tons of billets were made. This did not make the mill any more profitable for the owners but did at least make the plant more attractive (and a greater competitive threat) to the Carnegie interests. During this same period, Park obtained options on all the other partners' holdings, and when negotiations resumed, he was able to offer the entire stock of the company to Frick.

In October 1890, Frick raised his bid to $1 million, to be paid in bonds that would mature in five years. On the thirtieth of the month Park accepted the offer, and a couple of weeks later the plant was turned over to Carnegie. The purchase became a legend among steel manufacturers everywhere as the greatest bargain in the history of the industry. The Carnegie interests did not pay out a single dollar of cash for the plant, and by the time the bonds were due in 1895, the plant, made into a wonder of productivity by Carnegie management, had paid for itself six times over.

The old-line upper-class steel manufacturers had once again lost to Carnegie, and this defeat was even more galling than the one at Homestead. William Park quietly slipped away to New York City, where he lived for five years, waiting for his bonds to mature. When they did, he reentered the industry in a small way with Liggett Spring and Axle and later became chairman of Crucible Steel. This was the last attempt by the old Pittsburgh steel men to challenge Carnegie on his own ground. It is tempting to view this devastating defeat of Pittsburgh's old iron and steel families in simple terms. Conservative, out of step with the modern world of industry and labor relations, their two attempts to compete with Carnegie were the working out of a preordained plan: as the dust settled in the early 1890s, Carnegie and Bessemer steel were triumphant and a new order had emerged, manned by a new group of industrialists. It was the symbolic and actual end of the old prewar order of mercantile elite and small-scale iron manufacturers. This might make good literature, but it is bad history. The reality was quite different.

Badly beaten, but not defeated, most of these older Pittsburgh iron and steel men turned to concentrate on the finishing end of the industry, an area in which Carnegie did not participate, except in rails and bridge work. When they did install Bessemer operations— and a few did—they were small-batch ones, designed to provide steel billets for their own structural shapes.[38] The older steel masters were to find substantial success in this area, many of them running their mills well into the twentieth century, as is discussed in chapter 3. The story of those operations is far less dramatic than the challenge to Carnegie, but it was much more successful, and its telling reveals an industrial context of fundamental importance to the economic, political, and social structure of Pittsburgh in the late nineteenth and early twentieth centuries.

3

The Quiet Revolution:
Surviving by Adapting

"I could not compete with the steel rail production proposed for this Edgar Thomson Works," he said slowly. But he added, "They cannot compete with me if I concentrate on special alloys for tools and farm machinery. Nobody," he said slowly, "is opening up that field much."

Marcia Davenport, *The Valley of Decision*

MOST of Pittsburgh's independent iron and steel makers never directly challenged Carnegie or became involved in the large-batch rail market. And even those who did quickly learned their lesson, a deceptively simple one that has resurfaced in recent years as a maxim for businessmen: "Stick to your knitting."[1] In this case, sticking to their knitting often meant staying with familiar markets and technologies. If they did branch out into new markets and technologies, these old-line steel men made sure these endeavors suited their temperaments and abilities. As a result, the independent iron and steel manufacturers at the turn of the century in Pittsburgh engaged in a quest that has become the hallmark of small business, the search for a specialized market niche in which they could survive and prosper and, at the same time, be shielded from the economies of scale and cost efficiencies of large-scale operators like Andrew Carnegie.

It is difficult to make broad general statements about specialized niche marketing. It is, after all, by its very nature rather small, unique, and resistant to generalization. It was precisely those characteristics that made it difficult for the large-scale producers to enter these markets. If the markets had been amenable to generalization, products and market strategies could have been standardized and large-scale producers would have conquered them. Nonetheless, it is possible to isolate certain essential features of the market strategies and technological responses employed by Pittsburgh's independent iron and steel manufacturers during these years.

The Economic Advantages of Small Scale

Economic literature has generally focused on the advantages of big-ness when discussing economies of scale, but there has long been a recognition by many analysts that smallness itself could be an ad-vantage in certain markets and with particular technologies. Small-er firms, like their larger brethren, could take advantage of strategies of size in surviving and prospering in the marketplace. The great trick for the entrepreneur was to identify those market niches and develop the proper marketing and production techniques to service them.

James Soltow's examination of the metal fabricating and machinery-making industry in New England provided a compelling illustration of this intricate process. As he noted: "At any given time, there existed an objective structure of opportunity, deriving from such forces as the state of technology and science, income levels, population distribution, and the current structure of the in-dustry. Specifically, the opportunity for the small enterprise lay in occupying the interstices, or niches, which developed in the process of industrial growth."[2]

W. Arnold Hosmer, in a study conducted in the mid-1950s, iso-lated several such niches that the small entrepreneur must try to fill. He pointed out, for example, that small manufacturers should specialize in the manufacture of items with a limited total demand, a field limited enough that large firms, oriented to mass production and mass distribution, were not likely to enter.[3] As he noted, "Short runs of special styles create management difficulties and increase costs for large companies in both production and marketing. The more completely mechanized mass production becomes, the greater the problems in these unusual orders."[4]

Sometimes these smaller markets involved precision products that depended on craftsmanship or fine manual skill. Other times they were simply more regional markets that stressed a different kind of product differentiation, one, in Soltow's words, that had to be based on special services to customers, reputation for dependabil-ity and reliability, and personal sales representation.[5] Service, in fact, was one of the main products sold by small manufacturers,[6] so that even when the physical product of a small manufacturer appeared to be nearly identical to that of a large producer, and might even be more expensive, the small manufacturer often had hidden advantages in the marketplace. All of these intricate elements were woven together into a complex and dense web of marketing and technology in the iron and steel industry of the late nineteenth and early twentieth centuries.

The Fate of Wrought Iron and the Puddling Furnace in Pittsburgh

David Brody, in his masterful book on America's steelworkers, gave a somewhat inaccurate impression of the transformation of the iron and steel industry in the late nineteenth century. Focusing on Jones & Laughlin, and, to a lesser extent, on Carnegie Steel and Republic Iron and Steel, he penned an epitaph for puddled iron:

> The 1890's saw the widespread dismantling of iron mills. The largest producer, Jones and Laughlins, had operated 110 puddling furnaces. In 1884 the firm built a five-ton converter, then two more in 1890, and began reducing its iron production. It closed down thirty-three furnaces in February, 1892 because iron was being "crowded out." Its employees were advised to seek work elsewhere. . . . The basic steel companies, all iron manufacturers in 1890, employed barely a puddler among them in 1900.[7]

It's not that Brody was wrong in his facts about these companies, or even about the general trend in the industry in the late nineteenth century. Steel was replacing iron, and replacing it at an increasingly rapid rate. If one looks, for example, at the percentages of rolled products made of iron and steel, the death rattle of wrought iron seems all too evident. In 1867, 98 percent of all rolled products were made of wrought iron, as were 97 percent of all rails. Ten years later, 74 percent of all rolled products were still wrought iron, but only 44 percent of the rails were iron. Quite obviously, iron was holding its own fairly well to this point in virtually all product uses except rails, where Bessemer steel had established its preeminence. By 1887, just 44 percent of all rolled products were made of puddled iron, largely because by then only 2 percent of rails were made of it. In 1897, the proportion of puddled iron used for all rolled products had dropped to 21 percent, and no iron rails were made. Since rails for some time had not been a significant market for iron, it is quite clear that the decline of the 1890s was due to a drop in demand in other materials, primarily structural shapes. By 1907, only 11 percent of all rolled products were wrought iron, and that figure dropped to 8 percent by 1911.[8] These percentages seem to indicate that the situation for wrought iron manufacturers was pretty bleak indeed.

But this transformation, especially in Pittsburgh, was not nearly as full or complete as the general figures would imply. First of all, although the relative amounts of iron being produced were going down, the absolute amounts actually increased throughout much of this period. In 1867, 928,000 tons of rolled iron was produced. By 1877 this had risen to 1,319,000 tons, and in 1887 to 2,310,000 tons. Peak production in the nineteenth century came three years later with 2,518,000 tons. Thus, during a twenty-year period in which the percentage of iron products consumed was dropping, actual production was rising. Although the use of wrought iron for rolled products dropped drastically in 1897, when a total of 1,460,000 tons was produced, this rose to 2,033,000 tons in 1899. Then, over the first few years of the twentieth century, rolled iron production continued to rise, reaching 2,533,000 tons in 1902—the all-time greatest production year for rolled iron products. After that, even absolute production began dropping, until it was just 1,461,000 tons in 1911. The germane point here is that even as relative iron production was declining, there was still room for a great deal of productive capacity in cities like Pittsburgh.[9] In fact, the American Iron and Steel Institute (AISI) assured readers in 1892 that puddled iron in the United States was "not by any means a decaying industry."[10] Yet, the number of puddling furnaces operated in America during the years of the 1890s and first decade of the twentieth century did decline. From a peak of 5,165 furnaces in 1884, it slipped to 4,715 in 1894, and just 2,635 in 1907.[11]

What was the situation in Pittsburgh during these years? In 1894, two years after Jones & Laughlin began closing down its puddling department, Pittsburgh was still in many respects Iron City. Of the sixty-three iron and steel plants in Pittsburgh and the surrounding area, thirty (48 percent) made wrought iron. At a time when the number of puddling furnaces had declined to 4,700 nationally, there were still 1,050 single puddling furnaces in Pittsburgh, representing 22 percent of the national total. These furnaces produced about 808,000 tons of wrought iron annually.[12] At the same time, there were just eight Bessemer plants in the city, eighteen open hearth plants, and ten crucible operations. Wrought iron was still king in Pittsburgh in the mid-1890s, even though the output of the Carnegie works alone exceeded that of all thirty-one iron mills combined.[13]

By 1901, the number of plants producing wrought iron in the

Pittsburgh area had dwindled significantly. In that year, there were just nineteen such plants, containing 573 puddling furnaces with a capacity for about 605,000 tons of wrought iron. Of these, only a dozen remained independent entities, with production capacity of 363,000 tons.[14] At this time, there were sixty-three steel plants and rolling mills in Pittsburgh and Allegheny County, seven producing Bessemer steel, twenty-two making open hearth steel, ten producing crucible, and four making blister steel. Pittsburgh was no longer Iron City, but wrought iron production was not quite dead, and, in fact, manufacturers still found lucrative markets for its products.[15] We shall examine a few of those firms and their market strategies, better to understand the complex operation of the iron and steel industry at the turn of the century.

Most of the iron firms that managed to operate successfully in the late nineteenth century were not exciting or spectacular. As a result, there has been a tendency to dismiss them as unimportant. That is a mistake, because although they were certainly less dramatic than the Carnegie operations, they were far more typical of the iron and steel industry in Pittsburgh, and of American manufacturing generally, at the turn of the century. One such firm was the Sable Rolling Mill. One of the oldest and most conservative merchant iron firms in the city, it was run by Christopher Zug and his son Charles. The plant had been built in 1845 in partnership with the Graff family. When the Graffs erected their blast furnace in Pittsburgh in 1859, it gave the Zug and Graff iron firm an informally integrated structure. During the Civil War, the Sable mill emerged as one of the strongest and wealthiest in the city; by 1874 it had thirty-four puddling furnaces with an annual capacity of fifteen thousand tons of merchant iron, along with a nail factory in the city's Ninth Ward. R. G. Dun estimated that it was worth $1 million by this time.[16]

The Sable mill was crippled by a combination of factors in the mid-1870s. Partly, it was caused by the depression of the time, but even more by a dispute between Charles H. Zug and his sisters over the distribution of their father's estate.[17] The result was that the firm, with assets of between $800,000 and $900,000 and liabilities of only $400,000 to $600,000, was forced to file for bankruptcy. It is quite clear that on the business side, Sable was still doing well, but the family feud over inheritance rights caused great problems. The firm was reorganized in 1877, with Charles Zug and his son still running it, but with a number of new partners who brought in additional capital. By 1880, Sable mill was in good financial condition, and the company continued to prosper despite the viscisitudes of the 1880s and 1890s. By the turn of the century, Sable Iron was a small- to moderate-size iron mill (they made no steel) with an annual capacity for 22,500 tons of merchant bar iron. Their one concession to finding new markets and new products was the erection of a sheet mill, which produced 14,000 tons of sheet per year. Like many other small Pittsburgh iron firms, the Sable mill marketed its products with its own sales force, seldom relying on the services of metals or hardware brokers.[18] It was a business that depended on a reputation for high-quality products and personal service. Sable mill, as one of the old-line iron firms in the city, was steeped in reputation and rectitude, and this fact was of great benefit to the company in terms of its economic survival at the turn of the century. The quiet, conservative Sable Rolling Mill continued to be run profitably and successfully by the Zug family until it was dismantled around the time of World War I. Like many other Pittsburgh iron families, the Zugs found a safe and profitable market niche in the late 1870s and 1880s and never tried to produce steel or to challenge any of the larger firms in areas where their economies of scale gave them an advantage. Quiet, cautious Sable Iron and the Zug family did not make headlines and were seldom noticed. All they did was survive and make money.

Vesuvius Iron was similar to Sable Iron in many respects. Built in 1846, it was run for years by the Lewis, Dalzell, O'Hara, and Bailey families. By 1868, R. G. Dun estimated that it was worth between $500,000 and $600,000.[19] Six years later, it had twenty-four single puddling furnaces and produced twelve thousand tons of bar and sheet iron, rods, hoops, and nails. As it was for Sable Iron, the depression of the 1870s was hard on Vesuvius, and the plant sat idle for two years, until it was taken over by John Moorhead, Jr., member of another wealthy pre–Civil War Core upper-class iron family.[20]

Moorhead, who had just graduated from Yale, ran Vesuvius for nearly fifty years until his death in 1927. During these years, although Vesuvius increased its output slightly, it never changed its basic structure of operation. In 1884, the plant had twenty-eight single puddling furnaces and could produce 12,000 tons of iron, along with 105,000 kegs of cut nails. By 1894, it produced 22,500 tons of iron annually and no longer made cut nails, which had been rendered largely obsolete by wire nails. In 1901, still only puddling wrought iron, Vesuvius had forty single puddling furnaces with an annual capacity for 100,000 tons. No steel of any kind was ever produced in the works. Like Sable and other independent iron and steel firms, Moorhead marketed Vesuvius's products in traditional markets, using his own contacts and in-house sales force to pursue them. There was nothing fancy or innovative here, just old-line basic business enterprise, a business system inherited from the nineteenth century that lasted well into the twentieth.

The A. M. Byers Pipe Works was perhaps the most successful of the old Pittsburgh iron firms that stuck to their knitting. Taking as its motto "Wrought iron pipe or bust," Byers Pipe profitably pursued rather traditional technologies and markets until the 1960s. Much of the market for Byers's product came from the burgeoning oil and gas industry during the first half of the twentieth century. Its pipe was also used for irrigation systems and hydraulic mining.[21] It was a market that the Byers family executives began exploiting when the oil and gas industry was located in western Pennsylvania, and when the industry began migrating west and south, they used their contacts with industry executives, especially the Mellon-and-Guffey-owned Gulf Oil, to enhance their network of personal contacts.

Just as it is inaccurate to assume that Pittsburgh's wrought iron firms were all dying out at the turn of the century, it is wrong to conclude that all of them were able to find the elusive secret of success. A stark example of failure was the Pittsburgh Iron Mill, one of the oldest and most prestigious merchant iron firms in the city. Owned by the Painter family, it was worth over $1 million in the mid-1870s and as late as 1879 was the second largest iron mill in the city, producing twenty-seven thousand tons annually. But although Pittsburgh Iron underwent some linear expansion, it did not move successfully into profitable market areas. As a result, the Painters sold the plant to American Steel & Wire in 1898, turning their attention to the lucrative banking field. If Pittsburgh Iron did not survive, the Painters did, simply transferring their wealth and social connections to banking. Other old iron mills, such as Sligo Iron, Pennsylvania Iron, Kensington Iron, and Keystone Rolling Mill, had varied experiences during the later years of the nineteenth century. Sligo, like Sable, continued running profitably until it was sold in 1903, but Kensington Iron, Pennsylvania Iron, and Keystone Rolling Mill were dismantled in the late 1890s.

In the drive to find profitable markets and to develop the proper technologies and organizational structures, most of the independent iron manufacturers remained relatively small, unintegrated operations. Others, however, became more daring and expansive. Many of those ultimately turned their attention to steel products, but one of them ultimately returned to his roots in iron. That was Henry W. Oliver.[22] After Andrew Carnegie and B. F. Jones, Oliver was the most dynamic and powerful iron master in the Pittsburgh area. Head of Lewis, Oliver & Phillips (LOP), Oliver Wire, and a number of other firms, Oliver created a smaller, but nonetheless vertically and horizontally integrated, iron and steel empire during the late nineteenth century. He then sold off much of this to the new steel consolidations and settled back as an inordinately wealthy merchant iron and steel maker.

Oliver, like Carnegie and unlike many of the other older iron men, was a relative newcomer to Pittsburgh, and this fact may account for his more daring and impetuous behavior. Oliver immigrated to the city as a child in 1842 from Northern Ireland. He and Carnegie worked together as young boys in Allegheny, after which Oliver went to work for Clark & Thaw, a freight forwarding company. In 1859 he became a shipping clerk at Graff, Bennett & Co.'s spanking new Clinton blast furnace, the first in Pittsburgh. While working there, Oliver began making daring investments that became the hallmark of his later career. One of these turned out well for him, and by 1863 he had spare capital to invest in his own iron venture.

The iron firm that attracted Oliver's money was a small, struggling nut and bolt mill on Liberty Avenue, near the Allegheny River, run by William J. Lewis and John Phillips, who had purchased the plant with just three thousand dollars in 1860. Lewis was a master roll turner, and Phillips was a bricklayer. Neither had much money.[23] Henry Oliver and his brother, David, soon had the mill in good running order, and orders picked up, as the irrepressible Oliver proved to be an excellent salesman.[24] The three men next bought a small plant at Tenth and Muriel streets on the south side of Pittsburgh to keep up with their rapidly increasing orders. By 1866, the firm was ready to make its first significant expansion. They bought a mill building on the south side for twenty-five thousand dollars, rebuilt the works there during the year, and a short time later also purchased a mill David Oliver owned in Kittanning, Pennsylvania, for twenty thousand dollars.[25]

By 1874, the combined Lewis, Oliver & Phillips operations had three mills in Pittsburgh with forty-nine single puddling furnaces, eight trains of rolls, and an annual capacity for twenty thousand tons. Already one of the larger operations in the city, it was worth between $500,000 and $700,000, and R. G. Dun & Co. called it "an excellent house."[26] Even the economic downturn of the 1870s did not retard the young firm's development. At the depth of the depression Oliver leased the neighboring Birmingham Iron Works, so that by 1878 his plants could produce forty thousand tons annually, twice their capacity four years earlier. During these difficult depression years, LOP spent fifty thousand dollars annually on improvements to its mills, and since the market for merchant iron was depressed during much of this time, they began manufacturing a wide variety of iron specialty products for which there was still a ready market.[27] This was a pattern that would be followed by many Pittsburgh iron masters.

In 1880, Lewis left the partnership, also signing over his ownership of several patents.[28] By this time, Oliver had built up the business—the manufacture of nuts and bolts, wagon and other hardware, along with rolled merchant iron—into the predominant concern in its line in the country. Oliver was not content, however, and in 1881 he formed Oliver Wire Company to erect a wire-drawing plant not far from his Monongahela Rolling Mill. At the same time, he purchased the barbed wire plant and business of H. B. Scutt & Co. and moved it to Pittsburgh, also locating it nearby. This brought Oliver into the burgeoning barbed wire business in the 1880s, and at the same time he also began to produce wire nails with the organization of the Pittsburgh Wire Nail Company. This, too, was a recent innovation in the trade, soon to make the iron cut nail outmoded. Oliver was rapidly expanding his already extensive line of goods into potentially profitable new areas. With the success of his wire and wire nail plants, Oliver decided to erect a plant (Oliver & Roberts Wire) to make wire rods to supply the rods needed for his wire and nail business. This was an important small first step toward larger vertical integration by Oliver.

At the same time Oliver was developing these interests, he also turned his attention to steel manufacture. Like other merchant iron manufacturers, Oliver began discovering in the 1880s that customers were asking for a number of products to be made with steel. Oliver installed some Clapp-Griffiths furnaces, which he hoped would make a more pliable, but stronger, steel than Bessemer in his plant. The furnaces, however, did not work properly, and this problem forced Oliver to seek a five-year extension from his creditors. Oliver's business had recovered by 1884, and in 1885 he installed two new Clapp-Griffiths furnaces in his steel plant, capable of a daily output of 150 tons.[29] Finding that he could not keep up with the ever-increasing orders for specialty steels, Oliver next installed a small two-ton Bessemer converter in the plant. These various innovations increased the plant's capacity five times over what it had been just ten years earlier. Oliver also continued to pursue his policy of vertical integration by purchasing a blast furnace in New Castle, Pennsylvania. In 1889, he and Edward C. Converse set up the Monongahela Natural Gas Company to supply natural gas to his mill and those of National Tube. In 1891, Oliver leased, and later purchased, the Edith blast furnace in Pittsburgh and also organized Oliver Coke and Furnace to supply his mills with coke. During this same period, he also obtained an interest in Hainsworth Steel of Pittsburgh, but that purchase again plunged him into bankruptcy. As a result, he had to sell off many of the units he had acquired (Allegheny Furnace, Monongahela Natural Gas, and much of his coal and coke lands).

In order to save his enterprise, Oliver then allied himself with William Penn Snyder, an equally dynamic young steel and coke operator, and they formed Oliver and Snyder Steel in 1896. Into this firm went Hainsworth Steel, Edith Furnace, Oliver Coke and Furnace, and shares Oliver held in additional firms. By the mid-1890s, then, Henry Oliver controlled four firms: Oliver Iron & Steel, Oliver & Snyder Steel, Oliver Wire, and the recently purchased Monongahela Tin Plate (which moved him into yet another new and growing industry). By this point, Oliver felt that just one link was missing from his integrated empire: a cheap and dependable source of iron ore. This caused him to begin looking in the Mesabi region of Lake Superior for ores, and he accumulated vast holdings of that mineral, which he ultimately held in concert with Carnegie Steel and John D. Rockefeller. In 1901, with the creation of U.S. Steel, Oliver sold his one-sixth interest in the iron mining firm for $18.5 million in common and preferred stock in the steel trust.[30] He also sold a number of other properties to U.S. Steel subsidiaries—Monongahela Tin Plate, Oliver Wire, and Oliver & Snyder Steel—for another tidy nest egg.

Oliver retained Oliver Iron & Steel, which was composed of the original three iron rolling mills. Oliver ran this as a family business until he died, and his son-in-law, Henry R. Rea, continued the business until it was liquidated in 1923. Henry Oliver was a rather curious case. More aggressive and organizationally daring and innovative than most Pittsburgh iron masters, he finally sold off the large and heavily leveraged integrated iron and steel empire he had created to return to his roots: to running the small, but profitable, merchant and specialty iron and steel operation similar to that of other Pittsburgh iron and steel men. Also like them, Oliver had accumulated a great fortune, a matrix of accumulation that only increased over time with profits from his small iron and steel firm and other ventures. Oliver was one of the truly wealthy men of

Pittsburgh when he died, and his family had become an integral part of the local Core upper class.

Andrew Carnegie was the least typical of all of Pittsburgh's iron and steel manufacturers; rather it was men and firms like the Zugs at Sable Iron and John Moorhead at Vesuvius who constituted the archetype. Normally cautious and conservative, they were successful in finding profitable markets and adopting the proper technologies. Attaining great wealth and esteemed social status, few were willing to risk them as Oliver had with his impetuous plunging. Nor did most even want to pursue the expensive and aggressive kind of growth that the relatively cautious B. F. Jones did with J&L. That kind of expansion often forced one to become dependent on the money markets, with the possible loss of control that implied. These men were determined to run their mills, and to run them in their own way, so they chose a quieter and safer path of survival.

For most Pittsburgh iron and steel manufacturers in the late nineteenth century, the route to survival and profitability lay neither with breathtaking expansion and innovation nor with steadfast refusal to produce anything but wrought iron. In that sense, Henry Oliver provided a model for many Pittsburgh iron and steel men. They continually sought out new markets, markets of a more specialized nature that could be serviced by small production runs of specialty iron and steel. A majority of the older Pittsburgh iron and steel men followed this path.

The problems these independent Pittsburgh iron and steel men had in the late nineteenth and early twentieth centuries were threefold: first, to find and develop a secure, stable, and profitable market niche; second, to develop the requisite technology to create the products to fill that niche; and, third, to find some means of controlling the price and market structure without at the same time falling prey to the clutches of larger consolidations. The Zugs and the Moorheads accomplished these objectives quite well, but Oliver's experience was more mixed. He found the markets, created the technological and organizational structures, and worked to control those markets but ultimately sold his firms and lost most of those markets to larger consolidations. He then settled in to servicing a small merchant iron and hardware niche. Other Pittsburgh iron and steel men experienced a variety of results during this time, but for most, finding the proper market niche meant abandoning wrought iron at least partially and engaging in the production of steel products.

That judgment was one of the most wrenching decisions many old Pittsburgh iron masters had to make during this time. After

1890, however, it was not Bessemer steel, with its demands for large-batch continuous processing, that was the issue: it was the newly emergent technology of open hearth steel making. In 1899, Bessemer steel still accounted for 70 percent of the nation's steel output, but open hearth methods were rapidly growing in favor and were coming to dominate the market for structural steels and many specialty steel shapes.[31] More important for Pittsburgh's independent iron men, open hearth steel making provided less impetus to vertical integration and increased scale of production. The early furnaces were hand charged, and costs of production varied only slightly with size. Consequently, open hearth steel was better suited for small-scale production than Bessemer steel and could therefore be used for structural steel, angles, wire, sheet, and plates, without the necessity of developing large integrated production facilities. Open hearth steel making, then, although certainly compatible with large-scale operation, was also practical for those who wished to keep their operations small to service specialty markets and to avoid the great expense and risk involved in large-batch production.

The Conversion to Open Hearth Steel

During the later years of the nineteenth century wrought iron manufacturers experienced increasing competitive pressures to produce a higher-quality steel at more competitive prices. The answer for them was the development of open hearth steel production. Between 1880 and 1890, steel production for the first time surpassed that of iron in the United States: In the earlier year, steel production was just 29 percent of the total output; by 1890, steel production accounted for 61 percent of production, and its use had spread well beyond rails. The largest amount of this steel output was Bessemer, which accounted for 70 percent of all the steel made, a great portion of which still went into rails. By 1900 virtually every rail made in the United States was made of Bessemer steel. For other products, however, a critical dual transformation was taking place. Structural shapes that had formerly been made largely of wrought iron or crucible steel, and only incidentally of Bessemer steel, increasingly were made of open hearth steel. By 1904, open hearth constituted 72 percent of the iron and steel output in America.[32] This meant a new challenge for iron and steel men.

Despite the fact that it produced steel, and could produce it in quite large quantities, the open hearth furnace was essentially an enlarged puddling furnace. For this reason, wrought iron and crucible steel manufacturers, who had bitterly opposed the adoption of Bessemer steel making, were able to embrace the new technological procedure with less stress. Then, too, the open hearth furnace, unlike the Bessemer converter, did not demand expanded operations in the rest of the plant. It was a more variable and flexible process, one that fit more neatly into the existing iron and steel rolling operations.

A major change of great advantage to the owners of these mills, however, was that open hearth steel making was far from a rule of thumb operation. It was, in fact, a process heavily oriented to chemical engineering, and decisions on the correct refining process to produce high-quality metal were made not by the skilled workman at the furnace but by scientists in the laboratory. This was a great advantage to the steel mill owners, as we shall see in chapter 4, as it allowed them to gain some control over their high labor costs. In most other respects, however, open hearth production allowed them to continue to use relatively time-honored methods. Since the early furnaces were charged with cold metal, there was no great advantage to increased size of operations. Carnegie might well install massive open hearth operations at his Homestead plant, but this was to take advantage of the economies of scale brought by high throughput in other stages of his plant's operation. Costs of operation of the open hearth furnace varied little with size, so that open hearth steel could not compete with Bessemer steel at the low end of the market. Its competitive edge was from the higher-quality steel that could be produced with the process. So, although open hearth steel making could lend itself readily, particularly after the development of charging machines, to extremely large batch production, it was just as attractive for small-scale operation. In fact, the vast majority of firms using the open hearth process both in Pittsburgh and throughout the United States in the late nineteenth century produced a wide range of products in small batches requiring frequent roll changes.[33]

In 1884, there were just four plants making open hearth steel in Pittsburgh. The hearths ranged in size from 7 to 12 tons, and the largest operation, at the Shoenbergers' Juniata works, had two 12-ton furnaces, capable of producing just 12,000 tons of steel annually. This was about one-half of Juniata's productive capacity for puddled iron and about the same as the output of the largest crucible steel operations. By 1894, Andrew Carnegie had installed mammoth open hearth operations at the Edgar Thomson plant. There were six 20-ton, eight 25-ton, and one 35-ton furnaces, capable of producing a total of 180,000 tons of open hearth steel annually. To put this in some perspective, total production for the 39 open hearth furnaces in the entire country in 1882 had been just 162,000 tons. Yet the great expansion of Carnegie's open hearth operations by the mid-1890s had relatively little impact on the general scale of open hearth operations in the country. By that time, there were some 225 furnaces operating in eighty-eight plants, with a total capacity of 1,750,000 tons. Average output, outside the Carnegie mill, then, was about 18,000 tons. By 1894, there were eighteen open hearth operations in Pittsburgh, and although it is not always possible from the reports to distinguish open hearth from other steel products, or even from wrought iron, it is clear that range of operation varied enormously. Carbon Steel evidently produced about 100,000 tons of open hearth steel annually, while LaBelle Steel and Chartiers Iron and Steel apparently produced open hearth steel quite profitably in amounts as low as 4,000 to 5,000 tons per year.[34] Open hearth production, then, was a "friendly" technology, one that allowed independent iron and steel manufacturers to eliminate certain types of skilled labor, produce somewhat larger amounts of decent-quality steel for their specialized markets, and at the same time retain much of the production culture they had long cultivated in the wrought iron and crucible steel mills.

One of the very earliest innovators in the new open hearth process was Pittsburgh's oldest iron firm, Juniata Iron. By the late nineteenth century, the Shoenberger family had created a large, vertically integrated company with its own blast furnace operations. During the late 1870s and early 1880s Juniata was capable of producing about 25,000 tons of nails, horseshoes, and other products but found its traditional line of business hemmed in by the development of larger and more aggressive firms like Carnegie Steel and Jones & Laughlin (J&L). So the Shoenbergers, in conjunction with their plant manager, Thomas S. Blair, installed a twelve-ton Siemans-Martin acid open hearth furnace in 1879–81 capable of producing 12,000 tons of steel. This steel was used to make other specialty products, such as firebox steel, sheet steel, plate steel, and steel boiler plate, all in relatively protected market areas that could not be easily serviced by Carnegie or J&L.

This was a generally successful move for the Shoenbergers, so they also installed two six-ton Bessemer converters in the plant in 1886. By 1894 they made 100,000 tons of iron and steel annually, but Juniata was by then only the eighth largest mill in the city. In the mid-1890s, things began to unravel for both mill and family. First, the three Shoenbergers who had been running the operation all died within a few years of one another in the early 1890s, causing the company to be reorganized in 1894 as the Shoenberger Steel Company, capitalized at $1.8 million. The new officers (most of whom were related to the Shoenbergers by marriage) had problems coping with the depression of the 1890s and began negotiating to sell the plant to American Steel and Wire in 1899. The sale was completed in 1900, and a year later the Juniata mill became part of U.S. Steel. After seventy-five years, the independent career of Juniata Iron had ended. The fate of Juniata is often seen by students of the industry as allegorical for all of Pittsburgh independent mills, but its sale came about because of rather unique familial circumstances, rather than an inability to devise the proper technologies and market strategies.

Soho Iron was also one of the first Pittsburgh iron mills to install open hearth furnaces, with decidedly mixed results. Run for years by another branch of the Moorhead family, it was still a relatively small iron firm making galvanized, sheet, and plate iron by the early 1880s. During 1883, Maxwell and William J. Moorhead installed a twelve-ton open hearth furnace with the purpose of manufacturing soft steel for stamping purposes. The new furnace had a capacity of seven thousand tons.[35] Two years later they also built a new tube and pipe works to make additional iron and steel products, and in 1888 they made further extensive improvements to the mill, doubling the capacity of the open hearth works with two new fifteen-ton furnaces. By 1894, the plant had an annual capacity for thirty-two thousand tons of iron, along with sixteen thousand tons of steel plate. The Soho mill had by then become one of the larger establishments in Pittsburgh, capitalized at $1.6 million and employing five hundred to seven hundred hands in the works. Profits, however, were another matter. A consistent money loser throughout its history, it became bankrupt in 1894, partially because of the depression of the times. The mill was sold to another group, who ran it for three years, and in 1897 was sold again to J&L.[36] The path through technological innovation to products and markets was a thorny one, and achieving profitable survival was by no means a foregone conclusion, as the histories of both Juniata and Soho demonstrate.

A similar fate befell Spang Iron & Steel during this same period. Run by a number of the most prestigious old iron families in the city, it had a turbulent existence in the 1880s and 1890s. The plant had been built in 1880–81 with two ten-ton Siemans Pernot open hearth furnaces and a thirty-inch blooming mill. Spang Iron & Steel, however, did not have much success with these furnaces and by 1884 had replaced them with seventeen- and fourteen-ton Siemans-Martin open hearths. Still, the plant's capacity in 1884 was just six thousand tons. In 1887 they set up a Clapp-Griffiths steel plant with two three-ton converters to make soft steel by that process. That innovation, a variant on the Bessemer system, was not a success, and the unit was soon closed. By this point, however, the plant's operation had finally improved, so that by 1894 it could produce sixty thousand tons annually.[37] All of this was to no avail. The company went bankrupt during the depression of the 1890s. Its extensive and expensive innovations were so little valued by other manufacturers in the city that no one purchased the works, and it was ultimately dismantled. Despite the utter lack of success of Spang and the mixed results of Juniata and Soho, it is important to remember that the number of independent firms in Pittsburgh that suffered a similar fate was rather small. Most were quite successful in their quest for new technologies and markets.

Other old iron firms, such as McKeesport Rolling Mill and Solar Iron, made a more advantageous adaptation to the new technology. It was, however, Pittsburgh's old crucible steel firms who adopted the open hearth process with the greatest success. In 1875, just forty-four firms in the United States made cast, blister, or open hearth steel. Their total output was only 61,000 tons, two-thirds of which was made by the crucible process. Despite all the attention given to Bessemer and open hearth steel during the late nineteenth century, the output of crucible steel plants continued to increase during this time. Not only did the older Pittsburgh crucible firms survive but a number of large new plants came into existence. By 1884, total crucible steel production in America had risen to 115,000 tons, but it began to decline thereafter as a result of competition from open hearth steel. What is usually not recognized in this transformation is the fact that the larger open hearth producers did not generally make steel for the specialized markets served by the crucible steel makers. It was the crucible firms themselves that usually installed their own open hearth furnaces to supplement their crucible steel production. The special shapes they made were difficult to manufacture and had to be produced in small lots, so despite the spread of open hearth steel making to the large-batch manufacturers, the specialty steel producers were seldom in danger.[38]

Black Diamond Steel, largest of the crucible steel makers in Pittsburgh, was evidently doing a fine business during the late nineteenth century, but since the firm refused to release any information on its activities, it is difficult to say anything of substance. It did, however, win an award from the AISI in 1879 for making the best crucible steel in the country. The award was made specifically for rolling a crucible steel plate measuring 180 inches long, 53 inches wide, and 0.75 inch thick. The plate weighed twenty-seven hundred pounds.[39] A year later, R. G. Dun & Co. reported that Black Diamond was "a well conducted firm, in excellent repute, stands among the best concerns here, keep their affairs in hand, and have made money rapidly. . . . They are estimated to be worth in the neighborhood of one million dollars."[40]

In 1881, William Park introduced into the Black Diamond plant a 17-ton steam hammer that revolutionized many features of the industry. It allowed the firm to accomplish many tasks that before could only be done at the Krupp works in Germany.[41] Two years later, Park constructed two massive 30-ton open hearth furnaces for the works. About a year later, two more 30-ton furnaces were installed. This gave the Black Diamond plant capacity for 360 tons per day, the largest open hearth production of any steel plant in the world at that time.[42] The plant, which just a few years before could produce only 12,000 tons annually, by the late 1880s had a capacity of 140,000 tons. By the end of the 1890s Black Diamond was the largest and strongest crucible firm in the industry and had successfully added open hearth furnaces to its facilities, enabling it to serve new and profitable markets.

Several other crucible firms in Pittsburgh followed a similar pattern. Sheffield Steel, owned by the Singer and Nimick families, was the oldest continuing crucible steel firm in the city. Engaged in the manufacture of tool and other specialty steels, it was awarded second place in 1879 for the AISI award given to Black Diamond Steel. Sheffield installed a five-ton open hearth plant in its works in the early 1870s and replaced it with a ten-ton furnace in the early 1880s. By that time the mill's capacity had been expanded to twenty-three thousand tons. It continued its stable, prosperous growth throughout the 1890s. Hussey, Howe & Co. (the old Hussey, Wells Co.) by 1874 had a capacity for eighteen-thousand tons of crucible steel, making it at that time the largest such plant in the city, 50 percent larger than Black Diamond. Then, in 1886, the owners installed an open hearth works, consisting of one thirty-ton and one twenty-ton furnace. Used to make plates, machinery steel, and plow and spring steel, the open hearth works essentially doubled the plant's output. Hussey, Howe remained a profitable producer during the 1890s. The last of the older crucible firms was LaBelle Steel, owned by the Smith family. Built in 1862, the plant had a capacity for six thousand tons of spring, agricultural, and machinery steel in 1874. By 1884, this had expanded to ten thousand tons of specialty steel. In 1886 and 1887, however, the firm's owners installed two fifteen-ton open hearth furnaces in the plant. By 1894, capacity had increased to fifteen thousand tons. LaBelle continued to be a small, but profitable, operation throughout the 1890s.

Crucible and open hearth steel ultimately were in large measure the saving grace of the Pittsburgh iron and steel industry. But a number of wrought iron firms also made remarkably successful adaptations to specialized markets in the late nineteenth century, some of which required important technological innovations, some of which did not. The situation in Pittsburgh's iron and steel industry, aside from Carnegie Steel, seemed remarkably similar to what Scranton found in Philadelphia's textile industry: Pittsburgh iron and steel makers "constructed an alternate pathway to accumulation, overcoming a score of obstacles with strategies that differed systematically from those employed by the [Carnegie Corporation]."[43]

The Challenge of Vertical Integration

Not all the challenges to independent iron and steel manufacturers were on the plant floor. Some involved organizational changes that were at least as revolutionary and upsetting. Andrew Carnegie had not only brought Bessemer steel and large-batch production techniques to new levels in the industry but created massive vertically integrated structures that became emblematic to many observers of the steel industry at the turn of the century. One of the few independent iron and steel operations in Pittsburgh, outside Carnegie's works, to adopt a vertically integrated structure was Jones & Laughlin.

One of the earliest and largest of Pittsburgh's pre–Civil War iron firms, J&L developed integrated operations before the Civil War, owning blast furnaces, rolling mills, and finishing operations. But the vast majority of wrought iron and crucible steel mills never integrated backward to gain control of their sources of supply. By 1880, only American Iron, Juniata, Clinton, and Soho Iron had done so. Although a number of other Pittsburgh iron manufacturers, such as Henry Oliver, either bought or leased blast furnaces during the late 1880s and early 1890s, the characteristic structure for Pittsburgh iron and steel mills was to remain unintegrated throughout most of the nineteenth century.

J&L was the first Pittsburgh iron firm to engage in forward integration in the 1850s, by setting up its own warehousing and distribution facilities.[44] It soon became the largest iron producer in Pittsburgh, and one of the largest in the nation, and although never pursuing rails or Bessemer production with the verve and single-mindedness of Carnegie, it was a major player in both areas throughout most of its history. Benjamin F. Jones, the firm's chief executive officer, was one of the most respected Pittsburgh iron masters, and J&L was the only large integrated steel firm of the twentieth century to grow entirely through internal expansion, rather than through acquisition. Thus, it stands as the most successful independent Pittsburgh iron firm of the nineteenth century. It not only survived but grew to giant size and until the 1960s avoided being swallowed up by a larger consolidation.

J&L's first great expansion was during the Civil War, when its productive capacity (all wrought iron) increased from six thousand to thirty-six thousand tons. It was by that time the most extensive rolling mill operation in the state. This expansion was fueled by the fact that from 1856 to 1869 although the firm earned a total of nearly $1.7 million, no dividends were paid out: all profits were plowed back into improvements and expansion. Beginning in 1870, small dividends were paid, amounting to just a small portion of the earnings throughout the 1870s, and only after 1879 were they paid with any regularity. The general attitude of the firm's partners was that the needs of the business came first, and whatever was left over, if anything, would be made available for dividends. During the twenty years from 1854 to 1874, dividends amounted to just 4 percent of the total earnings. Over the next twenty years (1874–94), dividends climbed to 32.32 percent of total earnings.[45]

Until the mid-1880s, J&L remained essentially an iron manufacturer, using traditional iron puddling and rolling methods. In the early 1870s, however, B. F. Jones became the first Pittsburgh iron master to build a Bessemer plant in his works, a few years before Carnegie's Edgar Thomson Works. Jones hired Alexander Holley to build the Bessemer works for him, and Jones became an early member of the Bessemer Steel Association's rail pool. His works rolled several tons of steel rails annually, but the Bessemer works were not efficient and were closed down. Jones turned his attention back to merchant iron, while continuing to make some iron rails.

In the early 1880s, however, Jones decided to take his firm back into the world of steel: not to make steel rails, but to service the merchant iron market, which was increasingly demanding products made from soft steel. Like other Pittsburgh manufacturers, Jones at first went to Carnegie for Bessemer steel ingots to be rolled at the J&L plant. But Jones decided against joining the consortium to build Allegheny Bessemer Steel and instead installed two nine-ton Bessemer converters in his own works to make merchant steel. He had his first blow in August 1886, putting J&L back into the steel business.[46] A few months later, three new roll trains were erected at the mill, with capacity for two hundred tons per day.[47]

By the early 1890s, the J&L plant was a behemoth, second only to Carnegie Steel in the city. With capacity for 350,000 tons of steel billets and blooms, 50,000 tons of muck bar, and 450,000 tons of finished materials, it also ran two foundries with capacity for about 85,000 tons of various structural materials. In 1885 there were 2,900 workmen in the J&L plant, and ten years later there were 3,426. Jones continued his rapid expansion during the 1890s, adding more Bessemer converters, two 40-ton open hearth furnaces, and two new blooming and finishing mills. By 1901, J&L could produce 650,000 tons of ingots annually. The company had also become a completely integrated operation, with its own sources of ore and coke supplies, its own railways and transportation lines, blast furnaces, steel plants, rolling and finishing mills, along with warehousing and sales operations.

By that point, the profitability of the works was so great that Jones could pursue rapid expansion without sacrificing dividends. Dividends, which had remained low for years, increased in the 1880s and 1890s. Herbert Casson reported that B. F. Jones's income during these years averaged $325,000 per year, allowing him and the rest of his family to engage in an opulent life-style. They had, in Philip Scranton's words, achieved an enviable matrix of accumulation,[48] one that allowed them to pursue expensive and rapid technological change and expansion while developing a life-style that became increasingly characteristic of Pittsburgh's iron and steel aristocracy, and of the upper class in other cities. Other Pittsburgh iron and steel makers, if they could not match J&L's and Carnegie's productive capacity, could match their way of life. Their matrix of accumulation was large, impressive, and conspicuous.

Few of the other independent iron and steel mills in the Pittsburgh area became integrated operations during the nineteenth century. The reason for this failure to undertake what might be theoretically viewed as a rational business decision to integrate backward was quite clear and eminently sensible: an oversupply of pig iron throughout virtually this entire period. This caused a declining price spiral for pig iron, one that was reversed for only short periods before the end of the 1890s.[49] In this respect, then, as in most others, the bulk of the iron and steel firms—those that lay outside the Bessemer steel and iron and steel rail orbit—maintained a structure and management culture more similar to what existed in the English and European iron and steel industries.

Britain, the world leader in iron and steel prior to the late nineteenth century, also never developed the integrated structures that characterized the mass production end of the American Bessemer steel industry. As late as the eve of World War I, Britain's production was characterized as "amazingly scattered in small plants."[50] At that time, no firm produced more than 0.5 million tons of steel. A major reason for this difference between the two countries was that despite the fact that Britain had pioneered in Bessemer steel production, the process played a diminishing role in that country's industry after 1880. This is because Bessemer steel was most ideally suited for rails, and whereas America built over 100,000 miles of track in the twenty years from 1870 to 1890, the demand for rails in Britain grew more slowly. On the other hand, the demand for ship plates for Britain's expanding navy was the most dynamic sector of its market. In the 1890s, Britain still built about 90 percent of the world's ships, and open hearth steel was much better suited for that purpose. For this reason, Britain shifted earlier and more emphatically to open hearth production than the United States. Open hearth works, as noted, made fewer demands for economies of scale and integration of facilities, so the British iron and steel industry largely retained its nineteenth-century structure into the twentieth century.[51]

The vast majority of British firms by the early twentieth century were single-product companies characterized by little integration and even less diversification. They tended to service fairly highly specialized market niches, despite a plethora of rather large mergers in the British economy during this period.[52] The independent iron and steel firms in Pittsburgh, then, if deviant from the image generally propagated about the American steel industry, were strikingly similar to more traditional industrial and management structures in Britain and on much of the European continent.[53]

Thus, the independent iron and steel makers in Pittsburgh were hardly an aberration. If literature on the American scene has tended to glorify the large and the dynamic, to thrust forward images of

Andrew Carnegie and the large-scale integrated organization with its armies of professional managers and bureaucrats, it is useful to recall that all of the world was not America. Not even all of America was America, or at least the standard textbook version of the country. America, despite the Carnegies and Rockefellers, was still largely dominated by small business at the turn of the century.

The same was true of the iron and steel industry, of which Pittsburgh was the largest and most important center in the country. Long before Carnegie made his first Bessemer steel at the Edgar Thomson Works in 1875, Pittsburgh's mills dominated the industrial scene in the city, state, and nation. The dazzling brilliance of the Carnegie works obscured their role and accomplishments in the last quarter of the nineteenth century. But they did not fail, or even cease to grow and change. They continued as a strong backbone of more traditional segments of the wrought iron and crucible steel production. Then, with the emergence of open hearth steel, they often pioneered in its adoption, even if their works never rivaled in size those of better known steel makers. With their more traditional methods on the shop floor and in the office, these iron and steel masters were not simply a forgotten remnant of the past. They continued to grow and prosper until at least the outbreak of World War II and represented an American equivalent to the smaller, traditional family-dominated iron and steel firms in Britain and France.

4

Craftsman's Empire/
Mill Owner's Domain

"A cloud of smoke hangs over it by day. The glow of scores
of furnaces light the river banks by night. It stands at the
junction of two great rivers, the Monongahela which flows
down in a turbid yellowy stream. . . . All nations are jumbled
up here, the poor living in tenement dens or wooden shanties
thrown up or dumped down with very little reference to roads
or situation. . . . It is a most chaotic city."

Raymond A. Mohl, *The New City: Urban America
in the Industrial Age, 1860–1920*

T WO general perspectives on labor relations in the iron and steel
industry of the nineteenth century have been developed over the
past several decades. The first of these, as characterized by David
Brody's brilliant *Steelworkers in America*, cultivated an image of
labor relations in the industry keyed to the psychology of steel making. In this vision, the iron- and steel-making processes of an earlier
period, based on skilled hand labor, had been largely revolutionized
by technological and managerial changes that had reduced the mill
owner's dependence on skilled, unionized labor. Replacing whole
armies of skilled workers with continuous processing machines
manned by unskilled immigrants, steel masters gained the undisputed upper hand in a new nonunion era.

Brody further declared that the pressures for economy, large-
batch production, and continuous processing that characterized the
Bessemer steel industry altered the competitive situation for all iron
and steel manufacturers. As a result, he said, the "two groups [iron
masters and steel men] were, indeed, largely identical" by the late
nineteenth century.[1] If, then, one accepts that proposition, a study of
the policies and practices of large-scale Bessemer steel masters

would provide us with a window on the practices of the entire industry. And this, in fact, has been the general approach of virtually all commentators on iron and steel firm management in the late nineteenth century. The concept, though, that smaller-scale iron and steel men and large-batch Bessemer producers were identical is not accurate. In virtually every respect, the older iron masters and crucible and open hearth steel makers who pursued smaller and more specialized markets differed from the large-batch, mass production steel men. By extension, it should follow that they also differed significantly in their approaches to labor relations. Thus, our view of management in the iron and steel industry has largely been based on a nonrepresentative segment of the group.

Partially in response to Brody, with his emphasis on the weak and dependent nature of labor in the steel mills during this period, a new perspective on labor relations has emerged. Focusing largely on skilled workers within the industry, David Montgomery and other new labor historians have challenged Brody's viewpoint with graphic portrayals of the persistence of craftsman empires in the iron and steel mills. These empires, in Montgomery's account, rested on a base of workman's skills and a powerful working-class culture that reinforced the importance of those skills. This allowed the skilled iron and steelworker, in Montgomery's words, to exercise "an impressive degree of collective control over the specific productive tasks in which they were engaged and the human relations involved in the performance of those tasks, and these same workers stamped their own distinctive mark on the character of the labor movement of the age."[2] Further, these skilled workmen "not only made their struggles for control increasingly collective and deliberative, but also manifested a growing consciousness of the dependence of their efforts on those of workers in other crafts."[3]

Quite obviously, there is a significant gap between Brody's perspective, with its stress on the erosion of skills with the introduction of new machinery and management processes, and Montgomery's view of the retention of power by skilled operatives. Montgomery's insights on the iron and steel industry, and the extent of the transformation of its labor scene during this time, have been enhanced by a number of other scholars. Bernard Elbaum, Katherine Stone, and Michael Nuwer, applying the concept of internal labor markets to the steel industry of the late nineteenth and early twentieth centuries, discovered far greater persistence of skills, and of the prerogatives that accompanied them, than earlier commentators.[4] As Nuwer has commented: "The transition from batch to flow production did not eliminate the employer's dependence on work-force cooperation to coordinate production."[5] This, along with other works, has done much to give substance to our understanding of the world of the skilled and unskilled iron and steel workers in late nineteenth-century America.[6]

These two perspectives—Brody's and Montgomery's—have, nonetheless, left a significant gap in our understanding. We understand the mind-set of the large-batch Bessemer steel producer with his armies of unskilled immigrant laborers. We also understand the attitudes and culture of the skilled craftsmen, many of whom continued to labor in the smaller independent mills. What we do not have is an enhanced understanding of the role of the independent mill owner in all of this. Although much ink has been spilled detailing the thoughts and actions of Andrew Carnegie, Henry Clay Frick, and some of the executives of U.S. Steel in labor disputes, we know practically nothing about the ideology and values—the mill-owning culture—of nineteenth-century iron masters. Earlier chapters in this study have attempted to give some sense of this in relation to plant expansion, technological innovation, and market strategy, but it is important also to develop some idea of these iron and steel manufacturers' beliefs about the proper conduct of labor relations in the late nineteenth century.[7] It is the primary focus of this chapter to re-create the ideology and practice of labor relations in these independent iron and steel mills that dominated the scene in Pittsburgh. Of critical importance in this analysis is a recognition that the labor/management ideas of these independent iron and steel owners were the product of both the market position of their mills and the values and culture of their class.

Re-creating this mill owners' culture with regard to labor relations in the nineteenth century, however, is no simple task. The aristocratic owners of the smaller iron and steel mills in Pittsburgh were an intensely private and discreet group. Only B. F. Jones left a diary, and the only biography is that of Henry Oliver, which gives the reader little insight into his ideas of labor management. There was, however, a trade paper for the iron and steel industry (*Iron Age*), which, although it did not always clearly reflect the ideas of the Pittsburgh iron men, is nevertheless a valuable repository for at least some elements of their ideology. Similarly, the *Pittsburgh Bulletin*, an upper-class newspaper, occasionally addressed issues of broader concern and may serve as an indication of class attitudes. In large measure, however, we must observe nuances and attempt to discern trends from highly random artifacts that have been left behind. We must, in other words, become archeologists of the written word, sifting verbiage for hints of what may have been.

In analyzing the thoughts and actions of these iron and steel men, we should be aware of the fact that there existed a basic continuum of belief concerning the proper conduct of labor relations among nineteenth-century businessmen. The ideology of the iron masters lay at various points along this continuum at different times in the nineteenth century. On the far right was a militant, ideologically antiunion stance that manifested itself in a visceral hatred of the workers themselves. This is seen most clearly in the thoughts and actions of Henry Clay Frick in the Homestead Strike in 1892 and of a number of other Carnegie executives in the late nineteenth and early twentieth centuries. One of them summed up this attitude well in 1901: "If a workman sticks up his head, hit it."[8]

Next on the continuum was what might be termed a romantic, paternalist antiunionism. This was a rural, largely anti-industrial set of attitudes that visualized the creation of an ideal, utopian community for workers under the Christian guidance of the mill owner. This set of beliefs was most clearly articulated in the iron and steel industry by Daniel J. Morrell, head of Cambria Iron in Johnstown.[9] Although Morrell's iron mill was located near Pittsburgh, Morrell and the other owners were aristocratic Philadelphians, and Johnstown was a fairly rural, even bucolic environment. As a result, as Herbert Gutman has noted, Morrell developed an ideology of labor management relations that was strikingly paternalistic and resoundingly antiunion. Morrell called his ideology the "American System." In Morrell's vision, Cambria Iron, located in a remote, semirural area, would provide nearly all of the necessities for its workers, along with a number of other amenities. The company built and owned most of the houses, stores, schools, and libraries in the town, and Morrell wanted to create a model community that reflected what he called a "civilized, intelligent, Christian community." The American worker, he declared, deserved to "live in a house, not a hut," and to "wear good clothes and eat wholesome and nourishing food." One thing the workers could not have, however, was a union. Morrell's vision was of a totally paternalistic environment, one in which the workers trusted to the Christian benevolence of the owners to provide for their needs.[10]

At the next position on the left in the continuum was an attitude of honest, if grudging, acceptance of unionism as an expression of the legitimate goals of workers, with a willingness to negotiate with those workers' organizations in a tough but fair manner. This is the set of attitudes, I would argue, that was most characteristic of the majority of upper-class Pittsburgh iron and steel men in the nineteenth century. Credence for this viewpoint is offered by John A. Fitch, who wrote a pioneering history of iron and steel workers in the early twentieth century. He noted of the 1870s and 1880s:

> There were difficulties and strikes occasionally; there was a long and determined strike in the summer of 1882, and now and then there was a lockout. But on the whole this decade was the period of most effective agreement between the employers and the men that the association [Amalgamated Association of Iron & Steel Workers] had ever experienced. Each knew and respected the strength of the other and while hard blows were dealt on both sides, there was much mutual confidence and good will.[11]

The final, technically most liberal or progressive point on the continuum was that which postulated the concept of welfare capitalism and enlightened self-interest in labor relations. In this formulation, there were to be no independent labor unions (although there could be company unions) and company management itself would take care of the various needs of the workers, from higher pay to medical benefits and education, to recreational facilities and libraries. In some ways, of course, these ideas were not far from those of Daniel Morrell, but the fact that labor organizations, albeit not independent ones, were tolerated and even encouraged did give the workers a voice, one that was at times rather powerful.[12] These attitudes were sometimes espoused by owners of the smaller Pittsburgh iron and steel plants but appeared most often in the speeches and writings of the banking interests who controlled Illinois Steel in the nineteenth century and U.S. Steel in the twentieth.[13]

This is hardly the place to given an overview of labor organization and labor relations in the iron and steel industry, or even a history of such organization in Pittsburgh itself. But in order to have some understanding of the material to follow, it is necessary to present a brief outline of those items here. As William A. Sullivan has noted, the iron industry in Pennsylvania began in a rural environment, especially on "iron plantations." This fact, along with a highly paternalistic form of management practiced by such early eastern Pennsylvania mill owners as Daniel Morrell, whereby they provided housing, land for gardens, hunting rights, and other benefits, did much to retard the growth of union organization in those eastern areas.[14]

As the iron industry spread to Pittsburgh, however, it quickly encountered a very different environment. Although still a small city in the 1830s, Pittsburgh nonetheless took on the appearance of a compact, urban industrial environment. By 1850, Pittsburgh had established its preeminence as America's iron city, producing nearly half of the nation's iron. As a result, Pittsburgh became an overwhelmingly working-class community. Michael Holt, in his study of the city in the 1850s, estimated that one-third of Pittsburgh's white male work force were unskilled workers, 30 percent were skilled workers, and another 8.7 percent were small manufacturers, many of whom were self-employed artisans. Since there were a number of factories and working-class neighborhoods in Allegheny City, across the Allegheny River from Pittsburgh, which Holt did not consider in his calculations, the actual percentages were probably even higher.[15] By 1850, there were twelve small forges located within Pittsburgh's city limits (which did not include many of the communities that later became part of the city), and they employed an average of seventy-six workers each. The rolling mills, with which we have been primarily concerned in this study, were mostly in Allegheny City or other still-autonomous communities. They averaged 158 workers per plant at that time. It has been estimated that forty-five firms employed a total of 5,500 workers in the metropolitan iron industry. Iron workers, according to another estimate, accounted for about 49 percent of all workers in the area.[16] Since Pittsburgh was so highly industrialized at such an early stage, and since it was clearly an urban environment, one that encouraged communal fellow feeling among the workers, it early became a seedbed of labor union activity, and one of the principal areas of union organization was in the city's young iron industry.

The first group to organize in Pittsburgh's iron industry were the molders, who walked off the job in the first recorded industry strike in western Pennsylvania in 1842. That walkout proved a failure, and the men returned to work six months later, forced to accept a wage cut of fifty cents per ton.[17] Over the next several years, however, there were a number of other strikes, and slowly a union organization began to form.

All of these early strikes were single-craft actions, but in 1849–50 there was a major turning point in the industry's labor relations. Faced with wage cuts in December 1849, the puddlers, scrappers, refiners, boilers, and heaters all went out in January. It was, in the words of a contemporary, "a remarkably bitter" strike. Pittsburgh's iron manufacturers used every weapon at their disposal to break the incipient union. They imported immigrant strikebreakers, who restarted four of the mills with reduced wages in February. The striking workmen responded by attacking the mills and the strikebreakers working there, in what have been called the Rolling Mill riots of 1850. The iron manufacturers called on the police and courts to punish the workers but were dismayed when Governor Johnson pardoned them and remitted their fines. Nonetheless, the manufacturers won the confrontation, reduced workers' wages, and forced many of the strikers to seek employment in mills to the west.[18]

The 1850s, then, were generally years in which Pittsburgh's old-family iron manufacturers had things their own way. Retaining a good deal of control over political power in the city and county through their eminence in the Republican party, they were able to defeat strikes, keep wages down, and run their mills as they saw fit.[19] Even when the workers formed a union, they could not prevail. In April 1858, the iron workers of Pittsburgh got together and formed the Iron City Forge of the Sons of Vulcan, a union of boilers and puddlers. The reaction of the iron manufacturers was swift and brutal: mill owners blacklisted the union leaders and members and shared the lists with one another. Union members were rapidly dismissed as troublemakers. As a result, the union disintegrated within a short time.[20]

Up to the outbreak of the Civil War, then, the old Pittsburgh iron masters' labor ideology tended to reflect a point on the far right of the continuum. Providing few paternalistic benefits to their workers, they reacted in draconian manner to any threat to their autonomy in mill operation, "hitting the heads" of any worker who dared engage in union organizing or demand collective bargaining. Yet, it should be remembered that the owner, even at this time, had to share at least some power and decision making with his skilled workers, whether organized or not. The productive process in the iron and steel industry at that time of necessity demanded a team effort, one that was under the direction of the skilled craft worker. Puddlers, rollers, and molders assumed the role of labor supervisor and took control of the work and men under them.[21] The independent mill owner, then, despite his rigorous antiunion stand, was hardly an autonomous entity in the early nineteenth century. He was forced, by the very nature of the productive process in his mill, to engage in cooperative efforts with his skilled workers. The extent of his cooperation, whether voluntary or forced, expanded later in the century.

In 1861, the Sons of Vulcan was reorganized in Pittsburgh under the leadership of Miles S. Humphreys. With the great expansion of the iron and steel industry during the Civil War years, they were able to set up a national union, the Grand Forge of the United States, United Sons of Vulcan, in 1862. By 1865, the union had a number of forges scattered in eight states, but the center of union activity remained in Pittsburgh, with secondary areas of strength in Ohio and Wheeling. The key confrontation with employers soon developed over the issue of the sliding scale. It was over this matter that a fully articulated labor movement in the iron industry emerged and the nature of labor relations in the trade was solidified for some twenty years. It is also at this point that some of the ideas and reactions of Pittsburgh's old-line iron masters come more clearly into focus.

When the Civil War ended in 1865, the future did not look terribly promising for the nation's iron industry. The Sons of Vulcan was strictly a craft union, made up solely of boilers and puddlers, whose members' wages had risen to $9.00 a ton in 1864, compared to just $3.56 a ton when the war began.[22] After the war, however, prices began falling and the iron manufacturers were determined to reduce wages. Workers were just as resolute in their opposition. The result was a bitter strike that "was a contest over the principle of unionism as well as over wages."[23] The two sides battled for eight months before a historic resolution of the controversy, the sliding scale, was achieved.

According to John Jarrett, president of the Amalgamated Association of Iron and Steel Workers, the idea for the sliding scale, which became the integral element of labor relations in the iron industry and was regarded by the Sons of Vulcan as their greatest achievement, was first suggested by Benjamin F. Jones, head of American Iron Company (J&L).[24] The battle between union and management had gone on for eight months, and Jones had fought long and hard against the union, but now he, as well as the union members, was tired and eager to get the mills operating again. Jones wanted to find some mechanism that would tie the workers' wages to the mill's success, to find a means to create a community of interests between capital and labor. Union officials were at first skeptical but ultimately accepted the idea on a trial basis. Humphreys then devised the actual system so that the wages of puddlers could advance as iron prices went up and automatically recede during bad times. Previously, the only recourse workers had when prices went up was to strike for higher wages, and when iron prices fell, all that employers could do was institute a wage cut, which invariably caused a walkout and increased bitterness between the two sides.

The sliding scale was intended to end all of that. Although it never worked perfectly, it did go a long way toward achieving its goal. As John Jarrett commented many years later: "The puddlers realized that the profits of the iron manufacturers were enormous and that wages were out of proportion to profits, but they had no actual figures to determine what the profits were. The [sliding] scale was an experiment; and though not based on absolute knowledge, the rate was constantly increased."[25] Although there is no record of debates or discussions among the iron manufacturers, the sliding scale must have been a bitter pill for many to swallow. Nonetheless, Jones, as head of the manufacturer's committee, was able to persuade his fellow iron masters—James I. Bennett of Graff, Bennett; Henry Lloyd of Lloyd and Black; Barkley Preston of Everson, Preston; and Jacob Slagle of Juniata Iron—to sign the scale agreement.[26]

The result of the establishment of the sliding scale was to create an even more solid independent contracting system within the mill, wherein the skilled craftsmen—the puddlers, boilers, rollers, and so forth—were paid on a tonnage rate, and then hired semiskilled workers as their helpers, determining pay as they saw fit, without the intervention of the boss. Recent commentators have viewed this as a tremendous advance in the industry, and a significant step away from the earlier adversarial relationship: "The successful emergence of collective bargaining can be explained by the mutuality of interest of the contractors and the ironmasters arising from the importance and specificity of craft skills, the managerial status of the skilled workers and their financial stake in the industrie's [sic] prosperity resulting from the tonnage payment system. . . ."[27]

It took a while for the system to become routinized. During the first two years after the agreement was signed, iron prices dropped rapidly and wages were reduced accordingly. In 1866 the union gave ninety-day notice to terminate the scale. To preserve the sliding scale system, the iron manufacturers decided to give the workers an advance in scale. This advance lasted until 1867, when the manufacturers proposed to drop the rate. The puddlers refused, and the iron manufacturers locked them out of the mills. Again, it was a long lockout, lasting some five months, but in the end the manufacturers were defeated and agreed to pay the old wages. During the next several years, the wages of skilled tonnage workers within the industry were adjusted without major disputes. Since this was a time of high iron prices, however, wages automatically remained high, so there was little incentive for workers to change the system. The depression years from 1873 to 1879 ended this halcyon period, and three lockouts, along with a few other confrontations, darkened somewhat the relations between the manufacturers and the union.

Facing a severe downturn in prices brought on by the depression, the iron manufacturers asked for a conference with union leaders to discuss the card rate. At this conference in November 1874, the manufacturers gave thirty-day notice that they were terminating the sliding scale agreement. This threat worked the same magic with the union as it had with the manufacturers seven years earlier. The union proposed a fifty-cent reduction, while the manufacturers demanded one dollar. When they were unable to reach an agreement, the mill owners closed the city's iron plants for a period of four months in an effort to bring the union to its knees.[28]

This was the first protracted labor disturbance in several years in the iron industry, and on the surface the mill owners' action seemed similar to many earlier lockouts in which they had treated the workers with coldness and brutality. This time, however, they seemed almost sorrowful over the turn of events. James I. Bennett, one of the signatories to the original sliding scale agreement and certainly one of the most respected iron manufacturers in the city, appealed to the puddlers at a joint meeting held in December 1874: "There are a number of us who have been puddlers and laborers in the mills and can sympathize with you fully. We don't want to fight the union, but you can make us do it."[29] *Iron Age*, the Bible of the iron trade, commented ruefully of the shuttered plants, "All seemed deserted . . . the fires were out of the puddling furnaces and an air of chilliness and desertion generally pervaded the premises."[30] Nor was there a concerted effort by the mill owners to break the back of the union. When a few mills, such as Juniata Iron, attempted to bring in strikebreakers as they had in the past, the scabs were met by jeering crowds of puddlers, who "gathered about the mill and gave such expressions of displeasure that the workmen through [sic] up their jobs, fearing trouble."[31] Despite the fact that *American Manufacturer* talked of a reign of terror in the city due to these actions by the puddlers, these actions received little support from other mill owners.[32]

The extent to which the mill owners' ideology had changed by the 1870s and the degree to which labor/management relations had become routinized and normalized can be seen by the actions of a Pittsburgh mill that tried to use older heavy-handed tactics and the reaction of the older iron barons to these tactics. Only one firm in the city, the Pittsburgh Bolt Company, which significantly was owned by two men who had formerly been workers in the same mill, decided to take an all-out antiunion stance. Not part of Pittsburgh's upper-class establishment, and perhaps disdainful of men who they thought lacked their drive and ambition, the mill's owners, Edward Kaylor and R. H. Lewis, were determined to break the union and willing to use any means to do so. To this end, they brought in forty-eight black puddlers as strikebreakers in their mill. This was a provocation well beyond the usual in these labor disputes. Even the use of strikebreakers by this point was considered rather vulgar and bad form, but to use blacks at a time when they were a tiny minority of the population and virtually none could find work in the region's mills, mines, factories, or offices, was a provocation that transcended accepted behavior.[33] The strikers responded by sending a howling mob of two to three hundred men to the works. Kaylor then called on the local police department to disperse the crowd. The police refused, so Kaylor tried to convince the mayor to put the police at his disposal. Since the strikers were quiet and peaceful, however, the mayor deemed best not to interfere. The black puddlers then told Kaylor they were too frightened to come to work, and the confrontation came to an end. Significantly, none of the older Pittsburgh iron masters defended the owners of Pittsburgh Bolt. It may be surmised that they had an aversion to such tactics, tactics that were so antithetical to the patterns developing between the owners and the union and so opposed to the social and cultural traditions of the city.[34]

Soon after this incident, the lockout began collapsing. Keystone Mill, owned by the upper-class McCutcheon family, was the first to come to terms with the union, agreeing to resume operations under the previous scale. Four days later, Jacob Painter's Pittsburgh Iron Works fired up their furnaces after reaching agreement with the union. This occasioned a general meeting of Pittsburgh iron manufacturers in which they decided to capitulate fully to the union's demands. All of this is perhaps simply a sign of the manufacturers' weakness, yet there are important elements of accommodation to be noted. First, outside the Kaylor mill, there was no extensive use of strikebreakers, such as characterized earlier and later industry strikes. Second, owners and union leaders continued to discuss issues throughout the entire period. As John Fitch noted, in several instances "Pittsburgh employers requested the privilege of appearing before the convention of the association so that they might explain their position directly to the delegates."[35] This sort of mutual respect and accommodation, hammered out over many years in the context of intense confrontation and rivalry, would characterize relations between the two sides in the late 1870s and much of the 1880s.

The result of this lockout, as for so many others during this period, was a resounding victory for the iron workers. There are a number of germane points here. First, virtually every one of the older iron mills in the city, which were owned by the most prestigious of the pre–Civil War iron families, was unionized. At Pittsburgh Iron, the fourth largest mill in the city, which was owned by the Core upper-class Painter family, 216 of the 766 employees were members of the union.[36] Its owner, Jacob Painter, was also a regular member of the manufacturers' committee that negotiated the annual scale with the Amalgamated. Etna Rolling Mill, owned by the eminent Spang and Chalfant families, and Pittsburgh Forge and Iron, owned by the Wells and Verner families, were other typical examples of unionized old-family iron mills.[37] As John Fitch pointed out, "a list of manufacturers who signed the scale was practically a list of those engaged in the business."[38] Thus, we must remember that the acrimony of the lockout of 1874 took place within the context of a unionized environment, and none of the old-line Pittsburgh iron masters advocated a dramatic alteration of that environment.

Simply tolerating a union, however, is hardly evidence of a congenial stance toward workers and their organizations. More to the point are the kinds of attitudes and values displayed by these manufacturers. But these are elusive. None of the older manufacturers, unlike Carnegie, ever wrote an article outlining what professed to be his attitudes on the subject. To determine these we must, again, attempt to deduce these attitudes from their actions and from the words of agencies that might legitimately be taken as their representatives.

It must be remembered, first of all, that by the 1870s the monopoly that Pittsburgh's elite had held on political power in the city had eroded. The rise of immigrant political machines in the city had forced the elite at least to share power with their workers and middle-class residents in the city far more than they had a quarter-century before. Pittsburgh had been a Republican city since the 1860s, and that party had long been dominated by members of the city's industrial aristocracy. The party's hegemony had come with the shift of a number of working-class wards from the Democratic party during the Civil War. But little research has been done on the nature of city politics during these years, so that we do not know what kinds of compromises the iron barons were forced to make to gain the workers' allegiance. It does seem reasonable to assume that it entailed some degree of shared power, especially since the trade unionist William McCarthy was elected mayor in 1865 and 1875, and the Greenback party emerged to take votes away from Republicans whenever the party did not sufficiently reflect workers' needs.[39]

There were also in the 1870s and 1880s a number of seemingly minor examples of goodwill between employers and union. This goodwill, expressed within a context of confrontation over elemental issues of wages, hours, working conditions, and profits, manifested itself in a number of ways. *National Labor Tribune* in January 1884 reported that the annual reunion and picnic for members of the Amalgamated (which had succeeded the Sons of Vulcan) and their families would be held that summer. The officials of the Amalgamated in January had just concluded their wage conference with executives of the iron mills. President Weihe of the Amalgamated requested that employers shut down their mills in Pittsburgh, Wheeling, Youngstown, and Sharon so that workers and their families could attend the festivities. The manufacturers cordially consented and promised to urge other manufacturers to follow their lead.[40] Later that year, Weihe also asked employers to allow their workers to have June 5 off to attend another picnic, this one for both employees and employers, to be held at Beaver Falls. Management at Jones & Laughlin, Oliver Iron, and Shoenberger Iron, along with Carnegie Brothers, quickly gave affirmative response to the request, and most other mills in the area followed suit.[41]

There were a myriad other examples, none of which perhaps had initially been granted easily by mill owners, but all of which by the 1870s had become such an accepted part of the daily and annual ritual of life and work that they did not even have to be written into the bargaining agreements. The puddlers, heaters, and rollers, as independent contractors on a sliding scale of wages, were given a good deal of leeway over how they arranged their workday and week. Although the puddlers worked a long day, at least ten to twelve hours, to get in their five or six heats, the day was punctuated with innumerable breaks for relaxation. Jesse S. Robinson, in his history of the iron and steel workers' union, pointed out: "The puddler has always been accustomed to arrange for himself the time for starting and quitting. He objects to being hurried in order to produce a reasonable output."[42]

Similarly, the skilled workers did not work a seven-, or even six-day, week. Five and one-half days was the norm, with the half-day on

Saturday reserved for repairs of equipment. As Francis Couvares indicated, these arrangements were all left to local agreement and the custom of that particular shop and locale.[43] In addition, every summer the mills closed down for a month during the hottest season. Quite obviously it would have meant more money in the pockets of both owners and workers if the mills had been kept running during this time, but consensus on both sides held that it was not fair to make the workers labor in such overheated conditions. Then, too, the owners wanted to escape during this same period with their families to recently organized summer retreats in the nearby mountains.

Facts such as those presented here are fairly common knowledge among labor historians, who have treated them as evidence of the existence of a strong and autonomous working-class culture. As Couvares remarked, it meant that entrepreneurs in Pittsburgh's leading industries lacked real control over production.[44] Not to deny the importance of these elements for the creation of a working-class culture in the nineteenth century, it is equally critical to recognize that they had become part of a shared shop culture by the 1870s and 1880s. It was as much a part of the employer's culture as the worker's, so much so that it did not have to be spelled out in a contract. However bitter may have been the struggles over some of these issues at one point—and there is no clear evidence that these particular issues were especially contentious in the early iron industry—they had become routinized by the postbellum period. They defined the mill owner's culture as much as the mill worker's and probably were not considered a matter of power by either side by that time: it was simply an accepted part of a shared value system. We must not let the psychology of Bessemer steel making, which arose from a different culture and emanated from an alternative group of steel masters, color our assumptions about the world of the iron master of the 1870s and 1880s. There is no evidence that he was lusting to wrench these privileges—from the sliding scale to the one-month hiatus in the summer—from the workmen in his mill. They were seldom, if ever, a point of dispute or negotiation. It was the Bessemer mills that made them an issue.

Perhaps no incident exemplified the remarkable nature of the Pittsburgh iron master's ideology regarding workers, unions, strikes, and violence better than the traumatic Great Railroad Strikes of 1877 in the city. For many people in Pittsburgh and elsewhere this event was tantamount to social revolution, rather than simply a strike, and it was not unusual to hear normally calm voices raised in alarm over this specter. Later historians of the event have generally reflected the same attitude. Pittsburgh's elite, according to their account, reacted with moral outrage, believing that the workers' destruction of railway property was the beginning of a massive revolution. But was this the response of Pittsburgh's iron manufacturers?

The strike had been occasioned by wage cuts demanded by the Pennsylvania Railroad. A cut of 10 percent went into effect on July 10, 1877, and the next day most of the railroad workers at Martinsburg, West Virginia, walked off the job. This walkout soon degenerated into an ugly mob that burned and plundered railroad property. The strike and accompanying violence spread, until the outbreak hit Pittsburgh on July 19. There militiamen from Philadelphia were called to break up the mob, at the cost of twenty-six lives. Looting and rioting went on for another day until it ground to a halt. At the end of four days most of the property of the Pennsylvania Railroad within the city lay in smoking ruins. The nation's press, and political leaders at the state and federal level, were alarmed, fearing massive social revolution. Pittsburgh's iron men, however, appeared to take the whole affair in stride.

B. F. Jones, in his diary, was remarkably sympathetic and even-handed in his appraisal of the situation. On July 24, he placed blame for the situation squarely on the railroad officials who had cut wages. Although he more than likely understood the railroad's need to cut costs, he seemed annoyed at the way in which it was done. Furthermore, he greatly lamented the loss of life occasioned when the militia from Philadelphia was brought in: "A regiment came from Philadelphia, the men hooted at them and annoyed them . . . [and they responded] by killing and wounding quite a number of citizens. This started a riot and the working men throughout the country and city took it up. . . ."[45] Jones even remained reasonably even tempered when his skilled puddlers, who were bound by contract to stay at work, informed him they were supporting the strikers. Demanding a 25 percent raise in pay for the day laborers, the entire plant went out on July 24.

Jones's response was to be firm and not to give in to the strikers' demands. He wrote in his diary on July 26: "Hardly likely [the strikers] will get the wages asked and when they find out they are *not* to gain it there *may* be trouble."[46] He noted quite proudly, however, that when the strikers failed to persuade the firemen and foundry men to join them in the strike, they refused to use any force against them. That seemed to indicate to Jones that however inflamed his workers were by the events of July, they were still operating within the framework established over years of negotiation. Jones next decided to try hiring six strikebreakers to unload ore cars, a violation of this same agreement. The new men spent an entire day unloading cars, and Jones noted, "The [strikers] did not interfere with them."[47] The Amalgamated responded, however, by posting notices around the plant advising workers not to take jobs at American Iron. Jones calmly noted that only two of the six men returned the next day. Finally, on September 18, the strike was ended, with concessions on both sides. Jones noted: "Great rejoicing among all that the mill will start up tomorrow morning. So the strike is ended and we are all glad of it for it was becoming very monotonous."[48] Monotonous! Not "this union must be destroyed," or "the men will pay for this villanous act," or "the revolution is at hand"—but "monotonous." Could anything indicate more clearly the way in which even sometimes bitter labor/management relations had become routinized in Pittsburgh by the 1870s?

Nor was Jones the only iron master to react in that manner. When James Park, the majestic owner of Black Diamond Steel, rallied people at his church to help in the effort to quell the violence in the city, he made it very clear that they had no intention of opposing the strike, but only of returning the conflict to its local context.[49] When the mayor and trade unionist William C. McCarthy called on citizens to contain the violence and protect property during the riot, he insisted that their efforts not be directed toward the strike itself. Similarly, the citizens committee enlisted labor leaders in its cause. Joining the group were Joseph Bishop of the Amalgamated; John M. Davis of the Knights of Labor; Andrew Burtt, local teacher and champion of labor rights; and Thomas A. Armstrong, editor of *National Labor Tribune*. Davis, in fact, was co-author of the proclamation calling on "industrious workmen" to oppose "thieves and similar classes," and Miles Humphreys, president of the Amalgamated, made a speech at the Pennsylvania Railroad depot during the rioting denouncing the violence and looting. Members of the Amalgamated lodge at the Oliver Brothers iron plant stood guard around the plant throughout the entire disturbance, protecting the owner's mill property (by extension, the skilled laborer's property) from vandalism.[50]

Our best source, however, for the ideology and values of Pittsburgh's iron and steel manufacturers during these years is *Iron Age*, the industry's most important trade paper. Unfortunately, during the years prior to 1876, the paper was controlled not by men who shared the values of the Pittsburgh iron men, but rather by those who ran eastern iron mills, which were almost exclusively nonunion and whose owners were generally aggressively antiunion. They were in other words, who shared the ideology of Daniel Morrell.

During the 1870s, *Iron Age* was published by David Williams, whose father had established the paper in 1855 as *Hardware Man's Newspaper*. In 1859 the name was changed to *Iron Age*, and in 1864 the offices were moved to New York City. In 1869, Williams, whose forte was business management, not editing and writing, brought in James C. Bayles. Bayles was also a New Yorker, and both men shared the antiunion commercial sentiment of their seaboard class cohorts.[51] During these years prior to 1876, *Iron Age* stressed the essential harmony between capital and labor and reflected the philosophy of Henry Carey.

Henry Carey held that the interests of capital and the labor were "in perfect harmony with each other as each derives advantage from every measure that tends to facilitate the growth of capital."[52] Eric Foner, in his brilliant analysis of the development of Republican party ideology during the 1850s, has quite rightly recognized Carey as the single most powerful source of their economic ideas.[53] As Foner notes, northern Republicans had an essentially middle-class conception of the social order, and much of their glorification of northern labor during their campaign against slavery was rooted in the harmony of interests idea.[54] Similarly, it was precisely this lack of any harmony of interests between planter and slave that formed the basis of their attack on the southern labor system.[55] As Foner points out, the most striking example of the harmony of interests idea was the concept of the protective tariff, which Carey and Horace Greeley argued was designed primarily to advance the interests of labor. Just as significantly, there was no room for trade unions or strikes within the Republican/Carey system of thought. It was, after all, a harmonic ideal, but also one that was essentially paternalistic. Workers would be paid high wages because of the superior productivity of American labor, which in turn derived from capital investment in machinery and technology.[56] Thus, as Carey declared, the two were in perfect harmony.

Iron Age in the early 1870s perfectly reflected this Republican ideology. Free labor, individualism, and unlimited opportunity were the key concepts of *Iron Age*'s philosophy, as it developed a conservative defense of liberal capitalism in the North.[57] The unfettered operation of the corporation, claimed the journal, safeguarded the best interests of the worker, since the profitability of invested capital determined the size of the wages fund. The most austere workings of economic law, in turn, would be softened by employers' paternalism.[58] As *Iron Age* stated: "In nearly every instance of which we have any knowledge, employers have considered the best interests of their operatives, and have made every sacrifice of self interest which could redound to the advantage of those dependent upon them."[59]

Similarly, *Iron Age* viewed the growth of trade unions as the consequence of a personal defect of those associated with the labor movement. The labor leader was a demagogue who distorted the true relations between capital and labor.[60] As a result of these attitudes, *Iron Age* was strongly in favor of the use of the iron clad oath and the discharge system.[61] The constellation of these ideas— harmony of class interests, paternalism, community, antipathy to trade unions, use of the iron clad oath and the discharge system— was obviously close to the ideology expressed by Daniel Morrell, and, in fact, *Iron Age* was a powerful champion of Morrell's actions during the miner's strike at Cambria in 1874. It advised its readers that Morrell's handling of the situation was "the easiest and best means" for solving labor troubles, for it told the worker he could not "serve two masters."[62]

On immediate reflection, it would seem that the ideas expressed in *Iron Age* fit well with the ideology of average, upper-class Pittsburgh iron masters. Indeed, it seems almost axiomatic. They were, after all, strong Republicans; they believed in the protective tariff and certainly must have had at least a strong nostalgic attraction to the concept of harmony of interests. Yet, as we have observed, these Pittsburgh iron makers accepted, however grudgingly, the concept of trade unions; bargained honestly and fairly with them; made creative, if sometimes tough-minded, contributions to the collective bargaining process; and granted rather extraordinary concessions to the workers and their unions. How do we explain this seeming paradox? Why did rigidly Republican iron and steel manufacturers, who were firm devotees of Henry Carey's protective tariff, apparently stray so far from the fold in the 1870s and 1880s? There are a number of possible answers.

Carey, like the New England upper-class industrialists who developed the Lowell mills, found the factory cities of England absolutely abhorrent. American industrialization, Carey thought, was quite different. Viewing the small shops of his native Philadelphia, the nearby coal mines nestled in the valleys, the ironworks scattered along the riverbanks in rural settlements, and even the large cotton mills in Lowell, Carey found the essential preservation of a rural, agrarian ideal.[63] As Foner points out, Carey's ideas were highly romantic, since his image of the nation's future involved no fundamental social reorganization.[64] These ideas seemed to fit well the concept of Philadelphia's iron masters who built their mills (Cambria Iron, Pennsylvania Steel, Bethelehem Iron) in small villages, environments that allowed them, like Morrell, to perceive themselves as preserving older community values and concepts of class harmony in the cockpit of industrialism. And even Philadelphia itself in the late nineteenth century resembled more a congeries of small shops than a true large-scale industrialized city.[65]

Pittsburgh iron masters did not have this luxury, at least not for long. Pittsburgh, certainly by the early 1870s, had become the archetypal industrial city in America: it was America's Birmingham. The city's iron mills were hard, brutal places; Pittsburgh was, in some respects, an industrial nightmare; and relations between mill owners and men were, if based on mutual respect, nonetheless characterized by tough, relentless bargaining. By 1874, when Daniel Morrell was handily defeating the union in his isolated feudal domain, Pittsburgh's iron masters had been forced to accept and live with a more urban concept of labor management relations.

In fact, a new ideological consensus developed in Pittsburgh during the 1860s and 1870s, one that made itself felt on the editorial policies of *Iron Age* after 1876. The new consensus had begun with disenchantment over some of Carey's ideas, was enhanced by forced acceptance of trade unions and collective bargaining, and finally came to accept ideas from labor leaders as at least a partially legitimate element of the intellectual universe. Pittsburgh, home of *National Labor Tribune*, became a hotbed of ideological unionism in the 1860s. The key figure in this was Thomas A. Armstrong. In 1865 he and Andrew C. Cameron of Chicago drafted *The Address of the National Labor Congress to the Workingmen of the United States*, which was presented to the National Labor Union congress in Baltimore in that year. Calling for such items as the eight-hour day and cooperatives, they also strongly advocated the necessity for the thorough organization of workingmen into trade unions. Eschewing more strident arguments in favor of unions, however, they justified them as effective barriers against "strife, anarchy and confusion." Strikes were to be used only as a last resort.[66] Further, Armstrong and many of his colleagues in the iron and steel unions were staunch Republicans who supported the protective tariff. What was emerging in Pittsburgh at this time was a new ideological consensus, one that integrated a new tolerance and respect for labor unions with older ideas of the tariff and Republicanism. And it was a consensus that embraced both mill owner and worker.

Since Pittsburgh by the 1870s had become the center of the iron industry, and since *Iron Age* proclaimed itself the Bible of the industry, it was imperative that the journal hire an editor with roots in the Pittsburgh area, someone who better reflected this industrial city mentality, as opposed to the commercial mentality of Bayles. The man who would mold this rather inchoate intellectual consensus into a new conceptual framework was Joseph D. Weeks, who became associate editor and manager of the Pittsburgh office of *Iron Age* in 1876. Weeks was a native of Lowell, Massachusetts, who graduated from Wesleyan University in 1869. After working in several midwestern cities, he moved to Pittsburgh in 1871. There he married Mattie J. Fowler, daughter of an industrialist in the city. A year later Weeks became editor of *American Manufacturer*, which in 1874 was consolidated with *Iron World*. Two years later Weeks assumed his new position at *Iron Age*. Although he was only an associate editor, Weeks's title belied his real influence. During his decade with the trade journal, Weeks dominated the editorial matter concerning the iron and steel industry and events in Pittsburgh, while David Williams and James Bayles spent much of their time developing the journal *Metal Worker*.[67]

Weeks was tightly networked into the Pittsburgh iron and steel elite. In addition to his marriage to Mattie Fowler, he was a founder of both the Western Iron Association and the Western Pig Iron Association, cartels that were organized to fix iron prices. Weeks was also largely responsible for organizing the manufacturers to meet the Amalgamated Association as a unified group and presented the first wage scale to the workers from the organized body of iron manufacturers. In succeeding years Weeks presided over a number of wage conferences, largely enjoying the confidence of both sides in the dispute. A firm believer in the protective tariff, Weeks often testified before congressional hearings on the topic and was instrumental in organizing many activities in the iron and steel industry dedicated to its preservation. A founder of the American Association of Mining Engineers, Weeks served as president of the body in 1895 and was secretary to the Republican National Committee in 1892. Weeks, in other words, spoke for the large body of Pittsburgh iron and steel manufacturers in a number of important areas.[68]

Weeks changed *Iron Age's* rigidly antiunion attitudes. The journal not only had supported Morrell in his fight against the union in 1874 but took an unyielding attitude toward strikers' demands in various confrontations in Pittsburgh and elsewhere in 1875 and 1876. Weeks began counseling in the editorial pages that traditional antiunion measures had not been successful: the iron clad oath, discharge system, and other devices had simply stiffened worker resistance. Responding to the 1877 railroad strike, Weeks, like Jones, was generally sympathetic to the workers and blamed the railroads for the strike, calling them intolerant and oppressive.[69] Nor did he support demands for an enlarged militia or national army force to put down those or future riots.

Yet, simply to denounce the older techniques was obviously not enough. Weeks had to find an alternative to the existing system of confrontation, strike, and lockout that characterized relations between owners and workers in the iron and steel industry. This was especially true since he had to appease eastern mill owners as well as those in Pittsburgh. What he proposed was a system of arbitration. Weeks had worked out the elements of this system somewhat earlier in the pages of *American Manufacturer,* and his ideas represented a significant deviation from the concept of the harmony of interests between capital and labor that had earlier dominated the pages of *Iron Age* but were also a departure from the routine acceptance of collective bargaining by the old iron masters. Under this new system, equality between capital and labor would replace the old paternalism, and worker's unions would emerge as their authorized representatives for the purposes of arbitration.[70] Weeks was one of the most important proponents of the idea that became so popular in the late nineteenth century.[71]

Increasingly turning away from the ideas of Henry Carey, the economist laureat of Civil War Republicans, Weeks and Pittsburgh's iron men looked for a new prophet. As Paul Conkin has commented, "[A]s a perceptive prophet [Carey] lived too long. Unlike Moses, he was able to explore all the dark corners of his promised land."[72] His ideas may still have been attractive to seaboard aristocrats, but not to the men, owners and workers alike, who labored in the crucible of industrialism in Pittsburgh. For many, the new prophet appeared to be Francis Amasa Walker. The son of Amasa Walker, a traditional economist of Carey's generation, young Walker graduated from Amherst in 1860 and in 1872 was appointed professor of political economics at the newly organized Sheffield School at Yale. There Walker taught a new generation of Pittsburgh iron makers, the sons of old-family mill owners who would increasingly assume control of the family enterprises.[73]

More importantly for Pittsburgh labor ideology, Walker attacked the wages fund theory. He argued that the theory had been advanced mainly because it afforded a complete justification for the existing order of things respecting wages and demonstrated the futility of trade unions and strikes. Walker contended instead that the value of the product, not the amount of wealth possessed, determined the amount of wages that could be paid. Wages in the long run must be less than the product by enough that the employers could earn a fair profit, which, Walker believed, taught workers that by better production and harder work they could improve their own condition. This, of course, fit almost perfectly with the concept of the sliding scale. As Joseph Dorfman explains, Walker's theories had two important ramifications. First, they emphasized that captains of industry like the iron manufacturers, as distinct from capitalists like J. P. Morgan, were the chief agents of production. They were the "chief engineers of industrial progress, for they directed the efficient functioning of labor and capital."[74] This sort of acclaim made Walker's ideas even more attractive to old-family iron manufacturers.

The second ramification of Walker's ideas led to support of limited state interference on behalf of labor. State interference was justified in Walker's mind as necessary to bring about perfect competition. In the same light, Walker found some limited justification for strikes and trade unions. Although Walker's ideas became more conservative in the late 1880s and he became less tolerant of large national unions, his early ideas fit well with Weeks's emerging conviction that arbitration was the wave of the future. Under that system, unions of some sort were a necessity, the wages fund theory had no relevance, but strikes and overly aggressive action by unions would also be curtailed.[75]

Although Weeks had to be somewhat cautious in his espousal of unionism in the 1880s, it was nonetheless clear that the success of arbitration depended on some form of unionization of the workers. Furthermore, within the iron and steel industry there was increasing recognition that the recently formed Amalgamation Association and its early leaders, John Jarrett (1880–83) and William Weihe (1884–92), were precisely the kinds of safe, conservative union leaders whom management should encourage in its mills. Jarrett was in some respects almost indistinguishable from many manufacturers[76] and, in effect, made the transition from laborer to labor leader to lobbyist to trade association official and business executive within his lifetime. It was this sort of conservative union leadership that encouraged Weeks and many upper-class iron and steel manufacturers in Pittsburgh. Weihe did not travel quite as far as Jarrett in this regard, but he was also the epitome of the conservative union leader. He endeavored to adjust the union to the rapid mechanization of the steel industry and was generally accommodating to change.[77]

After Weeks took over at *Iron Age*, there were a number of labor/management confrontations in the iron and steel industry in Pittsburgh. It is instructive to examine a few of those in order to discern the ideology of the mill owners and *Iron Age*. There was a fairly clear pattern to these labor/management confrontations: The union made a demand; the owner responded that he would never accede to that demand; a lockout or strike followed. After an acceptable period of bluster, the owner gave in substantially to the union's demands and normality was resumed. Joseph Weeks viewed all of this as rather wasteful strife but, like the iron masters themselves, did not deny unions their right to bargain collectively. Weeks's main point of departure from both groups was that he posited the concept of arbitration as an alternative to this process.[78]

A fairly typical set of confrontations between the boilers and management took place at the Jones & Laughlin mill in 1878 and 1879. In June 1878, the boilers presented their demands to B. F. Jones. He refused to accept their ultimatum, and five days later the workers walked out. The mill had been shut down for five days when, on June 10, Jones signed an agreement for another year with the boilers. A year later, in May 1879, the boilers again went to Jones to present their demands. He refused to sign the new agreement and warned in his diary on May 26 that a "'lockout' is on the look out." A week later he noted, "The strike has commenced," and remarked that there "seems no chance of starting up for some time—both sides appear determined and time will only show which is the more so." Five days later, however, Jones reported, "Under existing circumstances it is impossible to further resist the demands of the Boilers."[79]

In between these two ritualistic confrontations, however, was yet another ritual. On September 25, 1878, President Rutherford B. Hayes visited Pittsburgh and toured American Iron Works. In a spirit of joint cooperation, management and labor thoroughly cleaned the mill from top to bottom before the president's arrival, and Jones let the mill workers off at noon on the day Hayes visited the mill so that they might continue to enjoy the festivities in town that afternoon and evening.[80] There was, then, a sense of mutual trust and respect that pervaded labor/management relations in the iron industry in Pittsburgh during the 1870s and 1880s. Adhering neither to the paternalistic harmony of interests of an earlier age nor to the antagonistic antiunion open shop ideals of the later 1890s, both the older iron manufacturers and *Iron Age* desired an alternative system at this time, one based on the seemingly contradictory elements of mutual respect and conflicting interests.

A major reason the iron manufacturers of Pittsburgh were able to become more accommodating toward the union was that, with the help of Weeks, they had developed their own "union," a manufacturers' association that had originally grown out of their desire to exert some control over the declining price levels in the industry. That group, the Western Iron Association, began playing a critical role in labor/management negotiations in the industry. When the boilers were locked out in 1879, for example, B. F. Jones did not negotiate with them alone but as part of a team of owners in the Western Iron Association. Although they were not particularly successful in resisting the union's demands, they probably did as well as could be expected. It would be nearly a decade before an employers' association in the iron industry could meet the Amalgamated on equal footing. The important point is that the individual mill owner was no longer alone in facing the union, and this made confrontations with a national union of ironworkers less daunting.

Joseph Weeks and *Iron Age* applauded these new efforts, while counseling the unions to be moderate in their demands. At the same time, true to his belief in arbitration, Weeks was critical of the use of strikes as a method of labor/management relations. Since arbitration was still only a dream, however, *Iron Age* decided that the sliding scale, which it had vehemently opposed since its inception in 1865, was now an acceptable means to fix and maintain workers' wages.[81] The scale, of course, had long been accepted by upper-class Pittsburgh iron manufacturers. For *Iron Age*, however, acceptance of the sliding scale involved a profound change in many deeply entrenched attitudes. It abandoned its adherence to the wages fund theory, now agreeing with *National Labor Tribune* that the scale was a method that would give more leverage to both workers and employers to combat both low prices and low wages.

A major turning point in labor relations for many contemporaries came in 1880, when John Jarrett was elected president of the Amalgamated, and all parties moved impressively toward a new consensus. Jarrett bent every effort toward making the Amalgamated a more conciliatory and accommodating agency during this time. He was particularly annoyed with the number of strikes, counseling union members, "Quite a number of strikes have emanated from very trivial causes." He advised Amalgamated members to "calmly keep on with our work and avoid unnecessary conflicts."[82] Jarrett proposed that strikes be resorted to only in the most extreme situations and moved to centralize the Amalgamated's operations so that local vice presidents had to report all strike votes immediately to the general office. Local lodges found it increasingly difficult to obtain executive committee approval of strikes in the early 1880s. At the same time *Labor Tribune* began advocating a similar policy, which argued that shutting down a mill for slight cause was an abuse of the Amalgamated's power.[83]

A major test for these new policies came with the dramatic strike against the newly organized Pittsburgh Bessemer Steel Company in January 1882. This strike has been noted by a number of scholars, but generally from the perspective either of its takeover by the Carnegie firm or within the context of the inexorable working out of the psychology of steel making. In the first perspective, the older iron masters appear as rather woolly-headed nincompoops who lacked Carnegie's pragmatism and hardheaded drive. From the other perspective, the outcome simply seems inevitable, a form of technological determinism. Although there is some truth to both perspectives, when the conflict is viewed within the context of the nature of labor relations that had painfully emerged in the industry to that point, and when the ideological, social, and cultural backgrounds of these older iron men are understood, a markedly different picture emerges.

The Allegheny Bessemer Works, as noted in the previous chapter, was developed by a consortium of Pittsburgh crucible steel manufacturers when Andrew Carnegie cut off their supply of Bessemer steel ingots. Originally intended to supply a small number of ingots to the consortium, by the time it opened, Andrew Kloman's rail mill had been attached and the owners were bent on competing head-on with Carnegie in that market. When Kloman suddenly died, however, the upper-class owners needed a man who had experience with large-batch production methods, a talent a number of them possessed, so they turned to William Clark, owner of the Solar Iron Mill in Pittsburgh. Clark was a former iron worker in the Pittsburgh mills who had moved to Youngstown, where he opened his own plant. He had returned to Pittsburgh shortly before taking over the Allegheny Bessemer mill. Unfortunately for the owners of the mill, Clark had an almost pathological animus against labor unions. Whether this was due to his own working-class origins, as was often the case, or the fact that he had become used to operating in a nonunion framework in the west, is not clear. What is clear is that Clark, who had not allowed the union in his Solar Iron Works, was disgusted when he found that lodges of the Amalgamated were already deeply embedded in the plant when he took over. From the foregoing, it should be clear that Clark's attitudes were hardly reflective of the great number of old-family Pittsburgh iron masters.

Almost from the moment Clark took over, the Amalgamated made a series of minor demands on him. Caught at a critical time of transition, he acceded to them but inwardly vowed he would have his revenge. By December 1881, Clark felt the time was ripe to take his stand. He issued an order requiring all employees to sign a "yellow dog" contract renouncing their right to belong to a union. Not a single member of the Amalgamated would sign, so on January 1, 1882, Clark ordered a lockout. A week later, Clark declared that even if his men did sign the contract, they could not return until they accepted a further reduction in wages. It should be clear to the reader at this point that Clark's actions were hardly characteristic of labor negotiations in Pittsburgh's iron and steel industry. Perhaps they represented an inevitable working of the new psychology of steel making among these iron masters, but that conclusion is not at all clear.

In response to Clark's actions, the Amalgamated, which had not become involved in the dispute, declared a strike at the mill's Homestead works. When Jarrett tried to negotiate with Clark, he found him totally unresponsive. Only under pressure from the city's newspapers did Clark finally agree to meet with Jarrett, but nothing came of the pro forma conference. Jarrett decided he could strike back at Clark by putting pressure on the old-family Pittsburgh steel men who owned the works. He announced: "If this condition of affairs continues at Homestead, the stockholders in the Homestead Works who have mills in Pittsburg [sic] may have to fight the Association in their own mills. We shall not much longer permit several firms to fight us in this concentrated shape."[84] Clark responded in an oppressive manner, evicting the workers from homes they rented from the company. The union announced that on March 11, 1882, it would expand the strike to the owners' other mills in the district.

By this point, the upper-class owners of Allegheny Bessemer (Singer, Miller, Park, and Hussey), men conditioned to negotiating with the Amalgamated in good faith, were thoroughly alarmed at the turn of events. Although they had tacitly endorsed Clark's earlier stand, they now began putting pressure on him to settle with the union. To Clark's disgust, the company owners unilaterally withdrew his demand for a yellow dog contract, substituting the milder request that the men had to give three days' notice of a work stoppage and the requirement that no more than three men give the notice at any one time. The wage reduction, however, was not rescinded because of the contention that improved machines in the plant made work easier and output higher.

With a broader strike imminent on March 11, the august owners of Allegheny Bessemer put great pressure on Clark to settle the dispute. Just hours before the sympathy strike was to go into effect, a verbal agreement was announced. A day later, however, that agreement was strained when Clark and the union leaders quarreled over its scope. Clark, who had opposed the agreement in the first place, steadfastly refused to relent and exploded the next day with even greater bitterness against the union. The result was violence at Homestead, with a pitched battle between deputy sheriffs and strikers, attacks on strikebreakers, and even a murder. Undaunted, Clark threatened to close the works indefinitely, rather than give in.

The old established steel men were befuddled by what had happened. William H. Singer expressed bewilderment that the Amalgamated had struck his Sterling Steel plant, "where there was no trouble existing between employers and employees."[85] Pressed beyond endurance by the city's newspapers and politicians, the upper-class owners finally took control of negotiations out of Clark's hands and insisted on a rapid settlement. Within a few days, the strike was ended. The result was almost total victory for the union, as virtually every one of its demands was granted by the owners. The Amalgamated's victory was made more complete when the hated Clark, thoroughly disgusted with the terms of agreement, tendered his resignation. It was speedily accepted by the owners.[86] All of this also put the Amalgamated, *National Labor Tribune,* and *Iron Age* in a difficult situation. William Clark was behaving in an unfortunately provocative and intransigent manner, but workers had also responded in an intemperate way.

Pittsburgh Chronicle, a conservative Pittsburgh newspaper, declared that the union should be held solely responsible for the violence that had occurred during the strike, and *National Labor Tribune,* for its part, disavowed the violence, arguing for a peaceful set of tactics by the union.[87] To demonstrate its reasonableness, the Amalgamated made a major concession. Giving up its demand for full union recognition, it proposed that the mill run one turn with nonunion men, while the union would double up on the other turn. The company accepted this proposal on March 19, and *Iron Age* hailed the proposition as highly sensible.[88]

Iron Age and *Labor Tribune* viewed the events of March 1882 as a major breakthrough in labor/management relations. Both journals embraced the concept of a labor organization—disciplined and stabilized—as the best means to maintain order and harmonious relations within the iron and steel industry. *Iron Age* particularly defended both the Western Iron Manufacturers Association and the Amalgamated as harbingers of a new era of harmony.[89]

The upper-class owners of Allegheny Bessemer, having settled a long and bitter strike that endangered the company's future and having gotten rid of the contentious Clark, breathed a collective sigh of relief. It was short-lived. The Amalgamated, embolded by its dramatic success in a large Bessemer mill, was heady with power. Workers had also learned the value of multiplant action, so a few weeks after settling the Allegheny Bessemer strike, they demanded a general wage advance across the country of 5 to 15 percent. Iron mill owners in the Pittsburgh valleys cursed the Homestead owners. Long accustomed to relatively amicable, individualized negotiations with the union and their workers, they were now dragged into a nationwide strike. They prepared for a long and bitter struggle with the union.

The owners of Allegheny Bessemer, traumatized by the earlier strike, immediately settled with the Amalgamated at the new, higher rates, dramatically increasing the mill's operating costs in a steadily deteriorating rail market. Other area mills refused to acquiesce, so that by June practically every iron mill in the country was shuttered. The strike dragged on for four months. The only other mills of consequence to remain running during this time were the Carnegie operations. The Edgar Thomson works were not unionized, and Carnegie agreed to the Amalgamated's terms in his other two unionized plants.

By August 1882, the owners of Allegheny Bessemer realized they could no longer operate their mill profitably, and on August 21 the plant was closed for lack of orders. A month later, the Amalgamated strike collapsed, and the workers, having been literally starved into submission by the mill owners, suffered a crushing defeat, their first failure since they were formed in 1876. As John Jarrett said, this defeat "has multiplied our troubles, demoralized quite a number of our lodges, and deprived the Association of no small amount of prestige, and robbed it of a large degree of power and influence."[90] The union felt a strong need to recoup its losses by the mid-1880s.

Another element that had emerged during the second strike in 1882, really for the first time in the Pittsburgh milieu, was the whole concept of the right to work claimed by nonunion workers and management.[91] *Iron Age* and the Pittsburgh iron mill owners viewed the issue of the right to work in terms of an open and free market, and in many respects their justification rang strongly of older Careyite notions that had been articulated during the Civil War. The worker, they declared, was a slave unless he was the owner of his own labor. If strikers did not allow him to work, if they used tactics to intimidate or dissuade him, then they made that worker a slave, just as surely as the slave owner enslaved the blacks before the Civil War. *Labor Tribune* and the Amalgamated, however, had a clear conception of their right to persuade through picketing and talking to actual or potential strikebreakers. What was involved for them were two equally profound and fundamental issues. The first was the issue of free speech and assembly, and the second was the equally important concept of the right of the worker to protect his job. Both sides, though, were categorical in their condemnation of the use of violence on either side. The right to work issue, nonetheless, was one that frustrated any full agreement between labor and management during this time.

At the same time, the Western Iron Association had emerged from the strike on a more united and powerful basis, and it issued a call to all western manufacturers to meet in Pittsburgh in June 1882. The association by then included nearly all the iron and steel manufacturers west of the Alleghenies, representing almost 150 rolling mills with about $190 million in invested capital.[92] Most significantly, the association united both iron and large-scale steel manufacturers for the first time. It also for the first time included many nonunion mills from outside Pittsburgh. In the past these mills had continued to operate during strikes and lockouts in the Pittsburgh area, forcing the manufacturers in Pittsburgh to come to terms more rapidly with the union. This was not to be the case in this strike.[93]

The Amalgamated on its part was crippled by a lack of unity in its ranks. The puddlers, who had the most to gain from the strike, supported it fully, but the finishing departments opposed the strike. This meant that the Amalgamated had only reluctant support from some of its members. Further, the Amalgamated in Pittsburgh, as we saw at Jones & Laughlin, had grown accustomed to short strikes. The Amalgamated would go out for five days, win most of their concessions, and go back to work. This time, however, they were facing a far more powerful and concerted managerial phalanx.

After a bitter four-month struggle, the result was a defeat, but not a rout, for the union. It was forced to accept the manufacturers' offer to continue the old scale rate but managed to defeat three other proposals made by the manufacturer's association. It was clear that the iron mill operators had new-found power in their association. It was equally clear, however, that the union, although somewhat bloodied, was unbowed. It had survived a four-month strike, coming on the heels of long strikes in Cincinnati and at Pittsburgh Bessemer Steel, and had defended itself well. *Iron Age*, the voice of the iron manufacturers, continued to endorse the Amalgamated. It was still willing, despite the long and bitter strike, to justify the union to manufacturers as an organization that possessed "an impressive list of virtues and functions." *Pittsburgh Commercial Gazette* reported that iron manufacturers themselves also continued to recognize a need for the Amalgamated, "although a minority were not persuaded of this view."[94] One manufacturer declared, "The Amalgamated never breaks its word with me and I would rather deal with an organized body."[95] For many other manufacturers, the problem of discipline in the mill and small strikes loomed large. To their mind, the Amalgamated at least battled only over major issues and fought those battles within acceptable and recognized bounds.

Despite the rather virulent antiunion rhetoric of the manufacturer's association, there were few nonunion mills in the Pittsburgh area, and labor relations during the series of bitter strikes in 1882 continued to be conducted within the confines of the older labor/management ideology. To attempt to destroy the union or to restart their mills on a nonunion basis still appeared to be folly to most of the iron masters in 1882. Nonetheless, the Amalgamated defeat in 1882 led to a persistent degeneration in union power over the next few years. Between 1882 and 1885, union membership declined from over 16,000 to just 5,702, and the number of lodges fell from 197 to 107. Average lodge membership fell from 81 to 53.[96] At the same time, the number of nonunion companies increased, as employers began trying to remove the union from their mills. Then, with the onset of the depression of 1884–85, pressure intensified to undermine the Amalgamated's influence. Despite the union's nationwide decline, however, it retained its strong position in the Pittsburgh area. Although union membership in the Pittsburgh district diminished by 43 percent during these four years, this was less than the 57 percent drop in other districts. Only 7 lodges were lost in the Pittsburgh area during this time.

Throughout most of 1880s *Iron Age* and Joseph Weeks continued to display a conciliatory attitude toward the Amalgamated and pressed even harder for acceptance of arbitration. Iron and steel manufacturers in the late 1870s continued to be skeptical of the idea: two-thirds of them declared in an informal survey that they preferred to settle their own affairs. The Amalgamated also rejected the concept of arbitration, as both sides desired to rely on the sliding scale. With the bitter strikes of the early 1880s, along with the decline of the Amalgamated's power, attitudes slowly began changing. First of all, Weeks's ideas on arbitration were incorporated in the Wallace Act, passed by the Pennsylvania legislature in 1883. The act provided for voluntary tribunals that could be organized on submission to a local court of common pleas or by a joint petition from both parties.[97] *Iron Age* declared editorially that the new law must be employed, and Weeks stated that the interests of the worker and employer were not identical, so for the worker to trust his interests to his employer was "absurd and dangerous."[98] The result, if there were no system of arbitration, claimed Weeks, was an endless series of large-scale and bitter strikes such as had occurred in 1882. Arbitration, by placing the issue in the hands of impartial adjudicators, would resolve differences in a fair, amicable, and, most importantly, peaceful manner.

The Pittsburgh iron manufacturers were evidently finally won over to the concept of arbitration. Under the urging of Joseph Weeks, they sought to apply it to an 1884 wage dispute with the Amalgamated. It was the manufacturers themselves who took the initiative in this. *Iron Age*, in fact, had called for a 10 percent reduction in wages, reflecting the depression conditions. When the Amalgamated rejected the manufacturer's initial demand for a reduction, the iron mill operators applied for an arbitration tribunal under the Wallace Act. *Iron Age* gratefully supported this action, arguing that it would simultaneously demonstrate the justness of the manufacturers' position and prevent stoppage of work. *Labor Tribune*, on the other hand, treated it as a ploy by manufacturers to undermine the position of the skilled workers. William Weihe, who had by then replaced Jarrett as president of the Amalgamated, decided not to oppose the application for an arbitration tribunal. Personally, however, he was suspicious of the move, suspecting it was a scheme to generate sentiment for the owner's position with the public.[99] As a result, the union did not support the application and the whole venture failed. Finding no other alternative, the manufacturers caved in to the union's demands to retain the old scale for another year, and *Labor Tribune* viewed this as a great victory for the more militant leadership of Weihe.

This was, however, probably the last gasp of the older, more conciliatory stance of Pittsburgh iron manufacturers. Despite the sharp decline in prices and a great drop in total output—in 1884 production dropped 16 percent in Allegheny County, the first time since 1875 that the area had experienced a decline—the Pittsburgh manufacturers were still paying their puddlers the same rate as during flush times. The older iron makers in Pittsburgh saw clearly where the problems lay and what had to be done. For one thing, iron manufacturers in the areas west of Pittsburgh were continually breaking ranks with the employer's association, agreeing to sign the scale after only a short time. This greatly undermined the power of the association, which was dominated by the older iron manufacturers of Pittsburgh. Similarly, the great growth in nonunion mills outside Pittsburgh meant that Pittsburgh mills lost increasing numbers of customers during these protracted work stoppages. At their 1883 convention, the Amalgamated reported that twelve new mills had been added to the nonunion list in 1883 and in 1884 stated that twelve more were added that year. By that time (1884) there were thirty-one nonunion mills operating, twenty-nine of them outside Pittsburgh.[100]

All of this meant that labor/management relations were going to change radically in the late 1880s and early 1890s. Pittsburgh iron manufacturers had lost faith in the Amalgamated, in their own employer's association, and, most particularly, in arbitration. They turned to new tactics. So, too, did *Iron Age*. Joseph Weeks left the journal in 1886, and almost immediately *Iron Age* began embracing a new set of attitudes essentially hostile to the concept of trade unionism. These changes marked a new era in labor relations in the iron and steel industry, one that would culminate in the Homestead strike of 1892 and the nonunion era of the early twentieth century.

5

And the Earth Shifted: The Revolutionary World of Iron and Steel, 1885–1920

> Paul Scott to union leader: "I'll put anybody I please in your shop."
> Union Leader: "Ye can have strikes here as much as Carnegie's mills, though."
> Paul Scott: "If that's what you're threatening over this Hunky, go ahead and strike. If you want what they got at Homestead, you'll get that. I don't run this mill like Homestead but by God I can if I have to. I can act like Henry Frick, too."
> Union Leader: "Your father would never have gone back on us like that."
>
> Marcia Davenport, *The Valley of Decision*

By the late 1880s a number of important factors were beginning to coalesce, creating a new pattern of labor relations and spelling future trouble for the union. There was, first of all, an increasing awareness of the importance of technology even for the old-line iron masters and rolling mill operators. For a number of years, there had been a series of important innovations in rolling techniques that had improved productivity in that end of the mill. That, however, was of little consequence as long as puddling technology remained stagnant. The attitude of mill owners for years had reflected the values of their puddlers, and little interest was evidenced for technological change in that area. But pressure began building in the 1880s to find either improvements or a replacement for the puddling process. One highly touted candidate was the Clapps-Griffith process, but that was not successful, nor was a mechanical puddling machine. As a result, puddling remained manual, but urgency increased during the

128

later part of the nineteenth century to reduce wages and costs throughout the iron rolling mill.

The thrust of the Bessemer steel-making process had been to substitute mechanical process for hand labor. This meant that less skilled labor could be used with those processes, as opposed to the highly skilled labor needed for puddling. But as larger numbers of mills substituted steel for iron, with the resultant rising unemployment of skilled puddlers, that group found their position declining relative to that of unskilled laborers in the late 1880s. Whereas the daily wages of skilled puddlers fluctuated substantially between 1879 and 1890, showing no clear net increase, the wages of unskilled laborers went up 27 percent.[1] This situation created a crisis for the Amalgamated, and they met in December 1887 to draw up scales for steel.

Despite these rather ominous developments, the Amalgamated grew steadily during the fifteen years from 1876 to 1891, when membership reached a peak of 24,068 members, organized into 290 locals in eight districts. It is important to recognize, however, that this union membership never comprised more than 25 percent of those working in the iron and steel industry. Furthermore, the great bulk of this membership was in the area west of the Allegheny Mountains, much of it particularly centered in Allegheny County and Pittsburgh. During the decade of the 1880s, virtually every iron mill in Allegheny County was unionized. At the same time, the Amalgamated largely failed to organize the eastern mills. With the exception of a few plants in Philadelphia, the large iron-producing valleys of the Schuylkill and Lehigh were relatively free of union influence. In 1880, a year during which union membership nearly doubled, Philadelphia accounted for less than 8 percent of the Amalgamated's membership and the rest of eastern Pennsylvania less than 2 percent. By 1892, when the union was at the peak of its power and influence, the eighth district, comprising Philadelphia and eastern Pennsylvania, had only 7 percent of the 20,975 members.[2]

With the rise of the steel industry, the Amalgamated spread into the new mills, carrying its policies with it. But it was never nearly as successful in the steel mills, with a great deal of variation between its ability to penetrate entirely new mills compared to steel departments in older mills. That is, if a steel department was added to a previously organized iron mill, the union was able to extend its influence quite readily, and the manufacturer seldom appeared to oppose this development. Thus it was that during the 1880s the steel workers became an important part of the Amalgamated, and by 1892 the number of lodges composed exclusively of steel workers nearly equaled the lodges of puddlers or boilers.[3] Yet, even as late as 1891 the steel delegates at the annual convention complained that few delegates (most of whom were puddlers from iron mills) understood the steel industry.[4]

The great problem for the Amalgamated came in organizing new steel mills built in a new location, such as Carnegie's Edgar Thomson Works. Of the four great steel mills built in Pittsburgh in the 1870s, only one, the Allegheny Bessemer Works at Homestead (soon to become part of the Carnegie empire), was successfully unionized. And, of course, the union was broken in this mill in the great lockout of 1892, which hastened the decline of the union in many of the other mills, both iron and steel.[5]

Even though the Amalgamated had been rather accommodating of the introduction of new machinery during the years it was directed by Jarrett and Weihe, this generosity was no longer sufficient for iron and steel mill owners. There was, indeed, a growing consensus that the mill owner had the right to direct the operation of his plant without outside interference, whether by the union or even the individual craftsman himself. Since so many of the large-batch process steel mills were nonunion, and since they were garnering an ever-larger share of the market, the older iron masters and crucible steel makers had reason to be concerned. No longer could they afford, as they added open hearth steel plants to their iron mills, simply to allow the Amalgamated to extend its influence over those new departments as they had in the past. A new antiunion mentality was developing among many of them. This new attitude collided head-on with plans by the Amalgamated in the late 1880s to make a strong push to organize steelworkers.

Thus, a great confrontation unfolded in the late 1880s in the few large steel mills where the Amalgamated already had representation. A critical battle occurred at the Edgar Thomson plant in 1885. The Amalgamated had never been strong in that mill, but Carnegie had negotiated with a couple of lodges there for a number of years. With the defeat of the union in the bitter nationwide strike of the summer of 1884, Carnegie astutely recognized that an opportunity was at hand to terminate the Amalgamated's influence in his giant mill. Therefore, in December 1884, the mill was closed and new, improved machinery was installed. About sixteen hundred men were thrown out of work by the closure, and in January 1885 the company proposed a new lower scale to the men, along with a resumption of the double turn or twelve-hour system. All of this meant a major reduction in the amount of labor needed in the plant.

The Amalgamated's first impulse was to fight Carnegie's action with every weapon at their disposal, but their lodges in the mill were not strong, and in early February the men accepted the company's terms and went back to work. Soon after that the two lodges of the Amalgamated in the plant collapsed and the company pronounced itself once again able to compete with nonunion mills.[6] The vacuum left by the Amalgamated at Edgar Thomson was filled by the Knights of Labor. In the mid-1880s a lodge of the Knights was formed in the plant, and it continued to negotiate with management until it was driven out in May 1887. With that action, the last vestige of unionism was eliminated in the Edgar Thomson plant. Only at the Homestead mill, which Carnegie had acquired from the old-line Pittsburgh iron men, with seven Amalgamated lodges, did Carnegie still have to deal with a union.[7]

Surprisingly, the Amalgamated and the labor movement generally were sympathetic to Carnegie in his move to eliminate the Knights from his mill. *Labor Tribune* accepted Carnegie's argument that he was forced to demand these reductions because he had to compete with nonunion plants, especially new steel mills in Chicago. The *Tribune* urged the Knights to accept Carnegie's wage reduction and twelve-hour-day proposals, with the idea that the union movement would soon begin a concerted attempt to organize the growing number of nonunion steel mills in the west.[8] That effort, however, was not fruitful. Only in mills where the Amalgamated already had strength, such as Carnegie's Homestead plant and the Jones & Laughlin mill, did membership increase. The nonunion segment of the industry simply became more adamant in their refusal to deal with the union. As the attitudes of these newer steel producers hardened, and as Carnegie moved to close the union out of all of his mills, the older Pittsburgh iron men also changed their attitudes.

In Pittsburgh, significantly, the antiunion thrust was led by a group of New England aristocrats running National Tube in McKeesport. Sharing the profoundly antiunion attitudes of their regional class cohorts, the owners moved early to eradicate the nascent union in their mill. In the summer of 1882, just a couple of months after an Amalgamated lodge had been organized in the plant, the firm's officers declared their intention to run the plant on a nonunion basis. In December of that year the lodge was disbanded, and after that time the company was unbending in its refusal to deal with any union organization, requiring their employees to sign iron clad oaths. Reminiscent of Daniel Morrell at Cambria, the Boston Brahmins who controlled National Tube were aided by their mill's location in McKeesport, far enough from Pittsburgh to make it difficult to organize mass picketing and boycotts.[9]

But the real crisis for the union, and the one that did much to change the attitudes of many of Pittsburgh's independent iron manufacturers, was in 1889. In that year Carnegie decided to challenge the growing unionism in his Homestead mill. Carnegie had run the formerly strife-torn mill for six years without a strike or labor troubles of any consequence; the men even accepted a severe pay cut in 1884. But trouble was building. Where there had been only two Amalgamated lodges in the plant in 1885, there were six in 1889. In May of that year Carnegie management proposed a radical new agreement with the Amalgamated. Carnegie was determined to break the power of the Amalgamated in the mill. He called for a sweeping reduction in rates. Furthermore, the scale was to run just from July 1889 to January 1892, so that future negotiations would take place in midwinter, a time of slack sales for the company, and a time when the men could less successfully withstand a prolonged strike or engage in extensive picketing. Finally, Carnegie required that each employee sign the scale individually, essentially repudiating the principle of collective bargaining. The Homestead lodges rejected the proposal, and in July 1889 the men went out on strike.

Carnegie responded by doing what was virtually unheard of in a union mill in Pittsburgh: he began importing large numbers of nonunion men to take the places of strikers. On July 10, the sheriff of Allegheny County attempted to bring a carload of workers into the mill, but massed strikers thwarted the effort. Two days later, the sheriff took 125 deputies to Homestead with the intention of taking over the plant, but again, literally thousands of strikers assembled before the plant gates and denied them admission. At this point, William L. Abbott, president of the Homestead firm, lost his nerve and signed a new three-year contract with the union. The union accepted a greatly reduced scale, but the company agreed to accept the Amalgamated as the exclusive bargaining agent at the plant. Carnegie was furious with Abbott for this action and promptly fired him. But Carnegie had successfully developed some new antiunion tactics during this strike, and the stage was set for the next great confrontation at Homestead when the scale expired in July 1892.

Often overlooked in the whole question of unionism at the

Homestead mill is the impact it had on many of the old-line upper-class iron and steel manufacturers in Pittsburgh. For iron and steel manufacturers long accustomed to dealing with the Amalgamated as a matter of course, the antiunion movement began as a small but persistent trend in the early 1880s. Manifested in only a few firms in the Pittsburgh area, such as National Tube, McKeesport Rolling Mill, and Apollo Iron and Steel, by the late 1880s it had extended to Carnegie's Edgar Thomson Works and a number of other mills. B. F. Jones, former chairman of the Republican National Committee and president of the American Iron and Steel Association, who thirty-four years before had come up with the idea of the sliding scale and who, moreover, had bargained faithfully with the Amalgamated during all those years, had a change of heart. He announced, "This company will make no terms with its men until there is a settlement at Homestead." As David Brody points out, Jones & Laughlin, which was by then a major steel producer, simply could not afford to pay higher wages than its principal rival, especially since Carnegie's Homestead plant had tonnage rates just half that of the unimproved mills at Jones & Laughlin.[10]

This antiunion attitude spread to a number of other mills, not all of which were major steel producers. Sheffield Steel announced that it would run on a nonunion basis. Sheffield is important because it was a typical, medium-size, upper-class Pittsburgh establishment. Although the firm's president, William Singer, was a Carnegie partner, he was also among the most respected of the old Pittsburgh iron and steel manufacturers. The conflict began at his mill in May 1888 as a strike against a reduction in wages that would have made Singer's scale lower than at other area firms. Both the Knights of Labor and the Amalgamated lodges in the plant rejected the proposal. The company's response was to expel both organizations from the mill, refusing any longer to recognize a union. William Singer stated, "None of our men will be asked to sign any agreement [iron clad oath], but they must withdraw from [the Amalgamated]."[11] By the second week of the strike, large crowds of strikers gathered outside the plant gates, and the company felt compelled to hire special police to deal with the situation. Despite these actions, the situation remained peaceful and no altercations developed between strikers and nonstrikers.

The workers at the Sheffield plant, however, were deeply upset over the firm's action, one that seemed out of character in the Pittsburgh milieu. A worker named McKeown wrote to the local papers attacking the firm for creating a potentially dangerous situation. He declared in exasperation: "We are all sensible American work-ingmen and citizens and do not approve of any mob law in conducting this strike. . . . If we cannot win the strike by keeping men out of the mill with persuasive argument then I am in favor of quitting now . . . to bring policemen here would be a menace to our men . . . it would have a tendency to incite men to violence. . . ."[12] The strike failed when a few skilled workers returned to work, and soon there was a "stampede . . . in order to secure jobs" by the rest of the workers. On July 21 the union admitted defeat, and Sheffield Steel became a major gap in the ranks of Pittsburgh's unionized iron and steel mills.

Soon struggles of this nature were occurring all over the city. Glendon Rolling Mill, an old-line iron spike firm owned by the aristocratic Dilworth family, began hiring nonunion workers in October 1888, and the Spang, Chalfant works refused to sign the steel-workers' scale. Police were used at the plant, and within a few days enough nonunion workers were secured to allow the mill to resume operations. The Spang, Chalfant mill was also run by eminent members of Pittsburgh's pre–Civil War upper class. The antiunion contagion continued to spread. Solar Iron, owned by the Clark family of Allegheny Bessemer infamy, remained true to its heavy-handed traditions by importing black strikebreakers. In 1890 Carbon Iron and Braddock Wire, both owned by new men on the Pittsburgh scene, succeeded in opening new mills with nonunion labor.[13] When the Carnegie Company abruptly signed with the union in 1889, however, many of the other iron and steel firms in the city also went along, thus blunting for a time the growing antiunion sentiment.

By the late 1880s, it was also clear that *Iron Age*, iron and steel manufacturers, and the mill workers themselves had turned decisively against the concept of arbitration. Its popularity in 1883–84 was not long-lived. A survey conducted by *Age of Steel* in 1886 asked whether arbitration, profit sharing, and industrial cooperation were suitable remedies for the industrial problems of the day. By a three-to-one margin both manufacturers and workers rejected arbitration. Both groups by the same margin believed that strikes and lockouts were now an unavoidable part of the labor management process. Only five of the twenty-two mill owners surveyed saw any hope in the use of profit sharing or other kinds of industrial cooperation and welfare capitalism. Most significant, however, was a new, almost unremitting hostility to trade unions among the mill owners. Whereas the manufacturers had earlier accepted a form of shared if antagonistic enterprise between employer and employee, they now posited a clear picture of employer domination and control similar to that pronounced and practiced by Daniel Morrell at Cambria Iron.[14] Strikes, which they had earlier viewed as a legitimate, if somewhat regrettable, part of the labor management system, were now condemned as caused by the "tyranny of unions who take away the rights of American laborers."[15] During this same period, *Iron Age*, with Joseph Weeks no longer in the editorial chair, began to present the nonunion mill as the model for the industry to follow.

Yet this growth of antiunion activity among Pittsburgh's iron and steel manufacturers must be viewed within its proper context. By 1890, the number of nonunion mills in the district was just nine out of sixty, 15 percent of the total. In fact, the Amalgamated actually enjoyed some rather impressive growth during this time. In just two years, from 1885 to 1887, membership more than doubled from 5,702 to 11,426. Much of this advance was in Pittsburgh, where there was an increase from fifty-five lodges with 2,811 members to seventy-five lodges with 6,880 members. The union had become strong enough by 1888 to be able to defeat manufacturers' demands for reduced wages. In addition, the 1888 conflict had resulted in the dissolution of the manufacturers' Western Iron Association, giving the Amalgamated additional leverage in its negotiations, which again could be carried on with individual mills. The number of strikes and lockouts declined in the late 1880s, and by 1890 the Amalgamated was stronger than it had been three years before. Membership reached an all-time high of 24,068 in 1891. Much of this increase had resulted from a change in recruiting policies by the Amalgamated, as they attempted to bring in larger numbers of less skilled workers in the steel mills.[16]

These antithetical forces—the increasing antiunionism of the iron and steel manufacturers and the expansive activities of the Amalgamated—were to reach their culmination in the Homestead lockout of 1892. That altercation need not be handled in any detail here, but a few salient points should be made. Since its abortive attempt to rout the union in 1889, the Carnegie firm had made some important changes. Most significant was the ascension of Henry Clay Frick to head of the Carnegie enterprises. Trained in the rough and tumble, antiunion mold of the western Pennsylvania coke fields, Frick would have no truck with any union. In Frick's mind, the Amalgamated was a serious obstacle to efficiency, and Carnegie was equally eager to be rid of its influence in the Homestead mill. Carnegie and Frick agreed on a two-point negotiating program with the workers. The first was a reduction in the minimum on the sliding scale. This was a vexsome, but fairly traditional, demand in the industry. The second point reflected events that had been occurring with increased regularity on the Pittsburgh scene since the late 1880s: Carnegie and Frick wanted to eliminate the union as bargaining agent. Frick knew this would cause a mammoth fight with the union, and he was prepared to use every weapon in the company's arsenal to win the titanic struggle. His attitudes toward labor were brutal: the union must be smashed, and employers should brook no interference with their power to set wages and define working conditions. Further, Frick was willing to use all resources at his disposal to win his case. There was virtually no limit to how far Frick would go. If most other iron and steel manufacturers were moderated by what they considered acceptable behavior in labor/management confrontations, Frick was not. Carnegie knew how far Frick was willing to go and gave him a blank check. The result was one of the bloodiest and most violent confrontations in American labor history, one that spelled the beginning of the end for the Amalgamated and for unionism in an important segment of the iron and steel industry.

It was a devastating defeat for the Amalgamated. The loss at Homestead meant that they had now lost control of all three of the giant Carnegie mills in Pittsburgh and with it any hope for a nationwide scale agreement for steel. The defeat also provided impetus to the growth of the antiunion movement in the industry. Jones & Laughlin, one of the earliest mills to be organized in the city, became completely nonunion in 1897. Shoenberger Iron and Steel overthrew the union in 1898. What Homestead did not do to the Amalgamated, the depression of the 1890s did. From over twenty-four thousand members in 1891, there were just ten thousand in 1894. Most steel mills in Allegheny County were put on a nonunion basis before 1900, and a number of the old iron mills, formerly the strongest bastions of unionism in the industry, became nonunion between 1890 and 1900.

This dramatic transformation called for a new labor ideology among the older iron and steel manufacturers. The ideas of the 1870s and early 1880s, so ably articulated by Weeks in *Iron Age,* were obviously no longer germane, or desirable. What would define the new situation? Would it be the militant, unyielding antiunionism of Frick? Would it be the slightly softer and paternalistic antiunionism of Daniel Morrell and the eastern aristocrats? Would it in some way be the garbled and confused ideals of Andrew Carnegie, owner of the largest mills and the most flamboyant individual in the profession? Or would it be a new form of welfare capitalism? The issue was hammered out in two widely separated locations: in the paneled New York conference rooms of U.S. Steel and in the dingy, crowded mill offices of the remaining independent iron and steel men. The result was a bifurcated labor management system in the industry, with welfare capitalism emerging in the mills owned by U.S. Steel and a general return to acceptance of unionism along with a strong dose of paternalism in the smaller mills.

The concept of welfare capitalism in the nation's iron and steel mills had been building since around 1890. Charles William Kirchoff became chief editor of *Iron Age* in 1889, and until he resigned in 1910, he worked to popularize the idea in the industry. Kirchoff, like most advocates of welfare capitalism, was antiunion but believed in trying to establish a system that went beyond both old-fashioned paternalism and the hardfisted tactics of the Carnegie executives. Thus, shortly after becoming editor, Kirchoff began pushing the idea of profit sharing, hoping to synthesize an essential harmony between worker and employer in a new, more meaningful manner. Kirchoff's plan had two distinct goals: One was the desire to promote hard work by employees, thereby raising the quality and lowering the cost of the product. Second was to create a mutuality of interests and bonds between employer and employee, thereby preventing strikes and lockouts.[17]

These ideas of welfare capitalism, however, seemed to have little attraction for the independent Pittsburgh iron and steel makers. The only two firms to adopt aspects of that system in the 1890s were run by outsiders, and both ultimately became part of U.S. Steel in the early twentieth century. Andrew Carnegie had begun providing a variety of benefits to his workers in the mid-1880s and later established the Carnegie Relief Fund to take care of injured workers or the families of workers killed on the job. Although it was not a systematic program of what came to be known as welfare capitalism, it did receive a good deal of publicity, both negative and positive, in the Pittsburgh area. The most extensive adoption of welfare capitalism in the area, however, took place in the mid-1890s, when George Gibson McMurtry began building a model town around his new mill. A native of Northern Ireland who immigrated to Pittsburgh after the Civil War, and a man who was not part of the older social establishment in the city, McMurtry in 1882 set up the Apollo Iron Works, which he made every effort to run as a nonunion shop during the years when virtually every Pittsburgh mill negotiated with the Amalgamated. This came to something of a climax in October 1893, when McMurtry took advantage of a labor dispute to lock the Amalgamated out of the mill and bring in strikebreakers. The strike dragged on, and throughout the early months of 1894 there were several reports of violence on both sides of the struggle.[18] The strike continued for well over a year.

Tiring of continual conflict with the union at Apollo, in 1895 McMurtry decided to build a new mill in a model town designed by Frederick Law Olmstead to be called Vandergrift. American Sheet Steel, as the new firm was named, built its new plant in an isolated and controlled environment, with the newest technological advances in steel production and sheet making. It also provided a series of benefits to the workers designed to tie them more closely to the goals and ideals of the firm's owners.[19] Vandergrift became a classic example of the new welfare capitalism, so much so that Ida Tarbell several years later extolled its virtues, an important element of which was individual homeownership for the firm's skilled workers. Another aspect that drew much praise was the prohibition of the sale of liquor in the town. Interestingly, the militant antiunion attitudes that generated the town's creation drew no criticism from Progressives. As Tarbell explained, the beauty of Vandergrift was that it managed to reestablish that essential harmony of interests between capital and labor:

> Its creator [McMurtry] looked upon the health, prosperity and content of his employees as part of his stock in trade. In building a new plant which was necessary to accommodate his growing business, he arranged for a town with the same care he arranged for his best machinery. "Don't imagine we're going to make it a hobby," he wrote in one of his announcements. "This town belongs to the rest of our business management."[20]

However attractive they were to reformers, the antiunion ideas of welfare capitalism did not appear to gain much favor with either the mass of workmen or even the independent Pittsburgh iron and steel manufacturers. There appears, despite a certain hardening of their ideas in the 1890s, to be a fairly clearly defined set of attitudes among the older Pittsburgh iron masters during the nineteenth century. The antiunion sentiments that surfaced in the early 1890s had not been characteristic of the mill culture that had developed among both workers and mill owners during the period from the 1860s to the 1880s. Throughout that time, there had been no rabid antiunionism, no excessive use of strikebreakers or violence in the labor confrontations with the Amalgamated. Through it all, however, the owners had remained masters of their mills. During the years when they had signed union agreements and shared control of the shop floor with skilled craftsmen, there is little sense that they felt they were powerless. If it was the craftsman's empire, it was still the mill owner's domain. While they battled over scale prices and other prerogatives, neither side lost its dignity.

Matters began to change in the late 1880s. Technology played a role in this. Bessemer steel production was cutting into at least some of the older iron and steel markets, and puddling technology and wages remained static in a dynamically changing environment. This was bound to make the iron barons restive. Then, too, the Amalgamated became more aggressive in the 1880s. Fearing a continuing erosion of their power in the industry and woefully unable to organize the new Bessemer mills, the Amalgamated often vented its frustration on the iron mills, where it could more easily wring concessions. Then, as the older iron and steel men watched tough, young steel executives easily rout the union in confrontations, it emboldened their actions. Finally, in the Homestead strike, one of their own, Henry Clay Frick, a member of a Core upper-class family with deep roots in the area, rejected the entire mill culture that many had assumed to be sacrosanct in the Pittsburgh area. And, despite almost universal condemnation by the press, religious leaders, and many political figures, Frick got away with it. Undoubtedly, this caused many of the older iron and steel men to stiffen their resolve against the union, and some of the old Pittsburgh mills pushed the Amalgamated out of their plants. Yet it often seemed to be done with a genuine sense of sorrow on both sides—it was a tragedy that both seemed fated to play out—and none of the older mill owners used the sort of tactics Frick had employed at Homestead. A major reason for this variant approach by the older iron mill owners was that they managed to find their own protected niche in the marketplace as the twentieth century dawned.

If the 1890s had been a time of turmoil for both management and union in the independent iron and steel mills in Pittsburgh, the dawn of the twentieth century brought seemingly profound transformations. The great merger movement of those years created a series of steel giants, especially U.S. Steel, which on the surface, at least, dominated the industry in a manner far beyond that achieved by Carnegie Steel. Then, too, U.S. Steel established a system of non-union labor relations in the industry that was a far cry from the unionized mills of the nineteenth century. Through it all, the independent mills of Pittsburgh emerged relatively unscathed from this great transformation.

The Great Merger Movement in Steel: Winners, Losers, and Survivors

At first glance it would seem axiomatic that the older iron and steel families lost control of their mills to the creation of the massive U.S. Steel. By the early years of the twentieth century, according to even the steel trust's own estimates, it controlled about 60 percent of the pig iron used for steel making purposes, 66 percent of the crude steel output, and around 50 percent of the finished steel output in the nation. Capitalized at $1 billion, and with Carnegie Steel of Pittsburgh its largest and most powerful unit, there could be little question of the fate of Pittsburgh's iron masters. P. Glenn Porter and Harold Livesay, in their fine study of industrialization in America, had no doubt concerning what had transpired: "In the Pittsburgh area in 1869, for example, there were numerous manufacturers of primary and finished iron and steel products; by the early years of the twentieth century most of these had become part of the large firms, such as United States Steel or Crucible Steel, which had come to dominate the industry."[21] The problem with this analysis, as with virtually every other examination of the steel industry, is that although it may well be accurate for the national scene, it ignores important developments on the local level. Although it is certainly precise to state that those old Pittsburgh firms and families were no longer as important in the industry as before, it is equally true that they did not simply vanish. A significant number of the old firms continued to function and prosper on a comparatively reduced scale, and a host of new firms were founded by these old iron-making families, often with money received from selling their older plants to the new consolidations.

In order to understand better what was happening at the turn of the century, we must first relate it to the analysis we have pursued in the preceding chapters.[22] Naomi Lamoreaux distinguishes between two types of firms in the iron and steel industry: those that mass-produced vast quantities of a cheap, homogeneous product (the large-batch producers) and those that manufactured small quantities of carefully differentiated, high-quality products.[23] The first group of producers were those most likely to be drawn into the large consolidations, whereas the latter generally remained outside them. In the iron and steel industry, Andrew Carnegie was the classic example of a producer of a cheap, homogeneous product. The vast majority of the iron and steel manufacturers in Pittsburgh, however, never tried to compete with Carnegie and were outstanding examples of producers of specialty goods. Nor were they greatly affected by the formation of U.S. Steel.

As noted in early chapters, these independent iron and steel makers survived by pursuing strategies of product differentiation and selling to specialized niche markets. Leaving the market of cheap, mass-produced Bessemer rails to Carnegie, these men sought out new markets for high-quality differentiated products, developed effective marketing strategies for these products, and innovated with the proper technology. Most were able to develop precisely the proper blend of innovation and caution to make a success of their mills. Their rate of survival during the nineteenth century stands as a monument to their success, but the organization of U.S. Steel in 1901 was their ultimate challenge.

The process that resulted in the formation of U.S. Steel absorbed twenty formerly independent firms in Pittsburgh. It had all begun in the mid-1890s, when American Steel and Wire, American Tin Plate, and National Tube took in several firms. With the formation of American Sheet Steel and American Steel Hoop in the later years of the decade, others were assimilated. Ironically, perhaps, given the sort of mythology that has emerged about the impact of U.S. Steel, the only firm in Pittsburgh directly affected by its organization in 1901 was Carnegie Steel, which, of course, became the key unit in the new holding company. Additionally, American Steel Casting in that year took in one firm, and the formation of Crucible Steel in 1900 also absorbed a number of older Pittsburgh crucible firms. Since Crucible Steel remained under the control of the families whose steel firms it absorbed, it hardly had the same kind of impact on Pittsburgh's independent steel makers. These local manufacturers continued to run their own plants, to live in Pittsburgh, and to function as part of the local aristocracy. Table 5.1 gives a breakdown of those firms absorbed by U.S. Steel.

As the table indicates, the Pittsburgh firms taken into U.S. Steel were a motley group. First of all, most were fairly small. Besides Carnegie Steel, only National Tube Works, which had already absorbed several mills in the Pittsburgh area, could be considered large. The only other firms of any size at all were Oliver & Snyder Steel and Shoenberger Steel (the old Juniata Iron Mill). There were, in addition, a number of firms of middling size and several quite

TABLE 5.1
Pittsburgh Companies Absorbed by Units of U.S. Steel

Company Name	Year Organized	Controlling Families	Production Type	Capacity (Tons)
American Sheet Steel				
Apollo I.&S.	1850	McMurtry/Vandergrift	O. H. steel	27,000
Chartiers I.&S.	1883–84	Kirkpatrick/Leech	Iron	4,500
Leechburg Iron	1872	Kirkpatrick/Leech	Iron & O. H. steel	10,000
McKeesport R. M.	1851	Wood	Iron & O. H. steel	18,000
West Penn Steel	1881	Jennings	O. H. Steel	7,000
Total American Sheet Steel				66,500
American Steel Hoop Company				
Pittsburgh Iron	1836	Painter	Iron	50,000
Solar Steel	1868	Clark	O. H. steel	35,000
Star Iron & Steel	1862	Lindsay/McCutcheon	Iron	12,000
Total American Steel Hoop				97,000
American Tin Plate Company				
Monongahela Tin Plate	1894–95	Oliver/Quay	Tin plate	12,000

Pittsburgh Tin Plate	1891–92	Parkin	Tin plate	5,500
Star Tin Plate	1895	Hemphill	Tin plate	12,500
U.S. Iron & T. P.	1873–74	Cronemeyer/Demmler	Tin plate	11,000
Total American Tin Plate				41,000
American Steel & Wire Company				
Braddock Wire	1885–86	Gates	Wire	50,000
Oliver Wire	1884	Oliver	Wire	70,000
Pittsburgh Wire	1891	Dempster/Cochrane	Wire	40,000
Oliver & Snyder Steel	1881	Oliver/Snyder	Bessemer steel	120,000
Shoenberger Steel	1824	Shoenberger	Iron and O. H. steel	100,000
Total American Steel & Wire				300,000
National Tube Company				
National Tube	1879	Converse	Iron and Bess. steel	320,000
Elba Iron Works	1862	Eaton/Converse	Iron	35,000
Total National Tube				355,000
Carnegie Steel Company				
Carnegie Steel	1863	Carnegie	Bess. and O. H. steel	1,822,000
Grand Total: Pittsburgh Companies in U.S. Steel				2,681,500

small companies taken into the new merger. Second, relatively few firms belonging to families of the older Pittsburgh upper class, especially that group which had been involved in the pre–Civil War iron and steel industry, were absorbed. In this category were McKeesport Rolling Mill (although W. D. Wood, the owner, was in most respects a Philadelphian rather than a Pittsburgher), Pittsburgh Iron (owned by the Painter family), and Shoenberger Steel (whose owners had moved to Cincinnati). Other firms belonging to Pittsburghers of more recent vintage were Henry Oliver's three companies, Kirkpatrick and Leech's two firms, Apollo Iron and Steel, Solar Steel, Star Tin Plate, and U.S. Iron & Tin Plate. Third, if there was a typical firm that was absorbed into U.S. Steel, it was owned by someone who in some important sense was external to the Pittsburgh upper-class social system: an outsider. This was certainly true of Carnegie Steel, the largest; National Tube, the second largest; Braddock Wire, Apollo Iron and Steel, Elba Iron Works; and to a certain degree, McKeesport Rolling Mill and Solar Steel. The Clark family, owners of Solar Steel, were fairly new to Pittsburgh, were of working-class origins, and had cost the old families control of Allegheny Bessemer Steel. Possibly as a result of these factors, the Clarks were not accepted by the Pittsburgh upper class.

Thus, with just a few important exceptions, firms already controlled by people who were in some respect outsiders to the Pittsburgh upper-class social system were those most likely to be sold to U.S. Steel. This was true even of Shoenberger Steel, the oldest iron and steel firm in the city, controlled by the Shoenberger and Fitzhugh families. Although the Shoenbergers were a particularly old and well-regarded family, both they and the Fitzhughs had long since moved out of Pittsburgh, transferring their primary social relationships to Cincinnati. The impact of the formation of U.S. Steel on the older upper classes of Pittsburgh, then, with the exception of the Painter family, was practically nil. Another reason for this minimal impact was that some of the families, such as the Olivers, Kirkpatricks, and Leechs, did not sell all of their mills to U.S. Steel and continued in the iron and steel business with their other plants.

In one sense, Crucible Steel, which was organized in 1900, had a greater impact on the old upper-class Pittsburgh firms. In another sense, at least during the first quarter-century or so of its existence, it had very little influence. Table 5.2 indicates that the firms taken into Crucible Steel in 1900, with one exception, were owned and controlled by Pittsburgh's oldest and most prestigious iron and steel

TABLE 5.2
Pittsburgh Companies Absorbed by Crucible Steel

Company	Year Organized	Controlling Families	Production	Capacity Type
Crescent Steel	1865	Miller/Metcalf/ Parkin	Crucible steel	27,000
Howe, Brown & Co.	1859	Howe, Brown	Crucible and O. H. steel	14,300
LaBelle Steel	1863	Smith	Crucible and O. H. steel	13,000
Black Diamond	1862	Park	Crucible and O. H. steel	135,600
Sheffield Steel	1848	Singer, Nimick	Crucible and O. H. steel	14,800
Aliquippa Steel	1892	Vilsack	Crucible and O. H. steel	12,000
Pittsburgh Steel	1845	DuPuy	Crucible and O. H. steel	13,500
Total Capacity Absorbed in Pittsburgh				230,200

families. The exception was Aliquippa Steel, owned by the Vilsack family, which was old, but Roman Catholic, and therefore not part of the establishment. What was significant about Crucible Steel was that these old upper-class families did not lose control of their firms. The board of directors of the consolidated firm in 1901 was composed of James H. Park of Black Diamond Steel; Herbert DuPuy of Pittsburgh Steel; Reuben Miller of Crescent Steel; Charles E. Clapp of Howe, Brown; G. Bruce Harton and William H. Singer of Sheffield Steel; and Frank B. Smith of LaBelle Steel, along with Andrew W. Mellon and a couple of others. Only the non-upper-class Vilsack family was not represented.

Even more important for the economic and social structure of upper-class Pittsburgh in the early twentieth century was the large number of firms organized prior to 1895 that survived the great merger wave of the late nineteenth century. After the dust had settled, twenty-three of these pre-1895 independent firms were still functioning in the city. Table 5.3 gives the relevant details for these companies, and as can be discerned, the independent firms included one large vertically integrated company, Jones & Laughlin; four other firms with over 100,000-ton capacity; a number of medium-

TABLE 5.3

Independent Iron and Steel Firms Organized prior to 1895 Still Surviving in Pittsburgh in 1901

Company	Year Organized	Controlling Families	Production Type	Capacity (tons)
Jones & Laughlin	1852	Jones/Laughlin	Bessemer and O. H. steel	1,325,000
Purchased Soho Mill	1859	Moorhead	Iron and O. H. steel	100,000
Anchor Nail & Track	1842	Chess	Iron	12,000
A. M. Byers & Co.	1862–63	Byers	Iron	16,000
Carbon Steel	1862	Raymond	O. H. steel	125,000
Clinton Iron & Steel	1846	Friend/Hoffstot	Iron	15,000
Etna Iron & Tube	1828	Chalfant	Iron	25,000
Ft. Pitt Foundry	1882	Hemphill	O. H. steel	16,500
Glendon Rolling Mill	1857	Dilworth	Merchant steel	58,000
Liggett Spring & Axle	1865	Not available	Merchant iron and steel	5,000
Monongahela I. & S.	1891	Carter	Merchant iron	15,000
Oliver Iron & Steel	1863	Oliver	Merchant iron	120,000
Pittsburgh Forge & I.	1864	Wells/Richardson	Merchant iron	44,000
Reliance Steel Casting	1889	Bailey/Kelly	Crucible and O. H. steel	2,500
Sable Iron Works	1845	Zug/Reid	Merchant iron	36,500
Sligo Rolling Mill	1825	Nimick	Merchant iron	24,000
Superior Steel	1892	Hammond	Strip steel	15,000
Vesuvius Iron & Steel	1846	Moorhead	Merchant iron	100,000
Vulcan Forge & Iron	1877	Gillespie/Lockhart	Merchant iron	27,500
Wayne Iron & Steel	1825	Brown	Crucible steel	23,000
Hussey, Binns & Co.	1875	Binns/Willson	Crucible steel	1,350
Hussy Steel	1891	Hussey/McCord	O. H. steel	20,000
Westmoreland Steel	1889–90	Burgwin/Kaufman	Crucible steel	7,000
Firth-Sterling Steel	1875	Firth	Crucible steel	3,700
Total: Pre-1895 Independent Firms				2,137,550

size firms; and several smaller ones. Most significant is that the management of these plants included most of the venerable names of Pittsburgh iron and steel making.

If, for example, we turn to a list of sixty iron and steel manufacturers in Pittsburgh in the mid-1870s, we find that of that group of families in the industry, only 27 percent are missing from the group of independent iron and steel manufacturers a quarter of a century later. Missing in 1901 from the list of independent manufacturers are the following families: Spang, Graff, Bennett, Clark, Carnegie, Lindsay, McCutcheon, Kloman, Painter, Lloyd, Everson, W. D. Wood, Nellis, Anderson, Shoenberger, and Blair. Of these, only Clark, Carnegie, Lindsay, McCutcheon, Painter, Shoenberger, and Wood were eliminated by the U.S. Steel consolidation. Of the rest, either they had gone out of business previously or all the male members of the family were deceased. As table 5.3 shows, independent iron and steel firms in Pittsburgh were still responsible for over 2 million tons of capacity after 1901, compared to 2.6 million tons of Pittsburgh capacity in U.S. Steel (of which 1.8 million came from Carnegie Steel) and 230,000 tons in Crucible Steel. But the saga of the surviving independent firms is only part of the story. Hidden by the ballyhoo of consolidation at the turn of the century, fourteen new independent iron and steel plants were organized in and around the city between 1898 and 1901. Table 5.4 gives the relevant information on the founding of these firms.

Most of these firms were founded by members of Pittsburgh's older upper class. Braeburn Steel, Colonial Steel, and West Leechburg Steel were founded by pre–Civil War iron and steel families; Allegheny Iron and Steel, Duquesne Steel Foundry, Pittsburgh Steel Foundry, Columbia Steel and Shafting, Nickle Steel and Forge, Union Steel Casting, and Union Steel were organized by members of other old Pittsburgh upper-class families. Pittsburgh Steel, Sharon Steel Hoop, and McKeesport Tin Plate were started by men who were relatively new to Pittsburgh, although none was of non-elite origin. Nor were most of these fly-by-night operations. Union Steel, the largest, was sold to U.S. Steel in 1902, and Columbia Steel and Shafting and Nickle Steel and Forge went out of business after a few years, but the other eleven firms remained in business for at least a quarter-century. The key to the success of these newly organized firms was the same as for those older Pittsburgh firms that survived as independent entities: product differentiation. Although many were innovative in technical respects, it was their ability to develop

TABLE 5.4
Independent Firms Organized in Pittsburgh at the Turn of the Century

Company	Year Organized	Controlling Families	Production Type	Capacity (tons)
Allegheny Iron & Steel	1900–1901	Hicks	O. H. steel	35,000
Braeburn Steel	1897	Metcalf	Crucible steel	14,200
Colonial Steel	1900–1901	Childs/Brown/Howe	Crucible steel	70,000
Columbia Steel & Shafting	1900–1901	Lee/Macrum	O. H. steel	2,000
Duquesne Steel Foundry	1900	Herron/Bakewell	O. H. steel	10,000
McKeesport Tin Plate	1901	Crawford	Tin plate	25,000
Mesta Machine	1899	Mesta/Robinson	O. H. steel	10,000
Nickle Steel & Forge	1899	Jamison	Crucible steel	6,000
Pittsburgh Steel Co.	1901	Rowe	Specialty steels	350,000
Pittsburgh Steel Foundry	1900	Johnston/Lockhart	O. H. steel	60,000
Sharon Steel Hoop	1900	Ker	Hoops	150,000
Union Steel	1900	Mellon/Frick	Specialty steels	850,000
Union Steel Casting	1899	Smith/Wainwright	O. H. steel	6,000
West Leechburg Steel	1898	Kirkpatrick	Specialty steels	18,000
Total				1,606,000

relatively unique, highly differentiated products that provided the path to success and profits in the twentieth century.

Not only did many of these firms survive; several of them went on to become large and highly successful entities in the twentieth century. Table 5.5 provides an analysis of the growth patterns of these independent companies over time. In 1901 there were forty independent iron and steel firms in Pittsburgh. They had a combined capacity for 3,766,050 tons in the Pittsburgh area, compared to 2,911,700 area tons controlled by U.S. Steel and Crucible Steel. These totals can be viewed in some slightly different ways, however, providing other perspectives on what was happening during these years.

In 1901, including Carnegie Steel, U.S. Steel absorbed plants with an annual productive capacity in the Pittsburgh area of 2,681,000 tons. Old Pittsburgh iron and steel families, along with other new independent steel makers (if we include Crucible Steel in their totals) controlled an aggregate annual productive capacity of 3,996,250 tons in the same year. However, if we consider the fact that much of the capacity that U.S. Steel inherited in the Pittsburgh area was the result of its takeover of Carnegie Steel (1,822,000 tons) and that Carnegie Steel had never been a local firm in either its social or economic context anyhow, the impact of U.S. Steel on local steel makers in Pittsburgh becomes even less significant. In fact, if one subtracts from the U.S. Steel totals those firms controlled by men who lived outside Pittsburgh (Carnegie Steel, National Tube, McKeesport Rolling Mill, and Braddock Wire), we are left with only 436,000 tons of productive capacity owned by indigenous iron and steel manufacturers whose firms were taken over by U.S. Steel. This total is exceeded by the productive capacity of the new plants (exclusive of Union Steel) started by independents in the Pittsburgh area from 1898 to 1901 (756,000 tons).

As mentioned previously, independent firms had a remarkable record of longevity (see table 5.5). In 1911, fully 80 percent of the forty independent firms still survived (and, in fact, a number of others were also organized during these years). After another decade, in 1920, only one additional firm had expired, leaving 78 percent that survived from 1901. The 1920s, the time of the "second great merger wave" in American industry, hit these firms with relative severity, so that only twenty, or 50 percent, still operated by 1930. The depression of the 1930s, which so ravaged the steel industry, was the final blow for many of them. Another nine firms went under or were merged with others during the Depression decade, leaving

TABLE 5.5
Independent Iron and Steel Firms in Pittsburgh during
the Twentieth Century

Independent Firms in 1901	Survival of Firms in Selected Years				Capacity
	1911	1920	1930	1938	
Allegheny Steel	•	•	•	•	868,000
Anchor Nail & Tack					
Braeburn Steel	•	•	•	•	8,000
A. M. Byers & Co.	•	•	•	•	422,000
Carbon Steel	•	•			
Clinton Iron & Steel	•	•			
Colonial Steel	•	•			
Columbia Steel					
Crucible Steel	•	•	•	•	1,300,000
Duquense Steel Foundry	•	•	•		
Etna Iron & Tube	•	•	•		
Firth-Sterling Steel	•	•	•	•	20,000
Ft. Pitt Foundry	•	•	•		
Glendon Rolling Mill	•	•			
Hussey, Binns & Co.	•	•			
Hussey Steel					
Jones & Laughlin Steel	•	•	•	•	3,420,000
Liggett Spring & Axle	•				
McKeesport Tin Plate	•	•	•	•	360,000
Mesta Machine	•	•	•	•	120,000
Monongahela Iron & Steel	•	•			
Nickle Steel & Forge					
Oliver Iron & Steel	•	•			
Pittsburgh Forge & Iron	•	•	•		
Pittsburgh Steel	•	•	•		
Pittsburgh Steel Foundry	•	•	•		
Reliance Steel Casting	•	•			
Sharon Steel Hoop	•	•	•	•	500,000
Sligo Rolling Mill	•	•			
Sterling Steel Foundry	•	•	•		
Superior Steel					
Union Steel					
Union Steel Casting	•	•			
U.S. Wire & Nail					
Vesuvius Iron & Nail	•	•	•		
Vulcan Forge & Iron	•	•	•	•	49,000
Wayne Iron & Steel	•	•			
West Leechburg Steel	•	•	•		

TABLE 5.5 (continued)

Independent Firms in 1901	Survival of Firms in Selected Years				Capacity
	1911	1920	1930	1938	
Westmoreland Steel					
Zug Iron & Steel	•	•	•		
Totals	32	31	20	11	7,878,110
40 Companies in 1900	(80%)	(78%)	(50%)	(28%)	

Note: Blank spaces indicate out of business.

eleven, or 28 percent, still independent on the eve of World War II. Extending the analysis to the postwar period, we find nine of the old independent mills still in operation in 1956, along with ten new independent firms that had been organized since the early 1930s.[24]

This would appear to be a significant record of continuity and survival and, given the tenor of most of the literature dealing with the steel industry, rather unexpected. Not only did these firms survive—they grew. Their capacity of 3,881,250 tons in 1901 had grown to 7,878,110 by 1938. Of course, the nation's overall steel capacity had expanded greatly, so relative productive capacity had slipped, but this was true of the Pittsburgh area generally. Controlling 30 percent of the nation's iron and steel total in 1900, Pittsburgh had slipped to 22 percent in 1930 and 20 percent in 1950, even though regional output was three times as large by the end of the period.[25] This, it seems to me, provides eloquent testimony to the ability of these independent firms in Pittsburgh to survive and prosper.

Historians have not generally paid much attention to these independent iron and steel firms in the twentieth century, and if they are mentioned at all, they are usually simply dismissed as small affairs. That is not wholly accurate. Certainly Jones & Laughlin and Crucible Steel were giant companies, but even Allegheny Steel, A. M. Byers & Co., Sharon Steel Hoop, and McKeesport Tin Plate were significant entities by the 1930s. We must, after all, not compare them only to U.S. Steel, Bethlehem Steel, or Republic Steel. The independent iron and steel mill was still the most typical unit on the Pittsburgh scene and controlled at least as much productive capacity in the area as U.S. Steel.

Labor/Management Relations in the Core
and on the Periphery

A very important area in this regard is the whole phenomenon of labor/management relations. Generally, our view of labor relations in the steel industry in Pittsburgh has been conditioned by what happened at the core steel firm, U.S. Steel. John Fitch in the *Pittsburgh Survey* in 1911 detailed the situation for Pittsburgh's steelworkers. Their union, the Amalgamated, had been bloodied in the Homestead strike and then suffered severe losses of lodges and membership in the late nineteenth century when Jones & Laughlin and other iron and steel firms shut the union out of their mills. Then, a great crisis occurred for the Amalgamated Association in 1901 when it called a strike against the new steel giant, U.S. Steel. Charles M. Schwab and the other Carnegie men wanted to use the same sort of tactics Frick had used against the union in Homestead in order to rout them from all the mills in the giant corporation, but Elbert Gary, representing J. P. Morgan and the financiers, counseled a more moderate, politically sensitive stance. The result was something of a compromise: the union was badly defeated and banished from nearly all the mills of U.S. Steel by 1909, but to deal with potentially adverse publicity and to control their restive work force of 168,000, U.S. Steel instituted a policy of welfare capitalism, setting up a safety program and establishing a range of benefits for its (primarily skilled) workers and introducing what David Brody called the nonunion era in the steel industry, which lasted until the 1930s.[26] It is a very important and well-documented story and did affect the lives of thousands of steelworkers but was hardly the only labor/management episode in the industry in Pittsburgh. In fact, one might legitimately argue that it was not even the most important.

As noted, the independent mills continued to play a large role in Pittsburgh's affairs, and at least a large minority of iron and steel workers still labored in mills with fewer than one thousand employees. Therefore, it is vitally important to determine what the situation was in those mills. Most analysts have been vague on the point. Fitch simply claimed, "The independent mills of the Pittsburgh District followed the lead of the Carnegie Steel Company and the other companies that are now in the combination, in breaking with the union . . . so that today conditions are practically uniform in all steel mills, under the absolute and unregulated control of the employers." David Brody was more careful in his analysis but essen-

tially reached the same conclusion. He granted that the Amalgamated lasted in some of the independent mills for a longer time but
by World War I felt it was pretty well finished.[27] On the other hand,
he found little evidence that these independent mills were attracted
by the expensive proposition of welfare capitalism.[28] That leaves a
question about what sort of labor/management ideology and system
these independent mills employed.

There is at least some documentation that many of these older
Pittsburgh mills continued to be run as union shops and that labor
relations remained much as they had been in the nineteenth century. When many skilled puddlers pulled out of the Amalgamated in
1907 to form a new Sons of Vulcan union, headquarters of the new
organization was established in Pittsburgh. The Sons of Vulcan had
sixteen lodges during the early years, most of which were in Pittsburgh and Youngstown.[29] There is little extant evidence concerning
which companies had lodges in their works, but information from a
couple of firms gives some idea of the relative stability of labor
relations in these peripheral firms.

Lockhart Iron and Steel, for example, happily signed with the
new union when it was organized in 1907. There is no particular
reason to believe they were forced to do this; it probably just seemed
the normal and proper thing to do. Three years later, when the Sons
of Vulcan demanded a large increase and went out on strike, the firm
was caught in a difficult situation because it had many back orders.
So it hired replacements: strikebreakers. All of this may look very
much like the kind of militant antiunionism we have been taught to
expect from these men, except for one glaring fact. Lockhart hired
union men: members of the Amalgamated. The Sons of Vulcan were
furious and demanded the discharge of the Amalgamated men, and
fighting broke out in the plant. To resolve the situation, Lockhart
officials promised that all workers could have jobs in the plant.
Technically, then, Lockhart had hired strikebreakers, but since they
were also union men there is no indication of a desire of management to run a nonunion shop.[30]

After the Sons of Vulcan fell apart in 1913, most of its members
drifted back to the Amalgamated, which continued to negotiate
with a small, but not insignificant, number of independent mills. In
1906, the independent bar iron manufacturers organized the Western
Bar Iron Association, composed of twelve independent companies,
to negotiate scales with the Amalgamated. Sheet and tin plate manufacturers had bargained in alliance with the American Sheet and
Tin Plate Company of U.S. Steel until it adopted the open shop in

1909; then the independent members set up the Western Sheet and Tin Plate Manufacturers to negotiate with the union. As late as 1916, the Western Bar Iron Association had fifteen members, and the Western Sheet and Tin Plate Association had ten. A number of these were located in the Pittsburgh area.[31]

Perhaps typical of those independent iron and steel firms in the Pittsburgh area that continued to negotiate with the union was A. M. Byers Co. Michael W. Santos has sensitively evoked a pattern of labor relations at the independent Pittsburgh iron mill that differed in myriad ways from the situation at the steel giants.[32] A. M. Byers was one of the old-line, pre–Civil War iron companies that refused to switch to steel production in the late nineteenth century, preferring to continue to make "quality iron products." Its skilled puddlers and finishers also remained members of the Amalgamated during the period of union busting in the late nineteenth and early twentieth centuries. And Byers management continued to negotiate with them in good faith. As Santos commented, in remarking how the family continued to run the firm until World War II: "Such long-range stability reinforced traditional managerial patterns and convinced Byers men of the patterns' continued efficiency. On the shop floor, that meant accepting unionization and worker control as long as they did not threaten profits."[33]

Byers continued to bargain collectively with the Amalgamated, and when its puddlers joined the Sons of Vulcan, they negotiated with that organization also. Although there were certain vicissitudes in this relationship over the decades, "the scope of anti-unionism at Byers was limited," Santos remarks, and even when the union was eradicated from the mill for a few years, the company maintained wages at or above the union scale. Further, Byers management continued to attempt to foster a cooperative environment between employer and workers that was strikingly similar to what had existed in the nineteenth century. They jointly sponsored union-company outings, with picnics, softball games, and the like. Even when the workers went out on strike, a cordiality was maintained that stood in stark contrast to the ham-fisted tactics of the major steel companies. A longtime employee recalled: "We had a 110-day strike [actually the strike lasted two months] there [at Byers] one time and it was in the winter time and our company was good. They gave us coal, they gave us coffee, they . . . gave us a canvas so we could put a tent over the lot they had . . . down alongside there on Sixth Street. They told us if we wanted Coke or stuff like that, go in and get it. [The] foreman would . . . [let] you in."[34]

As David Brody and others have so brilliantly elucidated, there was a psychology of steel making, one that focused on the use of technology to speed materials through the mill in a continuous, mass-production mode. It was also used to drive down costs by replacing expensive skilled manual labor with machines tended by cheaper semiskilled labor. Once the unions were driven out of the steel mills and wage levels and costs of production greatly reduced, a form of paternalism called welfare capitalism was initiated. In the older iron mills, however, a unionized paternalism similar to that which existed in the nineteenth century continued to function. A classic example of this older paternalistic attitude in the 1930s was the Byers plant.

Brody and a number of other historians argue that if iron mills did not take a strong antiunion stand, it was because puddling was impervious to mechanical innovation. If ever an innovation was found to eliminate that costly labor-intensive stage, they argue, then iron makers would act exactly like their colleagues in steel production. That axiom was tested after 1930, when Byers engineers perfected the Byers or Aston process that replaced the traditional puddling furnace with a Bessemer converter that purified the iron in a ten-minute blast. This allowed the Byers firm and other iron companies to take advantage for the first time of the kinds of economies of scale that the steel plants had long practiced. More significantly, it allowed them to get rid of their expensive puddlers and dispense with the union. Surely that is what Byers, driven by a technological imperative in the midst of a devastating depression, did. Just as surely, Byers did just the opposite. Building a new plant in Ambridge, Pennsylvania, to take advantage of the new puddling machine, it offered its puddlers other jobs in the mill and continued to bargain with the union, just as before.[35] As "big steel" and "little steel" battled the union tooth and nail during the 1920s and early 1930s, finally reaching an accommodation in the 1940s and 1950s, the Byers firm conducted its labor relations as it had for three-quarters of a century.[36]

It would be irresponsible to assume that all the independent iron and steel firms in Pittsburgh were like A. M. Byers. Nor were they similar to U.S. Steel and the other massive steel firms. Some were pathologically antiunion, of course, but most seem to have taken a middle road, negotiating with the union when they had to and paying union scale to their workers even if they were not unionized in order to maintain cordial relations with their work force. There is a fair amount of evidence that this was not unusual among the mass of smaller firms operating on the periphery. David Brody has pointed out that there were a number of advantages for small-scale producers who depended on craft unions to maintain an orderly labor market.[37] Similarly, studies conducted among a number of small firms in western Pennsylvania that failed between 1936 and 1954 indicate that in not one case was failure directly traceable to labor trouble.[38] Evidence is fairly strong that in the iron and steel industry, as in other corners of manufacturing, the smaller peripheral firms not only followed a different, often more unionized pattern of labor/management relations but suffered far less from labor problems than the larger core firms.

Labor relations in Pittsburgh's independent iron and steel mills were one element of a paternalistic ethic that most of these iron and steel families continued to pursue, one that carried over in important respects to the political, social, and cultural spheres. Just as they maintained their positions as specialized niche marketers in the iron and steel industry and over the years their mills survived and even expanded, and just as they continued their older patterns of labor relations, negotiating with the unions while retaining their dominance of the firm, so too did they continue to exercise impressive control and influence over Pittsburgh's social, cultural, and political activities. As chapter 6 demonstrates, they were not just "masters of the mill" but "masters of all they surveyed."

6

Masters of All They Surveyed

The Masters of Pittsburg are mostly of the Scotch-Irish race,
Presbyterians, keen and steady in the prosecution of their
affairs, indifferent to pleasure, singularly devoid of the usual
vanities and ostentations, proud to possess a solid and
spacious factory, and to live in an insignificant house. There
are no men of leisure in this town.

James Parton, "Pittsburg"

Newly fledged as Pittsburgh society is—or perhaps because it
is newly fledged—it has a narrowness and arrogance which
rather startle visitors from more democratic communities.
These traits do not show themselves in swagger and
ostentation. . . . But it may be set down as an axiom that the
solid basis of Pittsburgh society is money and that no
achievement and no personal charm not abundantly gilded
can effect an entrance. . . . "There never would arise in
Pittsburgh . . . a spontaneous invitation."

R. L. Duffus, "Is Pittsburgh Civilized?"

IN the early twentieth century the New York–based Charities and
Commons Publication Committee embarked on its famous multi-
volume *Pittsburgh Survey,* whose findings were to startle and energize a nation in the midst of the Progressive Era and create an agenda
for reform in cities throughout America.[1] In these volumes, the
authors in various ways described a city totally under the domination of the iron and steel industry. Much was made of the fact that
Pittsburgh had the most technologically advanced industrial sector
in the world, while its social and cultural sector were horribly im-
poverished. The *Survey* then took its analysis a step further in order
to identify the true culprit. Pittsburgh was dying, it said, because it
no longer had the resources to recreate itself as a community. This,

Edward I. Devine noted in one of the volumes, was because of the existence of "an absentee capitalism, with bad effects strikingly similar to those of absentee landlordism."[2] The theme was picked up by Robert Woods, a native of Pittsburgh who was by then a settlement house worker in Boston.[3] Pittsburgh's absentee capitalism, according to Woods, was a result of the "phenomenal concentration of capital, followed by highly centralized industrial administration." The result in Pittsburgh was that "the financial and even the administrative center of the great combinations has inevitably gravitated to New York, and the old type of self-reliant leader of industry is fast disappearing."[4]

Thus, the villain—U.S. Steel and other absentee corporations— had been identified and Woods also isolated another important factor in this decline, that of the disappearance of the old type of self-reliant leader who had helped create an earlier community feeling in the city. Who were these self-reliant leaders who were becoming extinct in Pittsburgh? Woods supplied the answer: "The leader was typified by Andrew Carnegie, B. F. Jones, whose firm continues to be the largest independent steel concern in Pittsburgh, the Parks, the Moorheads, the Olivers, the Laughlins."[5] These names, as the reader should be aware by this point, are, with the exception of Carnegie, all members of older upper-class iron and steel families in Pittsburgh. They had been replaced, in Woods's view, by "bureaucracies whose plans in detail are decided in New York, and whose local officials must guide their public actions so as to serve the corporations' interests."[6]

This makes for a dramatic scenario: an older, local, paternalistic elite has been overthrown by faceless bureaucrats and financiers from the remote financial center of world capitalism. The latter, in true colonial fashion, are draining the city of its wealth, leaving its citizens poor and desperate. Meanwhile, the city itself is unable to deal with its own problems because the absentee corporate interests control the political, social, and cultural institutes in the city. The problem with this image is that it does not square with the realities of power in Pittsburgh at the turn of the century. Several basic events had to happen before the scenario could be accurate: First, the older iron and steel families would have to lose control of their industry at the local level. Second, they would have to lose control of the political, social, and cultural institutions of the city. Third, they would have to be supplanted by a new social elite, a group that would become the new aristocracy of the city. And finally, even if all that did occur, it would be necessary to demonstrate that the political and social situation, in terms of social welfare policies, was in some way different from what it was before the transformation. Let us examine each of these areas.

We have seen, first of all, that the transformation in the iron and steel industry itself was hardly as complete as earlier theorists believed. Carnegie Steel and U.S. Steel were massive entities, to be sure, but Pittsburgh's independent iron and steel makers found differentiated markets in which to sell their goods, thus surviving and prospering for decades into the twentieth century. More importantly, they formed a powerful economic elite in the city that, through its control of banking and allied forms of finance, was able to have a powerful impact on the economy of the city and region. This has been a major point in most of the British studies dealing with the survival of aristocratic and mercantile groups in positions of power: it was accomplished through their influence and control of banking institutions. As W. D. Rubinstein has commented: "Above all, although there were indeed a substantial number of wealthy fortunes in certain manufacturing and industrial trades, like cotton manufacturing and engineering, the wealthy in Britain have disproportionately earned their fortunes in commerce and finance . . . rather than in manufacturing or industry. . . ."[7]

In Pittsburgh, of course, a larger proportion of the great fortunes were made in manufacturing, but financial and mercantile concerns remained key areas for control of the economy. We have seen how mercantile capital played a major role in the formation of the early iron and steel firms in Pittsburgh, and how the influence of bankers grew apace in the late nineteenth century. By the early twentieth century, some of the iron and steel families abandoned the mills, while in others one or two sons took over the mill as their brothers went into banking. Thus, by the early twentieth century, the older iron and steel elite, allied with other members of older upper-class families, dominated the banking and financial scene in Pittsburgh.[8]

An analysis of the *Pittsburgh Directory of Directors* for 1906 shows quite clearly that virtually every heir of a nineteenth-century iron and steel family, along with nearly every family they married into, held banking directorships in the city. Of greater significance, however, is the fact that the great majority of these directorships were held in the large, dominant central-city banks. At the same time, many of the officers of U.S. Steel subsidiary companies tended to hold their directorships in smaller regional banks that were located in the mill towns of their plants, such as the First National Bank of McKeesport. These findings are borne out by a broader study of banking in the city in the early twentieth century. Frank Lukaszewicz found that directors and executives of central-city banks in Pittsburgh tended to be members of old Scots-Irish Presbyterian families who had made their fortunes in iron, steel, and glass in the earlier nineteenth century. Directors of suburban banks tended more often to be German or Catholic Irish businessmen who had immigrated to the city after 1840. Their economic activities were generally centered on the periphery of the city, in real estate, construction, and other endeavors.[9] So, as in Britain and many other countries, it was banking that helped the independent iron and steel makers solidify their hold on the city's economy, despite the presence in the city of professional managers from powerful New York–based firms. These latter men were, after all, transient, whereas the older Pittsburgh families provided stability and continuity to the city's economic system. If it seems clear that a powerful influence was retained by these older families on the economic side, understanding the same phenomenon in the political and social context is even more intricate.

We saw in the previous chapter that despite increasing economic domination of city by outside centralizing forces and the emergence of a form of colonial economy, these iron barons retained substantial control of their own mills and, in an important sense, remained the lynchpins of the local economic system. Further, they were the local notables of the city. Solidly accepted as Pittsburgh's aristocracy, they jealously guarded entry to their bastions of social privilege. Their values dominated the public culture of the city and cast a long shadow over the cultural and social institutions of the city. In a word, they continued to display at least a modified hegemony over their environment, a hegemony that rested at least partially on a paternalistic worldview they had developed and many Pittsburghers accepted. These Pittsburgh iron men succeeded in separating themselves from the absentee bankers and bureaucrats of the large corporations, and from the crass politicians of the urban political machines. Far from attempting to return the city to a more pristine preindustrial age, these men wanted to keep it within the rubric of the independent steel mills that had dominated the city for so many years. Twentieth-century Pittsburgh, nearly as much as its nineteenth-century counterpart, was a world the iron barons made.

The Pittsburgh Survey's lament about the lack of "natural leaders" in the early twentieth century was not restricted to the economic system but was directed at politics as well. Although the

Survey bemoaned the lack of influence that the individual steel-worker had in his political affairs, the basic thrust of its critique centered on the need for greater community and the reemergence of a group of reform leaders who would demonstrate the sort of noblesse oblige that existed in earlier years. The *Survey* called for the development of the essential religion of social engineering, run by professional experts and supported by the better classes as a means to fill the horrible vacuum in social responsibility that had infected the city. This, it felt, had to emerge both in the public or political sphere and in the voluntary sector. Ironically, those leaders already existed, to a rather large degree, at that time.

The System of Politics in Pittsburgh

Historians do not know a great deal about the functioning of Pittsburgh's politics during the early years. Because it was a small, pedestrian city, most commentators have assumed that it conformed to patterns observed in walking cities. According to these theories, since rich and poor tended to mingle daily in close personal contact, their relationship was conditioned by a system of shared values, beliefs, and understandings. In this system, deference politics was the norm and members of the mercantile elite dominated the political universe of the young city. An additional assumption is that laws resulting from this system benefited all social groups, rich and poor, relatively equally. This assumption, to my knowledge, remains unverified.[10]

A few elements of that system are fairly clear. First, "despite economic and cultural divisions among its population, the early nineteenth century city continued to function as a community."[11] Similarly, the system of deference politics functioned throughout the period, with most elected offices being held by members of the patrician upper class. A study of Pittsburgh's mayors indicates that at least through the late 1820s they were drawn primarily from among the ranks of the city's economic dominants.[12] Elected members of council had similar backgrounds, with merchants and professionals making up some 58 percent of that group through 1828. Pittsburgh was a one-party, Federalist city, and these elite officeholders evidently looked on their terms in public office as an important part of their civic duty, rather than as a means of furthering their own political careers or that of their party organization.[13] It was, it seems, an "era of good feelings" in Pittsburgh as well as the nation. Finally, neither public officials nor the populace felt it was out of place for these economic notables to use their office to advance their own economic interests, which were generally assumed to coincide with the economic benefit of the community as a whole.[14]

The deferential, communitarian nature of Pittsburgh's politics began breaking down in the 1840s and 1850s. Studies of the political situation in Pittsburgh have stressed the impact that the change from a mercantile to a manufacturing city had on that structure. As the city grew larger and changed its economic and population base, its political system was also transformed in a number of important ways. The first significant change was in 1833, when the city abandoned citywide elections for councilmen and other officials and established a ward system of representation. The city was divided into four wards, each with its own representatives on the Select and Common councils. This, in Paul Kleppner's words, "symbolized a breakdown of the older sense of community and the emergence of identifiable, separate, and often conflicting interests that came to acquire territorial distinctiveness as the city's economic and spatial transformation progressed."[15]

There are few useful studies on this important period of Pittsburgh's politics, so all we can do is infer what may have been happening from intriguing shreds of evidence and a few limited but important studies. An analysis of Pittsburgh's city government by John Dankosky shows that until around 1833 the city's councilmen were primarily merchants, supported by old-style independent artisans in a system of deference politics.[16] After that point, as the city's iron and glass industries grew, merchants were supplanted by the new industrialists in control of the city. Dankosky also shows that other important policy-making institutions were undergoing a similar change. The Board of Trade (predecessor of the Chamber of Commerce) in 1837 was dominated by commercial interests, but by 1850 the commercial and manufacturing groups had equal influence. The same thing happened on the board of the Bank of Pittsburgh, where merchants dropped from 52 to 32 percent from 1834 to 1850. Since, as noted earlier, many of the industrial enterprises were financed by mercantile capital and a number of these men became partners in iron and steel enterprises, this transformation may not be quite as dramatic as it appears on the surface. Just as Pittsburgh's officeholders were changing during these years, so too were the electorate. The voters by the 1850s were largely factory workers rather than independent artisans, and a new system of political allegiance grew to support alliance.[17] This development, however, was a complex phenomenon that has been given little systematic attention. No one claims that this new manufacturing elite controlling Pittsburgh by 1850 was operating in a particularly "communitarian" fashion; neither, however, is there much sense that the city's working-class residents were as badly treated and exploited as they would later be. There still seemed to be some sense of shared enterprise and shared values between mill owner and mill worker, and this apparently was translated to the political realm. Nonetheless, the new system was less deferential than the old, with the Republican party's emerging to replace the Whig.

The great political issues in Pittsburgh, as elsewhere in the 1830s and 1840s, were primarily cultural rather than economic. First it was the anti-Masonic movement that energized the political scene, a movement that many historians have viewed as a mechanism the old mercantile elite used to forestall the victory of the new industrial elite. In Pittsburgh, however, the line between the two groups appears to be more blurred, and one cannot with confidence assert that the movement represented two contesting elite groups.[18] The anti-Mason agitation of the 1830s gave way to a powerful nativist influence in Pittsburgh's politics in the 1840s and 1850s. Although the movement in the 1840s appeared to consist of native-born workers' objecting to the new, less skilled immigrant workers flocking into the city, the nativism of the 1850s largely involved wealthy and middle-class individuals who objected to the life-style of the working-class immigrants: specifically, to their poverty, their drunkenness, and their bloc voting.[19]

Out of this vortex of cultural issues and class and ethnic hatred emerged the Republican party in Pittsburgh. The Republicans picked up on the anti-Catholic, protemperance, Sabbatarian sentiments of a large segment of the population and united those with strong antislavery sentiments.[20] The last item was developed, as Eric Foner has maintained, as a powerful producers' ideology that united manufacturer and mill worker both inside and outside the mill.[21] The Republican party almost completely dominated Pittsburgh's political scene for the next half-century. This dominance was based on an alliance of the working class and the city's middle and upper classes in a program that continued to stress a producers' ideology concerned with tariffs and industrial growth and allowing a modicum of personal freedom on a score of cultural issues.

The Republican party in the late nineteenth century is not generally thought of as the party of personal liberty. Its appeal on both the national and the local levels, in fact, was based at least partially on its strongly evangelistic anti-Catholicism, in which the party adopted a sense of mission to shape the world in its own image.[22] There is at least some evidence that this sense of mission was more muted among Pittsburgh's Republicans. With its producers' ideology, the Republican party almost always won a majority of the working-class wards in the city throughout the late nineteenth century.[23] In these wards, working men or area retailers were generally elected as councilmen and aldermen, and in upper-class wards members of elite groups were victorious. Thus, during a good portion of the late nineteenth century, Pittsburgh's elite withdrew from direct representation of the working class, and the sort of deference politics that entailed, leaving them to their own social and cultural representatives.[24]

The result of this kind of peer group representation can be seen in the functioning of the aldermanic courts in Pittsburgh, where the aldermen were not members of the city council but were akin to justices of the peace. As such, they handled a large portion of the cases dealing with assault, immorality, and family abuse in the working-class community. These aldermen, like the members of city council, were largely from the ranks of the working class or were small proprietors. They also reflected the social and cultural configuration of their ward and presumably were custodians of community values and beliefs.[25] The aldermen acted as an important buffer in the working-class community, protecting immigrant, largely Roman Catholic workers from the evangelical predilections of the upper-class Presbyterian Republicans. It was, in a word, one of the elements that allowed the Republican party to dominate a city made up overwhelmingly of working-class immigrants of non-Protestant heritage, groups who usually gave allegiance to the Democratic party.

Why did elite Republicans acquiesce in this sort of system in Pittsburgh? There is no clear answer to that question, but we may surmise that an important trade-off was involved. In return for adopting a laissez-faire attitude concerning issues of morality, the elite were freed from both government regulation of business and establishment of expensive, governmentally funded social welfare programs. Roy Lubove has shown that Pittsburgh in the nineteenth century was an open city for business as far as economic regulation was concerned. It was, as Sam Bass Warner, Jr., said of Philadelphia, a bastion of privatism, a system whereby communitarian concerns were left to private means for solution.[26] This saved growing businesses from governmental interference, kept the taxes of the elite at low levels, and resulted in the social and cultural dereliction of the city. At the time, however, it was viewed as a valid tradeoff by both sides. As a result, the working class relied on their own ethnic and labor organizations to provide for their welfare.[27]

This system of accommodation by the Republican party in Pittsburgh became formalized with the establishment of the Magee-Flinn machine in 1879. The two men, Christopher Magee and William Flinn, were in many respects the prototype of the new professional machine politicians of the late nineteenth century. Magee had served as city treasurer in the 1870s, during which time he became adept at controlling the expanding administrative functions of the city. He and Flinn, a traction magnate, then secured control of the common council and used that control to dominate the city's political system during the next two decades. The key to Magee's control in the city was his manipulation of patronage in working-class and ethnic districts. It is difficult, however, to know just whose interests Magee and Flinn were serving. On the one hand, older upper-class groups vilified the machine and its deleterious influence on the old system. On the other, organized labor also criticized the machine for distracting workers from their true interests.[28]

Without question, influence and control are exercised in many subtle ways that are as important to recognize as they are difficult to document. The Magee-Flinn machine was a curious hybrid that escapes simple categorization. Magee, despite the fact that certain members of upper-class groups heaped scorn on him in the city's newspapers, was nonetheless a marginal member of the city's upper class and was, in fact, an iron mill owner during part of this period. Further, he was a close friend of a number of old-line iron and steel men, particularly Henry W. Oliver. Despite these ties, and their Republican party affiliation, Magee and Flinn were remarkably proficient in attracting immigrant workers, saloon keepers, and small businessmen to their ranks. Their machine developed particularly close ties with traction enterprises and with banks that held public deposits. The machine's basic strategy was to run candidates for ward office who reflected the social and cultural background of that area, while running elite candidates for citywide offices.[29]

Despite the electoral success of the Magee-Flinn machine, a number of problems began plaguing both working-class and elite supporters during the late nineteenth century. The working class became most enraged over the unequal dispersion of city services.[30] Early in the century the city had established the principle that those who benefited from city services, such as water, paving, and sanitation should pay for them through special assessments. The result of this system was that poorer neighborhoods were significantly less well maintained than their wealthier counterparts. As a consequence, public health in the poorer working-class areas suffered terribly. Pittsburgh in the 1880s had the highest death rate from typhoid fever of any city in the country, and the incidence of the disease was disproportionately high in working-class wards.[31]

Ironically, perhaps, representatives of the working class were less concerned by these threats to the health of their constituents than by some blatantly unfair arrangements for paving suburban streets that emerged in the late nineteenth century. When the paving of streets depended on the ability or willingness of the property owner to pay an assessment for these services, the improvement of the streets in working-class wards lagged well behind that of more affluent areas. Pittsburgh's workers, however, did not seem to be very concerned about this. What did enrage them was when the city's upper class tried to change the system, proposing to have the entire city pay for street improvements made in the East End suburbs. Since the steel magnates lived on huge estates in this new area, the per-frontage-foot basis for assessing improvements would have cost them dearly to build the road infrastructure in the sprawling new suburbs. As a result, a "prominent and public-spirited citizen" proposed that the city sell bonds to cover these costs, and the city council agreed. The law was ultimately declared unconstitutional, but National Labor Tribune responded with a rage seldom directed at non–trade union issues, proclaiming, "Every poor man's lot and house is taxed to pay this great debt. His labor is taxed. His wages are attached before they are earned and for years to come."[32] Issues such as this began to erode working-class faith in the system of machine politics in Pittsburgh.

Members of the elite community were also becoming concerned. Poverty relief had traditionally been used as a form of social control in early nineteenth-century Pittsburgh. Cecelia F. Bucki, in her study of poor relief during this time, concluded, "The relief systems discussed . . . reveal much about interclass hostility and attempts at control . . . of one class over the other." She suggested, "Members of the benevolent class found it necessary to differentiate between the worthy poor and unworthy poor and conclude that poverty was a moral, not an economic, issue."[33] This procedure, however, had declined greatly by the late nineteenth century. The wealthy by then were particularly bothered by the actions of the aldermanic courts, which also reduced the power of the elite to enforce certain standards of morality in the urban ghettos. Thus, as the pathology of urban life grew in Pittsburgh's slums during the years after the Civil War, the elite sought answers to these problems.

The Western Pennsylvania Humane Society was formed in 1874 and given police powers by the state in 1877 to enable it to intervene in the child-rearing practices of families. The society, however, had to compete with the alderman for adjudication of cases, and invariably their attitudes diverged widely. In 1875, the Pittsburgh Association for the Improvement of the Poor (PAIP) was established. Louise Herron, founder of the PAIP, left no doubt where her sympathies lay, stating that it was necessary for the society to investigate the circumstances of "those who might be innocent sufferers [of poverty] or to deal harshly with imposters."[34] The boards of directors of both agencies were staffed overwhelmingly by the industrial, commercial, and professional elites of Pittsburgh and Allegheny.[35] Unlike their elite counterparts in the early nineteenth century, however, these directors did not visit the poor themselves but depended on hired agents to carry out their wishes.[36] As Bucki has noted, "At the same time as the distance between classes increased, the upper class showed an increasing interest in imposing their standards and morals upon an unruly, immoral and increasingly militant working class."[37]

By the 1890s, then, a strong feeling had evolved among the elite that it would be necessary to systematize social welfare activities in Pittsburgh and eliminate what they viewed as the baleful influence of the aldermanic courts. At the same time, it was necessary also to appeal to the real felt needs of the working class in the city, at least to promise them that something would be done about the horrid social conditions in the city. Simple pleas to morality and rectitude would no longer be sufficient in heterogeneous, industrial Pittsburgh. The days of blatant Scots-Irish hegemony were gone. Future reform would have to address the very real issues of poverty, social pathology, and disgraceful living conditions that had come to characterize the fate of so many of the city's workers.

Thus was born the great ferment of progressivism in Pittsburgh. Dissatisfied with the way in which the city was run, and particularly with the nature of machine politics, elite reformers began pushing for the centralization of decision making, the greater involvement of experts and professionals in the affairs of the city, and an end to the particularistic focus of the Magee-Flinn machine. Most especially, *The Pittsburgh Survey* wanted to get rid of the aldermen and their courts, which, it claimed, were corrupt and took advantage of new immigrants. Who were these new reformers? And what was their general position in the economic, social, and political life of the city?

The first two reformers to emerge to challenge the Magee-Flinn machine were Oliver McClintock and George W. Guthrie. Both were impeccable members of Pittsburgh's Core upper class who were married to iron and steel families, and McClintock's family also owned iron mills in the nineteenth century. These two men, though, were just the tip of the iceberg. The real key to reform was an Episcopalian minister and his congregation, along with a number of powerful civic organizations (the Civic Club, the Voters' League), the Pittsburgh Chamber of Commerce, and the Pittsburgh Board of Trade.

Samuel P. Hays has studied the Civic Club and Voters' League with an eye to their social configuration, subjecting the 645 members of these two organizations to an intensive analysis.[38] He points out that the preponderance of these members were from the city's upper class, 65 percent listed in various elite directories. He does note, however, "Few came from earlier industrial and mercantile families. Most of them had risen to social position from wealth created after 1870 in the iron, steel, electrical equipment and other industries."[39] Nevertheless, bankers and corporate officials and their wives comprised 52 percent of the reformers. This included, Hays notes, not only officials of Carnegie Steel, American Bridge, National Tube, and Jones & Laughlin but also executives of such "lesser steel companies" as Crucible, Pittsburgh, Superior, Lockhart, and H. K. Porter.[40] These groups, Hays points out, were interested in the rationalization of institutions and decision making in modern life, in which they particularly wished to push the level of control up from the ward to the city, the metropolis, the county, and even the state.

Hays's conclusions, I think, are somewhat misleading. Although it is quite clear that he found an industrial, as opposed to a mercantile, elite among these club members, it seems apparent to me that most of these men and women were from families who were part of the city's pre–Civil War upper class. My own analysis of the Civic Club membership shows that forty iron and steel families held memberships. Of these, eighteen were pre–Civil War iron and steel families and another seven were from other pre–Civil War elite families. Thus, of the iron and steel families involved in the Civic Club, over 60 percent were from older rather than newer families. A social analysis of the families as to class status reveals a similar pattern. Of the forty families, twenty-one were Core upper-class and another eight Non-Core upper-class families, generally the oldest and most distinguished in the city. Just over one-quarter were from the newer and less socially prestigious families. Broadening our focus somewhat, an analysis of the membership of the Civic Club in 1912 reveals that 175 (23 percent) of its members were from our iron and steel families or were married into them. Extending the analysis one more step, we find that 318 (42 percent) were included in the city's *Social Register*. Since the Civic Club did not practice closure, that is, anyone who wished to belong and was willing to pay the moderate dues was able to join, the high percentage in such a prestigious social directory is remarkable. As I have noted earlier, a large proportion of the families listed in *The Social Register* were old money. Even more important, as we shall see, the leadership of this and other reform organizations was composed of men and families who were intricately networked into the older upper class. The political scientist Peter H. Rossi has viewed this as a common pattern in city politics: "As the industrial elite withdrew from local politics as political office holders, the private sector developed as the sphere over which they could exercise control."[41]

The roots of the elite reform coalition, however, went deeper than the Civic Club and Voters' League. By all accounts, the earliest lynchpin of progressive reform in Pittsburgh was the Calvary Episcopal Church under the leadership of the Reverend George Hodges. Hodges headed Calvary for just five years, from 1889 to 1894, but, as his biographer has stated: "The Pittsburgh of today, with its park systems and civic center, owes much to the influence of George Hodges and his ringing messages. He gave Pittsburgh a great vision."[42] A follower of the Social Gospel program, Hodges was so successful at inspiring his congregation in the path of reform that politicians referred to them as "The D—— Calvary Crowd." The men who emerged as reform leaders among Calvary's congregation were George W. Guthrie, Henry D. W. English, James W. Brown, H. Kirke Porter, and Judge Joseph Buffington.

The Calvary Church was located in Pittsburgh's burgeoning East End, a new elite area, and throughout Hodges's ministry there he preached about the importance of building a bridge between the privileged East End and "Popular Alley" in the poorer section. To spread his word even further, every Monday morning his sermons were printed in the *Pittsburgh Dispatch*.[43] On the surface, at least, it might appear that the men and women of Calvary Church might represent precisely the new elite that Hays was talking about. After all, the older Pittsburgh aristocracy was Presbyterian and had either lived close to their mills along the riverbanks or in mansions in the city of Allegheny, on the other side of the Allegheny River. That conclusion, however, ignores some important transformations occurring in Pittsburgh's elite community in the late nineteenth century.

The area that was to become the East End was annexed by the City of Pittsburgh in 1868. It remained a rather isolated rural retreat, however, until the building of a streetcar line out Fifth Avenue in the late 1870s, followed in the 1880s by cable cars for the steep inclines. From the middle of the 1880s onward, a large number of palatial homes were built in the area, and Fifth Avenue, from Neville Street through the Shadyside area, became a vast and opulent millionaire's row. This, of course, might be taken as evidence that this was where Pittsburgh's new money was settling, but evidence indicates otherwise. A study of Shadyside, an important component of the East End, sheds some light on the situation. Renee Reitman examined 110 families in the area, and my calculation of her findings indicates that about 42 percent of them were new money, while 38 percent came from inherited wealth. Another 20 percent were professionals, most of whom had at least comfortable origins.[44] They were, as Hays suggested about members of the Civic Club and Voters' League, men who were in the very cockpit of Pittsburgh's industrialization, at least 40 percent of them involved in the iron and steel industry and nearly all the rest, except the professionals, in some other kind of industrial endeavor. Many of the merchants, for example, were either coal or iron merchants or were involved in shipping those materials. It is clear that this was an industrial elite, but since Reitman found a rather large amount of new money there, it is possible that they represent a group of new entrants on the social scene in Pittsburgh. Examination of a couple of other studies, however, belies that notion.

Joseph Rishel made a study of founding families of Allegheny County in which he found that when they began moving from their traditional residences on Penn Avenue in downtown Pittsburgh, the largest number moved to the East End.[45] These were among the oldest and most prestigious families in the city. Further, we find that the greater number of our iron and steel families also moved to the East End by the early twentieth century and that 83 percent of these families were listed in the city's *Social Register*.[46]

Evidence supports the conclusion that the East End was an area designed to integrate the newer and older elites. Although my analysis of iron and steel families indicates that only about a quarter of those in the East End were new money, it was nonetheless somewhat more open to the penetration of newer groups than were the older upper-class neighborhoods in Allegheny, about 95 percent of whose elite inhabitants were listed in *The Social Register*. The leaders of this new suburban culture, though, were younger members of older upper-class families. A new aristocracy was being created in the East End, one that not only brought in the most acceptable members of the newer elite families but also created a new social, cultural, and political culture for the city's upper class. In his analysis Francis Couvares has sensitively developed the process by which that took place.[47]

Couvares points out that when Pittsburgh's social elite moved to the East End, they not only changed residence but also profoundly changed their way of life. They went from a highly circumscribed Victorian life-style to a freer, more cosmopolitan, and more open pattern of living. He compares the new life-style to the dour provinciality of Pittsburgh's nineteenth-century iron elite, for whom luxury was a sin and recreation only a distraction from their proper business and religious pursuits. When younger members of the aristocratic iron and steel families moved to the East End, though, they "found escape not only from the vicious, but also from the confinement of their own narrow virtue." They built larger, more palatial homes, began giving lavish parties, and created a whole new suburban style in the area. This way of life brought with it a whole new point of view, what Couvares calls an official elite culture.[48] This culture not only stressed a stronger sense of class identity, with the creation of a panoply of social clubs and other organizations, but also wished to reach out to control the broader city, to reshape it in accordance with a newly emergent image of what Pittsburgh should be like. No longer sequestered in the dark, narrow homes of Allegheny, the young generation of Pittsburgh's iron and steel elite wanted to create a glittering jewel of a city. Many of these individuals had attended college in eastern cities, where their children were attending prep school. They were tired of apologizing for the dark, dirty, disreputable city in which they lived. Pittsburgh had to be remade in the image of the bright, open, and spacious East End.

Part of this transformation of Pittsburgh elite culture at the turn of the century coincided with the emergence of Episcopalianism. The Pittsburgh iron and steel elite, as noted earlier, had been traditionally Presbyterian. But as they developed a suburban elite culture in the East End, conversion to Episcopalianism, which became virtually a generic upper-class religion in America in the twentieth century, gained increasing popularity. Again, many of the members of these families attended Episcopal prep schools, which probably started the transformation. One clearly sees this conversion in a couple of studies. Among Rishel's founding families, just 13 percent were Episcopalian in 1820, but by 1900, 27 percent were members of that denomination.[49] Our iron and steel families showed a similar metamorphosis. The increasing number of Episcopalians among that group was not due to the introduction of new families but to a generational religious upheaval among the older families. Key elements of the new Episcopalianism in Pittsburgh were Calvary Church and George Hodges in the East End.

Hodges, along with several of his elite communicants, took a number of steps in the early 1890s that provided the impetus for broader reform movements in the early twentieth century. This was all part of a plan to systematize the social welfare process in the city. This was an area that Pittsburgh's upper classes (and those in other cities) had long used as a means of social control. Hodges, the Civic Club, and younger members of the upper class all wished to end earlier poor relief methods as representing "older traditions of paternalism, parochialism, and amateurism out of touch with any 'modernizing movements.'"[50] The Chamber of Commerce also supported Hodges and the Civic Club in this endeavor, establishing a special committee on charities chaired by Oliver McClintock.

The Civic Improvement Commission (usually simply called the Civic Commission) was established by Mayor George W. Guthrie to create a uniform approach to the problem of reform. Like the Civic Club, it was generally a bastion of influence for the older upper classes. Chairman of the commission was H. D. W. English, and members of the Black, Donnell, and Heinz families also served as officers. The commission was given broad powers to "plan and promote improvements in civic and industrial conditions which affect the health, convenience, education and general welfare of the Pittsburgh industrial district. . . ."[51] One of Hodges's most important steps in this regard was the establishment of Kingsley House, a settlement house modeled on similar establishments in England and America. In 1893 Hodges contacted Robert A. Woods, a former Pittsburgher who ran Andover House in Boston, to help him establish a similar concern. Getting financial support from wealthy members of his own congregation, he later received substantial contributions from affluent older Pittsburgh families in the Presbyterian churches.[52] Kingsley House, according to Roy Lubove, embodied two key aspects of the national settlement movement: religious idealism and dependence upon the social elite for funding and support.[53] It set up public playgrounds; public bathhouses; resident nursing services; a library and reading room; manual training and industrial work for boys; classes in housekeeping, sewing, and so forth, for girls; and a number of other services for the iron, steel, glass, and cork workers in the area in which it was located.[54]

Although Hodges was the important religious force behind Kingsley House, H. D. W. English was head of the lay organization and the single most important influence for reform on the Pittsburgh scene. English was a member of an older Blair County family and son of a Baptist minister who moved to Pittsburgh in 1871. English, then, was of genteel but nonaffluent origin. He soon began to network himself into Pittsburgh's older upper classes. After working for a newspaper on his arrival in Pittsburgh, English entered the life insurance business. Soon, he set up his own agency, which became one of the largest and most successful in the city. Of great importance for his rise was his marriage to Jennie Sellers (McLean), a member of Pittsburgh's upper class. English also joined the prestigious Duquesne and Union clubs (although not the more eminent Pittsburgh or Pittsburgh Golf clubs) and changed his allegiance to the tonier Calvary Episcopal church. He was listed in the 1912 *Social Register*. In the early twentieth century, English became a director of U.S. Glass and South Side Trust and served as a director and member of the executive committee of Crucible Steel. English's most important activities, however, were with the Chamber of Commerce and a range of civic and political organizations. He became the point man for the older upper-class groups in the Progressive reform surge of the early twentieth century.[55] In addition to the Chamber of Commerce, English also served as president of the Civic Commission and the Kingsley House settlement and, as such, "as much as any individual cemented the link between the business-professional elite and civic reform in Pittsburgh."[56] It was English, in fact, along with the Chamber of Commerce and Civic Club, who raised the money to bring the Charities and Commons group to Pittsburgh to make the *Survey.*[57]

This phalanx of elite forces, spearheaded by English, began to have an impact on the political scene in the early twentieth century. Despite the dissatisfaction of the wealthy with the machine and the system of politics that had emerged by the late nineteenth century, it was difficult to energize a following until the death of Christopher

Magee in 1901. Lincoln Steffens had called the Magee-Flinn machine the worst of all the urban machines but understood well the complex attraction that Chris Magee held for the city: "I have seen Pittsburghers grow black in the face denouncing his ring, but when I asked, 'What kind of man was Magee?' They would cool and say, 'Chris? Chris was one of the best men God ever made.' "[58] Whatever ability the Magee-Flinn machine had to charm Pittsburgh upper-class groups died along with Magee in 1901. As a result new reform or progressive political movements began springing up.

The first major reform actually occurred just before Magee's death, the result of a compromise worked out by the Pittsburgh machine, Matthew S. Quay's state machine, and the demands of elite reformers. It involved the passage of a new city charter, one that furthered some of the reformer's interests but maintained the power of the machine at the ward level. This charter reform greatly increased the mayor's power, giving him administrative authority over departments, and reduced the power of Select and Common councilmen, although they were still elected on a ward basis. The aldermanic courts were also left intact.

In 1906 the reformers were able to secure the election of George W. Guthrie, a member of the "Calvary crowd," as mayor. A short time later, another Calvary vestryman, James W. Brown, member of one of Pittsburgh's oldest iron and steel families, was elected to Congress. But the greatest single reform event in Pittsburgh was the invitation of the Charities and Commons group to undertake the sensational *Pittsburgh Survey* in 1907 and 1908. English, Buffington, and Guthrie, along with William H. Matthews, head worker at Kingsley House, were the key factors in getting the Survey started, supported by donations from the Civic Club, Henry J. Heinz, and the steel men Wallace Rowe and Benjamin Thaw. Kingsley House became the base for investigators of *The Pittsburgh Survey*, and John Fitch stayed there while preparing his *The Steelworkers* for the *Survey*. Although the *Survey* has been viewed as an attack on Pittsburgh's wealthy, it was, in fact, strongly supported by the city's older elite, especially members of the independent iron and steel mill families.

The Pittsburgh Survey attacked a number of evils in Pittsburgh; one of its principal targets was the political system. Robert A. Woods, one of the *Survey*'s organizers, warned in 1909 that the recent amalgamation of Pittsburgh and Allegheny would create problems for reformers and cited the Pittsburgh Chamber of Commerce, which was headed by English, as the kind of community movement needed to meet the needs of the new metropolitan community.[59] English, addressing the same group, stressed that the city should follow the lead of its business leaders, advising, "The consideration of great numbers of civic questions necessary to the economy of operation, reduction of water waste, etc. can be solved much more readily, much more intelligently, by a body of business men. . . ."[60] More than anything else, English and the Chamber wanted profound structural reform of Pittsburgh's political system. To this end, Mayor Guthrie set up the Civic Improvement Commission, with English as chairman. That organization listed as its purpose "to plan and promote improvements in civic and industrial conditions which affect the health, convenience, education, and general welfare of the Pittsburgh industrial district. . . ."[61] These problems were to be tackled on a broad canvas, but English, as head of the Chamber, as well as the Civic Commission, left no doubt that political reform was paramount.

The Chamber, in alliance with the Pittsburgh Board of Trade, the Civic Club, the Civic Commission, and the National Municipal League, spearheaded political reform in Pittsburgh, establishing what they called the "Pittsburgh Plan."[62] Under the old system of government, Pittsburgh was governed by a mayor and a bicameral council divided into two branches. The councilmen were elected by wards, each of the twenty-seven wards electing one Common councilman and one Select councilman, plus additional Common councilmen for additional population. Although the Chamber and other Pittsburgh elite groups complained about the extent of corruption within this system, it is also true that it gave the people—workers and lower-income individuals—greater voice in the affairs of the city.

In 1911, a new system was established. Under this new charter, reformers were able to effect the abolition of ward election of councilmen and school boards, while a new, citywide tax system was established. This ensured a diminution of working-class representation on the board and an increase in the number of elite or professional members of the body. A similar change took place on the school board, whereby ward-based school boards were replaced by a citywide board with members elected at large. As a result of these changes, the city council and the school board came to be dominated by members of the upper class, the advanced professional men, and the larger business groups.[63] Although this appears to be a rather crass attack on the principle of democracy and working-class power, reformers were able to sell the package as being in the interests of all the people. The older upper class evidently relied on their prestige, their lineage, and their deep roots in the community to give a greater authenticity to the movement and its curious reform ideology.

The political situation in Pittsburgh differed in some respects from that in other cities. In Birmingham, for example, the economic elite appeared to have little interest in retarding the development of citywide services such as schools, street paving, and sanitation, which had often been opposed by Pittsburgh's elite. In Birmingham, though, the iron and steel elites did work successfully to stop the passage of various kinds of government regulations that they thought would retard the growth of their business enterprises.[64] There is no clear sense in Birmingham that the Progressive Era effected significant change in the political patterns there, nor did it appear to give increased power to an economic elite, whether old or new.

Ronald Edsforth's study of Flint, Michigan, also exhibits some similarities to and differences from the situation in Pittsburgh. There, Edsforth found that the business class used paternalistic welfare capitalism and domination of a number of important civic organizations, and of the political process itself, to exercise powerful control of the city government and the workers' lives during this period. In most respects that would appear to conform to the Pittsburgh model, except that in the Flint instance it was an absentee corporation, General Motors, rather than the old localistic upper class, that was doing the controlling.[65] Whether Pittsburgh was unique is difficult to determine at this point, but it seems clear that political reform in Pittsburgh was just one part of a broad program by the older upper class to extend their dominion over the city. The creation of an agenda of cultural philanthropy was another part.

The Use of Cultural Philanthropy

There has long been a recognition that upper-class families have created new cultural institutions in the city as a means of social dominance and control. Studies of cultural philanthropy in Chicago, Boston, and New York, for example, have demonstrated the extent to which these programs were dominated by the economic elite and reflected attempts to impose a certain set of upper-class values and traditions on the rest of the populace. It was part, in Kathleen McCarthy's words, of a system of noblesse oblige designed to create a better society, and one that reflected the values of the dominant class.[66]

The situation in Pittsburgh, however, has been confused by the controversial and overweening presence of Andrew Carnegie. Francis Couvares, in his provocative study of Pittsburgh, asserts that the city's elite attempted to gain control of the culture and values of the city's working class through the establishment of a vast array of cultural benefactions intended to secure their dominance. The city's masses, according to Couvares, reacted indignantly, and the attempt by a set of American plutocrats to control the lives and thoughts of America's steelworkers was a failure. Thus, the use of philanthropy as a means of social control in Pittsburgh was largely unsuccessful.[67] That conclusion, however, ignores the very real success of other Pittsburgh iron and steel families. Although one cannot determine whether they did, in fact, lead to social control, it is clear that they were accepted with much gratitude. A comparison of the relative success of Carnegie with the benefactions of Henry Clay Frick and others is enlightening.

It is imperative to recognize that Andrew Carnegie was always an outsider to the Pittsburgh social scene, a man never fully accepted by that city's social upper class, even while fawned on by the nation's journalists. Carnegie had begun his major campaign of cultural philanthropy with his famous donation of libraries to Pittsburgh and to cities around the world. These donations did not excite the admiration of either the city's workers or its older upper class. The upper class, workers, and local journalists often heaped scorn on Carnegie when he gave libraries or other benefactions to the city. An example of this occurred in 1892, even before the Homestead lockout, when Arthur G. Burgoyne, one of the city's leading journalists, published a poem about Carnegie that ended in the following manner:

> On public libraries he spent
>   Of shekels not a few;
> A goodly slice to Pittsburgh went
>   And to Allegheny too;
> But still the loss he doesn't feel,
>   It cannot hurt his health,
> For his mills keep on with endless zeal
>   A-piling up the wealth.[68]

When Carnegie donated a library to Braddock, a local steelworker commented, "Carnegie builds libraries for the working men, but what good are libraries to me, working practically eighteen hours a day." In the thirty-three years that Carnegie donated libraries, 225 communities turned him down. As Paul Krause notes, this negative sentiment was especially strong in Pennsylvania, where twenty of the forty-six towns Carnegie solicited said "No."[69]

An important turning point for Pittsburgh came with the erection of the massive Carnegie complex in Oakland in the late 1890s. Carnegie was not old money and was not much liked by most of the older elite, but they did know a good thing when they saw it. The complex contained a music hall, library, museum, and art institute and was designed to pull Pittsburgh out of the sink of provincialism in which it had existed, bringing forth the new cosmopolitanism that the East Enders were so desirous of creating. So the aristocracy muted its criticism of this venture—after all, the complex would do much to fulfill their ideals of providing high culture to the city's masses. But that did little to create much enthusiasm for the Carnegie Complex in the rest of the city. Margaret Byington in her book on Homestead's mill workers summarized their feeling about Carnegie's philanthropies: "They resent a philanthropy which provides opportunities for intellectual and social advancement while it withholds conditions which make it possible to take advantage of them."[70] Although Pittsburgh's older families held their criticism of this benefaction, old-monied elite in other cities did not. Richard T. Crane, scion of the massive plumbing manufacturing empire in Chicago, was scathing in his attack on Carnegie and his method of philanthropy, referring to him as "the Dr. Jekyll of library building, and the Mr. Hyde of Homestead rioting and destruction."[71] Undoubtedly, many members of Pittsburgh's old upper-class families agreed.

Thus, to base the presumed failure of the Pittsburgh upper class to continue social and cultural dominance in the city on the rejection of Carnegie is misplaced. The people might take Carnegie's money, but, whether working class or elite, they would never accept his control or conditions. To understand the success of cultural benefactions it is better to look at the fate of those by Henry Clay Frick and other old-money Pittsburghers. Frick was not personally loved in Pittsburgh. By all accounts, he was a cold, difficult man and was widely disliked. Many looked on him as "an old curmudgeon, with a chunk of iron for a heart."[72] He was also personally held more responsible for the bloodshed at Homestead than Carnegie. But there was one critical difference: Frick was from an old, established family in western Pennsylvania and, even more important, had married into the eminent Childs family in Pittsburgh. Thus, unlike Carnegie, Frick was an impeccable member of the city's Core upper class and possibly as a result of that status did not experience the same negative responses to his philanthropies. Over the years, Frick was a major benefactor of many concerns in the city, providing much of the financing and support for Kingsley House.[73] He also gave money to hospitals, universities, and other institutions and provided a great deal of support to a number of projects for children in the city.[74] All of this, of course, was presented as pure altruism, but as Barbara J. Howe has commented: "When the rich had an opportunity to determine who would receive and who would not, they had the perfect chance to set forth the required standards for behavior for assistance."[75]

Frick's most public, and potentially most controversial, benefaction was the donation of 150 acres of land to the city in 1908, to be used for a park. His conditions for use contained all the features that caused trouble for other givers: the park was to be left relatively undeveloped and was not to be used for the organized leisure activities of the working classes. It was, in a word, a largely upper-class and middle-class preserve in the eastern end of the city where much of the elite had relocated. To run the park, Frick gave $2 million and required the establishment of a board of trustees to be controlled by the family and other members of the older upper class. Yet, a student of this benefaction indicates that public opinion was apparently largely in favor of the plan to leave Frick park undeveloped, and the benefaction incited little or no controversy. Nor did other gifts from upper class families.[76]

Frick was hardly Pittsburgh's only upper-class benefactor. Henry W. Oliver assisted in the building of the Nixon Theater, and Joseph Horne, department store owner, Core upper-class member, and connected by marriage to old iron and steel families, helped erect two downtown theaters. Schenley Park, a vast inner-city green space, was also donated by an old upper-class family.[77] Other older iron and steel families who gave significant benefactions to the city were B. F. Jones and William Thaw, along with H. J. Heinz and Andrew Mellon from other upper-class families, and Henry Phipps and Charles Schwab from the Carnegie group. Wealthy members of Pittsburgh's upper classes also set up the Buhl, Mellon, and Heinz foundations, which became powerful factors in the social and cultural life of the city. In fact, if one stands in the Oakland section of Pittsburgh and looks around, one sees overwhelming evidence of the philanthropic nature of Pittsburgh's older elite. Building after building bears the name of one of the city's industrial barons. And none created any particularly negative reaction. All of this, as mentioned, was part of a broader phenomenon in American life at the turn of the century:

the use of cultural philanthropy by the older upper classes to help them to control or influence their environment.

U.S. Steel and Absentee Capitalism

What about the main villain in all of this, U.S. Steel, the giant absentee corporation that was creating all of Pittsburgh's problems according to *The Survey?* It seems to have been largely a chimera in Pittsburgh. Although U.S. Steel controlled some large mills, both in the city proper and in the outlying mill towns, Pittsburgh's older elite retained control of most of their independent mills. Further, they continued to play a prominent part in the political, social, and cultural realms of the city. Even in those areas where the control of large corporations seemed most complete, there was a strong continuing influence of the older upper class. This can perhaps be seen most graphically in the mill towns that ringed the city. According to John Fitch and others, in these locales large steel companies were commonly understood to be the dominant political force. According to most accounts, none was more totally dominated by the huge steel corporation than the town of Duquesne, where the massive Carnegie Steel plant of U.S. Steel was located. In 1919, when union organizers tried to get a permit to hold a rally there, Mayor James C. Crawford refused them a permit, saying, "Jesus Christ himself couldn't hold a meeting in Duquesne." This was cited by Fitch and other contemporary observers as a perfect example of the overwhelming power and control of the steel corporation in the town.[78] It is not clear just why Crawford refused to grant the permit, but two points are abundantly evident: Crawford was indisputably a member of an older upper-class iron and steel family (his brother, Edward R. Crawford, was president of McKeesport Tin Plate Company), and he was an old and bitter foe of the Carnegie mill and its executives.

The Crawford family had moved to the Pittsburgh area in 1794 and became one of the earliest landed gentry families in the McKeesport region. Almost a century after the family had arrived the area was still largely rural, and the Crawford family remained a dominant factor there. With the building of Allegheny Bessemer Steel, which was taken over by Carnegie in 1889, a powerful new influence was introduced. Carnegie's goal was to build housing around the mill and run the whole area as a private fiefdom in order better to control the workers. Several of the local gentry, including two of the Crawfords, objected and petitioned the state to incorporate Duquesne as a borough. They were successful in this move, and in the first elections, held in 1890, James C. Crawford, Sr., was designated judge of elections. As the historian of the affair concluded: "This marked the beginning of Crawford power in Duquesne and the origin of the struggle between the two political groups—one representing the interest of Carnegie Steel Company and the other representing the interests of the Crawford family."[79]

Members of the Crawford family won elections to council, with John W. Crawford as burgess, and began creating an economic and political empire. The three Crawford brothers opened the First National Bank of Duquesne, the first bank in the town, and Edward Crawford, known as the "Tin Plate King" in later years, founded McKeesport Tin Plate in nearby McKeesport. In response, the Carnegie group formed a rival state-related bank—Duquesne Trust—and accused the Crawfords of machine politics. They pressed for the Carnegie Steel workers living in Duquesne to vote the Crawfords out of office and used the rhetoric of Progressive reform during elections in the early twentieth century. The split between the two groups continued into the 1930s, so much so that Harvey O'Connor, in his *Steel-Dictator*, said of the situation, "There are two cliques in town, Crawford and the First National, and then the Duquesne Trust Company crowd."[80]

The lesson here, it seems to me, is that even in situations where it seems as if the power of U.S. Steel and the other giant absentee firms is overwhelming and that upper-class family influence has been destroyed, appearances are often deceiving. As Karen Cowles comments: "The Crawfords were an old, conservative, landed family. . . . The anti-Crawford group consisted of men who were individually mobile . . . and rose to prominence with the Carnegie Steel Company."[81] If Duquesne was a closed town, it was news to Carnegie Steel, and it certainly had not been closed by them. In virtually every sphere of Pittsburgh's life in the early twentieth century, the city's older upper class continued to play a strong, and often dominant, role.

Pittsburgh's older upper class, it appears, were playing a precarious game around the turn of the century. Faced with massive challenges in the form of the rise of giant national corporations in the steel industry, of a powerful working-class culture, and of a heterogeneous population of immigrants from southern and eastern Europe, they demonstrated remarkable persistence. In the economic sphere they survived by finding market niches, areas where they could continue to run their businesses much as they had for over half a century. Similarly, in social, political, and cultural affairs, they presented themselves as the best men, as the saviors of the city. Using *The Pittsburgh Survey* as their instrument, they blamed Pittsburgh's problems on U.S. Steel and other large absentee corporations. Despite the fact that most of the city's problems stemmed from the days when the old elite were indisputably in control of the reins of power, they were nonetheless able to use the press and professional social welfare agencies to shift the blame to outsiders. Then, having identified the villain, these agencies agreed on the proper sort of leaders needed to restore a sense of community. In this the old elite also became niche marketers. Not part of the hated New York plutocracy, the old elite understood Pittsburgh and its problems. They were, they argued, part of a value system shared by the city's workers. And they were important industrialists in their own right, not part of the idle rich or a leisured class. These were men who continued to run many of Pittsburgh's oldest and most revered economic institutions. In large measure, Pittsburgh's citizens bought this argument and entrusted the old elite with its future, and that was perhaps a mistake. However great the promises at the turn of the century, elite-dominated reform failed to achieve much in the way of real social change. A little was done, to be sure, but by the eve of World War II Pittsburgh still had most of the health, housing, and poverty problems that had plagued the city a half-century before. As Herrick Chapman has noted: "Pittsburgh's elite used municipal reform to strengthen political control in the city, but it was not until the Pittsburgh Renaissance that a new generation of business leaders used their power to reshape the city itself."[82]

Conclusion

"When an epoch is closed, the following epoch is not generous, or even just, to it. What it achieved is taken for granted; what it failed to do is the outstanding and irritating fact."

John Dewey, quoted in John Patrick Diggins, *The Proud Decades: America in War and Peace, 1941–1960*

As war clouds gathered in Europe in 1939, the glory days of the independent Pittsburgh iron and steel masters were past. Only a relatively few mills remained in the city and its environs, and some of those would pass into oblivion in the decades after World War II. It was easy to forget them, and to ignore their very real accomplishments, since even when they had made up the bulk of iron- and steel-making capacity in the region in the early twentieth century they were overshadowed by U.S. Steel and the giant steel combines. But, as this study has attempted to demonstrate, they formed the core of Pittsburgh's industrial economy for nearly a century and were far more characteristic of the region's business environment than the more famous steel giants. What gave these independent iron and steel firms their durability and importance?

Much of the reason for the continuing influence and power of Pittsburgh iron and steel manufacturers on the economic, social, and political levels was rooted in the topography and spatial configuration of the city and surrounding area. Pittsburgh, unlike many cities in the nation's industrial heartland, was riven with rivers, valleys, and mountains. Squeezed into a narrow triangle by its rivers, Pittsburgh could only expand to the east and, during the early years, only as far as the steep slopes of Grant's Hill. Those who went beyond those barriers entered what remained fairly remote, inaccessible regions that were, nonetheless, a short distance from the city center. Thus, Pittsburgh's population became in some ways more dispersed than in other cities yet, at the same time, more mixed and more closely knit than elsewhere. This, as we shall see, had a dramatic impact on the city's people and their relationship to the elite. In addition, this same topography, while inspiring Pittsburgh to become one of the earliest industrial cities in America, also constrained its industries to smaller areas, allowing a higher degree of economic decentralization for a longer period.

During the early years of Pittsburgh's industrialization, the city's iron and steel mills clustered along the riverbanks, on which they were dependent for transportation. Hemmed in not only by rivers and hills but also by residences and commercial establishments, these locations had no room for giant mills. Even as late as 1880, Andrew Carnegie's Edgar Thomson Works was the only truly large establishment in Allegheny County, and with its fifteen hundred employees, it was located some distance from the city itself. Most mills in the city and the immediately outlying areas remained fairly small, seldom employing more than a few hundred hands and often operating more as a congeries of small shops than as large integrated enterprises. In these mills, skilled craftsmen continued to direct the labor of up to a dozen workers with relatively little direct interference from the owners. These owners retained a strong sense of dominion over their enterprises—a dominion understood and recognized by all, but one strictly limited by tradition and economic and technological necessity.

Most analysts of the city's iron and steel industry are pretty much in agreement on the nature of the situation until the 1890s. Then, however, many posit the overwhelming influence of what is often termed the "second industrial revolution." During this revolution, so the story goes, Pittsburgh's steel firms escaped the confines of the city's topography by relocating their plants in a large number of mill towns in places like Aliquippa, Braddock, Homestead, Clairton, Duquesne, and Monessen. In these new environments they secured thousands of acres of cheap undeveloped real estate, on which they erected massive mills employing thousands of workers. These workers, in turn, clustered in housing around the mill owned by the company, while the managers and officials lived in their own suburban enclaves, located miles from the smoke and noise of the mill and from the dilapidated housing of their workers. Land use had become specialized, residential living patterns had become divided by class, and the ownership and policy decisions of the massive new corporations themselves had shifted to boardrooms on Wall Street, while operating decisions were made by professional managers from central offices located in downtown Pittsburgh. There is, of course, some truth to this picture, but it is at best half-truth.[1]

There is no doubt that some aspects of the second industrial revolution occurred in Pittsburgh, but it was never as complete nor as rapid as most commentators would have us believe. Kenneth Warren, in his geographical analysis of America's steel industry, makes the point that even in the great valleys of the Allegheny and Ohio rivers, development of iron and steel facilities was rather slow and small scale. Whereas Montgomery and others talked of sites of thousands of acres, Warren notes that even Homestead had just 156 acres, and other mill sites often remained correspondingly small for decades.[2] These mills certainly were larger than those located in the city center, but hardly as large as the massive plants being built in the Chicago area. There, the openness of the land allowed for the building of larger facilities, and consequently greater centralization, than in the Pittsburgh area. Surely there was a second industrial revolution in America, but it came much more slowly to Pittsburgh and its iron and steel industry. This, in turn, allowed a greater persistence of small business as a significant entity in the city's iron and steel industry and permitted its independent iron and steel men to retain an impressive position of power within the city for a far longer period.

The rather unique topography of Pittsburgh also affected the city's residential patterns and aided the older social elite in retaining its influence in political and social affairs. Even in 1815, before the city had developed as a significant industrial enterprise, a propensity for decentralization had manifested itself. Although it was in some respects a classic "walking city" at that time, as the elite monopolized the central housing sites and the lower classes were forced to the periphery, John Swauger has demonstrated that a small, but significant, number of persons were already breaking away from this pattern. Although most of the elite who had to travel to work on a regular basis had to remain in the center city, a few who were independently wealthy and had no need to commute were already locating themselves in the equivalent of suburbs. Even more interesting, as transportation became available, working-class groups also showed a propensity to move to these areas, as long as transportation costs were not prohibitive. Thus, very early Pittsburgh displayed a proclivity for dispersion and decentralization in housing patterns that was to influence greatly its social and political relations.[3]

Thus, what developed in Pittsburgh throughout the nineteenth century was a series of small towns or communities within the larger city environment. On the broader level, Pittsburgh's residential patterns appeared similar to those in other cities.

Before the development of efficient public transportation in Pittsburgh, the middle and upper classes, as we have seen, resided in the center of the city, the working class on the outskirts. This residential pattern began disappearing after the Civil War, with the development of transportation. That led to the segregation of the city by class and function, with homogeneous residential developments and specialization of land use. The riverfront mill wards held a disproportionate number of working-class homes, and the elite had largely moved out to newer suburban enclaves, some distance from the noise and dirt of the mills.[4]

Just as with the second industrial revolution, there is much truth to this broad picture of residential development in Pittsburgh. But closer inspection reveals equally important truths that tell us much about the ability of Pittsburgh's elite to retain influence in their city. A glance at the development of a couple of these semiautonomous communities in Pittsburgh will provide us with some insight. Minersville today is an area indistinguishable from the rest of Pittsburgh. Located two miles east of downtown, it is now an integral and relatively undifferentiated part of the city. In the early nineteenth century, however, it developed as one of those classic village enclaves just outside downtown. Cut off from the city center by steep hills and poor transportation, Minersville early attracted a number of elite families, along with a collection of workers and owners of small retail establishments.[5]

Minersville was started in the early 1820s by John Herron, member of one of the city's oldest and most distinguished Scots-Irish families. Owner of a prosperous lumber company, Herron expanded that venture into a brickyard, gristmill, and saw mill. He soon became the foremost contract builder in early Pittsburgh. Needing a great deal of coal for his enterprises in Pittsburgh, Herron bought a large expanse of coal land in Minersville and built housing for his workers there. At first, Herron continued to live in downtown Pittsburgh, among other elite Pittsburghers, but in 1833 he moved his residence to a country estate in Minersville. There, he could keep a closer watch not only on his business but also on his workers and their daily moral life. Herron established a strongly paternalistic environment in Minersville and built a Presbyterian church for his workers there.[6] In the years after the Civil War, other elites, and still more workers, moved into Minersville and the community began to fragment. As density increased, as more workers moved in, and as several factories and retail establishments located in the area, it became less desirable as an elite residence. Several owners of large estates in the area then began subdividing their land for middle-class buyers, while the elite themselves moved out to new suburban areas in the East End.

Another isolated mill town within Pittsburgh had a similar history. Hazelwood had begun as an isolated elite community, then attracted a number of industrial concerns, including the blast furnaces of Jones & Laughlin. For a number of years it remained a mill village with the residences of elite owners, their workers, and owners of retail establishments in the area. During the 1880s and 1890s, however, the elite began moving out in large numbers transferring their residences to other parts of the East End. Hazelwood then became the habitat almost exclusively of the working class, who continued to live near the mills where they worked.[7]

When we see where the elites from Minersville and Hazelwood moved, we can better understand the subtlety of the transformation taking place. Most of the elite in these communities did not move large distances to Sewickley or Fox Chapel. The development of these suburbs coincided with that of the automobile in the 1920s. Instead they moved to Shadyside, just over the hill, a few blocks, or at most a few miles, from their mills and their former homes. Most of the very wealthy—the owners of the independent iron and steel mills and their social cohorts—settled in the western end of Shadyside, living on large estates in a highly homogeneous Scots-Irish Presbyterian environment. On the eastern end of Shadyside developed a densely compact middle-class suburb, with small lots and single-family homes.

After the 1890s, however, the pressure of development forced more social mixing in these areas. Portions of the large estates in the western portion of the East End were subdivided, allowing middle-class homes to be built there, while apartment buildings and duplexes began springing up in the eastern portion, accommodating better-off skilled workers who were renters. Nearly half the residents in the entire suburb in the early twentieth century rented. This allowed the older elite to retain a strong sense of hegemony over the middle-class and upper-working-class and white-collar elements in the city. They shared living space, they shared churches and other social institutions, and, most of all, they shared a common set of values.[8]

Yet, circumstances certainly had changed by the early twentieth century. The old, informal community ways of Minersville and Hazelwood were gone, and if the iron and steel elite could continue to exercise moral suasion over the middle classes and some workers, they had lost intimate contact with the masses of unskilled, immigrant, and black workers in their mills and in the city at large. To regain their former sense of control and influence, Pittsburgh's iron and steel elite had to develop new institutions and a new ideology, one they could share with the entire city.

The older Pittsburgh upper class, perhaps unlike those in many other eastern cities, refused to become part of the national, metropolitan upper class that E. Digby Baltzell describes in his *Philadelphia Gentlemen*. Although they sent their children away to fancy eastern prep schools and colleges and participated in a number of central elite institutions as the rest of the seaboard elite did, when it came time for marriage, the vast majority continued to find mates among local upper-class families. This was most true of the Core families. The higher the social prestige in Pittsburgh, the more likely they were to marry someone from home.[9] They refused to sell their mills to Carnegie or Morgan, and they remained close to home so that they might better control their environment. But control had become a more difficult proposition by the early twentieth century. The old-style community had broken down and new patterns were emerging, but the development was not as sudden or as complete as it appeared on the surface.

The iron and steel families had become accustomed to ruling by divine right. They were the city's most eminent personages, and their names graced most of Pittsburgh's businesses and public buildings. They lived in palatial homes in beautiful residential areas, attended the exclusive Duquesne or Pittsburgh or Pittsburgh Golf clubs. They had dinners, balls, cotillions, coming-out parties, and charity affairs that were fawned over in the *Bulletin* and the other Pittsburgh newspapers. They were the eastern counterpart to Booth Tarkington's "Magnificent Ambersons," whose "splendor lasted throughout all the years that saw their Midland town spread and darken into a city."[10]

But by the late nineteenth century, the working class that had poured into Pittsburgh no longer automatically accepted this sort of domination. The level of value integration that had existed in Pittsburgh in the early nineteenth century, when much of the working class was also Scots-Irish or German, and Presbyterian, or at least Protestant, had fragmented by the late nineteenth century.[11] In the early days, the owner's home had been close to the mill, where the workers' cottages were also clustered. There was a shared shop culture, abetted by a shared religioethnic culture. By the late nineteenth century, the owners had moved to their mansions in Shadyside, where they lived a style of life so different, so far removed from that of the Slavic and southern European workers who lived in tenements on streets around the mills, that they could have been on two different continents.[12]

It was clear that something had to be done about this, but equally clear that it had to be done in such a way that most people believed that it was being done either by the common man or at least in his name.[13] Thus came about a subtle transformation of the economic, civic, and political realms of Pittsburgh. The old iron and steel families, so the story went, no longer controlled their mills. The mills had been taken over by rapacious giant corporations controlled by New York financiers and their bureaucratic lackeys. All the problems, or at least most of them, that afflicted Pittsburgh in the early years of the twentieth century were laid at the feet of the steel trust and its minions. What was needed was reform. New organizations, more highly centralized and staffed by experts, should be given control over government, civic, and social welfare matters. And to direct these new institutions who better than members of the old upper class: men who were not tied to the steel trust (even though some were) or to the evil old political machine and its abuses (although some were); men who had risen above the fray of crass commercialism (although many still owned their own mills) and could act in a disinterested manner should be given trusteeship over the fate and future of the city. And, to a large extent, they were.

One key to their continuing influence in the city lay in the fact that, as is often the case in these matters, values changed far more slowly than institutions. Samuel P. Hays has argued: "With respect to organizational tendencies, the city was an extreme case. . . . With respect to changes in cultural values, however, the opposite was the case: the city reflects a more extreme example of cultural conservatism."[14] The old elite, more than any other group in society, represented tradition and a retention of older, simpler values. However much they differed from their immigrant workers, they had that much in common. As a number of scholars have noted, immigrant religion and ethnic traditions were often used by the workers as a shield against the dehumanizing influences of the city and the mill. Ironically, the independent mill owner himself, by appealing to Pittsburgh's past, to its religious traditions, and to the image of a seemingly simpler and gentler age, could speak the worker's language in some fundamental ways.

Yet Pittsburgh's social upper class were obviously not genteel old aristocrats who preached the gospel of anti-industrialism, an anti-industrialism that might cause Pittsburgh's workers to lose their jobs. These were men who had their feet conveniently in both camps. They represented both tradition and progress, continuity and change. They were not outmoded mercantilists baying helplessly at modern industrialism. These men ran large, modern industrial mills. True, they were not as large as those of U.S. Steel or Bethlehem, but they were profitable enterprises and loomed large on the Pittsburgh scene. When the iron and steel masters talked, the people of Pittsburgh listened.

This is, of course, hegemony and paternalism of a much different and far more complex sort. That is where the stories of both the Byerses and the Crawfords are so significant. The Byers family continued to run their mill successfully for decades, yet few journalists or scholars seemed to notice. They maintained an alternative (or enlightened?) form of paternalism for their workers throughout the nineteenth and much of the twentieth centuries that was far removed from the welfare capitalism practiced by U.S. Steel and other giant corporations, yet they more successfully retained the loyalty of their workers than any of the large entities. Similarly, the Crawford family ran Duquesne in a manner analogous to that practiced by landed gentry in an earlier time. Then, when abuses were uncovered, they were blamed not on the Crawfords but on their archenemies the executives of Carnegie Steel, the giant absentee-owned corporation.

As the barons of these iron and steel mills sat in their palatial homes or lounged in their opulent clubs and read accounts of how the local iron and steel industry had been taken over by the giant steel trust; of how the old type of self-reliant leader of political and social affairs was a thing of the past; of how there was a terrible vacuum at the center of Pittsburgh's society, culture, and politics that needed filling, they must have smiled. They, after all, knew full well that they were still running their mills profitably, and they also knew that most of the reform organizations coming to the fore to take control of the situation in Pittsburgh were strongly influenced by them and their friends, and they knew that the blame for at least some of the abuses could have been directed at them. So, they stayed out of the limelight; it suited their dour Presbyterian natures anyhow. They remained lords of all they surveyed.

APPENDIX A

Mills and Mill Owners by Social Class: 1850s

Name	Company	Blue Book Listing	Social Directory Listing 1904	Social Register Listing 1908	Family Rank
Anderson, Robert J.	Pittsburgh Steel				Marginal
Bennett, James I.	Graff, Bennett	•			Marginal
Black, Alexander M.	Kensington R. M.	•	•	•	Core
Blair, Thomas S.	Juniata Iron	•	•	•	Core
Brown, James	Wayne I. & S.	•	•	•	Core
Chalfant, James W.	Etna R. M.	•	•	•	Core
Dalzell, Robert	Vesuvius Iron	•	•	•	Core
Dilworth, Joseph	Glendon R. M.	•	•	•	Core
Everson, William H.	Pennsylvania Iron	•		•	Non-Core
Graff, H., J., C., M., and W.	Graff, Bennett	•	•	•	Non-Core
Howe, Thomas M.	Hussey, Wells	•	•	•	Core
Hussey, Curtis G.	Hussey, Wells	•	•	•	Marginal
Jennings, J. F.	Sheffield, LaBelle	•	•	•	Non-Core
Jones, Benjamin F.	American Iron	•	•	•	Core
Larimer, William	Sable Iron	•	•	•	Core
Laughlin, James	American Iron	•	•	•	Core
Lewis, George	Vesuvius	•		•	Non-Core
Lewis, William J.	Birmingham Iron	•			Elite
Lindsay, James	Sable Iron	•			Marginal
Lloyd, Henry	Kensington Iron	•	•	•	Non-Core
Lyon, William	Sligo R. M.	•	•	•	Core
Macrum, William	Pennsylvania Iron	•		•	Non-Core
Metcalf, William	Crescent Steel	•	•	•	Core
Miller, Reuben	Crescent Steel	•	•	•	Core
Moorhead, M. K.	McKeesport/Soho	•	•	•	Core
Nimick, A. and W. K.	Sligo/Sheffield	•	•	•	Core

(continued)

APPENDIX A (Continued)

Mills and Mill Owners by Social Class: 1850s

Name	Company	Blue Book Listing	Social Directory Listing 1904	Social Register Listing 1908	Family Rank
O'Hara, James	Vesuvius Iron	•	•	•	Core
Painter, Jacob	Pittsburgh Iron	•	•	•	Core
Park, James	Black Diamond	•	•	•	Core
Parkin, William	Crescent Steel	•			Marginal
Phillips, John	Birmingham Iron	•			Core
Porter, George	Glendon R. M.	•	•		Non-Core
Shoenberger, J. H. and G.	Juniata Iron	•			Non-Core
Singer, J. F.	Sheffield Steel	•	•	•	Core
Smith, Andrew	Pittsburgh Steel	•	•	•	Core
Spang, Charles H.	Etna R. M.	•	•		Non-Core
Wells, Calvin	Hussey, Wells	•		•	Elite
Wood, James	Eagle R. M.	•	•	•	Core
Wood, W. D.	McKeesport R. M.	•	•	•	Core
Zug, Christopher	Sable Iron	•	•	•	Core
Total: 40 Families		39	29	31	24 Core 60%
		98%	73%	78%	9 Non-Core 23%
					5 Marginal 13%
					2 Elite 5%

APPENDIX B

Mills and Mill Owners by Social Class: 1874

Name	Company	Blue Book Listing	Social Directory Listing 1904	Social Register Listing 1908	Family Rank
Anderson, Robert J.	Pittsburgh Steel				Marginal
Bennett, James I.	Clinton & Millvale	•			Marginal
Black, Alexander M.	Kensington R. M.	•	•	•	Core
Blair, Thomas S.	Juniata, Blair I & S	•	•	•	Core
Brown, H. G. and J. S.	Wayne I. & S.	•	•	•	Core
Byers, A. M. and E. M.	Byers, McCulloch	•	•	•	Core
Carnegie, A. and T.	Union I., E. T. Steel	•	•		Non-Core
Chalfant, J. W. and G. A.	Etna R. M.	•	•	•	Core
Chess, D., H., H. B., W.	Anchor Tack	•			Elite
Clapp, Dewitt C.	Black Diamond	•		•	Non-Core
Clark, W. and E. L.	Solar Iron	•			Non-Core
Demmler, J. H.	U.S. Iron & T. P.	•			Elite
Dilworth, Joseph	Glendon R. M.	•	•	•	Core
Everson, W. H. and J. Q.	Pennsylvania Iron	•		•	Non-Core
Graff, J., C., M., T. J. and W.	Ft. Pitt, C/M R. M.	•	•	•	Non-Core
Herron, Campbell B.	Etna R. M.	•			Core
Howe, Thomas M.	Hussey, Wells	•	•	•	Core
Hussey, C. G. and C. C.	Hussey, Wells	•	•	•	Marginal
Jones, Benjamin F.	American Iron	•	•	•	Core
Lauder, George	E T. Steel	•	•	•	Marginal

(continued)

APPENDIX B (Continued)

Mills and Mill Owners by Social Class: 1874

Name	Company	Blue Book Listing	Social Directory Listing 1904	Social Register Listing 1908	Family Rank
Laughlin, J., H. A., G. M.	American Iron	•	•	•	Core
Lewis, William J.	Mon. & Alleg. I.	•			Elite
Lindsay, James	Sable Iron	•			Marginal
Lloyd, Henry	Kensington Iron	•	•	•	Non-Core
McCutcheon, James	Star Iron	•		•	Non-Core
Metcalf, William	Crescent Steel	•	•	•	Core
Miller R. and W.	Crescent Steel	•	•	•	Core
Moorhead, M. K. and J.	McKeesport/Soho	•	•	•	Core
Nimick, A. and W. K.	Sheffield/Sligo	•	•	•	Core
Oliver, H. W., D. B., J.B.	Mon. & Alleg. I.	•	•	•	Core
Painter, J., A. E. W., P.	Pittsburgh Iron	•	•	•	Core
Park, J., D. C., W. G.	Black Diamond	•	•	•	Core
Parkin, William	Crescent Steel	•			Marginal
Patterson, H. W.	Pgh. Steel Cast	•			Elite
Phillips, John	Mon. & Alleg. I.	•			Core
Phipps, Henry	E. T. Steel	•	•	•	Non-Core
Porter, George	Glendon R. M.	•	•		Non-Core
Shoenberger, J. H., G. K.	Juniata Iron	•			Non-Core
Singer, G. and W. H.	Sheffield/Sligo	•	•	•	Core
Smith, A. D., D. M., D.	LaBelle Steel	•	•	•	Core
Spang, Charles H.	Etna R. M.	•	•		Non-Core
Speer, John Z.	Juniata Iron	•	•	•	Core
Wood, W. D. and R. G.	McKeesport R. M.	•	•	•	Core
Zug, C. and C. H.	Sable Iron	•	•	•	Core
Total: 44 Families		43	29	29	23 Core 52%
		98%	66%	66%	11 Non-Core 25% 6 Marginal 14% 4 Elite 9%

APPENDIX C

Mills and Mill Owners by Social Class: Late 1880s

Name	Company	Blue Book Listing	Social Directory Listing 1904	Social Register Listing 1908	Family Rank
Alldred, W. H.	Duquesne Steel			•	Elite
Bailey, J. M.	Reliance Steel	•	•	•	Core
Bennett, James I.	Clinton & Millvale	•			Marginal
Black, A. M. and G. P.	Kensington R. M.	•	•	•	Core
Blackburn, W. W.	Carnegie Steel	•	•	•	Core
Blair, Thomas S.	Juniata, Blair I. & S.	•	•	•	Core
Boulton, George	Duquesne Steel	•			Elite
Brown Family (5)	Wayne I. & S.	•	•	•	Core
Byers, A. M. and E. M.	Byers, McCulloch	•	•	•	Core
Carnegie, A. and T.	Union I., E. T. Steel	•	•		Non-Core
Cassidy, W. H. and E. T.	Oliver Wire	•		•	Core
Chalfant, J. W. and G. A.	Etna R. M.	•	•	•	Core
Chess, D., H., H. B., W.	Anchor Tack	•			Elite
Childs, O. H.	Soho Iron	•	•	•	Core
Clapp, C. E.	Black Diamond	•		•	Non-Core
Clark, W.	Solar Iron	•			Non-Core
Clarkson, T. C.	Sable I. & S.	•		•	Non-Core
Converse, E. C. and J.	National Tube	•			Marginal
Cronemeyer, W. C.	U.S. Iron & T. P.	•			Elite
Crosby, Horace	National Tube	•			Marginal
DeArmit, W. P.	Sterling Steel	•	•	•	Non-Core
Demmler, J. H.	U.S. Iron & T. P.	•			Elite

(continued)

APPENDIX C (*Continued*)

Mills and Mill Owners by Social Class: Late 1880s

Name	Company	Blue Book Listing	Social Directory Listing 1904	Social Register Listing 1908	Family Rank
Dilworth, J. R. and L.	Glendon R. M.	•	•	•	Core
Donnelly, C.	Elba Iron & Bolt	•	•	•	Non-Core
Eaton, J. and W. T.	National Tube	•	•	•	Non-Core
Edenborn, W.	Braddock Wire				Elite
Everson, W. H. and J. Q.	Pennsylvania Iron	•		•	Non-Core
Fitch, T. W.	Braddock Wire	•	•	•	Non-Core
Fitzhugh, C. L.	Juniata Iron	•	•	•	Non-Core
Flagler, J. H.	National Tube				Marginal
Frick, H. C.	Carnegie Steel	•	•	•	Non-Core
Friend, J. W.	Eagle, Pgh. Steel	•	•	•	Non-Core
Graff, J. and M.	Ft. Pitt, C/M R. M.	•	•	•	Non-Core
Hainsworth, W.	Pgh. Steel Cast				Elite
Hammond, W. J.	Pennsylvania I.	•			Elite
Hart, Pennock	Mcntsh-Hemp.	•	•	•	Marginal
Hemphill, James	Mcntsh-Hemp.	•	•	•	Non-Core
Herron, Campbell B.	Etna R. M.	•			Core
Hoffstot, F. N.	Eagle/Pgh. Steel	•			Marginal
Howe, Thomas M.	Hussey, Wells	•	•	•	Core
Hussey, C. G. and C. C.	Hussey, Wells	•	•	•	Marginal
Irwin, J. and J. Jr.	Pgh. Steel Cast	•	•	•	Core
Jennings, B. F.	LaBelle Steel	•	•	•	Non-Core
Johnston, W. G.	Pgh. Steel Cast.	•	•	•	Non-Core
Jones, B. F. and T. M.	American Iron	•	•	•	Core
Keating, A. F.	Sable Iron	•			Non-Core
Kirkpatrick, J. C.	Chartiers I. & S.	•	•	•	Non-Core
Lauder, George	E. T. Steel	•	•	•	Marginal
Laughlin Family (4)	American Iron	•	•	•	Core
Lazear, T. C.	Pgh. Steel Cast	•		•	Non-Core
Lewis, G. T. and W. J.	Mon./Alleg./ Vesuv.	•			Elite
Lindsay, J. H.	Keystone R. M.	•			Marginal
Lloyd, H. and J. W.	Kensington Iron	•	•	•	Non-Core
Lyon, W.	Pgh. Steel Cast	•	•	•	Core
McCutcheon, J. and J. H.	Star Iron	•		•	Non-Core

APPENDIX C (Continued)

Mills and Mill Owners by Social Class: Late 1880s

Name	Company	Blue Book Listing	Social Directory Listing 1904	Social Register Listing 1908	Family Rank
McDowell, N. M.	Keystone R. M.	•			Elite
Mackintosh, W. S.	Mcntsh-Hemp.	•	•	•	Marginal
McNeil, Hugh	Spang I. & S.	•			Elite
Metcalf, W. and O.	Crescent Steel	•	•	•	Core
Miller R. and R., Jr.	Crescent Steel	•	•	•	Core
Moorhead Family (5)	Soho Iron	•	•	•	Core
Nimick, A. and F. B.	Sligo R. M.	•	•	•	Core
Oliver, H. W., J. B.	Mon. & Alleg. I.	•	•	•	Core
Painter Family (4)	Pittsburgh Iron	•	•	•	Core
Palmer, W. P.	Carnegie Steel	•		•	Marginal
Park Family (4)	Black Diamond	•	•	•	Core
Parkin, W.	Crescent Steel	•			Marginal
Patterson, H. W.	Pgh. Steel Cast.	•			Elite
Phillips, John	Mon. & Alleg. I.	•			Core
Phipps, Henry	E. T. Steel	•	•	•	Non-Core
Porter, J. C.	Spang I. & S.	•			Non-Core
Read, C. H.	Duquesne Steel				Marginal
Rhodes, J.	Pioneer Tube	•	•	•	Elite
Roberts, H.	Oliver Wire				Elite
Rowe, W. H.	Braddock Wire	•		•	Non-Core
Schenck, F. E.	U.S. Iron & T. P.	•			Elite
Scully, Family (4)	Elba Iron & Bolt	•	•	•	Core
Shinn, W. P.	Carnegie Steel	•			Non-Core
Shoenberger, J. H. and G. K.	Juniata Iron	•			Non-Core
Singer, G. and W. H.	Sheffield/Sligo	•	•	•	Core
Smith Family (4)	LaBelle Steel	•	•	•	Core
Spang, Charles H.	Etna R. M.	•	•		Non-Core
Speer, John Z.	Juniata Iron	•	•	•	Core
Stewart, David A.	Carnegie Steel	•	•	•	Non-Core

(continued)

APPENDIX C (*Continued*)

Mills and Mill Owners by Social Class: Late 1880s

Name	Company	Blue Book Listing	Social Directory Listing 1904	Social Register Listing 1908	Family Rank
Travelli, Charles I.	Pgh. Steel Cast.	•			Non-Core
Verner, J. K.	Pgh. Forge & I.	•	•	•	Core
Wade, William	Mcntsh-Hemp.	•			Non-Core
Walker, John	Carnegie Steel	•	•	•	Core
Wells, Calvin	Pgh. Forge & I.	•		•	Elite
Wheeler, C. Y.	Sterling Steel	•		•	Elite
Wilson, J. R. and J. T.	Carnegie Steel	•			Elite
Wood Family (4)	McKeesport R. M.	•	•	•	Core
Zug, C. and C. H.	Sable Iron	•	•	•	Core
Total: 93 Families		87	50	59	32 Core 34%
		94%	54%	63%	30 Non-Core 32% 13 Marginal 14% 18 Elite 19%

APPENDIX D

Mills and Mill Owners by Social Class: Late 1890s

Name	Company	Blue Book Listing	Social Directory Listing 1904	Social Register Listing 1908	Family Rank
Abbott, W. L.	Carnegie Steel	•	•	•	Marginal
Andrews, J., E. E., and W. W.	Soho Iron				Elite
Bache, W. P.	Apollo I. & S.				Marginal
Bailey, J. M., C.	Reliance Steel	•	•	•	Core
Beaver, W. D.	Pittsburgh T. P.				Elite
Beymer, A. S.	Apollo I. & S.	•			Elite
Black, G. P. and W. H.	Kensington R. M.	•	•	•	Core
Blackburn, W. W.	Carnegie Steel	•	•	•	Core
Brown Family (5)	Wayne I. & S.	•	•	•	Core
Buchanan, J. I.	Apollo I. & S.	•	•	•	Elite
Byers Family (3)	Byers, McCulloch	•	•	•	Core
Carnegie Family (4)	Carnegie Steel	•	•		Non-Core
Chalfant, J. W. and G. A.	Etna R. M.	•	•	•	Core
Chess, H., H. B., W.	Anchor Tack	•			Elite
Chickering, K.	Elba Iron				Elite
Childs, O. H.	Soho Iron	•	•	•	Core
Clapp, C. E., D. C.	Black Diamond	•		•	Non-Core
Clark, F. L. and T. S.	Solar Iron	•			Non-Core
Cole, E. H.	Elba Iron				Elite
Crawford, E. R.	U.S. Iron & T. P.				Elite
Cronemeyer, W. C.	U.S. Iron & T. P.	•			Elite
Curry, H. M.	Carnegie Steel	•	•	•	Non-Core
Dallas, Charles R.	Soho Iron				Elite
Demmler, J. H.	U.S. Iron & T. P.	•			Elite

(continued)

APPENDIX D (Continued)

Mills and Mill Owners by Social Class: Late 1890s

Name	Company	Blue Book Listing	Social Directory Listing 1904	Social Register Listing 1908	Family Rank
Dilworth Family (3)	Glendon R. M.	•	•	•	Core
Donelly, C.	Elba Iron & Bolt	•	•	•	Non-Core
DuPuy, Herbert	Pittsburgh Steel	•	•	•	Non-Core
Everson, W. H. and T. B.	Pennsylvania Iron	•		•	Non-Core
Farrell, J. A. and W. H.	Pittsburgh Wire				Marginal
Firth, L. J.	Firth-Sterling	•		•	Elite
Fitch, T. W.	Braddock Wire	•	•	•	Non-Core
Frick H. C.	Carnegie Steel	•	•	•	Non-Core
Friend, J. W.	Eagle, Pgh. Steel	•	•	•	Non-Core
Gates, John W.	Braddock Wire				Elite
Gayley, James	Carnegie Steel	•	•		Marginal
Gillespie, T. J.	Lockhart I. & S.	•		•	Non-Core
Graff Family (5)	Carbon Steel	•		•	Non-Core
Hart, Pennock	Mcntsh-Hemp.	•		•	Marginal
Hemphill Family (3)	Mcntsh-Hemp.	•		•	Non-Core
Henry, John	Chartiers Iron				Elite
Herron, Campbell B.	Etna R. M.	•			Core
Hoffstot, F. N.	Eagle/Pgh. Steel	•			Marginal
Howard, W. N.	West. Penn. Steel				Non-Core
Howe, Thomas M.	Hussey, Wells	•	•	•	Core
Husler, E. G.	Williams Co.	•			Elite
Hussey, C. G. II	Hussey, Wells	•	•	•	Marginal
Jennings, E. H. and J. G.	LaBelle Steel	•	•	•	Non-Core
Johnston, W. G.	Pgh. Steel Cast.	•	•	•	Non-Core
Jones, B. F. and B. F. II	American Iron	•	•	•	Core
Kaufman, J. S.	Aliquippa Iron	•			Elite
Kelly, J. A.	Reliance Steel	•			Non-Core
Kirkpatrick, J. C.	Chartiers I. & S.	•	•	•	Non-Core
Lash, H. W.	Carbon Iron				Elite
Lauder, George	Carnegie Steel	•	•	•	Marginal
Laughlin Family (3)	American Iron	•	•	•	Core
Leech, M. W.	Chartiers I. & S.	•	•		Non-Core
Leishman, J. A. G.	Carnegie Steel	•	•	•	Marginal
Lindsay, Homer J.	Carnegie Steel	•		•	Marginal

APPENDIX D (Continued)

Mills and Mill Owners by Social Class: Late 1890s

Name	Company	Blue Book Listing	Social Directory Listing 1904	Social Register Listing 1908	Family Rank
Lloyd, H. and J. W.	Kensington Iron	•	•	•	Non-Core
Lockhart, Charles	Lockhart I. & S.	•	•	•	Core
Luke, Arthur F.	National Tube				Elite
Lupton, H. B.	Oliver Wire	•		•	Marginal
Lyon, J. S.	Sterling Steel	•	•	•	Core
McCutcheon Family (3)	Star Iron	•		•	Non-Core
Mackey, Charles W.	Sterling Steel	•			Elite
McMurtry, G. G.	Apollo I. & S.	•			Marginal
Metcalf, W.	Crescent Steel	•	•	•	Core
Miller, R., Jr., and W.	Crescent Steel	•	•	•	Core
Nimick, F. B.	Sligo R. M.	•	•	•	Core
Oliver Family (5)	Oliver I. & S.	•	•	•	Core
Painter, A. E. W. and P.	Pittsburgh Iron	•	•	•	Core
Palmer, J. C.	Elba Iron	•			Elite
Park Family (3)	Black Diamond	•	•	•	Core
Parkin, Charles	Crescent Steel	•			Marginal
Phipps, Henry and L. C.	Carnegie Steel	•	•	•	Non-Core
Quay, R. R.	Oliver I. & S.	•			Elite
Richardson, F. E.	Pgh. Forge & I.	•	•	•	Core
Schwab, C. M.	Carnegie Steel	•			Elite
Scully Family (3)	Elba Iron & Bolt	•	•	•	Core
Shaw, David	Pittsburgh Steel				Elite
Shoenberger, J. H.	Juniata Iron	•			Non-Core
Singer, G. and W. H.	Sheffield/Sligo	•	•	•	Core
Smith, F. B.	LaBelle Steel	•	•	•	Core
Smith, James	Oliver I. & S.	•			Elite
Snyder, William P.	Oliver I. & S.	•	•	•	Non-Core
Spang, Charles H.	Etna R. M.	•	•		Non-Core
Speer Family (3)	Juniata Iron	•	•	•	Core
Steele, W. C.	Spang I. & S.	•			Elite
Steiner, G. A.	Juniata Iron	•			Elite
Tener, S. W.	Oliver I. & S.	•			Non-Core
Tiers, C. P.	Pittsburgh Steel	•			Elite
Tindle, C. W.	Pittsburgh T. P.	•		•	Non-Core

(continued)

APPENDIX D (*Continued*)

Mills and Mill Owners by Social Class: Late 1890s

Name	Company	Blue Book Listing	Social Directory Listing 1904	Social Register Listing 1908	Family Rank
Trump, A.	Pittsburgh Steel	•			Elite
Verner, J. K.	Pgh. Forge & I.	•	•	•	Core
Vilsack, J. G.	Aliquippa Steel	•			Elite
Voegetley, W. P.	Pittsburgh, T. P.	•			Elite
Walker, John	Carnegie Steel	•	•	•	Core
Walker, T. M.	Pittsburgh Wire	•			Elite
Wells, Calvin	Pgh. Forge & I.	•		•	Elite
Wood Family (6)	McKeesport R. M.	•	•	•	Core
Young, E. M. S.	Superior Steel	•			Elite
Zug Family (4)	Sable Iron	•	•	•	Core
Total: 101 Families		86 84%	51 50%	56 56%	29 Core 28% 27 Non-Core 26% 13 Marginal 13% 33 Elite 32%

APPENDIX E

Pittsburgh Rolling Mills and Crucible Steel Works: 1874

Firm	Year Built	Puddling Furnaces (No.)	Bessemer Converter	Capacity (Tons)
Iron Rolling Mills				
American Iron	1852	75		50,000
Anchor Nail	1837	20		6,000
Birmingham Iron	1836	20		9,000
Byers, McCullough	1862	25		?
Clinton & Millvale	1841	41		20,000
Etna Rolling Mill	1828	14		20,000
Ft. Pitt I. & S.	1842	25 (B/Cr)		18,000
Glendon R. M.	1857	24		8,000
Juniata Iron	1828	29		15,000
Kensington Iron	1828	16		5,000
Keystone Iron	1865	19		11,000
McKeesport Iron	1854	7/10 F		4,000
Mon. & Alleg. I.	1864	49		20,000
Ormsby Iron	?	20/5 H		?
Pennsylvania I.	1844	30		?
Pgh. Forge & I.	1864	15		10,000
Pittsburgh Iron	1833	50		17,000
Sable Iron	1845	34		15,000
Sligo Iron	1825	?		?
Soho Iron	1859	?		?
Solar Iron	1869	?		?
Star Iron	1862	14		8,000
Superior R. M.	1865	?		?
J. E. Thomson	Under cons.	0	2 5-T	?
Union Iron	1862	21		27,000
U.S. Iron & T. P.	1873–74	8		8,000
Vesuvius Iron	1846	24		12,000
Wayne I. & S.	1829	?		?
J. Woods'	1850	?		?

(continued)

APPENDIX E (*Continued*)

Pittsburgh Rolling Mills and Crucible Steel Works: 1874

Firm	Year Built	Crucible Pots	Capacity (Tons)
Crucible Steel Works			
Black Diamond	1862	72/6	12,000
Blair I. & S.	?	?	?
Crescent Steel	1867	4 H	4,000
Hussey & Wells	1859	7 24-P	13,000
LaBelle Steel	1863	4 25-T	6,000
Pgh. Steel Cast.	1871	19 M	?
Pgh. Steel Wks.	1843	?	7,000
Sheffield Steel	1848	?	5,500

APPENDIX F

Pittsburgh Rolling Mills and Steel Works: 1884

Firm	Year Built	Puddling Furnaces (No.)	Open Hearth	Bessemer Converter	Capacity (Tons)
Iron Rolling Mills					
Alleg., Mon. & Birm. Mills	a	107		1 2-T[b]	97,500
American Iron	1852	76			75,000
Anchor Nail	1837	24			15,000
Apollo I. & S.	1882	6			8,000
Birmingham Iron	1836[c]				
Byers, McCullough	1862	26			15,000
Chartiers I. & S.	1884	4			4,000
Clinton & Millvale	1841	26			35,000
Eagle Rolling Mill	1848	17			?
Elba Iron & Bolt	1862	29			25,000
Etna Rolling Mill	1828	29			14,000
Ft. Pitt Foundry	1882	0	2 7-T		?
Ft. Pitt I. & S.	1842	22/2 30-P Cr			12,000
Glendon R. M.	1857	20			30,000
Glenwood Steel	1879		1 5-T		?
Juniata Iron	1828	29	2 12-T		26,000
Kensington Iron	1828	20			6,000
Keystone Iron	1865	30			12,000
Linden Steel	1879		1 10-T/1 7-T		27,000
McKeesport Iron	1854	24/12 F			8,000
Mon. & Alleg. I.	1864[c]				
National Tube	1879–82	48			53,000
Oliver & Rob Wire	1884	2 H			?
Pennsylvania I.	1844	14			11,000
Pgh. Bess. Steel	1880–81		2 4-T		125,000
Pgh. Forge & I.	1864	34			29,000
Pittsburgh Iron	1833	67			33,000
Republic Iron	1863	20			20,000

(continued)

APPENDIX F (Continued)

Pittsburgh Rolling Mills and Steel Works: 1884

Firm	Year Built	Puddling Furnaces (No.)	Open Hearth	Bessemer Converter	Capacity (Tons)
Sable Iron	1845	34			18,000
Sligo Iron	1825	34			16,000
Soho Iron	1859	21			7,200
Solar Iron	1869	21			12,000
Spang I. & S.	1880–81		2 7-T		6,000
Star Iron	1862	37			12,000
Superior R. M.	1865	32			(Idle)
J. E. Thomson	1875	0		3 10-T	500,000
Union Iron	1862	38			45,000
U.S. Iron & T. P.	1874–83	5/2-H			3,300
Vesuvius Iron	1846	28			18,000
Wayne I. & S.	1829	28/4 48-P Cr			22,000

Firm	Year Built	Crucible Pots	Open Hearth	Bessemer Converter	Capacity (Tons)
Crucible Steel Works					
Black Diamond	1862	?			
Crescent Steel	1867	10 H			6,000
Hussey & Wells	1859	2 30-P/14 Pd	1 7-T		4,500
LaBelle Steel	1863	2 25-T/2 30-T			10,000
Liggett Spring	1865–82	1 30-T			2,500
Nellis Agri.	1870	5 4-P Cr/6 F			?
Pgh. Steel Cast.	1871	2 24-P		1 5-T	40,000
Pgh. Steel Works	1843–82	?			10,000
Sheffield Steel	1848	8 Cnv/8 Pd			23,000

[a] Allegheny and Monongahela mills were built in 1864, Birmingham in 1836.
[b] Lewis, Oliver & Phillips installed a Clapps-Griffith "Bessemer" converter in 1884, but it was not successful.
[c] Part of Allegheny, Monongahela, and Birmingham (owned by Lewis, Oliver & Phillips).

APPENDIX G

Pittsburgh Rolling Mills and Steel Works: 1894

Firm	Year Built	Puddling Furnaces (No.)	Open Hearth	Bessemer Converter	Capacity (Tons)
Iron Rolling Mills					
Alleg. Mon. & Birm. Mills	[a]	123/30 H		2 2-T[b]	154,000
American Iron	1852	92/40 H		2 9-T	1,027,000
Anchor Nail	1837	24/6 H			?
Apollo I. & S.	1882	18 H	2 20-T		27,000
Apollo Sheet I.	1886–89	8 H			6,000
Birmingham Iron	1836[c]				
Byers, McCullough	1862	25/5 H			13,500
Carbon Steel	1862–88	4 Sms H		2 15-T/4 30-T	100,000
Carnegie Steel		46 H	18 O. H.	8 Bess.	2,000,000
Chartiers I. & S.	1884	4/11 H			4,500
Clinton	1841	33/11 H			31,500
Eagle Rolling Mill	1848	21			?
Elba Iron & Bolt	1862	30/6 H			35,000
Etna Rolling Mill	1828	29/9 H			25,000
Ft. Pitt Foundry	1882	0	2 12-T/2 20-T		16,500
Glendon R. M.	1857	32 H			45,000
Hainsworth	1881–91[d]			2 6-T	120,000
Juniata Iron	1828	13/13 H	2 12-T	2 6-T	100,000
Kensington Iron	1828	20			9,000
Keystone Iron	1865	36/7 H			22,500

(continued)

APPENDIX G (Continued)

Pittsburgh Rolling Mills and Crucible Steel Works: 1884

Firm	Year Built	Puddling Furnaces (No.)	Open Hearth	Bessemer Converter	Capacity (Tons)
Leechburg Iron	1872	5/15 H			10,000
Linden Steel	1879		1 25-T/2 15-T		40,000
Lockhart I. & S.	1877–82	31/7 H			16,500
McKeesport Iron	1854	12/12 F	2 20-T		18,000
Millvale	1850	43/18 H^e			50,000
Monongahela I. & S.	1891	20			13,500
National Tube	1879–82	120/25 H		2 8-T	320,000
Oliver & Rob Wire	1884	4 H			200,000
Pgh. Forge & I.	1864	38/14 H			26,100
Pittsburgh I. & S.	1833	16 H			50,000
Pittsburgh Wire	1891	2 H			40,000
Pgh. Works (Consol. Wire)	?	6 H^f			50,000
Republic Iron	1863	50/16 H^g			51,300
Sable Iron	1845	42/11 H			22,500
Sligo Iron	1825	38/12 H			24,000
Soho Iron	1859	30/10 H			16,500
Solar Steel	1869	11 H	2 12-T		35,000
Spang I. & S.	1880–81		3 10-T	2 3-T	60,000
Star I. & S.	1862	38/11 H			12,000
U.S. Iron & T. P.	1874–83	4/3 H			11,000
Vesuvius Iron	1846	28/10 H			22,500
Wayne I. & S.	1829	34/Cr			23,000
West Penn St.	1881		1 10-T		6,500

Firm	Year Built	Crucible Pots	Open Hearth	Bessemer Converter	Capacity (Tons)
Crucible Steel Works					
Aliquippa Steel	1892	8 H/Cr	1 12-T		18,400
Black Diamond	1862	?			

APPENDIX G (Continued)

Pittsburgh Rolling Mills and Steel Works: 1894

Firm	Year Built	Crucible Pots	Open Hearth	Bessemer Converter	Capacity (Tons)
Cold Rolled St.	1892	1 H			5,000
Crescent Steel	1867	32 H/Cr			11,000
Howe, Brown	1859	2 30-P/13 Pd	1 30-T/1 20-T		25,500
Hussey, Binns	1890	1 24-P/18 H			1,350
LaBelle Steel	1863		2 25-T/2 30-T/Cr		15,000
Liggett Spring	1865–82		1 30-T		?
Pgh. Steel Cast.	1871	1 18-P/2 24-P		1 10-T	6,500
Pgh. Tool Steel	1889–90	3 H			5,000
Reliance Steel	1889	1 24-P			440
Sheffield Steel	1848	8 Cnv/8 Pd		1 10-T	20,800
Sterling Steel	1843–82	15 H/Cr[h]			3,500
Superior Steel	1892	4 H			7,500
West Penn St.	1886	9 H			7,000

[a]Allegheny and Monongahela mills were built in 1864, Birmingham in 1836.
[b]Lewis, Oliver & Phillips installed a Clapps-Griffith "Bessemer" converter in 1884, but it was not successful.
[c]Part of Allegheny, Monongahela, and Birmingham (owned by Lewis, Oliver & Phillips).
[d]Formerly Pittsburgh Steel Casting.
[e]Formerly part of Clinton.
[f]Formerly Braddock Wire.
[g]Now part of National Tube.
[h]Formerly Pittsburgh Steel Works.

APPENDIX H

Pittsburgh Iron and Steel Plants Absorbed into Consolidations:
1895–1905

U.S. Steel	Crucible Steel
Apollo Rolling Mill	Black Diamond Steel
Apollo Sheet Iron	Crescent Steel
Carnegie Steel Company	Howe, Brown & Co.
Chartiers Iron & Steel	LaBelle Steel
Elba Iron Works of National Tube	Pittsburgh Steel Works
Works Co.	Sheffield Steel
Hainsworth Steel	Aliquippa Steel
Juniata Iron & Steel	
Leechburg Iron	Jones & Laughlin bought
McKeesport Iron & Steel	Soho Iron
National Tube Works Co.	
Oliver & Roberts Wire	American Steel Casting bought
Pittsburgh Wire	Pittsburgh Steel Casting
Pittsburgh Works of Consolidated	
Wire	
Republic Iron Works of National	
Tube Works Co.	
Solar Steel Works	
Star Iron and Steel	
U.S. Iron & Tin Plate	
West Penn Steel	

APPENDIX I

Pittsburgh Iron and Steel Families by Social Class

Core	Non-Core	Marginal	Elite
Black	Byers	Abbott	Andrews
Blackburn	Carnegie	Anderson	Beaver
Blair	Clapp	Bache	Beymer
Brown	Clarkson	Bennett	Boulton
Cassidy	Curry	Cole	Buchanan
Chalfant	DeArmit	Converse	Chess
Childs	Donnelly	Crosby	Chickering
Dalzell	DuPuy	Farrell	Crawford
Dilworth	Eaton	Flagler	Cronemeyer
Herron	Everson	Gayley	Dallas
Howe	Fitch	Hart	Demmler
Irwin	Fitzhugh	Hoffstot	Edenborn
Jones	Frick	Hussey	Firth
Larimer	Friend	Lauder	Gates
Laughlin	Gillespie	Leishman	Hammond
Lockhart	Graff	Lindsay, H. J.	Hainsworth
Lyon	Hemphill	Lindsay, J. H.	Henry
Metcalf	Howard	Lupton	Husler
Miller	Jennings	Mackintosh	Kaufman
Moorhead	Johnston	McMurtry	Lash
Nimick	Keating	Palmer, W. P.	Lewis, W. J.
O'Hara	Kelly	Parkin	Luke
Oliver	Kirkpatrick	Read	Mackey
Painter	Lazear		McDonald
Park	Leech		McDowell
Phillips	Lloyd		McNeil
Richardson	McCutcheon		Patterson
Scully	Palmer		Quay
Singer	Phipps		Rhodes
Smith	Porter		Roberts
Speer	Rowe		Schenck
Verner	Shinn		Schwab
Walker	Shoenberger		Shaw

(continued)

APPENDIX I (*Continued*)

Pittsburgh Iron and Steel Families by Social Class

Core	Non-Core	Marginal	Elite
Wood	Snyder		Smith, J.
Zug	Spang		Steele
	Stewart		Steiner
	Tener		Tiers
	Tindle		Trump
	Travelli		Vilsack
	Wade		Voegetly
			Walker, T.
			Wheeler
			Wilson
			Young

ABBREVIATIONS

In tables and appendixes

Agri.	Agricultural	B	boiling
Alleg.	Allegheny	Cnv	converting
Bess.	Bessemer	Cr	crucible
Birm.	Birmingham	F	forges
Cast.	Casting	H	heating
C/M	Clinton Mill	M	melting
Consol.	Consolidated	P	pot
E. T.	Edgar Thomson	Pd	puddling
Hemp.	Hemphill	Sms	Siemans
I.	Iron	T	ton
I. & S.	Iron and Steel		
Mon.	Monongahela		
O. H.	open hearth		
Pgh.	Pittsburgh		
R. M.	rolling mill		
St.	Steel		
T. P.	tin plate		
Vesuv.	Vesuvius		

In bibliography

AER	American Economic Review
BHR	Business History Review
EEH	Explorations in Economic History
JAH	Journal of American History
JEBH	Journal of Economic and Business History
JEH	Journal of Economic History
JPE	Journal of Political Economy
JUH	Journal of Urban History
LH	Labor History
PMHB	Pennsylvania Magazine of History and Biography

PSQ	*Political Science Quarterly*
QRE	*Quarterly Review of Economics*
SSH	*Social Science History*
WPHM	*Western Pennsylvania Historical Magazine*

NOTES

Introduction

1. (New York: Charles Scribner's Sons, 1980), 671.

2. Harold Vatter, *Small Enterprise and Oligopoly: A Study of the Butter, Flour, Automobile, and Glass Container Industries* (Corvallis: Oregon State College Press, 1955).

3. John Kenneth Galbraith, *The Rise of the New Industrial State* (Boston: Houghton Mifflin, 1966). See also Robert Averitt, *The Dual Economy* (New York: W. W. Norton, 1971), and Joseph Bowring, *Competition in the Dual Economy* (Princeton: Princeton University Press, 1986), for more recent statements of this concept.

4. Alfred D. Chandler, Jr., *The Visible Hand: The Managerial Revolution in American Business* (Cambridge, Mass: Harvard University Press, 1977), presents the most sophisticated statement of Chandler's vision of the development of the American business system.

5. Alfred D. Chandler, Jr., "The Beginnings of 'Big Business' in American Industry," *Business History Review* 33 (Spring 1959): 1.

6. Chandler, *Visible Hand*, 1.

7. Despite Chandler's preoccupation with large business, his work was highly sensitive to nuance. Although smaller firms were never the focus of his interest, he was always acutely aware of their continuing importance in many industries or segments of industries. See both *The Visible Hand* and *The Essential Alfred Chandler: Essays toward a Historical Theory of Big Business*, ed. Thomas McCraw (Boston: Harvard Business School Press, 1989), 459.

8. Ralph Hidy in 1970 lamented the dearth of studies of small business in American life and called for greater future attention to its role in the American business system. Ralph Hidy, "Business History: Present Status and Future Needs," *Business History Review* 44 (Winter 1970): 483–97.

9. Chandler, *Visible Hand*, 6.

10. McCraw, *Essential Alfred Chandler*, 451–52.

11. Alfred D. Chandler, Jr., and Richard Tedlow, *The Coming of Managerial Capitalism* (Homewood, Ill.: Richard D. Irwin, 1985), 404.

12. George J. Stigler, "The Economies of Scale," *Journal of Law and Economics* 1, (October 1958): 54.

13. Ibid., 56.

14. Ibid., 71.

15. Leonard W. Weiss, "The Survival Technique and the Extent of Suboptimal Capacity," *Journal of Political Economy* 72 (1964): 246–61. See also his "The Extent of Suboptimal Capacity: A Correction," *Journal of Political Economy* 73 (1965): 300–301.

16. Weiss, "Survival Technique," 249–52.

17. John A. James, "Structural Change in American Manufacturing, 1850–1890," *Journal of Economic History* 43, no. 2 (June 1983): 433–51.

18. Ibid., 436.

19. Ibid., 445.

20. Chandler would not disagree with this conclusion. He pointed out, for example, "[The] steel industry in 1917 still had the largest number of nonintegrated companies of any industry in which the large firm clustered" (*Essential Alfred Chandler*, 459). Many of Chandler's ideas in this area are based on studies by Glenn Porter and Harold Livesay in "Oligopoly in Small Manufacturing Industries," *Explorations in Economic History* 7, no. 5 (Spring 1970): 371–79. See also Louis P. Cain and Donald G. Patterson, "Factor Biases and Technical Change in Manufacturing: The American System, 1850–1919," *Journal of Economic History* 41, no. 2 (June 1981): 341–58. Cain and Patterson, however, assume constant returns to scale and make no link between technical change and industry structure.

21. Jeremy Atack, "Returns to Scale in Antebellum United States Manufacturing," *Explorations in Economic History* 14 (October 1977): 337–59; "Industrial Structure and the Emergence of the Modern Industrial Corporation," *Explorations in Economic History* 22 (1985): 29–52; "Firm Size and Industrial Structure in the United States during the Nineteenth Century," *Journal of Economic History* 46, no. 2 (June 1986): 463–75.

22. Atack, "Firm Size and Industrial Structure," 468.

23. Ibid., 471.

24. Ibid., 472.

25. Atack, "Industrial Structure," 47.

26. Ibid.

27. Lewis Atherton, *The Pioneer Merchant in Mid-America*, University of Missouri Studies, (Columbia: University of Missouri Press, 1939); "Itinerent Merchandising in the Antebellum South," *Bulletin of the Business Historical Society* 19 (1945): 35–59; *The Southern Country Store, 1800–1860* (Baton Rouge: Louisiana State University Press, 1949). Other studies are Thomas D. Clark, *Pills, Petticoats and Plows: The Southern Store* (Norman: University of Oklahoma Press, 1944); Fred Mitchell Jones, "Middlemen in the Domestic Trade of the United States," *Illinois Studies in the Social Sciences* 21 (1937): 1–18, and his "Retail Stores in the United States, 1800–1860," *Journal of Marketing* 2 (October 1936): 134–42. I am

indebted to Mansel Blackford for informing me of several of these studies in his yet unpublished "Small Business in America: An Historiographic Survey." Chandler in his studies also recognized the importance of these mercantile networks, especially in the nineteenth century, and although he acknowledged their continuation into the twentieth century, they were of decreasing significance.

28. Martha Taber, *A History of the Cutlery Industry in the Connecticut Valley*, Smith College Studies in History, no. 41 (Northampton, Mass.: History Department, Smith College, 1955).

29. Theodore Marburg, *Small Business in Brass Manufacturing: The Smith & Griggs Co. of Waterbury* (New York: New York University Press, 1956).

30. James Soltow, *Origins of Small Business: Metal Fabricators and Machinery Makers in New England, 1890–1957*, (Philadelphia: American Philosophical Society, 1965), 55; and "Origins of Small Business and the Relationships between Large and Small Firms: Metal Fabricating and Machinery Making in New England, 1890–1957," in *Small Business in American Life*, ed. Stuart Bruchy (New York: Columbia University Press, 1980), 192–211.

31. Soltow, "Origins of Small Business and the Relationships," 203.

32. Bruce Laurie and Mark Schmitz, "Manufacture and Productivity: The Making of an Industrial Base, Philadelphia, 1850–1880," in *Philadelphia: Work, Space, Family, and Group Experience in the Nineteenth Century*, ed. Theodore Hershberg (New York: Oxford University Press, 1981), 43–92.

33. Ibid., 43.

34. Ibid., 76.

35. Ibid., 85.

36. One of nineteenth-century Philadelphia's industries was iron and steel, and Laurie and Schmitz's analysis of it is revealing. First of all, since practically all iron firms used inanimate power sources, the vast majority were factories in both 1850 and 1870 (85.4 and 95.1 percent). Although average plant size increased during those thirty years, the number of firms also more than doubled, from thirty-four to seventy-three, suggesting continued ease of entry, despite greater capital requirements and size (the average number of employees increased from 37 to 53.2 during this time). Productivity increases, however, were remarkably low for iron and steel, indicating that returns to scale were disappointing.

37. Philip Scranton, *Proprietary Capitalism: The Textile Manufacture at Philadelphia, 1800–1885* (Philadelphia: Temple University Press, 1983); and "Milling About: Paths to Capitalist Development in the Philadelphia Textile Industry, 1840–1865" (Paper presented at the Social Science History Association Meetings, Nashville, 22–25 October 1981).

38. Scranton, *Proprietary Capitalism*, 7.

39. Ibid.

40. Ibid., 4

41. Ibid., 417. Scranton now has another volume on Philadelphia textiles that covers the period from 1885 to 1941: *Figured Tapestry: Production, Markets, and Power in Philadelphia Textiles, 1885–1941* (New York: Cambridge University Press, 1989).

42. Anthony F. C. Wallace, *Rockdale: The Growth of an American Village in the Early Industrial Revolution* (New York: A. A. Knopf, 1978); Gary Kulik, "Pawtucket Village and the Strike of 1824: The Origins of Class Conflict in Rhode Island," *Radical History Review* 17 (Spring 1978): 5–37; and Jonathon Prude, *The Coming Industrial Order: Town and Factory Life in Rural Massachusetts, 1810–1860* (Cambridge, England: Cambridge University Press, 1983).

43. It is important to reiterate that Chandler, for all his stress on bigness, never made that claim about the iron and steel industry (see n. 20). Nonetheless, one would have to read his work very carefully not to come away with the impression that the large integrated firm was predominant.

44. Mansel G. Blackford, *A Portrait Cast in Steel: Buckeye International and Columbus, Ohio, 1881–1980* (Westport, Conn.: Greenwood Press, 1982). Earlier, he had published an account of a small, family-owned firm in *Pioneering a Modern Small Business: Wakefield Seafoods and the Alaskan Frontier* (Greenwich, Conn.: JAI Press, 1979).

45. Amos Loveday, Jr., *The Rise and Decline of the American Cut Nail Industry: A Study of the Interrelationships of Technology, Business Organization, and Management Techniques* (Westport, Conn.: Greenwood Press, 1983).

46. Soltow, "Origins of Small Business and the Relationships," 201.

47. David Brody, "Labor and Small Scale Enterprise during Industrialization," in Bruchy, *Small Business in American Life*, 263–79.

48. Michael Santos, "Laboring on the Periphery: Managers and Workers at the A. M. Byers Company, 1900–1956," *Business History Review* 61 (Spring 1987): 113–33; and "Brother against Brother: The Amalgamated and the Sons of Vulcan at A. M. Byers Co., 1907–1913," *Western Pennsylvania Historical Magazine* 111 (April 1987): 195–212. See also his thesis, "Iron Workers in a Steel Age: The Case of the A. M. Byers Company, 1900–1969" (D.A. thesis, Carnegie-Mellon University, 1984).

49. The classic view of paternalism was molded by Henrietta Larson's presentation and analysis of the views of Samuel Watkinson Collins, head of Collins Company, a leading American manufacturer of cutting tools, in the early nineteenth century. He addressed his workers twice, in 1833 and 1846, with tellingly different results. In 1833 we saw classic paternalism: the workers were skilled, had recently come from nearby farms and villages, and shared a strong cultural and social identity with Collins, who acted as a father figure to them. By 1846, these personal relations had broken down to an extent; the relationship was largely commercial rather than personal. In the first instance, the workers accepted a reduction of wages "cheerfully" and "unanimously," stressing that the "welfare of our village and . . . pros-

perity of the manufacturing interest" were of primary concern. When the workers petitioned Collins for higher wages in 1846, he replied with a purely market response in refusing their entreaties. This is viewed as the beginning of a market mentality on both sides, which led to the development of trade unionism and an adversary stance in labor relations. Labor unions, by that formulation, could hardly exist in a paternalistic environment. Henrietta Larson, "An Early Industrial Capitalist's Labor Policy and Management," *Bulletin of the Business Historical Society* 17, no. 5 (November 1944): 132–41.

50. There is a vast literature on this subject. I will attempt to provide only a few major works to give the reader some direction: William Miller, "American Historians and the American Business Elite," "The Recruitment of the American Business Elite," and "The Business Elite in Business Bureaucracies: Careers of Top Executives in the Early Twentieth Century," and Frances W. Gregory and Irene D. Neu, "The American Industrial Elite of the 1870's: The Social Origins," all in *Men in Business*, rev. ed., ed. William Miller (New York: Harper & Row, 1962), 309–28. John N. Ingham, "The Robber Barons and the Old Elites: A Case Study in Social Stratification," *Mid-America* 42, no. 3 (July 1970): 190–204, and "Rags to Riches Revisited: The Role of City Size and Related Factors in the Recruitment of Business Leaders," *Journal of American History* (December 1976): 615–37. For a more general analysis, see Anthony Giddens, *The Class Structure of Advanced Societies* (London: Hutchinson University Library, 1973). The latter volume has an extensive bibliography of literature.

51. Geoffery Ingham, *Capitalism Divided? The City and Industry in British Social Development* (London: Macmillan, 1984), 2. See also Asa Briggs, *Victorian Cities* (New York: Harper & Row, 1979), 184–240; Dennis Smith, *Conflict and Compromise: Class Formation in English Society, 1830–1914: A Comparative Study of Birmingham and Sheffield* (London: Routledge & Kegan Paul, 1982); W. D. Rubinstein, "Wealth, Elites and the Class Structure of Modern Britain," *Past and Present* 76 (August 1977), 99–126, and *Men of Property* (London: Croon Helm, 1981); and Walter L. Arnstein, "The Survival of the Victorian Aristocracy," in *The Rich, the Well-Born and the Powerful*, ed. Frederick L. Jaher (Urbana: University of Illinois Press, 1973), 203–57.

52. David C. Hammack, "Problems in the Historical Study of Power in the Cities and Towns of the United States, 1800–1960," *American Historical Review* 83, no. 2 (April 1978): 323–49; and see his "Small Business and Urban Power: Some Notes on the History of Economic Policy in Nineteenth-Century American Cities," in Bruchy, ed., *Small Business in American Life*, 317–37.

53. Hammack, "Problems in the Historical Study of Power," 326.

54. See Peter Bachrach and Morton Baratz, *Power and Poverty: Theory and Practice* (New York: Oxford University Press, 1970), for a leading statement of this approach.

55. The most well-known exponent of the pluralist approach is Robert

A. Dahl in *Who Governs? Democracy and Power in an American City* (New Haven: Yale University Press, 1961).

56. Michael Aiken, "The Distribution of Community Power: Structural Bases and Social Consequences," in *The Structure of Community Power*, ed. Michael Aiken and Paul E. Mott (New York: Random House, 1970), 487–525.

57. Nelson Polsby, "Pluralism in the Study of Community Power: or *Erklärung* before *Verklärung* in *Wissensociologie*," *American Sociologist* 9 (1969): 118–22.

58. Hammack, "Problems of Historical Study of Power," 329; and James Bryce, *The American Commonwealth*, 2 vols. (New York: Macmillan, 1888).

59. Frederick C. Jaher, "The Boston Brahmins in the Age of Industrial Capitalism," in *The Age of Industrialism in America: Essays in Social Structure and Cultural Values*, ed. Frederick C. Jaher (New York: Free Press, 1968), 188–262; "Nineteenth Century Elites in Boston and New York," *Journal of Social History* 6 (1972): 32–77; "Style and Status in Late Nineteenth Century New York," in Jaher, ed., *The Rich, the Well Born*, 258–64; *The Urban Establishment* (Urbana: University of Illinois Press, 1982). Stow Persons, *The Decline of American Gentility* (New York: Columbia University Press, 1973).

60. Edward Pessen, "The Social Configuration of the Ante-Bellum City: An Historical and Theoretical Inquiry," *Journal of Urban History* 2 (1976); Michael Katz, *The People of Hamilton, Canada, West: Family and Class in a Mid-Nineteenth Century City* (Cambridge, Mass.: Harvard University Press, 1975); Michael Frisch, *Town into City: Springfield, Massachusetts and the Meaning of Community, 1840–1880* (Cambridge, Mass.: Harvard University Press, 1972).

61. Moisei Ostrogorski, *Democracy and the Organization of Political Parties* (New York: Macmillan, 1902).

62. Hammack, "Problems in the Historical Study of Community Power," 333.

63. Samuel P. Hays, "The Politics of Reform in Municipal Government in the Progressive Era," *Pacific Northwest Quarterly* 55 (1965): 157–69, gives the best overview of this perspective. Frederick C. Jaher develops the social side of this equation in much detail, although he does not tie it into the political arena in the same manner as Hays. See "The Boston Brahmins" in Jaher, ed., *Age of Industrialism in America*, 188–262; "Nineteenth Century Elites in Boston and New York," *Journal of Social History* 6 (1972): 32–77; "Style and Status in High Society in Late Nineteenth Century New York," in Jaher, ed., *The Rich, the Well Born* 258–84; and *The Urban Establishment*, 1–4, 7–9, 11–12.

64. There are myriad books on urban machines, written from virtually every vantage point. Those of greatest significance for the argument stated here are Martin Shefter, "The Emergence of the Political Machine: An Alternative View," in Willis D. Hawley et al., *Theoretical Perspectives on Urban*

Politics (Englewood Cliffs, N.J.: Prentice Hall, 1976), 14–44; Joel A. Tarr, *A Study in Urban Politics: Boss Lorimer of Chicago* (Urbana: University of Illinois Press, 1971), and "The Urban Politician as Entrepreneur," in *Urban Bosses, Machines, and Progressive Reformers*, ed. Bruce M. Stave (Lexington, Mass.: D. C. Heath, 1972); Zane L. Miller, *Boss Cox's Cincinnati: Urban Politics in the Progressive Era* (New York: Oxford University Press, 1968); Lyle Dorsett, *The Pendergast Machine* (New York: Oxford University Press, 1968); J. Joseph Huthmacher, "Urban Liberalism and the Age of Reform," *Mississippi Valley Historical Review* 49 (1962): 231–41; John D. Buenker, *Urban Liberalism and Progressive Reform* (New York: Charles Scribner's Sons, 1973).

65. I will not try to list all these works here, but they start with James Bryce, *The American Commonwealth*, 2 vols. (New York: Macmillan, 1888); received mass circulation with the writings of Lincoln Steffens in *Shame of the Cities* (New York: McClure, Phillips, Co., 1904); and were followed by works by a number of other early historians.

66. Hays, "The Politics of Reform in Municipal Government in the Progressive Era," *Pacific Northwest Quarterly* 55, no. 4 (October 1964): 157–69; and "The Changing Political Structure of the City in Industrial America," *Journal of Urban History* 1 (November 1974): 6–38.

67. The literature on these issues is voluminous. Some of the most important works are C. Wright Mills and Melville J. Ulmer, "Small Business and Civic Welfare," in *The Structure of Community Power*, ed. Michael Aiken and Paul E. Mott (New York: Random House, 1970), 124–54; Irving A. Fowler, "Local Industrial Structures, Economic Power, and Community Welfare," *Social Problems* 6 (Summer 1958): 41–51; and Roland J. Pellegin and Charles H. Coates, "Absentee-Owned Corporations and Community Power Structure," *American Journal of Sociology* 61 (March 1956): 413–19 (which argues for greater influence by absentee-owned corporations than most commentators would agree on). Robert O. Schulze found that just the opposite in his study of Ypsilanti: "The Bifurcation of Power in a Satellite City," in *Community Political Systems*, ed. Morris Janowitz (New York: Free Press, 1961), 19–80. M. K. Jennings, in his study of Atlanta (*Community Influentials: The Elites of Atlanta* [New York: Free Press, 1964]), found that local economic elites had a higher rate of participation in community organizations than representatives of absentee-controlled corporations. Paul E. Mott, "The Role of the Absentee-Owned Corporation in the Changing Community," in Aiken and Mott, eds., *Structure of Community Power*, 170–77, isolated three elite groups in Ypsilanti—political, local economic, and absentee-corporate—and indicated that the final group had more power than most observers recognized. He also argued that their lack of direct involvement in decision-making hid a powerful influence that was exerted in a number of ways.

68. Soltow, "Origins of Small Business: Metal Fabricators," 50.

69. Blackford, *Portrait Cast in Steel*, 65–66, 132–37, 184–89.

70. David C. Hammack, "Small Business and Urban Power," 317–37.

71. Carl V. Harris, *Political Power in Birmingham, 1871–1921* (Knoxville: University of Tennessee Press, 1977); see esp. chap. 3. Another study of an iron and steel center is that by James McKee on Lorain, Ohio. Lorain, a small steel-making city of fifty thousand, was dominated by one large mill, which employed half the population. McKee recognized that the upper stratum, made up of the managers of the industrial, banking, and utility firms, the owners and operators of the larger local business enterprises, and a small group of local professionals, at one time controlled decision making in the city. But an ethnically, religiously, and racially heterogeneous population, along with the rise of the CIO, which united these formerly antagonistic groups, drastically altered the system of power. The economic elite, however, continued to wield inordinate influence in civic welfare areas. James B. McKee, "Status and Power in the Industrial Community: A Comment on Drucker's Thesis," *American Journal of Sociology* 58 (January 1953): 364–70.

72. Shelby Stewman and Joel A. Tarr, "Public-Private Partnerships in Pittsburgh: An Approach to Governance," in *Pittsburgh-Sheffield, Sister Cities*, ed. Joel A. Tarr (Pittsburgh: Carnegie-Mellon University Press, 1986), 141.

73. Herrick Chapman, "Pittsburgh and Europe's Metallurgical Cities: A Comparison," in *City at the Point: Essays on the Social History of Pittsburgh*, ed. Samuel P. Hays (Pittsburgh: University of Pittsburgh Press, 1989), 411.

74. For further elaboration of this latter point, see John N. Ingham, "Steel City Aristocrats," in Hays, ed., *City at the Point*, 265–94.

75. For an overview of political developments in Pittsburgh, see Michael F. Holt, *Forging a Majority: The Formation of the Republican Party in Pittsburgh, 1848–1860* (New Haven: Yale University Press, 1969); Samuel P. Hays, "The Development of Pittsburgh as a Social Order," *Western Pennsylvania Historical Magazine* 57 (October 1974): 431–48, and his "Politics of Reform in Municipal Government in the Progressive Era," 157–69. Roy Lubove, *Twentieth Century Pittsburgh: Government, Business and Environmental Change* (New York: John Wiley & Sons, 1969); Bruce M. Stave, *The New Deal and the Last Hurrah: Pittsburgh Machine Politics* (Pittsburgh: University of Pittsburgh Press, 1970); Paul Kleppner, "Government, Parties and Voters in Pittsburgh," in Hays, ed. *City at the Point*, 151–80. For an overview of social welfare policies and civic organizations in Pittsburgh see Lubove, *Twentieth Century Pittsburgh*, along with his "Pittsburgh and the Uses of Social Welfare History," in Hays, ed., *City at the Point*, 295–325.

76. Scranton, *Proprietary Capitalism*, 8.

Chapter 1

1. Quoted in Richard C. Wade, *The Urban Frontier* (Chicago: University of Chicago Press, 1959), 10. Wade is virtually the sole exception to the neglect by historians of Pittsburgh's early years.

2. Ibid., 45.

3. Glenn Porter and Harold Livesay, *Merchants and Manufacturers: Studies in the Changing Structure of Nineteenth-Century Marketing* (Baltimore: Johns Hopkins University Press, 1971), 8.

4. Richard Wade asserts that during the next couple of decades the economic and social leaders of the town were merchants and that most of them were Scots-Irish Presbyterians (*Urban Frontier*, 106–7).

5. Joseph F. Rishel, "The Founding Families of Allegheny County: An Examination of Nineteenth Century Elite Continuity" (unpublished Ph.D. diss., University of Pittsburgh, 1975), 34–47. Rishel's dissertation has recently been published in revised form by the University of Pittsburgh Press.

6. Arthur Cecil Bining, "The Rise of Iron Manufacture in Western Pennsylvania," *Western Pennsylvania Historical Magazine* 16 (November 1933): 239.

7. James Riddle, *The Pittsburgh Directory for 1815* (Pittsburgh: Duquesne Smelting Co. Rpt. 1940), 50–51.

8. William A. Sullivan, *The Industrial Worker in Pennsylvania, 1800–1840* (Harrisburg, Pennsylvania Historical & Museum Commission, 1955), 13–14.

9. James M. Swank, *History of the Manufacture of Iron in All Ages* (Philadelphia: American Iron and Steel Association, 1892), 227–28.

10. Samuel Jones, *Pittsburgh in the Year 1826* (Pittsburgh: Johnston & Stockton, 1826), 50–57.

11. Louis C. Hunter, "Financial Problems of Early Pittsburgh Iron Manufacturers," *Journal of Economic and Business History* 2 (May 1930): 527.

12. Ibid., 531.

13. Bining, "Rise of Iron Manufacture," 252–53.

14. Porter and Livesay, *Merchants and Manufacturers*, 69, 107.

15. Ibid., 73–77, 101.

16. Ibid., 65–66.

17. Ibid., 71–72, 101.

18. Jones, *Pittsburgh in the Year 1826*, 53.

19. John A. Jordan, *Encyclopedia of Pennsylvania Biography*, 31 vols. (New York: Lewis Historical Publishing Co., 1914–63), 5:1484–86 (hereafter *EPB*); J. Fletcher Brennan, *A Biographical Encyclopedia and Portrait Gallery of the State of Ohio* (Cincinnati: J. C. Yorston & Co., 1880), 6:1457–58; Annie Clark Miller, *Chronicle of Families, House and Estates of Pittsburgh and Its Environs* (Pittsburgh: privately printed, 1927), 41–43; *Iron Trade Review* 75, 21 Aug. 1924, 475–779; *U.S. Steel News* 1 (June 1936): 5; James M. Swank, *Iron Manufacturing and Coal Mining in Pennsylvania* (Philadelphia: American Iron and Steel Association, 1878), 38–40. (Note: In the sources, the family name is spelled both Shoenberger and Schoenberger. I have chosen the former for this work.)

20. Hunter, "Financial Problems," 523–24; and Jones, *Pittsburgh in the Year 1826*, 50–51.

21. George Irving Reed, ed., *Century Cyclopedia of History and Biogra-*

phy of Pennsylvania, 2 vols. (Chicago: Century Publishing Co., 1904), 2:90–91; Jordan, *EPB* 6:1884–87.

22. Hunter, "Financial Problems," 523–24.

23. The Lyon and Stewart families were listed in the 1904 Pittsburgh *Social Directory,* perhaps the most exclusive published barometer of upper-class status. They were also included in the 1908 Pittsburgh *Social Register,* as was the Spang family. The Shoenbergers were not listed in either, since by the early twentieth century they were living in Cincinnati. Narrative evidence from the nineteenth century, however, affirms their eminence, including the fact that John H. Shoenberger, when he left Pittsburgh, donated his home as the clubhouse for the Pittsburgh Club, the most exclusive gentleman's club in the city. Under a more comprehensive schema of social status I developed in an earlier work (John N. Ingham, *The Iron Barons: A Social Analysis of an America Urban Elite, 1874–1965* [Westport, Conn.: Greenwood Press, 1978]), the Shoenbergers ranked as a Non-Core upper-class family in the city, as did the Stewarts and Spangs. The Lyon family was Core upper-class, the most prestigious ranking. These rankings are discussed in more detail in chapter 2. The variable status of the *Social Directory* and *Social Register* was established in an exhaustive study of 4,675 individuals and families in Pittsburgh by George Bedeian, "Social Stratification within a Metropolitan Upper Class: Early Twentieth Century Pittsburgh as a Case Study" (Seminar paper, History Department, University of Pittsburgh, 1974).

24. Swank, *Iron Manufacturing,* 230–31.

25. Louis C. Hunter, "Influence of the Market upon Technique in the Iron Industry in Western Pennsylvania up to 1860," *Journal of Economic and Business History* 1 (1929): 252–53.

26. George Thurston, *Pittsburgh's Progress, Industries and Resources* (Pittsburgh: A. A. Anderson & Co., 1886), 113.

27. Hunter, "Financial Problems," 525.

28. The Zug family were also of German extraction and had moved to Pittsburgh from Cumberland County in 1835 in the person of Christopher Zug. The son of a poor farmer, Zug entered the retail trade in Pittsburgh when he arrived in the city and then worked for an iron manufacturing firm. In 1846 he joined with Henry Graff and John Lindsay in starting the Sable Mill. His son, Charles H. Zug, joined the firm in the mid-1850s and continued to run it until the 1890s. Lindsay was a native of Northern Ireland who became a partner in Sable Iron when it was organized in 1845 (Margaret I. Lindsay, *The Lindsays of America* [Albany: J. Mansell's Sons, 1889]; *Iron Age,* 27 Sept. 1894, 530).

29. *Pittsburgh Bulletin,* 23 May 1896, 20 Feb. 1897; John Newton Boucher, *A Century and a Half of Pittsburgh and Her People,* 4 vols. (New York: Lewis Historical Publishing Co., 1906), 4:141–43; *Iron Age,* 25 Feb. 1897, 20.

30. *Encyclopedia of Contemporary Biography of Pennsylvania,* 3 vols.

(New York: Atlantic Publishing & Engraving Co., 1889), 1:204 (hereafter *ECB*); *Biographical Encyclopedia of Pennsylvania in the Nineteenth Century* (Philadelphia: Galaxy Publishing Co., 1874), 649.

31. Reed, ed., *Century Cyclopedia* 2:110–11; *Iron Age*, 16 July 1903.

32. R. G. Dun & Co. (Pa.) 5:384; *Magazine of Western History* 3 (1885), 183–87; Jordan, *EPB*, 7:2405–8, 5:2694–97; Reed, ed., *Century Cyclopedia* 2:31–33, 132–34; G. H. Thurston, *Pittsburgh As It Is* (Pittsburgh: W. S. Haven, 1857), 112.

33. R. G. Dun & Co. (Pa.) 10:131: *National Cyclopedia of American Biography*, 58 vols. (New York: J. T. White & Co., 1894–1964) (hereafter *NCAB*), 13:290, 22:446–47; *Pittsburgh Bulletin*, 13 Aug. 1904; *Iron Age* 5 Jan. 1889, 24 Aug. 1904; *Book of Prominent Pennsylvanians* (Pittsburgh: Leader Publishing Co., 1913), 144–45; Reed, ed., *Century Cyclopedia* 2:27–29; John N. Boucher, ed., *History of Westmoreland County, Pennsylvania*, 3 vols. (New York: Lewis Historical Publishing Co., 1906), 3:118–19.

34. *Iron Age*, 25 Sept. 1924, 795; *History of Allegheny County, Pennsylvania* (Chicago: A. Warren & Co., 1889) 2:438–39; *History of Allegheny County* (Philadelphia: Events Publishing, 1876), 193; R. G. Dun & Co. (Pa) 9:463.

35. Eagle Rolling Mill was built in 1848 by James Wood, a native of New York City who had served as a riverboat captain and in the 1830s moved to Pittsburgh, where he opened a cotton mill. He then started the Eagle Mill and also went to Youngstown, Ohio, where he erected the first blast furnace in the area. In later years Wood built a number of other furnaces as he too created an informally integrated rolling mill operation. His daughter, Rebecca Wood, married Porter R. Friend, who carried on the iron business in partnership with James T. Wood, the elder Wood's son. After the Civil War, Porter and Rebecca Friend's son, James Wood Friend, became a prominent iron and steel manufacturer in the city (Reed, ed., *Century Cyclopedia* 2:91–97; *Pittsburgh Directory*, 1865; *Iron Age*, 4 June 1896; John W. Jordan, *Genealogical and Personal History of Western Pennsylvania*, 3 vols. (New York: Lewis Historical Publishing Co., 1915), 1:386–90.

36. Pennsylvania Iron was built in 1844 by William Everson and his son, William H. Everson. Both men were natives of Staffordshire, England, who immigrated to Pittsburgh in 1835. The elder Everson retired in 1850, and his son continued to manage the firm, taking in William C. Macrum as a partner. Macrum and Everson also organized and ran the Commercial Banking Company, which later became the Marine National Bank. In addition, William H. Everson was a key factor in the organization of the Republican party in Pittsburgh in the mid-1850s (*Pittsburgh Bulletin*, 18 Apr. 1896; *Iron Age*, 16 Apr 1896; Jordan, *EPB* 5:1669–71; *Pittsburgh Gazette*, 16, 17 Dec. 1901).

37. McKeesport Rolling Mill was built in 1851 by William Dewees Wood and Richard Gilpin of Philadelphia. Like so many of the Pittsburgh ironmasters in the 1820s, Wood and Gilpin were members of families that

controlled important iron-making operations in eastern Pennsylvania. Wood was the son of Alan Wood, the first man to manufacture sheet iron in the United States and owner of Alan Wood & Co. Gilpin was also a partner in that concern and was W. Dewees Wood's father-in-law. Four years later, Gilpin retired to his native Philadelphia, and Wood took in two new partners at the McKeesport operation: George F. McClene and Maxwell K. Moorhead. McClene was a native of Wilmington, Delaware, and the inventor of an important patent process for making galvanized metal that was used in the mill. Maxwell K. Moorhead was the son of Gen. James Kennedy Moorhead, by the 1850s considered to be the "first citizen" of the city. Maxwell Moorhead and Wood struggled for control of their operations for a number of years; Wood returned to Philadelphia for a time in the late 1850s. Finally, in 1861, the two men agreed to end their partnership; Moorhead was to keep the Soho mill and Wood to retain the McKeesport one (Frederick A. Virkus, ed., *The Abridged Compendium of American Genealogy*, 7 vols. [Chicago: A. N. Marquis Co., 1925–   ], 1:515–16; *Iron Age*, 21 Jan. 1897, 28; *Pittsburgh Bulletin*, 17 Jan. 1897; Jordan, *EPB* 16:15–16; *Magazine of Western History* 2 (1884), 478–90; George O. Seilhammer, *Leslies' Republican Party* (New York: L. A. Williams Publishing Co., 1899), 2:457–58; Elizabeth Moorhead, *Whirling Spindle: The Story of a Pittsburgh Family* (Pittsburgh: University of Pittsburgh Press, 1942); *James Kennedy Moorhead: Memorial Volume* (Pittsburgh: privately printed, 1880); *Dictionary of American Biography*, 22 vols. (New York: Charles Scribner's Sons, 1927–58) (hereafter *DAB*), 13:147–48; *Pittsburgh Leader*, 3 Jan. 1899; *NCAB* 12:326–27, 34:136–37; *Pittsburgh Bulletin*, 3 Jan. 1899; *Iron Age*, 12 Jan. 1899; 4 Oct. 1900, 25; R. G. Dun & Co. (Pa.) 5:112, 601; Crosby C. McLean, Jr., *The Wood Family of Montgomery County*, Pennsylvania (n.p., n.d.).

38. Glendon was built to manufacture railroad spikes in 1858 by Joseph Dilworth. He was the son of William Dilworth, an early Pittsburgh resident and a member of the state legislature who was involved in the contracting business. Joseph Dilworth joined Dilworth Brothers, the largest wholesale grocery firm in the city, which had been founded by his brothers, George W. and John S. Dilworth. Later, Joseph set up Dilworth, Bidiwell & Co. to distribute black powder and gunpowder for du Pont and Hazard in Pittsburgh (Jordan, *EPB* 31:61–63; Boucher, *Century and a Half* 3:45; George Thornton Fleming, ed., *History of Pittsburgh and Environs*, 6 vols. [New York: The American Historical Society, 1922], 4:101–2; Western Pennsylvania Biographical Association, *Western Pennsylvanians* [Pittsburgh: WPBA, 1923], 294; Frank C. Harper, *Pittsburgh of Today*, 5 vols. [New York: American Historical Society, 1931], 5:213–14; *Iron Age*, 15 June 1911, 1449; 27 Sept. 1928, 802; 6 Sept. 1934, 46).

39. Birmingham Rolling Mill was owned by William J. Lewis and John Phillips in the late 1850s. Lewis was born in Pittsburgh, the son of an immigrant from Wales. His father died when Lewis was quite young, so he was apprenticed as a roll turner at the Birmingham plant. He worked there

for eight years, then became a superintendent at another mill for a time. Later he joined in partnership with his brother-in-law, John Phillips, to purchase the Birmingham plant. Phillips was a Pittsburgh native whose father was a blacksmith and manufactured wrought iron bolts. John Phillips apprenticed with his father and then became a bricklayer; later, he and his brother converted that operation into an important contracting firm that constructed several buildings in the Pittsburgh area (Reed, ed., *Century Cyclopedia* 2:161, 194–95; Henry Oliver Evans, *Iron Pioneer: Henry W. Oliver, 1840–1901* [New York: E. P. Dutton, 1942], 33; R. G. Dun & Co. [Pa.] 7:133; *Iron Age*, 7 Feb. 1907.)

40. Porter and Livesay, *Merchants and Manufacturers*, 67. For information on Jones, Laughlin, and American Iron, see *DAB* 10:162–63; *ECB* 1:42; Fleming, *History of Pittsburgh* 3:832; Reed, ed., *Century Cyclopedia* 2:1, 40; *Magazine of Western History*, 2 (1884), 566–71; 3, 189–93; *History of Allegheny County* 2 (1889), 233; Erasmus Wilson, ed., *Standard History of Pittsburgh, Pennsylvania* (Chicago: H. R. Cornell & Co., 1898), 984; *NCAB* 13:222; *Pittsburgh Iron City*, 23 Dec. 1953, 3; Boucher, *Century and a Half* 4:214; Jordan, *Genealogical and Personal History* 3:1132–33; Jordan, *EPB* 1:359, 9:207; *Iron Age*, 28 Dec. 1882, 15; 21 May 1903, 44; Thomas E. Lloyd, "History of Jones and Laughlin Steel Corporation," Jones and Laughlin Steel Company Papers, Archives for an Industrial Society (AIS), Hillman Library, University of Pittsburgh; B. F. Jones Diary (AIS); Jones and Laughlin Papers (AIS); R. G. Dun & Co. (Pa.) 5:131, 152, 180, 275.

41. Porter and Livesay, *Merchants and Manufacturers*, 59.

42. Ibid., 61.

43. Ibid., 58.

44. David Brody, *Steelworkers in America: The Non-Union Era* (Cambridge, Mass.: Harvard University Press, 1960).

45. Chapter 4 details the demands this type of production made on workers and its impact on labor-management relations.

46. U.S. Bureau of Labor, *Eleventh Special Report of the Commissioner of Labor: Regulation or Restriction of Output* (Washington, D.C.: U.S. Government Printing Office, 1904), 246, quoted in Michael Nuwer, "From Batch to Flow: Production Technology and Work-Force Skills in the Steel Industry, 1880–1920," *Technology and Culture* 29 (October 1988): 813–14.

47. David Montgomery, *Workers' Control in America* (Cambridge, England: Cambridge University Press, 1979), 9.

48. American Iron and Steel Association (AISA), *Directory of Iron and Steel Plants in the United States and Canada* (Washington, D.C.: AISA, 1874), and John W. Bennett, "The Iron Workers of Woods Run and Johnstown: The Union Era" (Unpublished Ph.D. diss., University of Pittsburgh, 1977), 10.

49. AISA, *Directory of Iron and Steel Works in the United States and Canada* (New York: AISA, 1874–1940), 1884, and B. F. Jones Diary (AIS).

50. *The Autobiography of Andrew Carnegie* (Boston: Houghton-Mifflin,

1920), 130. Iron making was hardly the only business characterized by this technique; it was, indeed, the normal way in which most businesses operated at that time. Once, Carnegie asked his friend Frank Doubleday, head of the Doubleday publishing house, what he had made that month. Doubleday replied that he didn't know, since his statements were only drawn up once a year. "Do you know what I would do if I were in that kind of business?" Carnegie asked. "No," replied Doubleday. "I would get out of it" was Carnegie's response. And so he did (Harold C. Livesay, *Andrew Carnegie and the Rise of Big Business* [Boston: Little, Brown, & Co., 1975], 111).

51. Harry H. Campbell, *The Manufacture and Properties of Iron and Steel* (New York: Hill Publishing Co., 1907), 90–91.

52. F. W. Harbord and J. W. Hall, *The Metallurgy of Steel*, 7th ed., vol. 2, *Mechanical Treatment* (London: C. Griffin & Co., 1923), 6.

53. Bradley Stoughton, *The Metallurgy of Iron and Steel* (New York: McGraw-Hill, 1923), 79–80.

54. H. M. Howe, *Metallurgy of Steel* (New York: Scientific Publishing Co., 1890), 296–316. See also Geoffrey Tweedale, *Sheffield Steel and America: A Century of Commercial and Technological Interdependence, 1830–1930* (Cambridge, England: Cambridge University Press, 1987) 37.

55. Tweedale, *Sheffield Steel*, chap. 2.

56. Ibid., 36.

57. Ibid., 15.

58. Ibid., 16; K. C. Barraclough, *Steelmaking before Bessemer*, vol. 2, *Crucible Steel: The Growth of Technique* (London: Metals Society, 1984), 219; Swank, *History of the Manufacture*, 389, and Harrison Gilmer, "The Birth of the American Crucible Steel Industry," *Western Pennsylvania Historical Magazine* 36, no. 1 (1953): 21–22, 24.

59. G. H. Thurston, *Pittsburgh As It Is* (Pittsburgh: W. S. Haven, 1857), 113.

60. *NCAB* 33:211; R. G. Dun & Co. (Pa.) 5:190, 193, 404; 6:396; *ECB* 1:50–52; Daniel W. Howe, *Howe Genealogies*, (Boston: New England Historical Genealogical Society, 1929); *Manufactures and Manufacturers of Pennsylvania of the Nineteenth Century*, (Philadelphia: 1875), 178; *History of Allegheny County* (1889), 2:262; John W. Jordan, ed., *Colonial and Revolutionary Families of Pennsylvania*, 17 vols. (New York: Lewis Historical Publishing Co., 1911–65), 3:1172–74, 14:383–95; Fleming, *History of Pittsburgh* 5:851–53; *Magazine of Western History* (1884), 2:550–56; 3:329–48, 626–35; *Iron Age*, 5 Aug. 1909; Samuel Calvin Wells, *Ancestry and Descendants of Col. Daniel Wells, 1760–1815* (Greenfield, Mass.: n.p., n.d.); *Pittsburgh Gazette*, 26 Apr. 1893; Erasmus Wilson, *Standard History of Pittsburgh, Pennsylvania* (Chicago: H. R. Cornell Co., 1898), 1001–3; Hussey, Wells & Co., *Steel Memorial*, 1 Dec. 1865; *In Memoriam of Calvin Wells* (Philadelphia, 1910); Tweedale, *Sheffield Steel*, 20–21; Harrison Gilmer, "Birth of the American Crucible Steel Industry," *Western Pennsylvania Historical Magazine* 36 (1953): 27–30.

61. *DAB* 14:205–6; *Pittsburgh Gazette*, 23, 24 Feb. 1875; Fleming, *History of Pittsburgh* 4:69–71; Jordan, *EPB* 9:176–81, 13:165–67; *Western Pennsylvanians*, 404; R. G. Dun & Co. (Pa.) 5:73, 93, 310; *Magazine of Western History* 4 (1886): 524–28; Gilmer, "Birth of the American Crucible," 30–32; *Iron Age*, 27 Oct. 1898, 22; *Pittsburgh Bulletin*, 27 Oct. 1898; M. A. Miller, *Meet the Blair Family* (Holidaysburg, Pa.: Blair County Historical Society, n.d.); Jordan, *Colonial and Revolutionary Families* 6:692–93; George P. Donehoo, *Pennsylvania: A History*, 5 vols. (New York: Lewis Historical Publishing Co., 1926), 5:125–26.

62. *NCAB* 23:336; Harper, *Pittsburgh of Today* 5:764–65; Jordan, *EPB* 1:138, 5:1667–68; Reed, ed., *Century Cyclopedia* 2:174–75; *Encyclopedia of Contemporary Biography* 2:39–40; *Iron Age*, 2 Apr. 1903, 26; 23 Sept. 1909, 926; R. G. Dun & Co. (Pa.) 5:138.

63. *Iron Age*, 22 Dec. 1898, 18; Reed, ed., *Century Cyclopedia* 2: 103; Jordan, *EPB* 5:1662–66; *Pittsburgh Gazette*, 20, 21 Apr. 1875; R. G. Dun & Co. (Pa.) 1:110, 138, 462.

64. Thomas Maxwell Potts, *Our Family Ancestors* (Armstrong, Pa.: the author, 1895); Harper, *Pittsburgh of Today* 5:955; *Iron Age*, 21 Aug. 1890; 2 June 1904, 42; 9 Dec. 1909; 22 Mar. 1917, 750; *Magazine of Western History* 2 (1884): 556–62; Jordan, *Colonial & Revolutionary Families* 6:330–34; Fleming, *History of Pittsburgh* 5:149–50; Leland M. Williams, *Prominent and Progressive Pennsylvanians of the Nineteenth Century*, 3 vols. (Philadelphia: The Record Publishing Co., 1898), 148; Engineer's Society of Western Pennsylvania, *Proceedings* 21 (1905): 225–29; *DAB* 6:583–84; *NCAB* 22:232–33; American Society of Civil Engineers, *Transactions* 71 (December 1911); American Institute of Mining Engineers, *Transactions* 41 (1911); American Society of Mechanical Engineers, *Transactions* 32 (1911); Jordan, *EPB* 1:152.

65. Wayne Iron and Steel, founded in 1829, was one of the oldest firms in the city. A few years later, James Brown, a wealthy merchant and brewer, purchased the firm. In 1849, he built a crucible steelworks at the plant, but it was not successful. In the 1860s a workable plant was installed, but Wayne always produced more iron than steel in the early years. The Browns also owned a couple of blast furnaces, and several members of the Brown family were involved in other steel ventures in the city, including Hussey, Wells & Co. (Reed, ed., *Century Cyclopedia* 2:92; *History of Allegheny County, Pennsylvania* [Philadelphia, 1876], 1052–53; *Memoirs of Allegheny County, Pennsylvania*, 2 vols. [Madison, Wis.: Northwestern History Association, 1904], 2:213; R. G. Dun & Co. [Pa.] 8:86).

66. Pittsburgh Steel had been built by Jones, Boyd & Co. in 1845 in an attempt to make cast steel. Later, crucible furnaces were installed, and in 1865 it was sold to Robert J. Anderson. Anderson was born in Pittsburgh and worked for a number of years for a wholesale drug firm. In 1855 he became a partner in the Anchor Tack Mill until taking over Pittsburgh Steel. Although always producing more iron than steel, the firm became one of the

more important producers in the Pittsburgh area (*Iron Age*, 28 Feb. 1884; R. G. Dun & Co. [Pa.] 6:344–45).

67. Fort Pitt Iron and Steel was another venture of the protean Graff family. The plant was originally built in 1842 as a puddled iron producer but in the 1860s began making steel. It, too, produced more iron than steel until the 1890s, when it became Carbon Steel Company (R. G. Dun & Co. [Pa.] 5:58; 9:222).

68. LaBelle Steel was built in 1862 by George Reiter and John Snavely. Little is known of either man. In 1874, Reiter bought out Snavely and a few months later took in the Sutton family as partners. They, in turn, forced out Reiter and brought in Andrew D. Smith and Benjamin F. Jennings. Andrew Smith was the son of Hugh Smith, a native of Ireland who developed massive coal holdings in Pittsburgh and Wheeling. Andrew joined his father in the business and later also became a partner in the Parks' Black Diamond works. The Smiths became the dominant entity in LaBelle Steel. Benjamin F. Jennings was the son of John F. Jennings, who had organized Sheffield Steel with the Singer and Nimick families (Reed, ed., *Century Cyclopedia*, 2:140; *Pittsburgh Bulletin*, 29 Oct. 1898; *Iron Age*, 27 Oct. 1898, 10 Dec. 1903; *ECB* [1889], 1:139–42; *Magazine of Western History* 3 (1885): 513–20).

69. Michael F. Holt, *Forging A Majority: The Formation of the Republican Party in Pittsburgh, 1848–1860* (New Haven: Yale University Press, 1969), 31–35.

70. Ibid., 33.

71. Ibid., 35.

72. Harold L. Twiss, "The Pittsburgh Business Elite, 1850–1890–1929" (Seminar Paper, History Department, University of Pittsburgh, 1964), 6, 9, 16.

73. James Carl Holmberg, "The Industrializing Community: Pittsburgh, 1850–1880" (Unpublished Ph.D. diss., University of Pittsburgh, 1981).

74. These class categories and the rationale for creating them are discussed in far greater detail in my *Iron Barons*, 127–52.

Chapter 2

1. *Engineering* 25, 19 Apr. 1878, 295.

2. Peter Temin, *Iron and Steel in the Nineteenth Century: An Economic Inquiry* (Cambridge, Mass.: MIT Press, 1964), 164–65.

3. Alfred D. Chandler, Jr., *The Visible Hand: The Managerial Revolution in American Business* (Cambridge, Mass.: Harvard University Press, 1977), 267; Joseph F. Wall, *Andrew Carnegie* (New York: Oxford University Press, 1970), 342.

4. Chandler, *Visible Hand*, 1.

5. Temin, *Iron and Steel*, 274–75.

6. Lynn Gordon Mapes, "*Iron Age*: An Iron Manufacturer's Journal and the 'Labor Problem' in the Age of Enterprise" (Unpublished Ph.D. diss., University of Rochester, 1973), 5.

7. Ibid., 6.

8. George Littleton Davis, "Greater Pittsburgh's Commercial and Industrial Development, 1850–1900" (Unpublished Ph.D. diss., University of Pittsburgh, 1951), 8, 176; Temin, *Iron and Steel*, 275.

9. Health and Welfare Federation of Allegheny County, Bureau of Social Research, *Population Trends of Allegheny County* (Pittsburgh, 1945), 1–2, 4, 7.

10. Victor Anthony Walsh, "Across the 'Big Wather': Irish Community Life in Allegheny City, 1850–1885" (Unpublished Ph.D. diss., University of Pittsburgh, 1983), 375.

11. Nora Faires, "Ethnicity in Evolution: The German Community in Pittsburgh and Allegheny City, Pennsylvania, 1845–1885" (Unpublished Ph.D. diss., University of Pittsburgh, 1981), 126.

12. Francis Couvares, *The Remaking of Pittsburgh: Class and Culture in an Industrializing City, 1877–1919* (Albany: State University of New York, 1984), 88.

13. John A. Fitch, *The Steel Workers*, vol. 3 of *The Pittsburgh Survey*, ed. Paul Underwood Kellogg (New York: Charities and Commons Publication Committee, 1911).

14. AISI, *Directory of Iron & Steel Plants in the U.S. and Canada* (Washington, D.C.: AISI, 1874).

15. Percentages in the Totals column for membership in the *Social Directory* and *Social Register* appear smaller than might be expected, as, to a lesser extent, do those for some of the Core families. These seeming anomalies are related. Because the high-status Core families were so persistent from decade to decade, they keep percentages for the above categories at a high level. Lower-status Elite families, on the other hand, seldom persisted beyond a few years, so their percentage of the final total was far higher than in any given year.

16. See John N. Ingham, *The Iron Barons: Social Analysis of an American Urban Elite, 1874–1965* (Westport, Conn.: Greenwood Press, 1978), for a full description of these family groups and how they were generated. See George Bedien, "Social Stratification within a Metropolitan Upper Class: Early Twentieth Century Pittsburgh as a Case Study" (Unpublished seminar paper, History Department, University of Pittsburgh, 1974) for a delineation of the comparative social standing of the three published directories.

17. AISI, *Directory of Iron and Steel Plants, 1884*.

18. George Stigler, "The Economics of Scale," *Journal of Law and Economics* 1 (1958): 54–71.

19. Wall, *Andrew Carnegie*, 474–75; James H. Bridge, *The Inside History of the Carnegie Steel Company* (New York: Aldine Book Co., 1903), 151. Singer & Nimick made tool steel, cast steel, patent rolled saw plates, spring

and plow steel, axles, tires, and the like. Hussey & Wells made refined cast steel for edge tools; homogeneous plates for locomotives, boilers, and fire boxes; and cast steel forgings for crank pins, car axles, and the like. Black Diamond produced a line of goods similar to that of Hussey & Wells.

20. R. G. Dun & Co. (Pa.) 3:335.

21. Bridge, *Inside History*, 151.

22. Stockholdings were as follows: William G. Park of Black Diamond, $50,000; Curtis G. and Durtis C. Hussey of Hussey, Wells, $50,000 jointly; William H. Singer of Singer, Nimick, $50,000; Reuben Miller of Crescent Steel, $40,000; and Andrew Kloman, $20,000 (Bridge, *Inside History*, 151). With the exception of Kloman, these men were all indisputably part of Pittsburgh's aristocracy. Park and Singer were Core upper class, Hussey was Marginal upper class, but all three families were listed in the 1904 *Social Directory* and the 1908 *Social Register* and belonged to the most prestigious social clubs in the city. Kloman, on the other hand, was far from upper class in any way, and none of his heirs was ever listed in any social directory or belonged to any of the best social clubs.

23. Bridge, *Inside History*, 152.

24. Kloman's son remained a partner in the Pittsburgh Bessemer venture until it was sold to Carnegie, but the whole affair pushed him into bankruptcy. With assets of $124,000, young Kloman had debts of more than $400,000 and was unable to pay them off even at the rate of twenty-five cents on a dollar. His creditors then sued the Kloman estate to recover part of what was owed them, and as a result young Kloman was left without resources. He died some fifty years later, in 1939, as a penniless drifter on the streets of Pittsburgh. His only possession at the time of his death was a letter from Andrew Carnegie's wife granting him a pension of fifty dollars a month (R. G. Dun & Co. [Pa.] 8:335; *Pittsburgh Sun Telegraph*, 27 July 1939).

25. Bridge, *Inside History*, 152.

26. AIME, "Memorial to Alexander Holley," 31 (quoted in Temin, *Iron and Steel*, 181).

27. Samuel Rezneck, "Patterns of Thought and Action in an American Depression, 1882–1886," *American Historical Review* 41 (January 1956): 284–307.

28. Bridge, *Inside History*, 156; Wall, *Andrew Carnegie*, 487–88.

29. Bridge, *Inside History*, 161.

30. See chapter 4 for an in-depth discussion of the first Homestead strike and the general labor attitudes and practice of older Pittsburgh iron and steel men.

31. John Newton Boucher, ed., *A Century and a Half of Pittsburgh and Her People*, 4 vols. (New York: Lewis Historical Publishing Co., 1908) 4:315–16; *National Cyclopedia of American Biography* 26:363–64; *Iron Age*, 13 July 1916, 116.

32. *Iron Age*, 16 Jan. 1908, 223.

33. George Thornton Fleming, ed., *History of Pittsburgh and Environs*, 6 vols. (New York: American Historical Society, 1922), 5:38; John W. Jordan, ed., *Encyclopedia of Pennsylvania*, 31 vols. (New York: Lewis Historical Publishing Co., 1911–65), 5:1624–27.

34. The firm's 7,000 shares were divided in the following manner: Edward L. Clark, 5,365 shares (77 percent); William G. Park, David E. Park, and Richard Gray Park, 218 shares each (total Park family holdings, 9 percent); Horace P. Smith, 107 shares (1.5 percent); Robert B. Brown, 427 shares (6 percent); George Boulton, 443 shares (6 percent) (*Iron Age*, 22 Mar. 1888).

35. *Iron Age*, 23 Jan. 1930; *Mining and Metallurgy* 9 (March 1930): 188–89.

36. Herbert Casson, *The Romance of Steel* (New York: A. S. Barnes & Co., 1907), 114.

37. Bridge, *Inside History*, 176–77.

38. By the mid-1890s, several of the old Pittsburgh iron and steel manufacturers (Jones and Laughlin, Juniata Iron and Steel, Pittsburgh Steel Casting, National Tube, and Hainsworth Steel) were running small Bessemer operations, but none tried to compete in the rail market, and none became a significant producer of Bessemer steel.

Chapter 3

1. The phrase is used often in Thomas J. Peters and Robert H. Waterman, Jr., *In Search of Excellence: Lessons from America's Best Run Companies* (New York: Harper & Row, 1982).

2. James H. Soltow, "Origins of Small Business and the Relationships between Large and Small Firms: Metal Fabricating and Machinery Making in New England, 1890–1957," in *Small Business in American Life*, ed. Stuart Bruchy (New York: Columbia University Press, 1980), 195.

3. W. Arnold Hosmer, "Small Manufacturing Enterprises," *Harvard Business Review* 35 (November–December 1957): 118–19.

4. Hosmer, "Small Manufacturing Enterprises," 119.

5. Soltow, "Origins of Small Business," 203.

6. Hosmer, "Small Manufacturing Enterprises," 121.

7. David Brody, *Steelworkers in America: The Nonunion Era* (Cambridge, Mass.: Harvard University Press, 1960). 8. Carnegie, Brody pointed out, shut down its eighty-four puddling furnaces in the 1890s, and Republic Iron and Steel, when it was formed in 1899, began abandoning the iron mills in its twenty-seven plants and erected in their stead a large steel plant in Youngstown. By 1914, Brody notes, Republic had become strictly a steel producer.

8. Peter Temin, *Iron and Steel in Nineteenth Century America: An Economic Inquiry* (Cambridge, Mass: MIT Press, 1964), app. C, table C.7, 276–77.

9. Ibid., app. C, table C.6, 274–75.

10. AISI, *Bulletin*, 24 February 1892.

11. Victor S. Clark, *History of Manufactures in the United States*, vol. 3, *1893–1928* (New York: McGraw-Hill, 1929), 83. If these figures are accurate, it would indicate that the productivity of puddling furnaces had increased dramatically by 1907. The average annual production per furnace in 1884 was about 332 tons; in 1894 it was 254 tons, and a whopping 835 tons in 1907.

12. AISI, *Directory of Iron and Steel Plants in the United States and Canada* (Washington, D.C.: AISI, 1894). I have computed the figures on the number of puddling furnaces and their capacity from the company reports in the directory. I suspect the figures are inflated well above actual production, especially in that Depression year, but it does give some sense of the tremendous continuing importance of puddled iron in Pittsburgh in the mid-1890s.

13. The various units of the Carnegie works had a capacity for about 2.2 million tons, mostly Bessemer steel (AISI, *Directory*, 1894).

14. Ibid., 1901.

15. After 1901, the American Iron and Steel Institute stopped noting puddling furnaces and separating the capacity for same in their firm-by-firm reports, so it is impossible to trace further the general fate of Pittsburgh iron puddling.

16. R. G. Dun & Co. (Pa.) 5:287.

17. See Bradley Hall, "Elites and Spatial Change in Pittsburgh: Minersville as a Case Study," *Pennsylvania History* 48 (October 1981): 326–27. Hall took his information from the *Orphans Court Proceedings* of Allegheny County.

18. See E. D. McCallum, *The Iron and Steel Industry in the United States: A Study in Industrial Organization* (London: P. S. King & Son, 1931), 189–96, for a helpful description of marketing techniques in the industry. He points out that only about 10 percent of steel sales were through independent jobbers and warehouses.

19. R. G. Dun & Co. (Pa.) 5:80.

20. Moorhead purchased the mill for $160,000 (AISI, *Bulletin*, 10 Dec. 1879).

21. Clark, *History of Manufactures*, vol. 3, 127–28.

22. *DAB* 7:19–20; *NCAB* 16:110, 22:286; *New York Times*, 9 Feb. 1904; Henry Oliver Evans, *Iron Pioneer: Henry W. Oliver, 1890–1904* (New York, 1942); Henry Oliver Rea, *Henry William Oliver: Ancestry and Descendants* (Dungannon, Northern Ireland: Tyrone Printing Co., 1959); *Pittsburgh Bulletin*, 2 Dec. 1905; *Iron Age*, 1 Nov. 1888, 30 Nov. 1905, 15 Feb. 1906, 21 Jan. 1915, 30 Jan. 1919, 30 Oct. 1934; Herbert Casson, *The Romance of Steel* (New York: A. S. Barnes & Co., 1907).

23. George Irving Reed, ed., *Century Cyclopedia of History and Biography of Pennsylvania*, 2 vols. (Chicago: Century Publishing Co., 1904), 2:161; Evans, *Iron Pioneer*, 33; R. G. Dun & Co. (Pa.) 7:133.

24. Oliver Iron and Steel Company, Papers, Archives for an Industrial Society, Hillman Library, University of Pittsburgh (hereafter cited as OIS Papers); R. G. Dun & Co. (Pa.) 2:133.

25. Henry William Oliver Scrapbook, 28 Feb. 1840 to 8 Feb. 1904, Articles of Agreement between Lewis, Oliver, and Phillips, 11 Sept. 1866, OIS Papers.

26. R. G. Dun & Co. (Pa.) 12:298.

27. R. G. Dun & Co. (Pa.) 12:311.

28. R. G. Dun & Co. (Pa.) 12:494; OIS Papers.

29. *Iron Age,* 12 Mar. 1885.

30. Evans, *Iron Pioneer,* 273–74.

31. U.S. Bureau of the Census, Twelfth Census of the United States: 1900, vol. 10, *Manufactures,* pt. 4, *Special Reports on Selected Industries* (Washington, D.C.: U.S. Government Printing Office, 1901), 3–95.

32. Ibid., U.S. Bureau of the Census, *Thirteenth Census of the United States, 1910,* vol. 10, *Manufactures, 1909, Reports for Principal Industries,* 205–61.

33. Bernard Elbaum and Frank Wilkinson, "Industrial Relations and Uneven Development: A Comparative Study of the American and British Steel Industries," *Cambridge Journal of Economics* 3 (1979): 281.

34. AISI, *Directory of Iron and Steel Plants,* 1874, 1884, and 1894.

35. R. G. Dun & Co. (Pa.) 14:378.

36. *Iron Age,* 15 Feb. 1883, 28 Feb. and 15 Mar. 1884.

37. Ibid., 17 Feb. 1887.

38. Temin, *Iron and Steel,* 225–26.

39. AISI, *Bulletin,* 31 May 1879, 133.

40. R. G. Dun & Co. (Pa.) 14:378, 442.

41. *Iron Age,* 15 Feb. 1883.

42. Ibid., 14 Apr. 1887.

43. Philip Scranton, *Proprietary Capitalism: Textile Manufacture at Philadelphia, 1800–1885* (Philadelphia: Temple University Press, 1983), 42–43. Scranton, of course, was referring in his book to the large-scale textile operations at Lowell and elsewhere. I have added "Carnegie Corporation" to make the quotation better fit the situation we have observed in Pittsburgh.

44. Glenn Porter and Harold Livesay, *Merchants and Manufacturers: Studies in the Changing Structure of 19th Century Marketing* (Baltimore: Johns Hopkins University Press, 1971), 146–47.

45. *Jones and Laughlin: Growth of an American Business,* in the Jones and Laughlin Papers at the Archives for an Industrial Society, Hillman Library, University of Pittsburgh (hereafter cited as J&L Papers).

46. *Iron Age,* 26 Aug. 1886.

47. Ibid., 23 Dec. 1886.

48. Philip Scranton, *Proprietary Capitalism,* 4.

49. William J. Hogan, *Economic History of the Iron and Steel Industry,* 5 vols. (Lexington, Mass.: D. C. Heath, 1971), 1:236.

50. T. H. Burnham and G. O. Hoskins, *Iron and Steel in Britain, 1870–1930* (London: Allen & Unwin, 1943), 236.

51. Bernard Elbaum and Frank Wilkinson, "Industrial Relations and Uneven Development: A Comparative Study of the American and British Steel Industries," *Cambridge Journal of Economics* 3 (1979): 279–80. See also Donald N. McCloskey, *Economic Maturity and Industrial Decline: British Iron and Steel, 1870–1913* (Cambridge, Mass: Harvard University Press, 1973), 53.

52. Peter L. Payne, "Industrial Entrepreneurship and Management in Great Britain," in *The Cambridge Economic History of Europe*, vol. 7, *The Industrial Economies: Capital, Labour, and Enterprise*, pt. 1, Britain, France, Germany, and Scandinavia, ed. Peter Mathias and M. M. Postan (Cambridge, England: Cambridge University Press, 1978), 206–7; and Leslie Hannah, "Mergers in British Manufacturing Industry, 1880–1918," *Oxford Economic Papers*, n.s., 26 (1974): 11.

53. Ann Wendy Mill, "Comment and Debate: French Steel and Metal-Working Industries: A Contribution to Debate on Economic Development in Nineteenth Century France." *Social Science History* 9, no. 3 (Summer 1985): 307–38. Germany, however, created an industrial form in iron and steel closer to the model developed for the United States; see Juergen Kocka, "Entrepreneurs and Managers in German Industrialism," in Mathias and Postan, eds., *Cambridge Economic History of Europe*, vol. 7, pt. 1, 492–589, and Steven B. Webb, "Tariffs, Cartels, Technology, and Growth in the German Steel Industry, 1879 to 1914," *Journal of Economic History* vol. 40, no. 2 (June 1980): 309–29.

Chapter 4

1. David Brody, *Steelworkers in America: The Nonunion Era* (Cambridge, Mass.: Harvard University Press, 1960), 8.

2. David Montgomery, *The Fall of the House of Labor: The Workplace, the State, and American Labor Activism, 1865–1925* (Cambridge, England: Cambridge University Press, 1987), 13. See also his "Workers' Control of Machine Production in the Nineteenth Century," *Labor History* 17 (Fall 1976): 485–509. The phrase "Craftsmen's Empire" is from Francis G. Couvares, *The Remaking of Pittsburgh: Class and Culture in an Industrializing City, 1877–1919* (Albany: State University of New York Press, 1984), chap. 2. Couvares essentially follows Montgomery's analysis in his re-creation of the iron mills of nineteenth-century Pittsburgh.

3. Montgomery, "Workers' Control," 506.

4. Bernard Elbaum, "The Making and Shaping of Job and Pay Structures in the Iron and Steel Industry," in *Internal Labor Markets*, ed. Paul Osterman (Cambridge, Mass.: MIT Press, 1984), 71–108. See also Barnard Elbaum and Frank Wilkinson, "Industrial Relations and Uneven Development: A

Comparative Study of the American and British Steel Industries,"
Cambridge Journal of Economics 3 (1979): 275–303; Katherine Stone, "The
Origins of Job Structures in the Steel Industry," *Review of Radical Political
Economics* 6 (Summer 1974): 61–97; Michael Nuwer, "From Batch to Flow:
Production Technology and Work-Force Skills in the Steel Industry, 1880–
1920," *Technology and Culture* 29 (1988): 808–38.

     5. Nuwer, "From Batch to Flow," 838.

     6. Other recent works include Andrea Graziosi, "Common Laborers,
Unskilled Workers: 1880–1915," *Labor History* 22 (Fall 1981): 511–44; Ir-
win M. Marcus et al., "Change and Continuity: Steel Workers in Home-
stead, Pennsylvania, 1889–1895," *Pennsylvania Magazine of History and
Biography* 111 (January 1987): 61–75; James Holt, "Trade Unionism in the
British and U.S. Steel Industries, 1888–1912: A Comparative Study," *Labor
History* 18, no. 1 (Winter 1977): 5–35; John W. Bennett, "The Iron Workers
of Woods Run and Johnstown: The Union Era" (Unpublished Ph.D. diss.,
University of Pittsburgh, 1977). See also older accounts such as James J.
Davis, *The Iron Puddler: My Life in the Rolling Mills and What Came of It*
(Indianapolis: Bobbs, Merrill, 1922).

     7. About the only exception to this neglect of the mill owner's values
and attitudes by labor historians working on the iron and steel industry
have been two excellent articles on the A. M. Byers Co. by Michael W.
Santos: "Brother against Brother: The Amalgamated and the Sons of the
Vulcan at the A. M. Byers Company, 1907–1913," *Pennsylvania Magazine
of History and Biography* 111, no. 2 (April 1987): 195–212; and "Laboring
on the Periphery: Managers and Workers at the A. M. Byers Company, 1900–
1956," *Business History Review* 61 (Spring 1987): 113–33. See also his thesis, "Iron Workers in a Steel Age: The Case of the A. M. Byers Company,
1900–1969" (Unpublished Ph.D., diss. Carnegie-Mellon University Press,
1984).

     8. John A. Garraty, "United States Steel Corporation versus Labor: The
Early Years," *Labor History* 1 (1960): 8.

     9. See Herbert G. Gutman, "Two Lockouts in Pennsylvania, 1873–
1874," *Pennsylvania Magazine of History and Biography* 83 (July 1959):
307–26, reprinted in Gutman's *Work, Culture and Society in Industrializing America* (New York: Random House, 1976).

     10. Gutman, *Work, Culture*, 335. An interesting insight into this at-
titude developed during the Civil War. Cambria Iron, like so many other
mills in the American North, organized companies of soldiers right in the
plant. At Cambria, the company executives acted as officers, while the
workers were enlisted men. The officers marched the men off to war under
the American flag, retaining the sense of community and deference that
were characteristic of these antebellum factories. "Captain" William R.
Jones, who was plant superintendent at Cambria at the time and later Carnegie's right-hand man, got his title of captain from the company of soldiers
he organized and led off to war.

11. John A. Fitch, *The Steel Workers*, vol. 3 of *The Pittsburgh Survey*, ed. Paul Underwood Kellogg (New York: Charities and Commons Publication Committee, 1911) 87.

12. See David Brody, *Workers in Industrial America: Essays on the Twentieth Century Struggle* (New York: Oxford University Press, 1980), chap. 2, "The Rise of Welfare Capitalism." Brody gives a balanced account of the role of corporate welfarism and company unions, seeing them as more honestly attractive to workers than many earlier students had granted. See also David Montgomery, *Worker's Control in America: Studies in the History of Work, Technology and Labor Struggles* (New York: Cambridge University Press, 1979), esp. chaps. 2, 4, 5; and Daniel Nelson, *Managers and Workers: Origins of the New Factory System in the United States, 1880–1920* (Madison: University of Wisconsin Press, 1975).

13. See Stuart Brandes, *American Welfare Capitalism, 1880–1940* (Chicago: University of Chicago Press, 1976), and Gerald G. Eggert, *Steelmasters and Labor Reform, 1886–1923* (Pittsburgh: University of Pittsburgh Press, 1981), for a detailed account of the rise of the idea of welfare capitalism at U.S. Steel.

14. William A. Sullivan, *The Industrial Worker in Pennsylvania, 1800–1840* (Harrisburg: Pennsylvania Historical and Museum Commission, 1955), 69–70. See also George Swetnam, "Labor-Management Relations in Pennsylvania's Steel Industry, 1800–1959," *Western Pennsylvania Historical Magazine* 62 (October 1979): 321–22.

15. Michael F. Holt, *Forging a Majority: The Formation of the Republican Party in Pittsburgh* (New Haven: Yale University Press, 1969), 29.

16. Ibid., 19; Catherine Elizabeth Reiser, *Pittsburgh's Commercial Development, 1800–1850* (Harrisburg: Pennsylvania Historical and Museum Commission, 1951), 124, 145, 192; James C. Holmberg, "The Industrializing Community: Pittsburgh, 1850–1880" (Unpublished Ph.D. diss., University of Pittsburgh, 1981), 85–87.

17. George McNeill, ed., *The Labor Movement: The Problem of Today* (Boston: A. M. Bridger, 1887), 269.

18. Ibid., 270–71; Swetnam, "Labor-Management Relations," 322–23. See James Linaberger, "The Rolling Mill Riots of 1850" (Unpublished seminar paper, History Department, University of Pittsburgh, n.d.), for the most extensive account of this strike.

19. McNeill, *Labor Movement*, 271.

20. Idem.; *National Labor Tribune*, 1 Aug. 1874.

21. David Brody, "Labor and Small-Scale Enterprise during Industrialization," in *Small Business in American Life*, ed. Stuart Bruchy (New York: Columbia University Press, 1980), 271.

22. Fitch, *Steel Workers*, 78.

23. Ibid., 79.

24. McNeill, *Labor Movement*, 273.

25. Quoted in Peter B. Doeringer, "Piece Rate Wage Structure in the

Pittsburgh Iron and Steel Industry, 1880–1900," *Labor History* 9, no. 2 (Spring 1968): 265.

26. *National Labor Tribune*, 7 Feb. 1874.

27. Elbaum and Wilkinson, "Industrial Relations," 284.

28. Carroll D. Wright, "The Amalgamated Association of Iron and Steel Workers," *Quarterly Journal of Economics* 7 (July 1893): 408.

29. *Pittsburgh Commercial*, 7 Dec. 1874.

30. *Iron Age*, 10 Dec. 1874.

31. Lynn Gordon Mapes, "*Iron Age*: An Iron Manufacturer's Journal and the 'Labor Problem' in the Age of Enterprise" (Unpublished Ph.D. diss., University of Rochester, 1973), 56, quoting from AISI, *Bulletin*, 15 Jan. 1875.

32. *American Manufacturer*, 17 Dec. 1874, quoted in Mapes, "Iron Age," 56.

33. There were just 1,152 blacks in Pittsburgh's population of over 50,000. See Lawrence Glasco, "Double Burden: The Black Experience in Pittsburgh," in *City at the Point: Essays on the Social History of Pittsburgh*, ed. Samuel P. Hays (Pittsburgh: University of Pittsburgh Press, 1989), 73.

34. Mapes, "Iron Age," 55, 57.

35. Fitch, *Steel Workers*, 87–88.

36. Although actual union membership fell short of potential membership in the mill (25 to 40 percent were probably eligible), this does not seem to be due to any undue employer harassment.

37. Mapes, "Iron Age," 21.

38. Fitch, *Steel Workers*, 87.

39. See Bennett, "Iron Workers," chap. 6; Couvares, *Remaking of Pittsburgh*, 25–29, 62–69; David Montgomery, *Beyond Equality: Labor and the Radical Republicans, 1862–1872* (New York: Random House, 1967), 211, 389–92; Paul L. Krause, "Road to Homestead" (Ph.D. diss., Duke University, 1987), chap. 3, 33–36, chap. 4, 34–67; John French, "'Reaping the Whirlwind': The Origins of the Allegheny County Greenback-Labor Party in 1877," *Western Pennsylvania Historical Magazine* 64 (April 1981): 97–119; and Richard Oestreicher, "Working-Class Formation, Development, and Consciousness in Pittsburgh, 1790–1960," in Hays, ed., *City at the Point*, 111–50.

40. *National Labor Tribune*, 7 Jan. 1884.

41. *National Labor Tribune*, 22 May 1884.

42. Jesse S. Robinson, *The Amalgamated Association of Iron, Steel and Tin Workers* (Baltimore: Johns Hopkins University Press, 1920), 105–9.

43. Couvares, *Remaking of Pittsburgh*, 14–15.

44. Ibid., 15. David Montgomery has made the same point in his *Fall of the House of Labor*, 17–20.

45. B. F. Jones Diary, AIS.

46. Ibid., emphasis in the original.

47. Ibid., 25 Aug. 1877.

48. Ibid., 18 Sept. 1877.

49. Couvares, *Remaking of Pittsburgh*, 7.

50. Ibid., 8.

51. Most of the foregoing material on *Iron Age* is abstracted and re-analyzed from Lynn Gordon Mapes's excellent "Iron Age."

52. Henry C. Carey, *Principles of Political Economy*, 3 vols. (Philadelphia: Carey, Lea, Blanchard, 1837–40), 1:339.

53. Eric Foner, *Free Soil, Free Labor, Free Men: The Ideology of the Republican Party before the Civil War* (New York: Oxford University Press, 1970).

54. Ibid., 18–20.

55. Ibid., 39.

56. Joseph Dorfman, *The Economic Mind in American Civilization*, 3 vols. (New York: Viking Press, 1945–49), 2:791–92.

57. Mapes, "Iron Age," 30–31.

58. Ibid., 34–35.

59. *Iron Age*, 25 Dec. 1873, cited in Mapes, "Iron Age," 36.

60. Mapes, "Iron Age," 37–38.

61. Ibid., 43.

62. Gutman, "Two Lockouts," 336.

63. Paul K. Conkin, *Prophets of Prosperity* (Bloomington, Ind.: Indiana University Press, 1980), 293.

64. Foner, *Free Soil*, 37.

65. Bruce Laurie and Mark Schmitz, "Manufacture and Productivity: The Making of an Industrial Base, Philadelphia, 1850–80," in *Philadelphia: Work, Space, Family, and Group Experience in the 19th Century*, ed. Theodore Hershberg (New York: Oxford Press, 1981), 43–92; and Sam Bass Warner, Jr., *The Private City: Philadelphia in Three Periods of Its Growth* (Philadelphia: University of Pennsylvania Press, 1968), 50. New York City was also made up largely of smaller shops. Although the mean firm size was about the same as Philadelphia and Pittsburgh, there was a larger proportion of workers in the largest mills in the latter city. In Allegheny County in 1850, 43.8 percent of manufacturing employees worked for firms of one hundred or more employees. Philadelphia had just 43 percent in firms of over fifty workers.

66. Montgomery, *Beyond Equality*, 24.

67. *DAB* 10:602–3; *NCAB* 13:27.

68. It should be noted that Weeks, while an editor at *American Manufacturer and Iron World*, did not betray the same guarded affection for unions and labor as he did at *Iron Age*. In 1874, he had described union leaders in the pages of that journal as "frequently and most generally idle, cunning fellows, who lead a lazy life at the expense of the hard working and credulous laborer" (*American Manufacturer*, 21 May 1874). About a month later, he criticized unions "because they exercise a tyranny over that portion of labor that does not choose to surrender itself to these unions. . . . Union-

ism, except to those who are unionists, is utter and despotic selfishness"
(Ibid., 18 June 1874). Both are quoted in Sharon Trusilo, "The Ironworkers'
Case for Amalgamation," *Western Pennsylvania Historical Magazine*
(1988): 57–58. What caused Weeks to change his attitudes in such a short
time is impossible to say.

69. *Iron Age*, 22 Aug. 1877.

70. Mapes, "Iron Age," 92.

71. In 1879 Weeks wrote his *Report on the Practical Operation of Ar-
bitration and Conciliation . . . in England*, which was followed two years
later by the volume *Industrial Conciliation and Arbitration in New York,
Ohio and Pennsylvania*. His magnum opus, *Labor Differences and Their
Settlement*, appeared in 1886. Arbitration achieved great popularity in
America during this same period, advocated by such prominent reformers as
Richard T. Ely, ("Arbitration," *North American Review* 193 [October 1886]:
317–21), Washington Gladden (*Applied Christianity* [Boston: Houghton-
Mifflin, 1886]), and Lyman Abbott ("Compulsory Arbitration," *Arena* 7
[December 1894]). See William Akin, "Arbitration and Labor Conflict: The
Middle Class Panacea, 1886–1900," *Historian* 29 (Nov. 1967): 565–83, for a
general overview of these ideas.

72. Conkin, *Prophets of Prosperity*, 307.

73. For an analysis and discussion of the education patterns of the sons
of Pittsburgh's iron barons, see John N. Ingham, *The Iron Barons: A Social
Analysis of an American Urban Elite, 1874–1965* (Westport, Conn.: Greenwood Press, 1978), 149ff.

74. Dorfman, *Economic Mind*, 3:103–4.

75. Ibid., 3:106–8.

76. Jarrett was such an adamant supporter of the protective tariff that he
withdrew the Amalgamated from the Federal Organization of Trade and
Labor Unions in 1881–82 when that organization refused to endorse it.
Despairing of falling bar iron prices that affected labor's wages because of
the sliding scale, Jarrett also called for further horizontal consolidation in
the industry. Further, while president of the Amalgamated, he urged more
circumspect use of the strike as a weapon in labor negotiations. When
Jarrett left his post at the Amalgamated, *Iron Age*, along with many executives in the iron and steel industry, unsuccessfully supported his nomina-
tion as head of the new Bureau of Labor Statistics. In the late 1880s and
1890s, Jarrett turned his attention to the tinplate industry, setting himself
up as a lobbyist in Washington. He developed strong ties to the Republican
party and played a crucial role in having a high duty on tin plate included in
the McKinley Tariff of 1890. From 1892 to 1900 Jarrett was an executive of
the Tin Plate and Sheet Metal Association; later he was in business in
Pittsburgh. Gary M. Fink, ed., *Biographical Dictionary of American Labor
Leaders* (Westport, Conn.: Greenwood Press, 1974), 172–73.

77. In his later years Weihe developed close ties with the Republican

party. In 1896 he was appointed deputy immigration inspector at Ellis Island by the Republicans; he served until 1908 (Fink, *Biographical Dictionary*, 370).

78. It is on this fundamental point that I disagree with the otherwise excellent analysis in Lynn Gordon Mapes's dissertation on *Iron Age*. Mapes asserts that there was a profound conflict between the editorial ideas of *Iron Age* and the industrial realities faced by the iron manufacturers, who were, according to him, profoundly and unabashedly antiunion. Evidence, however, does not appear to support this conclusion. Although no one would deny that these older iron manufacturers would have preferred to run their plants without a union if they could, the fact is that by the mid-1870s most, if not all, had come to terms with its existence within the industry. Neither, however, did they ever apparently become convinced of the utility of arbitration.

79. B. F. Jones Diary, AIS, 1, 3, 4, 6, 19 June 1878; 2, 7 June 1879.

80. Ibid., 25 Sept. 1878.

81. Mapes, "Iron Age," 100.

82. Ibid., 105.

83. Amalgamated Association, *Proceedings* (1881): 578-79, (1882): 667, 669, (1883): 935; *National Labor Tribune*, 18 June 1881, all cited in Mapes, "Iron Age," 106.

84. J. H. Bridge, *The Inside History of Carnegie Steel* (New York: Aldine Book Co., 1903), 155.

85. Ibid., 156.

86. Ibid., 153-56.

87. *National Labor Tribune*, 18 Mar. 1882.

88. *Iron Age*, 29 Mar. 1882.

89. *Iron Age*, 22 June 1882.

90. Ibid.

91. Mapes, "Iron Age," 111.

92. *Pittsburgh Commercial Gazette*, 26 May and 8 June 1882.

93. On 1 June 1882, 24,000 men in the western areas went on strike. In Pittsburgh alone this involved between 18,000 and 20,000 men in 36 mills with 875 puddling furnaces. The magnitude of the union's defeat was clear when one considers the numbers involved (Mapes, "Iron Age," 123).

94. Ibid., 130.

95. *Pittsburgh Commercial Gazette*, 31 July 1882, cited in Mapes, "Iron Age," 130.

96. Fitch, *Steel Workers*, 297.

97. Mapes, "Iron Age," 138.

98. Joseph D. Weeks, *Labor Differences and Their Settlement* (New York: Society for Political Education, 1886), 11.

99. Mapes, "Iron Age," 147-50.

100. Ibid., 152-53. See Mary Ellen Freifeld, "The Emergence of the American Working Classes: The Roots of Division, 1865-85," (Unpublished

Ph.D. diss., New York University, 1980), 477–534, for an in-depth discussion of a number of these critical strikes in steel plants in the early 1880s.

Chapter 5

1. David E. Novack and Richard Perlman, "The Structure of Wages in the American Iron and Steel Industry, 1860–1890," *Journal of Economic History* (September 1962): 334–47.

2. Lynn Gordon Mapes, "Iron Age: An Iron Manufacturer's Journal and the 'Labor Problem' in the Age of Enterprise" (Unpublished Ph.D. diss., University of Rochester, 1973), 15.

3. Fitch, *The Steel Workers*, vol. 3 of *Pittsburgh Survey*, ed. Paul Underwood Kellogg (New York: Charities and Commons Publication Committee, 1911), 88–89.

4. James Holt, "Trade Unionism in the British and United States Steel Industries, 1880–1914: A Comparison," *Labor History* 18 (Winter 1977): 11.

5. Harold Livesay, *Andrew Carnegie and the Rise of Big Business* (Boston: Little, Brown, 1975), 136–37.

6. Fitch, *Steel Workers*, 112–14. See also Paul L. Krause, "The Road to Homestead" (Unpublished Ph.D. diss., Duke University, 1987), for a more detailed analysis of the situation in the Edgar Thomson mill.

7. Fitch, *Steel Workers*, 114–16.

8. Ibid., 116.

9. Ibid., 118. Significantly, the only pre-Civil War iron mill in Pittsburgh area to attempt running on a nonunion basis in the early 1880s was McKeesport Rolling Mill, also owned by eastern aristocrats (the Wood and Lukens families of Philadelphia). The McKeesport location had shielded them somewhat from the worst of the boycotts and picketing. That attempt to eradicate the union failed but a few years later the mill became one of the earliest nonunion iron mills in the city (*Iron Age*, 24 Mar. 1881).

10. Brody, Steelworkers in America, 52, 57.

11. *New York Times*, 7 July 1888.

12. *Pittsburgh Commercial Gazette*, 11 July 1888, cited in Mapes, "Iron Age," 181.

13. Mapes, "Iron Age," 182–83.

14. *Age of Steel*, 2 Jan., 6 Feb. 1886, cited in Mapes, "Iron Age," 158.

15. *Iron Age*, 30 Apr. 1886.

16. See Mapes, "Iron Age," 155–57, 169–71. Western Iron had evidently fallen apart as a result of bickering among its members, especially over geographic issues.

17. Mapes, "Iron Age," 173. The best general survey of welfare capitalism is Stuart Brandes, *American Welfare Capitalism: 1880–1940* (Chicago: University of Chicago Press, 1976). An important addition to the literature is David Brody, "The Rise and Decline of Welfare Capitalism," in

Workers in Industrial America: Essays on the Twentieth Century Struggle
(New York: Oxford University Press, 1980). An interesting investigation of
the interaction of workers with a company's system of welfare capitalism is
Gerald Zahavi, "Negotiated Loyalty: Welfare Capitalism and the Shoe-
workers of Endicott Johnson, 1920–1940," *Journal of American History* 70
(December 1983): 102–20. The best study of developments at U.S. Steel on
this issue is John Garraty, "The United States Steel Corporation versus
Labor: The Early Years," *Labor History* 1 (Winter 1960): 3–38. Important
studies of other parts of the steel industry are those by Marlene H. Rikard:
"An Experiment in Welfare Capitalism: The Health Care Services of the
Tennessee Coal, Iron and Railroad Company" (Unpublished Ph.D. diss.,
University of Alabama, 1983) and "A Case Study of Welfare Capitalism and
Industrial Communities: The Tennessee Coal, Iron and Railroad Company
of Birmingham, Alabama, 1907–1950" (paper presented to the conference
Steel and Coal Communities in Comparative Perspective, 1900–1990:
United States and Germany, in Pittsburgh, 20–22 Apr. 1990). For an impor-
tant work dealing with the paternalistic welfare capitalism of smaller steel
firms in Chicago, see Lizabeth Cohen, "From Welfare Capitalism to Capitalism's Decline: Industrial Relations in Chicago's Steel Industry" (paper
presented to the conference Steel and Coal Communities), *Making a New
Deal: Industrial Workers in Chicago, 1919–1939* (New York: Cambridge
University Press, 1990), and "Learning to Live in the Welfare State: Industrial Workers in Chicago between the Wars, 1919–1939" (Unpublished
Ph.D. diss., University of California, Berkeley, 1986).

18. Ray Burkett, "Vandergrift: Model Worker's Community" (Unpublished seminar paper, University of Pittsburgh, n.d.).

19. The firm ultimately became part of U.S. Steel, and McMurtry served
as chairman of the U.S. Steel subsidiary American Steel and Wire for a
number of years (Pennsylvania Society of New York, *Yearbook* [New York:
Pennsylvania Society, 1916], 70; *Pittsburgh Index*, 14 Dec. 1918; *Iron Age*,
21 Nov. 1901, 5–9; 12 Aug. 1915, 366–67; Engineering Society of Western
Pennsylvania, *Proceedings* 31 [1915–16]: 936; R. G. Dun & Co. [Pa.] 13:105).

20. Ida Tarbell, *New Ideals in American Business* (New York: Macmillan, 1916), 153. See also Eugene J. Buffington, "Making Cities for Workmen," *Harper's Weekly*, 8 May 1909, for a similar laudatory account of
Vandergrift.

21. P. Glenn Porter and Harold Livesay, *Merchants and Manufacturers:
Studies in the Changing Structure of 19th Century Marketing* (Baltimore:
Johns Hopkins University Press, 1971), 136. It should perhaps be noted that
even on a national level, this statement is not quite accurate. As Michael W.
Santos has pointed out, as late as 1910, "the majority of workers in all
categories of iron and steel manufacture labored in firms of under a thousand employees." Even by the 1920s they were still a large minority of the
workers, and near Pittsburgh, "countless iron mills dotted the landscape
well into the 1930's and 1940's." Michael W. Santos, "Laboring on the Pe-

riphery: Managers and Workers at the A. M. Byers Company, 1900–1956," *Business History Review* 61 (Spring 1987): 115. This concept has been further extended by Richard Edwards in *Contested Terrain: The Transformation of the Workplace in the Twentieth Century* (New York: Basic Books, 1979), 34–35, in which he points out that although the American economy is dominated by big business, even in the 1970s some 11 million to 12 million firms were small- to medium-sized businesses that continued to be run on an entrepreneurial basis. In the smallest firms, "the entrepreneur often plays the role of the chief workman, setting the pace of work. . . . In slightly bigger firms, the owning family typically runs the firm, filling key managerial slots and keeping watch over supervisory staff."

22. The best analysis of the great merger movement in iron and steel at the turn of the century is Naomi Lamoreaux, *The Great Merger Movement in American Business, 1895–1904* (Cambridge, England: Cambridge University Press, 1985). Lamoreaux is far more sensitive to nuance within an industry, especially iron and steel, than other commentators. See also Anthony Patrick O'Brien, "The Great Merger Wave of 1898–1902," *Journal of Economic History* 48, no. 3 (September 1988): 639–49; Ralph L. Nelson, *Merger Movements in American Industry, 1895–1956* (Princeton: Princeton University Press, 1959); George J. Stigler, "Monopoly and Oligopoly by Merger," in *Organization of American Industry* (Homewood, Ill.: R. D. Irwin, 1968), 95–107; and Alfred D. Chandler, Jr., "The Beginnings of Big Business in American Industry," *Business History Review* 33 (Spring 1959): 1–31. Works focusing on the iron and steel industry include S. R. Dennison, "Vertical Integration and the Iron and Steel Industry," *Economic Journal* 49 (June 1939): 244–58; Richard B. Mancke, "Iron and Steel: A Case Study of the Economic Causes and Effects of Vertical Integration," *Journal of Industrial Economics* 20 (July 1972): 220–29; Edward Sherwood Meade, "The Genesis of the United States Steel Corporation," *Quarterly Journal of Economics* 15 (August 1901): 517–50; and Donald O. Parsons and Edward John Ray, "The United States Steel Consolidation: The Creation of Market Control," *Journal of Law and Economics* 20 (April 1975): 181–219. For a simpler, broad-gauged overview of combination in the steel industry see Leonard W. Weiss, *Case Studies in American Industry* (New York: John Wiley & Sons, 1971), 145–212.

23. Lamoreaux, *Great Merger Movement*, 16.

24. H. G. Cordero, *Iron and Steel Works of the World, 1956–57* (London: Quin Press, 1956).

25. Pittsburgh Regional Planning Association, *Region in Transition* (Pittsburgh: University of Pittsburgh Press, 1963), 271.

26. See Garraty, "United States Steel Corporation versus Organized Labor"; David Brody, *Steelworkers in America: The Nonunion Era* (Cambridge, Mass.: Harvard University Press, 1960), chap. 8; Gerald Eggert, *Steelmasters and Labor Reform, 1886–1923* (Pittsburgh: University of Pittsburgh Press, 1981) chap. 2; Fitch, *Steel Workers*, chaps. 10 and 11.

27. Fitch, *Steel Workers*, 192, Brody, *Steelworkers in America*, 68–75.

28. Brody, *Steelworkers in America*, chap. 4. Studies conducted in the 1920s indicated that the vast majority of workers in corporate welfare systems were in large firms with more than fifteen thousand employees; just 3 percent were in plants with fewer than one thousand workers. (Brody, "Labor and Small Scale Enterprise," 277).

29. Jesse S. Robinson, *The Amalgamated Association of Iron, Steel and Tin Workers* (Baltimore: Johns Hopkins University Press, 1920), 186–87.

30. Brody, *Steelworkers in America*, 74–75.

31. Robinson, *Amalgamated Association*, 143–44.

32. Santos, "Laboring on the Periphery," 113–33; "Brother against Brother: The Amalgamated and the Sons of Vulcan at the A. M. Byers company, 1907–1913," *Pennsylvania Magazine of History and Biography* 111, no. 2 (April 1987): 195–212. See also his "Iron Workers in a Steel Age: The Case of the A. M. Byers Company" (Unpublished D.A. diss., Carnegie-Mellon University, 1984). Peter Gottlieb, in *Making Their Own Way: Southern Blacks' Migration to Pittsburgh, 1916–1930* (Urbana: University of Illinois Press, 1987), analyzes the careers of black migrants in Pittsburgh, some of whom worked in Byers' South Side plant.

33. Santos, "Laboring on the Periphery," 118. Mansel G. Blackford, *A Portrait Cast in Steel: Buckeye International and Columbus, Ohio, 1881–1980* (Westport, Conn.: Greenwood Press, 1982) covers a small cast steel firm that functioned much as Byers Pipe did over the years.

34. Santos, "Laboring on the Periphery," 131. There were, however, limits to management's forebearance. Company personnel records show, for example, one Theo. Zuckowinz, a pitman, who was fired in 1917 as an agitator, with the comment, "Should not be re-employed. Walked out of the #3 pit and tried to get other men to go along with him." Personnel Records, A. M. Byers Company, Archives for an Industrial Society, Hillman Library, University of Pittsburgh (AIS).

35. Santos, "Laboring on the Periphery," 126.

36. As Santos notes, the union was not eliminated from the Byers plants until the 1960s, after the Byers family had sold out to General Tire and Rubber Company. The new managers were impelled by modern ideas of rational management, and they began diversifying Byers's operations and undercutting the power of the union (which was by then an AFL-CIO affiliate). As new management took Byers out of iron and steel manufacture, they embarked on rigorous cost control programs. This brought about a drastic change in labor relations at Byers. As Santos notes, "The result was to undermine the cornerstone that supported the system for so long at Byers—a view of its mutual beneficiality" ("Iron Workers in a Steel Age," 112). Massive layoffs were begun, as whole units in the plant were closed. Reading the Byers personnel records for the 1960s is an exercise in woe. Workers were placed on indefinite layoff but were denied severance pay, as the company refused to admit their departments had been permanently closed. One

worker petitioned the firm repeatedly for five years in the early 1960s, telling them of his difficulties and evidently expecting the sort of paternalistic concern to which he had grown accustomed. Management replied, "Regret to learn that you are having financial difficulties, but we cannot make an exception for one employee to the general rule that is applied to all" (Personnel Records, A. M. Byers Co., AIS).

37. Brody, "Labor and Small Scale Enterprise," 268.

38. A. M. Woodruff and T. G. Alexander, *Success and Failure in Small Manufacturing* (Pittsburgh: University of Pittsburgh Press, 1958; rpt., Westport, Conn.: Greenwood Press, 1974), 31.

Chapter 6

1. The *Pittsburgh Survey* was first published in three special articles in *Charities and Commons*, beginning 2 Jan. 1909, then as *The Pittsburgh Survey*, 6 vols., ed. Paul Underwood Kellogg (New York: Charities and Commons Publication Committee, 1910–14). For astute discussions of the ideological underpinnings of the survey and many of its authors, see John F. McClymer, "The Pittsburgh Survey, 1907–1914: Forging an Ideology in the Steel District," *Pennsylvania History* 41 (1974): 169–88; Samuel P. Hays, introduction to new edition of Margaret Byington, *Homestead: The Households of a Mill Town* (New York, 1910; new ed., Pittsburgh, 1974); Charles Hill and Steven Cohen, "John A. Fitch and the Pittsburgh Survey," *Western Pennsylvania Historical Magazine* 67, no. 1 (January 1984): 17–32; and Steven Cohen, "Reconciling Industrial Conflict and Democracy: The Pittsburgh Survey and the Growth of Social Research in the United States" (Unpublished Ph.D. diss., Columbia University, 1981).

2. Edward I. Devine, "Pittsburgh: The Year of the Survey," in *Pittsburgh Survey*, vol. 3, *The Civic Frontage*, 3

3. Woods was in many respects the archetypical Progressive reformer. Of middle-class background, he quickly attached himself to the older upper-class, "good government" groups in Boston and became closely allied with Josiah Quincy III when the latter was elected mayor of Boston in 1895. In 1903, Woods helped organize the Good Government Association in Boston (dubbed the "goo goos" by machine politicians) and contested the election of John Fitzgerald for mayor in 1905. The strategy of Woods and the other members of the Good Government Association was to push for the election of aldermen on an at-large basis, with a longer term and more political independence for the mayor (Allen F. Davis, *Spearheads for Reform: The Social Settlements and the Progressive Movement, 1890–1914* [New York: Oxford University Press, 1967], 174–80).

4. Robert Woods, "Pittsburgh: An Interpretation," in *Pittsburgh Survey* 3:14.

5. Ibid., 24.

6. Idem.

7. W. D. Rubinstein, *Men of Property* (London: Croon Helm, 1981), 61.

8. See Harold L. Twiss, "The Pittsburgh Business Elite, 1850–1890–1929" (Unpublished seminar paper, Department of History, University of Pittsburgh, 1964), and George Bedeian, "Social Stratification within a Metropolitan Upper Class: Early Twentieth Century Pittsburgh as a Case Study" (Unpublished seminar paper, Department of History, University of Pittsburgh, 1974). Twiss, in analyzing the directors of downtown Pittsburgh banks over a seventy-five-year period, found that very few were self-made and that the vast majority were from families who were part of the older aristocracy discussed here. Bedeian analyzed a total of 4,675 prominent individuals in early twentieth-century Pittsburgh. He concluded that those families from the upper levels of society "comprised an important, but interlocking group, welded together through marriage and business, who formulated the crucial corporate and financial decisions which affected the modern and technological growth of twentieth century Pittsburgh" (110).

9. Frank Lukaszewicz, "Regional and Central Boards of Directors of Pittsburgh Banks in 1912" (Unpublished seminar paper, History Department, University of Pittsburgh, 1965).

10. See Samuel P. Hays, "The Changing Political Structure of the City in Industrial America," *Journal of Urban History* 1 (1974): 8ff., for a concise statement of the characteristics of Pittsburgh during these years. His analysis is followed closely by Paul J. Kleppner, "Government, Parties and Voters in Pittsburgh," in *City at the Point: Essays on the Social History of Pittsburgh*, ed. Samuel P. Hays (Pittsburgh: University of Pittsburgh Press, 1989), 151–80; and Bradley W. Hall, "Elites and Spatial Change in Pittsburgh: Minersville as a Case Study," *Pennsylvania History* 48 (October 1981): 311–34. For studies of other pedestrian cities, see Sam Bass Warner, Jr., *The Private City: Philadelphia in Three Periods of Its Growth* (Philadelphia: University of Pennsylvania Press, 1968); Michael H. Frisch, *Town into City: Springfield, Massachusetts and the Meaning of Community, 1840–1880* (Cambridge, Mass.: Harvard University Press, 1972); Stephanie Grauman Wolf, *Urban Village: Population, Community and Family Structure in Germantown, Pennsylvania, 1683–1800* (Princeton: Princeton University Press, 1976), and Richard Wade, *The Urban Frontier: Pioneer Life in Early Pittsburgh, Cincinnati, Louisville, and St. Louis* (Chicago, 1964).

11. Kleppner, "Government, Parties and Voters," 153.

12. Thomas J. Kelso, "Pittsburgh's Mayors and City Councils, 1794–1844: Who Governed?" (Unpublished seminar paper, Department of History, University of Pittsburgh, 1963).

13. Ibid., 7–8.

14. Kleppner, "Government, Parties and Voters," 155.

15. Ibid., 157.

16. John Dankosky, "Pittsburgh City Government, 1816–1850" (Unpublished seminar paper, History Department, University of Pittsburgh, 1971).

17. Samuel P. Hays, "The Development of Pittsburgh as a Social Order," *Western Pennsylvania Historical Magazine* 57 (October 1974): 431–48. Michael Holt, *Forging a Majority: The Formation of the Republican Party in Pittsburgh, 1848–1860* (New Haven: Yale University Press, 1969), 175–219, draws a similar conclusion.

18. Scott C. Martin, "Fathers against Sons, Sons against Fathers: Anti-Masonry in Pittsburgh" (Unpublished seminar paper, History Department, University of Pittsburgh, n.d.), sees a clear socioeconomic difference between the masons and Antimasons; Duane E. Campbell, "Anti-Masonry in Pittsburgh" (Unpublished seminar paper, Department of History, Carnegie-Mellon University, n.d.), does not. The evidence in either case is not compelling. Ronald P. Formisano, *The Birth of Mass Political Parties: Michigan, 1827–1861* (Princeton, N.J.: Princeton University Press, 1971), investigates the issue in another environment.

19. See Holt, *Forging a Majority*, 25–28, and Robert Kaplan, "The Know Nothings in Pittsburgh" (Unpublished seminar paper, Department of History, University of Pittsburgh, 1977).

20. Holt, *Forging a Majority*, 123–74, 263–303; Miller Myers, "An Analysis of Voting Behavior in Pittsburgh, 1848–1856" (Unpublished seminar paper, History Department, University of Pittsburgh, 1963); Paul Kleppner, "Lincoln and the Immigrant Vote: A Case of Religious Polarization," *Mid-America* 48 (July 1966): 176–95.

21. Eric Foner, *Free Soil, Free Labor, Free Men: The Ideology of the Republican Party before the Civil War* (New York: Oxford University Press, 1970), chaps. 1 and 2.

22. Paul Kleppner, *The Third Electoral System, 1853–1892: Parties, Voters, and Political Cultures* (Chapel Hill: University of North Carolina Press, 1979), esp. 143–97.

23. Carmen DiCiccio, "The 1890's Political Realignment and Its Impact on Pittsburgh's Political Structure" (Unpublished seminar paper, Department of History, University of Pittsburgh, 1983).

24. Hays, "Development of Pittsburgh," 443–44. Herbert Gans, *The Urban Villagers: Group and Class in the Life of Italian-Americans* (New York: Free Press, 1962), 3–41, 142–226, discusses this phenomenon among a more modern group.

25. S. J. Kleinberg, *The Shadow of the Mills: Working Class Families in Pittsburgh, 1870–1907* (Pittsburgh: University of Pittsburgh Press, 1989), 278.

26. Roy Lubove, *Twentieth Century Pittsburgh: Government, Business and Environmentalism* (New York: John Wiley & Sons, 1969); see Sam Bass Warner, Jr., *The Private City: Philadelphia in Three Periods of Its Growth* (Philadelphia: University of Pennsylvania Press, 1968), xi, 3, for his definition of privatism.

27. See Kleinberg, *Shadow of the Mills*, 270–77, for an excellent analysis of the functioning of these organizations in Pittsburgh's working-class community.

28. Francis G. Couvares, *The Remaking of Pittsburgh: Class and Culture in an Industrializing City, 1877–1919* (Albany: State University of New York Press, 1984), 63–65.

29. My own analysis of Pittsburgh and Allegheny city governments in 1874 reveals a continuing powerful influence by old-family iron and steel manufacturers, particularly on the Select, as opposed to Common, Council. Four members of Pittsburgh's Select Council in that year were iron and steel manufacturers (Harry Darlington, Henry Lloyd, Frank S. Bissell, and John D. Scully). In addition, another six were men who were married into these iron and steel families, giving a total of ten members of the Select Council. On the Common Council, there were no iron and steel men, but three men who were married into their families were members. Most importantly, W. B. Negley, from an old, upper-class Pittsburgh family, served as president of the Common Council. In Allegheny, the situation was similar. Five men who were iron manufacturers or married with those families served on the Select Council, and one iron man (William H. Lockhart) served on the Common Council. Iron and steel manufacturers also held a number of other important positions, however. James Brown was controller of Allegheny, Robert Dilworth was clerk of the Common Council, and James Park, Jr., was president of the Park Commission. The situation had not changed much by the early 1880s. In Pittsburgh, the mayor was R. W. Lyon, from an old Pittsburgh iron family, and the city attorney was W. C. Moreland, from Carnegie Steel. Eight men from iron and steel or allied families sat on the Select Council; four were on the Common Council. In Allegheny, the influence of older families had been seriously diluted. Although James Brown was still controller and Robert Dilworth clerk, only two men from iron families were on the Select Council, and none was on the Common Council. Offsetting this somewhat, however, was a greater presence on the Allegheny County Board of Controllers, of which David B. Oliver was president. Another four iron and steel men sat on the Board of Controllers.

Analysis of the entire list of Select and Common Councilmen for the period from 1879 to 1909, however, reveals clearly a diminished direct influence of the economic elite on politics. Of the 678 men to serve in Pittsburgh during this period, 22 were members of old iron and steel families and another 7 were members of families married into them. Expanding the category a bit, just 42 manufacturers and bankers served during this time, 6 percent of the total. Another 122 held managerial positions in firms, or were professionals of one kind or another; 228 were small shopkeepers and 130 were in various lower white-collar professions; 146 were craftsmen and less skilled workers of various kinds (Carmen Peter DiCiccio, "Social Biographies of Pittsburgh's Bicameral Council, 1879–1906" [Unpublished papers, compiled 18 Apr. 1990).

30. Sam Bass Warner, Jr., *Streetcar Suburbs: The Process of Growth in Boston, 1870–1900* (Cambridge, Mass.: Harvard University Press, 1962), 31, asserts that city services were distributed on an equal basis, since they were

needed "to cover the whole city at once." Kleinberg, *Shadow of the Mills,* 85–99 indicates that was certainly not the case in Pittsburgh.

31. See Kleinberg, *Shadow of the Mills,* 87–93, and Clayton R. Koppes and William P. Norris, "Ethnicity, Class and Mortality in the Industrial City: A Case Study of Typhoid Fever in Pittsburgh, 1890–1910," *Journal of Urban History* 11 (May 1985): 269–75.

32. *National Labor Tribune,* 18 July 1874, quoted in Kleinberg, *Shadow of the Mills,* 87.

33. Cecelia F. Bucki, "The Evolution of Poor Relief Practice in Nineteenth Century Pittsburgh" (Unpublished seminar paper, Department of History, University of Pittsburgh, 1977), 4, 2.

34. John Newton Boucher, ed., *A Century and a Half of Pittsburgh and Her People,* 4 vols. (Pittsburgh, 1908), 3, 441.

35. Bucki, "Evolution of Poor Relief," 28.

36. Kleinberg, *Shadow of the Mills,* 283–84. See also Keith Melder, "Ladies Bountiful," *New York History* 48 (1967): 231–55, and John Rousmaniere, "Cultural Hybrid in the Slums," *American Quarterly* 20 (1970): 45–66, for somewhat contrasting aspects of this phenomenon in other cities.

37. Bucki, "Evolution of Poor Relief," 31.

38. Samuel P. Hays, "The Politics of Reform in Municipal Government in the Progressive Era," *Pacific Northwest Quarterly* 55 (October 1964): 157–69.

39. Ibid., 160.

40. Idem.

41. Peter H. Rossi, "Power and Politics: A Road to Social Reform," *Social Service Review* 35 (December 1961): 359–69.

42. Julia Shelley Hodges, *George Hodges* (New York: The Century Co., 1926), 99. Hodges had originally moved to Pittsburgh in 1881 as assistant pastor at Calvary.

43. From a letter by H. D. W. English dated 26 July 1919; reprinted in Hodges, *George Hodges,* 115–16.

44. Renee Reitman, "The Elite Community in Shadyside, 1880–1920" (Unpublished seminar paper, Department of History, University of Pittsburgh, 1964).

45. Joseph Rishel, "The Founding Families of Allegheny County: An Examination of Nineteenth Century Elite Continuity" (Unpublished Ph.D. diss., University of Pittsburgh, 1975), 150–54.

46. See John N. Ingham, *The Iron Barons: A Social Analysis of an American Urban Elite, 1874–1964* (Westport, Conn.: Greenwood Press, 1978), 109–13, for a fuller analysis of the residential and social class patterns of the city's iron and steel families.

47. Couvares, *Remaking of Pittsburgh,* 96–119.

48. Ibid., 104–5.

49. Rishel, "Founding Families of Allegheny County," 189.

50. Roy Lubove, *Twentieth Century Pittsburgh*, 25.

51. Ibid., 35.

52. Henry Clay Frick donated his old residence in the Hill District to house the organization in 1901, and Charles L. Taylor donated a sixty-five-acre farm in Butler County, which became the Lillian Home, the site of summer outings. Henry Frick, Herbert DuPuy, Joseph Buffington, Andrew and Richard Mellon, James Guffey, members of the Lockhart family, Charles Taylor, and other members of the older Pittsburgh elite also served as teachers of the children at the Kingsley House and served as referees of sporting events there (Trisha Early, "The Pittsburgh Survey" [Unpublished seminar paper, Department of History, University of Pittsburgh, 1972], 22.)

53. Lubove, "Pittsburgh and Uses of Social Welfare History," 308.

54. Kingsley House, *Handbook of Settlements* (Pittsburgh: privately printed, 1901). See also William H. Matthews, *The Meaning of the Social Settlement Movement* (Pittsburgh: Kingsley House, 1909), for further elaboration of these ideas.

55. *The Story of Pittsburgh*, 118; George Thornton Fleming, ed., *The History of Pittsburgh and Environs*, 6 vols. (New York: American Historical Society, 1922), 4:239–40; Arthur G. Burgoyne, *All Sorts of Pittsburghers, Sketched in Prose and Verse* (Pittsburgh: Leader All Sorts Publishing Co., 1892), 113; Erasmus Wilson, ed., *The Standard History of Pittsburgh, Pennsylvania* (Chicago: H. R. Cornell & Co., 1898), 1068–69; Pittsburgh Chamber of Commerce, *Pittsburgh First* 7, no. 49 (April 1926): 4; *Pittsburgh Gazette Times*, 29 Mar. 1926.

56. Roy Lubove, *Twentieth Century Pittsburgh: Government, Business and Environmental Change* (New York: John Wiley & Sons, 1969), 24.

57. Seed money to begin the survey came from Mayor George Guthrie, English, and Justice Joseph Buffington of the circuit court, who also had been a steel mill owner (American Sheet Steel) in the nineteenth century. All were members of Calvary Episcopal Church (John F. McClymer, "The Pittsburgh Survey, 1907–1914: Forging an Ideology in the Steel District," *Pennsylvania History* 41 [April 1974]: 170).

58. Lincoln Steffens, *Shame of the Cities* (New York: McClure, Phillips & Co., 1904), 104.

59. *Proceedings of the Pittsburgh Conference for Good City Government and the Fourteenth Annual Meeting of the National Municipal League* (Pittsburgh: National Municipal League, 1909), 390–91.

60. Ibid., 415.

61. Pittsburgh Civic Commission, *Plan and Scope* (n.p., n.d.).

62. Mary Young, "The Pittsburgh Chamber of Commerce and the Allied Boards of Trade in 1910" (Unpublished seminar paper, Department of History, University of Pittsburgh, 1966).

63. Hays, "The Politics of Reform," 165.

64. Carl V. Harris, *Political Power in Birmingham, 1871–1921* (Knoxville: University of Tennessee Press, 1977), chap. 10.

65. Ronald Edsforth, *Class Conflict and Cultural Consensus: The Making of Mass Consumer Society in Flint, Michigan* (New Brunswick, N.J.: Rutgers University Press, 1987).

66. See Kathleen McCarthy, *Noblesse Oblige: Charity and Cultural Philanthropy in Chicago, 1849–1929* (Chicago: University of Chicago Press, 1982); Helen Lefkowitz Horowitz, *Culture and the City: Cultural Philanthropy in Chicago from the 1880's to 1917* (Lexington: University of Kentucky Press, 1976); and Kenneth Kusmer, "The Functions of Organized Charity in the Progressive Era: Chicago as a Case Study," *Journal of American History* 60 (December 1973): 657–78, on Chicago; Nathan I. Huggins, *Protestants against Poverty: Boston's Charities, 1870–1900* (Westport, Conn.: Greenwood Press, 1971); and Paul Goodman, "Ethics and Enterprise: The Values of a Boston Elite, 1800–1860," *American Quarterly* 18 (Fall 1966): 437–51, on Boston; Daniel M. Fox, *Engines of Culture: Philanthropy and Art Museums* (Madison: State Historical Society of Wisconsin, 1963); Russell Lynes, *The Tastemakers* (New York: Harper & Row, 1949); and Robert H. Bremner, *American Philanthropy* (Chicago: University of Chicago Press, 1960), on general developments.

67. See Couvares, *Remaking of Pittsburgh*, chap. 7. This issue of elite hegemony over cultural institutions is complex and controversial. The leading theorist in this regard is Antonio Gramsci (*Selections from the Prison Notebook*, ed. and trans. Quintin Horace and Geoffrey N. Smith [New York: International Publishers, 1971]), who believes the elite tends to use cultural institutions of all kinds to establish its hegemony and legitimate elite rule. See T. J. Jackson Lears, "The Concept of Cultural Hegemony: Problems and Possibilities," *American Historical Review* 90 (June 1985): 567–93, for a useful discussion of the strengths and weaknesses of Gramsci's theory.

68. Arthur G. Burgoyne, *All Sorts of Pittsburghers*, quoted in Paul L. Krause, "Patronage and Philanthropy in Industrial America: Andrew Carnegie and the Free Library in Braddock, Pa.," *Western Pennsylvania Historical Magazine* (1984): 127–28.

69. Krause, "Patronage and Philanthropy," 143.

70. Byington, *Homestead: Households of a Mill Town*, 178.

71. "The Multimillionaires of Chicago," *Chicago Tribune*, 9 June 1907, quoted in McCarthy, *Noblesse Oblige*, 117.

72. *Pittsburgh Press*, 21 Dec. 1952, quoted in Marianne Maxwell, "Pittsburgh's Frick Park: A Unique Addition to the City's Park System," *Western Pennsylvania Historical Magazine* 68, no. 3 (July 1985): 243–64.

73. Ronald J. Butera, "A Settlement House and the Urban Challenge: Kingsley House in Pittsburgh, Pennsylvania, 1893–1920," *Western Pennsylvania Historical Magazine* 25–47.

74. Lily Lee Nixon, "Henry Clay Frick and Pittsburgh's Children," *Western Pennsylvania Historical Magazine*.

75. Barbara J. Howe, "Clubs, Culture, and Charity: Anglo-American Up-

per Class Activities in the Late Nineteenth Century City" (Unpublished Ph.D. diss., Temple University, 1976), 554.

76. Maxwell, "Pittsburgh's Frick Park," 256.

77. To me, nothing expresses the curious amalgam of public purpose and private use that the upper classes espoused in much of this giving so well as Schenley Park. When Mary Schenley's estate donated the park to the city, it also allowed the Pittsburgh Golf Club, an austere upper-class institution, to continue to have exclusive use of the golf course on park grounds. Only later, after much litigation, was this disallowed and the course made public. See Couvares, *Remaking of Pittsburgh*, chap. 7, for a fuller discussion of all of this.

78. S. Adele Shaw, "Closed Towns: Intimidation as It Is Practiced in the Pittsburgh Steel District," *Survey* 43, 8 Nov. 1919, 58–64; John A. Fitch, "Democracy in Steel: A Contrast between the Rhine and the Monongahela," *Survey* 41, 4 Jan. 1919. Fitch also noted that the mill towns were a principal means of controlling the work force in the mills in his *The Steel Workers*, vol. 3 of *The Pittsburgh Surveys*, ed. Paul Underwood Kellogg (New York: Charities and Commons Publication Committee, 1911). That theme was picked up and enhanced by Brody, *Steelworkers in America*, and Lubove, "Pittsburgh and the Uses of Social History."

79. Karen Cowles, "The Industrialization of Duquesne and the Circulation of Elites, 1891–1933," *Western Pennsylvania History Magazine* 62, no. 1 (January 1979): 9.

80. Harvey O'Connor, *Steel-Dictator* (New York: John Day Co., 1935), 272.

81. Cowles, "Industrialization of Duquesne," 15–16.

82. Herrick Chapman, "Pittsburgh and Europe's Metallurgical Cities: A Comparison," in Hays, ed., *City at the Point*, 424.

Conclusion

1. David Montgomery, *Worker's Control in Industrial America: Studies in the History of Work, Technology, and Labor Struggles* (Cambridge, England: Cambridge University Press, 1979), gives a good account of the preceding version of the "second industrial revolution," especially for the iron and steel industry. Ronald Edsworth, *Class Conflict and Cultural Consensus: The Making of a Mass Consumer Society in Flint, Michigan* (New Brunswick, N.J.: Rutgers University Press, 1987), chaps. 1 and 2, does the same for the automobile industry and Flint.

2. Kenneth Warren, *The American Steel Industry, 1850–1970* (Oxford, England: Clarendon Press, 1973), 134–38.

3. John Swauger, "Pittsburgh's Residential Patterns in 1815," *Annals of the Association of American Geographers* 68, no. 2 (June 1978: 265–77.

4. See Joel A. Tarr, *Transportation, Innovation, and Changing Spatial*

Patterns in Pittsburgh, 1850–1934 (Chicago: Public Works Historical Society, 1978); and S. J. Kleinberg, *The Shadow of the Mills: Working Class Families in Pittsburgh, 1870–1907* (Pittsburgh: University of Pittsburgh Press, 1989).

5. Bradley W. Hall, "Elites and Spatial Change in Pittsburgh: Minersville as a Case Study," *Pennsylvania History* 48 (October 1981): 331–34.

6. John Herron himself continued to commute into Pittsburgh to attend the elite First Presbyterian Church, whose pastor was his cousin, Dr. Francis Herron. This is an interesting example of the curious blend of decentralization and centralization in nineteenth-century Pittsburgh. First Presbyterian was a central elite institution, as were the various social clubs that Herron and his wife attended. Yet, they resided in a dispersed area and acted as virtual country squires in relation to their dependent working-class population.

7. Joel A. Tarr and Denise Di Pasquale, "The Mill Town in the Industrial City: Pittsburgh's Hazelwood," *Urbanism Past and Present* 7 (Winter/Spring 1982): 1–14. See also Joan Miller, "The Early Development of Hazelwood" (Unpublished seminar paper, History Department, University of Pittsburgh, n.d.).

8. Francis G. Couvares, *The Remaking of Pittsburgh: Class and Culture in an Industrializing City, 1877–1919* (Albany: State University of New York Press, 1984); Robert J. Jucha, "The Anatomy of a Streetcar Suburb: A Development History of Shadyside, 1852–1916," *Western Pennsylvania Historical Magazine* 62 (October 1979): 301–19; and Renee Reitman, "The Elite Community in Shadyside, 1880–1920" (Unpublished seminar paper, Department of History, University of Pittsburgh, 1964). See also Ethel Spencer, *The Spencers of Amberson Avenue: A Turn-of-the-Century Memoir* (Pittsburgh: University of Pittsburgh Press, 1983); and Annie Dillard, *An American Childhood* (New York: Harper & Row, 1987), two remarkably moving and perceptive views of what it was like to grow up in Shadyside, the first at the turn of the century, the second around World War II.

9. E. Digby Baltzell, *Philadelphia Gentlemen: The Making of a National Upper Class* (New York: Free Press, 1958), chap. 2; John N. Ingham, *The Iron Barons: A Social Analysis of an American Urban Elite, 1874–1965* (Westport, Conn.: Greenwood Press, 1978), 127–53, and "The American Urban Upper Class: Cosmopolitans or Locals?" *Journal of Urban History* 2 (November 1975): 76–87.

10. Booth Tarkington, *The Magnificent Ambersons* (New York: Doubleday, Page, 1918), 1.

11. See Cecelia Bucki, "The Evolution of Poor Relief in Nineteenth Century Pittsburgh" (Unpublished seminar paper, History Department, University of Pittsburgh, 1977), for an analysis of this transformation.

12. See Couvares, *Remaking of Pittsburgh*, chap. 7.

13. Samuel P. Hays reports that one businessman-reformer told a labor audience that his slate of candidates represented labor "better than you do yourself" ("The Politics of Reform in Municipal Government in the Progressive Era," *Pacific Northwest Quarterly* 55, no. 4 [October 1964]: 160).

14. Samuel P. Hays, "Pittsburgh: How Typical?" in *City at the Point: Essays on the Social History of Pittsburgh*, ed. Samuel P. Hays (Pittsburgh: University of Pittsburgh Press, 1989), 386–87.

BIBLIOGRAPHY

Government Materials

U.S. Bureau of the Census. *12th Census of the United States, 1900.* Vol. 10, *Special Reports on Selected Industries,* Washington, D.C.: U.S. Government Printing Office, 1900.

———. *13th Census of the United States, 1910.* Vol. 10, *Manufacturers, 1909, Reports for Principal Industries.* Washington, D.C.: U.S. Government Printing Office, 1910.

U.S. Bureau of Labor. *11th Special Report of the Commissioner of Labor, Regulation of Output.* Washington, D.C.: U.S. Government Printing Office, 1904.

Manuscript Collections

American Steel & Wire Company Collection, Baker Library, Harvard University, Boston, Mass.

Annual Reports of American Corporations, Records Division, Baker Library, Harvard University, Boston, Mass.

A. M. Byers Company, Personnel Records, Archives for an Industrial Society (AIS), Hillman Library, University of Pittsburgh, Pittsburgh, Pa.

R. G. Dun & Co. Collection, Baker Library, Harvard University, Boston, Mass.

Benjamin Franklin Jones Diary, AIS.

Jones and Laughlin Corporation Papers, AIS.

Oliver Iron and Steel Company Papers, AIS.

Books, Articles, and Unpublished Dissertations and Papers

Abbott, Lyman. "Compulsory Arbitration." *Arena* 7 (December 1894).

Age of Steel. July 1890–July 1906 (after 1902: *Iron and Machinery World*).

Aiken, Michael. "The Distribution of Community Power: Structural Bases and Social Consequences." In *The Structure of Community Power,* edited by Michael Aiken and Paul E. Mott, 487–525. New York: Random House, 1970.

Akin, William. "Arbitration and Labor Conflict: The Middle Class Panacea, 1886–1900," *Historian* 29, no. 4 (1967): 565–83.

Amalgamated Association of Iron, Steel and Tin Workers. *Proceedings* (1870–1900). Microfilm copy from Cornell University Library, Ithaca, N.Y.

American Institute of Electrical Engineers. *Transactions* 1–83 (1884–1964).

American Iron and Steel Association. *Bulletin* 1–46. New York: AISA

———. *Directory of Iron and Steel Works in the United States and Canada, 1874–1940.* New York: AISA.

American Iron and Steel Institute. *Annual Statistical Report.* Philadelphia: AISI, 1913–45.

———. *Biographical Directory.* New York: AISI, 1911.

———. *Bulletin* 1–5. New York: AISI, 1913–17.

American Manufacturer & Iron World 11–78 (1872–1906).

American Society of Civil Engineers. *Transactions* 1–99 (1867–1935).

American Society of Mechanical Engineers. *Transactions* (1911).

American Society of Mining Engineers. *Transactions* (1911).

Arnstein, Walter L. "The Survival of the Victorian Aristocracy." In *The Rich, The Well-Born and the Powerful*, edited by Frederick C. Jaher, 203–57. Urbana: University of Illinois Press, 1973.

Atack, Jeremy. "Firm Size and Industrial Structure in the United States during the Nineteenth Century." *JEH* 46, no. 2 (June 1986): 463–75.

———. "Industrial Structure and the Emergence of the Modern Industrial Corporation," *EEH* 22 (1985): 29–52.

———. "Returns to Scale in Antebellum United States Manufacturing." *EEH* 14 (October, 1977): 337–59.

Atherton, Lewis. "Itinerant Merchandising in the Antebellum South." *Bulletin of the Business Historical Society* 19 (1945): 35–59.

———. *The Pioneer Merchant in Mid-America.* University of Missouri Studies. Columbia: University of Missouri Press, 1939.

———. *The Southern Country Store, 1800–1860.* Baton Rouge: Louisiana State University Press, 1949.

Atlas of the Cities of Pittsburgh and Allegheny and Adjoining Boroughs. Philadelphia, 1872.

Averitt, Robert. *The Dual Economy.* New York: W. W. Norton, 1971.

Bachrach, Peter, and Morton Baratz. *Power and Poverty: Theory and Practice.* New York: Oxford University Press, 1970.

Backert, A. O., ed. *The ABC of Iron and Steel.* Cleveland: Penton Publishing, 1919.

Bakewell, B. G. *The Family Book of Bakewell, Page & Campbell.* Pittsburgh: privately printed, 1896.

Baldwin, Leland. *Pittsburgh: The Story of a City.* Pittsburgh: University of Pittsburgh Press, 1937.

Baltzell, E. Digby. *Philadelphia Gentlemen*. Glencoe, Ill.: The Free Press, 1958.

_____. "Who's Who in America and the Social Register: Elite and Upper Class Indexes in Metropolitan America." In *Class, Status and Power*, edited by Reinhard Bendix and Seymour M. Lipset. Rev. ed. Glencoe, Ill.: The Free Press, 1966.

Barraclough, K. C. *Steelmaking before Bessemer*. Vol. 2, *Crucible Steel: The Growth of a Technique*. London: Metals Society, 1984.

Baxter, Harold. "Growth of the Steel Industry." *Mining Reporter* (July 1906): 60–61.

Bedeian, George. "Social Stratification within the Upper Class: Early 20th Century Pittsburgh as a Case Study." Seminar paper, History Department, University of Pittsburgh, 1974.

Bennett, John William. "Iron Workers in Woods Run and Johnstown: The Union Era, 1865–1895." Ph.D. diss., University of Pittsburgh, 1977.

Berglund, Abraham. *The U.S. Steel Corporation: A Study of Growth and Combination in the Iron and Steel Industry*. New York: Columbia University Press, 1907.

_____. "U.S. Steel Corporation and Industrial Stabilization." *QRE* (August 1924): 607–30.

Bining, Arthur Cecil. "The Rise of Iron Manufacture in Western Pennsylvania." *WPHM* 16 (November, 1933): 235–56.

Biographical Encyclopedia of Pennsylvania in the 19th Century. Philadelphia: Galaxy Publishing Co., 1874.

Biographical Review. Vol. 24, *Containing the Life Sketches of Leading Citizens of Pittsburgh Pa. & Vicinity*. Boston: Biographical Review Publishing Co., 1897.

Blackford, Mansel G. *A Portrait Cast in Steel: Buckeye International and Columbus, Ohio, 1881–1980*. Westport, Conn.: Greenwood Press, 1982.

_____. *Pioneering a Modern Small Business: Wakefield Seafoods and the Alaskan Frontier*. Greenwich, Conn.: JAI Press, 1979.

Book of Prominent Pennsylvanians. Pittsburgh: Leader Publishing Co., 1913.

Boucher, John N., ed. *A Century and a Half of Pittsburgh and Her People*. 4 vols. New York: Lewis Historical Publishing Co., 1908.

_____. *History of Westmoreland County, Pennsylvania*. 3 vols. New York: Lewis Historical Publishing Co., 1906.

Bowring, Joseph. *Competition in the Dual Economy*. Princeton, N.J.: Princeton University Press, 1986.

Brandes, Stuart D. *American Welfare Capitalism, 1880–1940*. Chicago: University of Chicago Press, 1976.

Brecher, Jeremy. *Strike*. Boston: South End Press, 1972.

Bremner, Robert H. *American Philanthropy*. Chicago: University of Chicago Press, 1960.

Brennan, J. Fletcher. *A Biographical Encyclopedia and Portrait Gallery of the State of Ohio.* Cincinnati: J. C. Yorston & Co., 1880.

Bridge, James H. *The Inside History of Carnegie Steel.* New York: Aldine Book Co., 1903.

Briggs, Asa. *Victorian Cities.* New York: Harper & Row, 1984.

Brody, David. "Labor and Small Scale Enterprise." In *Small Business in American Life,* edited by Stuart Bruchy, 253–79. New York: Columbia University Press, 1980.

————. "The Old Labor History and the New: In Search of the American Working Class." *LH* 20 (1979): 111–26.

————. *Steelworkers in America: The Nonunion Era.* Cambridge, Mass.: Harvard University Press, 1960.

————. *Workers in Industrial America: Essays on the Twentieth Century Struggle.* New York: Oxford University Press, 1980.

Bruchy, Stuart W., ed. *Small Business in American Life.* New York: Columbia University Press, 1980.

Bryant, Keith L., and Henry Dethloff. *A History of American Business.* Englewood Cliffs, N.J.: Prentice-Hall, 1983.

Bryce, James. *The American Commonwealth.* 2 vols. New York: Macmillan, 1888.

Bucki, Cecelia. "The Evolution of Poor Relief Practice in 19th Century Pittsburgh." Seminar paper, History Department, University of Pittsburgh, 1977.

Buenker, John D. *Urban Liberalism and Progressive Reform.* New York: Charles Scribner's Sons, 1973.

Buffington, Eugene J. "Making Cities for Workmen." *Harper's Weekly* 53 (8 May 1909): 15–17.

Burgoyne, Arthur G. *All Sorts of Pittsburghers, Sketched in Prose and Verse.* Pittsburgh: Leader All Sorts Publishing Co., 1892.

Burkett, Ray. "Vandergrift: A Model Worker's Community." Seminar paper, History Department, University of Pittsburgh, 1971.

Burnham, T. H., and G. O. Haskins. *Iron and Steel in Britain, 1870–1930.* London: Allen & Unwin, 1943.

Butera, Ronald J. "A Settlement House and the Urban Challenge: Kingsley House in Pittsburgh, Pennsylvania, 1893–1920." *WPHM* 66, no. 1 (1983): 25–47.

Cain, Louis P., and Donald G. Peterson. "Factor Biases and Technical Change in Manufacturing: The American System, 1850–1919." *JEH* 41, no. 2 (June 1981): 341–58.

Calhoun, Craig. *The Question of Class Struggle.* Chicago: University of Chicago Press, 1982.

Campbell, Duane E. "Anti Masonry in Pittsburgh." Seminar paper, History Department, Carnegie Mellon University, Pittsburgh, n.d.

Campbell, Harry Huse. *The Manufacture and Properties of Iron and Steel.* New York: Hill Publishing Co., 1907.

Carey, Henry C. *Principles of Political Economy.* 3 vols. Philadelphia: Carey, Lea, Blanchard, 1837–40.

Carnegie, Andrew. *Autobiography.* Boston: Houghton Mifflin, 1920.

Carnegie Brothers Co. *The Edgar Thomson Steel Works and Blast Furnaces.* Pittsburgh: J. Eichbaum Co., 1890.

Casson, Herbert. *The Romance of Steel.* New York: A. S. Barnes, 1907.

Chandler, Alfred D., Jr. "Beginnings of Big Business in American Industry." *BHR* 33 (Spring 1959): 1–31.

_____. "The Structure of American Industry in the 20th Century: A Historical Overview." *BHR* 43 (1966): 255–81.

_____. *The Visible Hand: The Managerial Revolution in America.* Cambridge, Mass: Harvard University Press, 1977.

_____, and Louis Galambos. "The Development of Large Scale Economic Organizations in Modern America." *JEH* 30 (March 1970): 212–16.

_____, and Richard Tedlow. *The Coming of Managerial Capitalism.* Homewood, Ill: Richard D. Irwin, 1985.

Chapman, Herrick. "Pittsburgh and Europe's Metallurgical Cities: A Comparison." In *City at the Point: Essays on the Social History of Pittsburgh,* edited by Samuel P. Hays, 407–35. Pittsburgh: University of Pittsburgh Press, 1989.

Chemical Engineering 1– (September 1902–   ).

[The] *City's Blue Book, Councilmen and City Officials.* Pittsburgh, 1904–05.

Civic Club of Allegheny County. *Fifteen Years of Civic History, October, 1895–December, 1910.* Pittsburgh: Nicholson Printing Co., 1910.

Clark, Thomas D. *Pills, Petticoats and Plows: The Southern Store.* Norman: University of Oklahoma Press, 1944.

Clark, Victor S. *History of Manufactures in the United States.* 3 vols. New York: McGraw-Hill, 1929.

Cohen, Lizabeth. "From Welfare Capitalism to Capitalism's Decline: Industrial Relations in Chicago's Steel Industry." Paper presented to Conference on Steel and Coal Communities in Comparative Perspective, Pittsburgh, 20–22 April 1990.

_____. *Making a New Deal: Industrial Workers in Chicago, 1919–1939.* New York: Cambridge University Press, 1990.

Cohen, Steven R. "Reconciling Industrial Conflict and Democracy: *The Pittsburgh Survey* and the Growth of Social Research in the United States." Ph.D. diss., Columbia University, 1981.

Cole, Arthur H. "Marketing Non-Consumer Goods before 1917." *BHR* 33 (1959): 420–28.

Colvin, William H. *Crucible Steel Company of America: Fifty Years of Speciality Steel Making in the USA.* New York: Newcomen Society in North America, 1950.

Conkin, Paul K. *Prophets of Prosperity.* Bloomington: Indiana University Press, 1980.

Constitution, By-Laws and List of Members of the Allegheny Country Club, Sewickley, Pennsylvania. Pittsburgh: privately printed, 1911.

Cook, Earnshaw. *Open-Hearth Steel Making.* Cleveland: American Society for Metals, 1937.

Cordero, H. G. *Iron and Steel Works of the World, 1956–57.* London: Quin Press, 1956.

Cotter, Arundel. *The Authentic History of the U.S. Steel Corp.* New York: Doubleday, Page & Co., 1907.

Couvares, Francis G. *The Remaking of Pittsburgh: Class and Culture in an Industrializing City, 1877–1919.* Albany: State University of New York Press, 1984.

Cowles, Karen. "The Industrializing of Duquesne and the Circulation of Elites, 1891–1933," *WPHM* 62 (January 1979): 1–17.

Cronemeyer, William C. "The Development of the Tinplate Industry," *WPHM* 13 (1930): 23–55.

————. "Heroes of American History: John Henry Demmler, the Preserver of the American Tin Plate Industry." *Progressive* (1 October 1926): 562–66.

"Crucible Steel Company of America." *Fortune* 20 (November 1939): 74–79.

Crum, W. L. "On the Alleged Concentration of Economic Power." *AER* 24 (1934): 69–83.

Dahl, Robert. *Who Governs? Democracy and Power in an American City.* New Haven: Yale University Press, 1961.

Daly, Janet. "The Political Context of Zoning in Pittsburgh, 1900–1923." Seminar paper, History Department, University of Pittsburgh, 1984.

Dankosky, John. "Pittsburgh City Government, 1816–1850." Seminar paper, History Department, University of Pittsburgh, 1971.

Daugherty, Carroll R. *The Economics of the Iron and Steel Industry.* 2 vols. New York: McGraw-Hill, 1937.

Davenport, Marcia. *The Valley of Decision.* New York: Charles Scribner's Sons, 1943.

Davis, Allen F. *Spearheads for Reform: The Social Settlements and the Progressive Movement, 1890–1914.* New York: Oxford University Press, 1967.

Davis, John J. *The Iron Puddler: My Life in the Rolling Mills and What Came of It.* Indianapolis: Bobbs Merrill, 1932.

Davis, Mike. "Why the U.S. Working Class Is Different." *New Left Review* 123 (1980): 3–46.

Dennison, S. R. "Vertical Integration in the Iron and Steel Industry." *Economic Journal* 40 (June 1930): 244–58.

Devine, Edward I. "Pittsburgh: The Year of the Survey." In *The Pittsburgh Survey*, edited by Paul Underwood Kellogg. Vol. 5, *The Civic Frontage.* New York: Charities and Commons Publication Committee, 1914.

DiCiccio, Carmen. "The 1890's Political Realignment and Its Impact on

Pittsburgh's Political Structure." Seminar paper, History Department, University of Pittsburgh, 1983.
_____. "Social Biographies of Pittsburgh's Bicameral Council, 1879–1909." Unpublished paper, compiled 18 April 1990.
Dickson, William Brown, ed. *Genealogy of the Dickson Family*. Montclair, N.J.: privately printed, 1908.
_____. *History of the Carnegie Veterans Association*. Montclair, N.J.: Mountain Press, 1938.
Dictionary of American Biography. 22 vols. New York: Charles Scribner's Sons, 1927–1958.
Diggins, John Patrick. *The Proud Decades: America in War and Peace, 1941–1960*. New York: W. W. Norton, 1988.
Dillard, Annie. *An American Childhood*. New York: Harper & Row, 1987.
Dinkey, Gertrude Flora. *Genealogy of the Flora–Dinkey Families*. Pittsburgh: privately printed, 1946.
Dixon, Margaret Collins Denny. *Denny Genealogy*. New York: National Historical Society, 1944.
Doeringer, Peter B. "Piece Rate Wage Structure in the Pittsburgh Iron and Steel Industry, 1880–1900," *LH* 9 (Spring 1968): 262–74.
Donehoo, George P. *Pennsylvania: A History*. 5 vols. New York: Lewis Historical Publishing Co., 1926.
Dorfman, Joseph. *The Economic Mind in American Civilization*. 3 vols. New York: Viking Press, 1945–49.
Dorsett, Lyle. *The Pendergast Machine*. New York, Oxford University Press, 1968.
Duffus, R. L. "Is Pittsburgh Civilized?" *Harper's Magazine* 161 (October 1930): 537–45.
Dunbar, Donald E. *The Tin Plate Industry*. Boston: Houghton Mifflin, 1915.
Dupuy, Charles M., & Herbert Dupuy. *A Genealogical History of the Dupuy Family*. Philadelphia: private printed, 1910.
[The] Duquesne Club. *Directory*. Pittsburgh: privately printed, 1881– .
Early, Trisha. "The *Pittsburgh Survey*." Seminar paper, History Department, University of Pittsburgh, 1972.
Edsforth, Ronald. *Class Conflict and Cultural Consensus: The Making of a Mass Consumer Society in Flint, Michigan*. New Brunswick, N.J.: Rutgers University Press, 1987.
Edwards, Richard. *Contested Terrain: The Transformation of the Workplace in 20th Century America*. New York: Basic Books, 1979.
Edwards, Richard. *Industries of Pittsburgh: Trade, Commerce & Manufactures*. Pittsburgh: R. Edwards, 1879.
Eggert, Gerald G. *Steelmasters and Labor Reform, 1886–1923*. Pittsburgh: University of Pittsburgh Press, 1981.
Elbaum, Bernard. "The Making and Shaping of Job Structures in the Iron and Steel Industry." In *Internal Labor Markets*, edited by Paul Osterman, 71–107. Cambridge, Mass: MIT Press, 1984.

————, and Frank Wilkinson. "Industrial Relations and Uneven Development: A Comparative Study of the American and British Steel Industries." *Cambridge Journal of Economics* 3 (1979): 275–303.

Encyclopedia of Contemporary Biography of Pennsylvania. 3 vols. New York: Atlantic Publishing and Engraving Co., 1889.

Encyclopedia of Genealogy and Biography of the State of Pennsylvania. 2 vols. New York, 1904.

Engineer's Society of Western Pennsylvania. Proceedings 1– (1860–   ).

Engineering News-Record. 1897.

Englander, Ernest J. "The Inside Contract System of Production and Organization: A Neglected Insight of the History of the Firm," *LH* 28 (Fall 1987): 429–46.

Erickson, Charlotte. *British Industrialists: Steel & Hosiery, 1850–1950.* Cambridge, England: Cambridge University Press, 1959.

Evans, Gilbert. *Manufacture of Seamless Tubes, Ferrous and Non-Ferrous.* Cleveland: Sherwood Press, 1935.

Evans, Henry Oliver. *Iron Pioneer: Henry W. Oliver, 1840–1904.* New York: E. P. Dutton, 1942.

Faires, Nora. "Ethnicity in Evolution: The German Community in Pittsburgh and Allegheny City, 1845–1885." Unpublished Ph.D. diss., University of Pittsburgh, 1981.

Fink, Gary, ed. *Biographical Dictionary of American Labor Leaders.* Westport, Conn: Greenwood Press, 1974.

Fitch, John A. "Democracy in Steel: A Contrast Between the Rhine and the Monongahela." *Survey* 41 (4 January 1919): 453–54.

————. *The Steel Workers.* Vol. 3 of *The Pittsburgh Survey,* edited by Paul Underwood Kellogg. New York: Charities and Commons Publication Committee, 1911.

————. "Unionism in the Iron and Steel Industry." *PSQ* 24, no. 1 (March 1909): 57–79.

Fleckinstein, John V. "The Reluctant Revolution: A View of Popular Attitudes in Pittsburgh to the Merger of U.S. Steel as Reflected in the Press." Seminar paper, History Department, Carnegie Mellon University, n.d.

Fleming, George Thornton, ed. *The History of Pittsburgh and Environs.* 6 vols. New York: American Historical Society, 1922.

Fohlen, Claude. "Entrepreneurship and Management in France in the Nineteenth Century." In *Cambridge Economic History of Europe.* Vol. 7, pt. 1, 347–81. Cambridge, England: Cambridge University Press, 1978.

Foner, Eric. *Free Soil, Free Labor, Free Men: The Ideology of the Republican Party before the Civil War.* New York: Oxford University Press, 1970.

Formisano, Ronald P. *The Birth of Mass Political Parties: Michigan, 1827–1861.* Princeton, N.J.: Princeton University Press, 1971.

Fowler, Irving A. "Local Industrial Structures, Economic Power, and Community Welfare." *Social Problems* 6 (Summer 1958): 41–51.

Fox, Daniel M. *Engines of Culture: Philanthropy and Art Museums.* Madison: State Historical Society of Wisconsin Press, 1963.

Fox Chapel Golf Club. Pittsburgh: privately printed, 1939.

Freifeld, Mary Ellen. "The Emergence of the American Working Classes: The Roots of Division, 1865–1885." Ph.D. diss., New York University, 1980.

Frisch, Michael H. *Town into City: Springfield, Massachusetts and the Meaning of Community, 1840–1880.* Cambridge, Mass.: Harvard University Press, 1972.

_____, and Daniel Walkowitz, eds. *Working Class America: Essays on Labor, Community and American Society.* Urbana: University of Illinois Press, 1983.

Fritz, John. "The Progress of the Manufacture of Iron and Steel." American Society of Mechanical Engineers, *Transactions* (1897): 39–69.

Galbraith, John Kenneth. *The Rise of the New Industrial State.* Boston: Houghton Mifflin, 1966.

Gans, Herbert. *The Urban Villagers: Group and Class in the Life of Italian-Americans.* New York: Free Press, 1962.

Garraty, John A. "The United States Steel Corporation versus Labor: The Early Years." *LH* 1 (1960): 3–38.

Gaventa, John. *Power and Powerlessness: Quiescence and Rebellion in an Appalachian Village.* Urbana: University of Illinois Press, 1980.

Genealogy of the Darlington Family. West Chester, Pa.: privately printed, 1900.

Genovese, Eugene D. *The Political Economy of Slavery.* New York: Random House, 1965.

_____. *Roll, Jordan, Roll: The World the Slaves Made.* New York: Random House, 1974.

George, Peter. *The Emergence of Industrial America.* Albany: State University of New York Press, 1982.

Giddens, Anthony. *The Class Structure of Advanced Societies.* London: Hutchins University Library, 1973.

Gilmer, Harrison. "Birth of the American Crucible Steel Industry." *WPHM* 36 (1953): 17–36.

Gladden, Washington. *Applied Christianity.* Boston: Houghton Mifflin, 1886.

Glasco, Lawrence. "Double Burden: The Black Experience in Pittsburgh." In *City at the Point: Essays on the Social History of Pittsburgh,* edited by Samuel P. Hays, 69–109. Pittsburgh: University of Pittsburgh Press, 1989.

Glazier, William. "The Great Furnace of America." In *Peculiarities of American Cities.* Philadelphia, 1883. In *Pittsburgh,* edited by Roy Lubove,

22. *Documentary History of American Cities*. New York: Franklin Watts, 1976.

Goodman, Paul. "Ethics and Enterprise: The Values of a Boston Elite, 1800–1860." *American Quarterly* 18 (Fall 1966): 437–51.

Gottlieb, Peter. *Making Their Own Way: Southern Blacks' Migration to Pittsburgh, 1916–1930.* Urbana: University of Illinois Press, 1987.

Grace, Eugene G. *Charles M. Schwab.* Bethlehem, Pa.: private printed, 1947.

Gramsci, Antonio. *Selections from the Prison Notebooks,* translated and edited by Quintin Horace and Geoffrey N. Smith. New York: International Publishers, 1971.

Graziosi, Andrea. "Common Laborers, Unskilled Workers, 1880–1915." *LH* 21 (1980): 512–44.

Greater Pittsburgh, Official Bulletin of the Chamber of Commerce of Pittsburgh. *Pittsburgh First* 7, no. 49 (April 1926).

Greater Pittsburgh and Allegheny County.

Gregory, Frances, and Irene Neu. "The American Social Elite of the 1870's: The Social Origins." In *Men in Business,* edited by William Miller, 193–211. Rev. ed. New York: Harper and Row, 1962.

Gresham, John M. *Biographical and Historical Encyclopedia of Westmoreland County, Pennsylvania.* Philadelphia: Press, Dunlap and Clark, 1890.

Grosse, R. M. "Determinants of the Size of Iron and Steel Firms in the United States, 1820–1880." Ph.D. diss., Harvard University, 1948.

Gulick, C. A. *Labor Policy of the United States Steel Corporation.* New York: Columbia University Press, 1924.

Guthrie, George W. "Pittsburgh Victory." *National Conference City Government* (1902): 145–60.

Gutman, Herbert G. "Two Lockouts in Pennsylvania, 1873–1874." *PMHB* 83 (July 1959): 307–26.

―――. *Work, Culture and Society in Industrializing America.* New York: Random House, 1976.

―――. "The Worker's Search for Power." In *The Gilded Age,* edited by H. Wayne Morgan, 31–54. Rev. ed. Syracuse, N.Y.: Syracuse University Press, 1970.

Hacker, Louis M. *The World of Andrew Carnegie, 1865–1901.* Philadelphia: Lippincott, 1968.

Hall, Bradley W. "Elites and Social Change in Pittsburgh: Minersville as a Case Study." *Pennsylvania History* 48 (October 1981): 311–34.

Hammack, David C. "Problems in the Historical Study of Power in Cities and Towns of the United States, 1800–1960." *American Historical Review* 83, no. 2 (1978): 323–49.

―――. "Small Business and Urban Power: Some Notes on the History of Economic Policy in Nineteenth Century American Cities." In *Small Business in American Life,* edited by Stuart Bruchy, 317–37. New York: Columbia University Press, 1980.

Hannah, Leslie. "Mergers in British Manufacturing Industry, 1880–1918."
   Oxford Economic Papers n.s. 26 (1974): 1–20.
Harbord, F. W., and J. W. Hall. *The Metallurgy of Steel.* 7th ed. Vol. 2,
   Mechanical Treatment. London: C. Griffin & Co., 1923.
Harlow, Alvin F. *Andrew Carnegie.* New York: J. Messner, 1953.
Harper, Frank C. *Pittsburgh of Today,* 5 vols. New York: American Histor-
   ical Society, 1931.
Harris, Carl V. *Political Power in Birmingham, 1871–1921.* Knoxville: Uni-
   versity of Tennessee Press, 1977.
Hartman, Blanche T. *A Genealogy of the Nesbit, Ross, Porter, Taggert Fami-
   lies of Pennsylvania.* Pittsburgh: privately printed, 1929.
Harvey, George. *Henry Clay Frick: The Man.* New York: privately printed,
   1928.
Hatcher, Harlan. *A Century of Iron and Men.* Indianapolis: Bobbs Merrill,
   1950.
Hays, Samuel P. "The Changing Political Structure of the City in Industrial
   America." *Journal of Urban History* 1 (November 1974): 6–38.
_____. "The Development of Pittsburgh as a Social Order." *WPHM* 57 (Oc-
   tober 1974): 431–48.
_____. "The Politics of Reform in Municipal Government in the Progres-
   sive Era." *Pacific Northwest Quarterly* 55, no. 4 (October 1964): 157–
   69.
_____, ed. *City at the Point: Essays on the Social History of Pittsburgh.*
   Pittsburgh: University of Pittsburgh Press, 1989.
Health and Welfare Federation of Allegheny County. Bureau of Social Re-
   search. *Population Trends of Allegheny County.* Pittsburgh, 1945.
Heilbroner, Robert L. *The Economic Transformation of America.* New York:
   Harcourt, Brace, Jovanovich, 1977.
Hendrick, Burton J. *Life of Andrew Carnegie.* 2 vols. New York: Doubleday,
   Doran, 1932.
Herron, William Alfred, and William Herron Hazlip. *Our Herron Family of
   Allegheny County, Pennsylvania.* Pittsburgh: privately printed, 1960.
Hidy, Ralph W. "Business History: Present Status and Future Needs." *BHR*
   44 (Winter 1970): 483–97.
Hill, Charles, and Steven Cohen. "John A. Fitch and the *Pittsburgh Survey.*"
   WPHM 67 (January 1984): 17–32.
History of Allegheny County, Pennsylvania. Philadelphia: Evarts Publish-
   ing Co., 1876.
History of Allegheny County, Pennsylvania. 3 vols. Chicago: A. Warner &
   Co., 1889.
History of the Pittsburgh Club, 1879–1979. N.p.: privately printed, 1979.
Hodges, Julia Shelley. *George Hodges.* New York: Century Co., 1926.
Hogan, William T. *Economic History of the Iron and Steel Industry in the
   United States.* 5 vols. Lexington, Mass.: D. C. Heath, 1971.
Holbrook, Stewart H. *Iron Brew.* New York: Macmillan, 1939.

Holmberg, James. "The Industrializing Community in Pittsburgh, 1850–1880," Ph.D. diss., University of Pittsburgh, 1981.

Holt, James. "Trade Unionism in the British and U.S. Steel Industries, 1880–1914." *LH* 18 (Winter 1977): 5–35.

Holt, Michael. *Forging a Majority: The Formation of the Republican Party in Pittsburgh, 1848–1860*. New Haven: Yale University Press, 1969.

Horowitz, Helen Lefkowitz. *Culture and the City: Cultural Philanthropy in Chicago from the 1880's to 1917*. Chicago: University of Chicago Press, 1976.

Hosmer, W. Arnold. "Small Manufacturing Enterprises." *Harvard Business Review* 35 (November–December 1957): 118–19.

Howe, Barbara J. "Clubs, Culture and Charity: Anglo-American Upper Class Activities in the Late 19th Century City." Ph.D. diss., Temple University, 1976.

Howe, Daniel W. *Howe Genealogies*. Boston: New England Historical Genealogical Society, 1929.

Howe, H. M. *Metallurgy of Steel*. New York: Scientific Publishing Co., 1890.

Huggins, Nathan I. *Protestants against Poverty: Boston's Charities, 1870–1900*. Westport, Conn.: Greenwood Press, 1971.

Hunt, R. W. "The Evolution of American Rolling Mills." American Society of Mechanical Engineers. *Transactions* (1892): 45–69.

Hunter, Louis C. "Factors in the Early Pittsburgh Iron Industry." In *Facts and Factors in Economic History: Articles by Former Students of Edwin Francis Gay*, 424–45. Cambridge, Mass.: Harvard University Press, 1932.

———. "Financial Problems of the Early Pittsburgh Iron Manufacturers." *JEBH* 2 (May 1930): 520–44.

———. "Influence of the Market upon Technique in the Iron Industry in Western Pennsylvania up to 1860." *JEBH* 1 (February 1929): 239–81.

Hussey, Wells & Co. *Steel Memorial*. N.p., 1865.

Huthmacher, J. Joseph. "Urban Liberalism and the Age of Reform." *Mississippi Valley Historical Review* 49 (1962): 231–41.

In Memoriam of Calvin Wells. Philadelphia, 1919.

Industrial and Engineering Chemistry. Vol. 1– (1909–).

Ingham, Geoffrey. *Capitalism Divided: The City in Industry in British Social Development*. London: Macmillan, 1984.

Ingham, John N. "The American Urban Upper Class: Cosmopolitans or Locals?" *JUH* 11 (November 1975).

———. *The Iron Barons: A Social Analysis of an American Urban Elite, 1874–1965*. Westport, Conn.: Greenwood Press, 1978.

———. "Rags to Riches Revisited: The Role of City Size and Related Factors in the Recruitment of Business Leaders." *JAH* 63 (December 1976): 615–37.

———. "Robber Barons and the Old Elites: A Case Study in Social Stratification." *Mid-America* 52 (July 1970): 190–204.

_____. "Steel City Aristocrats." In *City at the Point: Essays on the Social History of Pittsburgh*, edited by Samuel P. Hays, 265–94. Pittsburgh: University of Pittsburgh Press, 1989.

Iron 1–41 (1873–93).

Iron Age 11– (1873–   ).

Iron and Steel Engineer 1– (1924–   ).

"Iron and Steel Industries of America." *Engineering* (July 1891).

Iron and Steel Institute. *Journal* 1– (1870–   ).

Iron Trade Review (after 1930 called *Steel*) (1898–   ).

J & L—The Growth of an American Business. Pittsburgh: Jones and Laughlin Corp., 1953.

Jaher, Frederic Cople. *The Age of Industrialism in America: Essays in Social Structure and Cultural Values*. New York: Free Press, 1968.

_____. "Nineteenth Century Elites in Boston and New York." *Journal of Social History* 6 (1972): 32–77.

_____. *The Rich, the Well Born and the Powerful: Elites and Upper Classes in History*. Urbana: University of Illinois Press, 1973.

_____. *The Urban Establishment: Upper Strata in Boston, New York, Charleston, Chicago, and Los Angeles*. Urbana: University of Illinois Press, 1982.

James, John A. "Structural Change in American Manufacturing, 1850–1890." *JEH* 43 (June 1983): 433–75.

Jennings, M. Kent. *Community Influentials: The Elites of Atlanta*. New York: Free Press, 1964.

Johnston, William G. *Life and Reminiscences from Birth to Manhood*. Pittsburgh: Johnston Publishing Co., 1901.

Jones, Fred Mitchell. "Middlemen in the Domestic Trade of the United States." *Illinois Studies in the Social Sciences* 21 (1937): 1–81.

_____. "Retail Stores in the United States, 1800–1860." *Journal of Marketing* 2 (October 1936): 134–42.

Jones, Samuel. *Pittsburgh in the Year 1826*. Pittsburgh: Johnston & Stockton, 1826.

Jones, Wayne V. *Mary Ann (Berkstrasser) Negley and Her Descendants*. Texas: by the author, 1963.

Jordan, John W. *Colonial and Revolutionary Families of Pennsylvania*. 17 vols. New York: Lewis Historical Publishing Co., 1911–65.

_____. *Encyclopedia of Pennsylvania Biography*. 32 vols. New York: Lewis Historical Publishing Co., 1914–63.

_____. *Genealogical and Personal History of Allegheny Valley, Pennsylvania*. 3 vols. New York: Lewis Historical Publishing Co., 1913.

_____. *Genealogical and Personal History of Western Pennsylvania*. 3 vols. New York: Lewis Historical Publishing Co., 1915.

Jucha, Robert J. "Anatomy of a Streetcar Suburb: A Developmental History of Shadyside, 1852–1916." *WPHM* 62 (October 1979): 301–20.

Judd, Barbara. "Edward M. Bigelow: Creator of Pittsburgh's Arcadian Parks." *WPHM* 59 (January 1975): 53–67.

Kaplan, Robert. "The Know Nothings in Pittsburgh." Seminar paper, History Department, University of Pittsburgh, 1977.

Katz, Michael. *The People of Hamilton, Canada, West: Work, Family and Class in a Mid-Nineteenth Century City.* Cambridge, Mass.: Harvard University Press, 1975.

Kellogg, Paul Underwood, ed. *The Pittsburgh Survey.* 6 vols. New York: Charities and Commons Publication Committee, 1909–14.

Kelso, Thomas J. "Allegheny Elites, 1850–1907." Seminar paper, History Department, University of Pittsburgh, 1964.

Kent, Raymond P. "The Development of Industrial Unionism in the American Iron and Steel Industry." Ph.D. diss., University of Pittsburgh, 1938.

Kerr, K. Austin. "Labor-Management Cooperation: An 1897 Case." *PMHB* 99 (January 1975): 45–71.

———, and Mansel Blackford. *Business Enterprise in American History.* Boston: Houghton Mifflin, 1986.

Kindl, F. H. *The Rolling Mill Industry.* Cleveland: Penton Publishing Co., 1913.

Kingsley House. *Handbook of Settlements.* Pittsburgh: privately printed, 1901.

Kirkland, Edward C. *Dream and Thought in the American Business Community, 1860–1900.* Ithaca, N.Y.: Cornell University Press, 1956.

Kitson, John. "The Iron and Steel Industry of America." *Contemporary Review* 59 (May 1891): 625–44.

Kleinberg, S. J. *The Shadow of the Mills: Working Class Families in Pittsburgh, 1870–1907.* Pittsburgh: University of Pittsburgh Press, 1989.

Kleppner, Paul. "Government, Parties and Voters in Pittsburgh." In *City at the Point: Essays on the Social History of Pittsburgh,* edited by Samuel P. Hays, 151–180. Pittsburgh: University of Pittsburgh Press, 1989.

———. "Lincoln and the Immigrant Vote: A Case of Religious Polarization." *Mid-America* 48 (July 1966): 176–95.

———. *The Third Electoral System, 1853–1892: Parties, Voters, and Political Culture.* Chapel Hill: University of North Carolina Press, 1979.

Knox, Howard A. *Development of the American Tin Plate Industry.* Pittsburgh: Carnegie-Illinois Steel Co., United States Steel Corp., 1944.

Kocka, Jurgen. "Entrepreneurs and Manufacturers in German Industry." In *Cambridge Economic History of Europe,* Vol. 11, pt. 1, 492–589.

Koppes, Clayton R., and William P. Norris. "Ethnicity, Class and Mortality in an Industrial City: A Case Study of Typhoid Fever in Pittsburgh, 1890–1910." *Journal of Urban History* 11 (May 1985): 269–75.

Kraditor, Aileen. *The Radical Persuasion, 1890–1917: Aspects of the Intellectual History and the Historiograhy of Three American Radical Organizations.* Baton Rouge: Louisiana State University Press, 1981.

Krause, Paul L. "Patronage and Philanthropy in Industrial America: Andrew

Carnegie and the Free Library in Braddock, Pa." *WPHM* 71, no. 2 (1988): 127–46.

_____. "The Road to Homestead," Ph.D. diss., Duke University, 1987.

Kulik, Gary. "Pawtucket Village and the Strike of 1824: The Origins of Class Conflict in Rhode Island." *Radical History Review* 17 (Spring 1978): 5–37.

Kusmer, Kenneth. "The Functions of Organized Charity in the Progressive Era: Chicago as a Case Study." *Journal of American History* 60 (December 1973): 657–78.

Laidler, Harry W. *Concentration of Control in American Industry.* New York: T. Y. Crowell, 1931.

Lamoreaux, Naomi. *The Great Merger Movement in American Business, 1895–1904.* Cambridge, England: Cambridge University Press, 1985.

Landes, David S. *The Unbound Prometheus.* New York: Cambridge University Press, 1969.

Larson, Henrietta M. "An Early Industrial Capitalist's Labor Policy and Management." *Bulletin of the Business Historical Society* 17, no. 5 (November 1944): 132–41.

Laurie, Bruce, and Mark Schmitz. "Manufacture and Productivity: The Making of an Industrial Base, Philadelphia, 1850–1880." In *Philadelphia: Work, Space and Group Experience in the Nineteenth Century,* edited by Theodore Hershberg, 43–93. New York: Oxford University Press, 1981.

Lears, T. J. Jackson. "The Concept of Cultural Hegemony: Problems and Possibilities." *AHR* 90 (June 1985), 567–93.

Levine, A. L. *Industrial Retardation in Britain, 1880–1914.* New York: Basic Books, 1980.

Lewis, Kenneth B. *Steel Wire in America.* Stamford, Conn.: Wire Association, 1952.

Leyburn, James G. *The Scotch-Irish.* Chapel Hill: University of North Carolina Press, 1962.

Linaberger, James. "The Rolling Mill Riots of 1850." Seminar paper, History Department, University of Pittsburgh, n.d.

Lindsay, Margaret I. *The Lindsays in America.* Albany: J. Munsell's Sons, 1889.

Livesay, Harold C. *Andrew Carnegie and the Rise of Big Business.* Boston: Little, Brown, 1975.

_____, and P. Glenn Porter. "Vertical Integration in American Manufacturing, 1899–1945." *JEH* 29 (1969): 494–500.

Lonich, David. "A General Statement about Working Class Housing in Pittsburgh, 1900–1910," Ph.D. diss., University of Pittsburgh, 1979.

Loomis, Elias. *Descendents of Joseph Loomis in America.* N.p.: privately printed, 1908.

Lorant, Stefan. *Pittsburgh: The Story of an American City.* Garden City, N.Y.: Doubleday, 1964.

Love, Philip H. *Andrew W. Mellon.* Baltimore: F. H. Coggin & Co., 1929.

Loveday, Amos J., Jr. *The Rise and Decline of the American Cut Nail Industry: A Study of the Interrelationships of Technology, Business Organization and Management Techniques.* Westport, Conn: Greenwood Press, 1983.

Lubove, Roy, ed. "Pittsburgh and the Uses of Social Welfare History." In *City at the Point: Essays on the Social History of Pittsburgh,* edited by Samuel P. Hays, 295–305. Pittsburgh: University of Pittsburgh Press, 1989.

―――. *Twentieth Century Pittsburgh: Government, Business and Environmental Change.* New York: John Wiley, 1969.

―――. *Pittsburgh.* Documentary History of American Cities. New York: Franklin Watts, 1976.

Lukaszewicz, Frank. "Regional and Central Boards of Directors of Pittsburgh Banks in 1912." Seminar paper, History Department, University of Pittsburgh, 1965.

Lukens, Lewis N. "Family Memoranda: An Essay upon the Lukens Family." Typewritten ms. Philadelphia: Historical Society of Pennsylvania, 1933.

Lynes, Russell. *The Tastemakers.* New York: Harper & Row, 1949.

McCarthy, Kathleen. *Noblesse Oblige: Charity and Cultural Philanthropy in Chicago, 1849–1929.* Chicago: University of Chicago Press, 1982.

McClain, Raymond. "The Immigrant Years: Irene Kaufmann Settlement, 1895–1915." Seminar paper, History Department, Carnegie Mellon University, n.d.

McCloskey, Donald M. *Economic Maturity and Entrepreneurial Decline: British Iron and Steel, 1870–1913.* Cambridge, Mass.: Harvard University Press, 1973.

McClymer, John F. "The *Pittsburgh Survey,* 1907–1914: Forging an Ideology in the Steel District." *Pennsylvania History* 41 (April 1974): 169–88.

McCraw, Thomas, ed. *The Essential Alfred Chandler: Essays toward a Historical Theory of Big Business.* Boston: Harvard Business School Press, 1989.

McHugh, Jeanne. *Alexander Holley and the Makers of Steel.* Baltimore: Johns Hopkins University Press, 1980.

McKee, James B. "Status and Power in the Industrial Community: A Comment on Drucker's Thesis." *American Journal of Sociology* 58 (January 1953): 364–70.

McKie, James W. *Tin Cans and Tin Plate.* Cambridge: Harvard University Press, 1959.

McLean, Crosby C., Jr. *The Wood Family of Montgomery County, Pennsylvania.* Privately printed, n.d.

McNeill, George E., ed. *The Labor Movement: The Problem of Today.* Boston: A. M. Bridger, 1887.

Magazine of Western History 2–4 (1884–86).

Mancke, Richard B. "Iron and Steel: A Case Study of the Economic Causes and Effects of Vertical Integration." *Journal of Industrial Economics* 20 (July 1972): 220–29.

[The] *Manufactories and Manufacturers of Pennsylvania of the Nineteenth Century.* Philadelphia: Galaxy Publishing Co., 1875.

Mapes, Lynn Gordon. "*Iron Age:* An Iron Manufacturer's Journal and the 'Labor Problem' in the Age of Enterprise." Ph.D. diss., University of Rochester, 1973.

Marburg, Theodore. *Small Business in Brass Manufacturing: The Smith & Griggs Co. of Waterbury.* New York: New York University Press, 1956.

Marcus, Irwin M., Jennie Bullard, and Rob Moore. "Change and Continuity: Steel Workers in Homestead, Pennsylvania, 1889–1895." *PMHB* 111 (January 1987): 61–75.

Martin, Scott. "Fathers against Sons, Sons against Fathers." Seminar paper, History Department, University of Pittsburgh, n.d.

Matthews, William H. *The Meaning of the Social Settlement Movement.* Pittsburgh: Kingsley House, 1909.

Maxwell, Marianne. "Pittsburgh's Frick Park: A Unique Addition to the City's Park System." *WPHM* 68 (July 1985): 243–64.

Meade, Edward Sherwood. "The Genesis of the United States Steel Corporation." *Quarterly Journal of Economics* 15 (August 1901), 517–50.

Melder, Keith. "Ladies Bountiful." *New York History* 48 (1967): 231–55.

Mellon, Rachel H. L. *The Larimer, McMasters and Allied Families.* Philadelphia: J. B. Lippincott, 1903.

Mellon, William Larimer. *Judge Mellon's Sons.* Pittsburgh: privately printed, 1948.

Memoirs of Allegheny County, Pennsylvania. 2 vols. Madison, Wis.: Northern History Society, 1904.

Metzger, Elizabeth. "A Study of Social Settlement Workers in Pittsburgh, 1893–1927." Seminar paper, History Department, 1974.

Mill, Ann Wendy. "Comment and Debate: French Steel and Metal Working Industries: A Contribution to Debate on Economic Development in 19th Century France." *SSH* 9 (Summer 1985): 307–38.

Miller, Annie Clark. *Chronicles of Families, Houses and Estates of Pittsburgh and its Environs.* Pittsburgh: privately printed, 1927.

Miller, Mervin A. *Meet the Blair Family.* Holidaysburg, Pa.: Blair County Historical Society, 1946.

Miller, William, ed. *Men in Business.* Rev. ed. Cambridge, Mass.: Harvard University Press, 1962.

Miller, Zane. *Boss Cox's Cincinnati: Urban Politics in the Progressive Era.* New York: Oxford University Press, 1968.

Mills, C. Wright, and Melville J. Ulmer. "Small Business and Civic Welfare." In *The Structure of Community Power,* edited by Michael Aiken and Paul E. Mott, 124–54. New York: Random House, 1970.

Mining and Metallurgy 1–29 (1902–48).

Misa, Thomas Jay. "Science, Technology, and Industrial Structure: Steel-making in America, 1870–1925." Ph.D. diss., University of Pennsylvania, 1987.

Mitchell, A. W. "The Labor Relations of a Large Steel Company: Jones and Laughlin." Ph.D. diss., University of Pittsburgh, 1939.

Mohl, Raymond A. *The New City: Urban America in the Industrial Age, 1860–1920.* Arlington Heights, Ill.: AHM Press, 1985.

Montgomery, David. *Beyond Equality: Labor and the Radical Republicans, 1862–1872.* New York: Random House, 1967.

————. *The Fall of the House of Labor.* New York: Cambridge University Press, 1987.

————. "To Study the People." *LH* 21 (1980): 485–512.

————. *Workers' Control in America: Studies in the History of Work, Technology and Labor Struggles.* New York: Cambridge University Press, 1979.

————. "Worker's Control of Machine Production in 19th Century America." *SSH* 17 (Fall 1976): 485–509.

Moorhead, Elizabeth. *Clouded Hills.* Indianapolis: Bobbs, Merrill, 1929.

————. *Whirling Spindle: The Story of a Pittsburgh Family.* Pittsburgh: University of Pittsburgh Press, 1942.

James Kennedy Moorhead: Memorial Volume. Pittsburgh: privately printed, 1880.

Morgan, C. H. "Some Land Marks in the History of the Rolling Mill." American Society of Mechanical Engineers. *Transactions* (1901) 31–64.

Moritzer, Julius. "The Great Steel Makers of Pittsburgh." *American Monthly Review of Reviews* 21 (April 1900): 432–44.

Mott, Paul E. "The Role of Absentee-Owned Corporations in the Changing Community." In *The Structure of Community Power,* edited by Michael Aiken and Paul E. Mott, 170–77. New York: Random House, 1970.

Muller, Edward K. "Metropolis and Region: A Framework for Enquiry into Western Pennsylvania." In *City at the Point: Essays on the Social History of Pittsburgh,* edited by Samuel P. Hays, 181–212. Pittsburgh: University of Pittsburgh Press, 1989.

Muller, G. F. "The City of Pittsburgh." *Harpers* 62 (1881): 49–69.

"Multimillionaires of Chicago." *Chicago Tribune* (9 June 1907).

Munslow, Alan. "Andrew Carnegie and the Discourse of Cultural Hegemony." *Journal of American Studies* 22 (1988): 213–24.

National Cyclopedia of American Biography. 58 vols. New York: J. T. White & Co., 1892–1964.

National Industrial Conference Board. *Mergers in Industry: A Study of Certain Economic Aspects of Industrial Concentration.* New York: National Industrial Conference Board, 1929.

National Iron and Steel: Coal and Coke Blue Book. Pittsburgh: R. L. Polk, 1907.

Navin, Thomas R., and Marian V. Sears. "The Rise of a Market for Industrial Securities, 1887–1902." *BHR* 29 (1955): 105–38.

Nelson, Ralph L. *Merger Movements in American Industry, 1895–1956.* Princeton, N.J.: Princeton University Press, 1959.

Nevin, Adelaide Mellier. *The Social Mirror: A Character Sketch of the Women of Pittsburgh and Vicinity during the First Century of the County's Existence.* Pittsburgh: T. W. Nevin, 1888.

Nevins, Allan. *John D. Rockefeller: The Heroic Age of American Capitalism.* 3 vols. New York: Charles Scribner's Sons, 1940.

———. *Study in Power: John D. Rockefeller: Industrialist or Philanthropist?* 2 vols. New York: Charles Scribner's Sons, 1953.

Nixon, Lily Lee. "Henry Clay Frick and Pittsburgh's Children." *WPHM* 29 (1946): 65–72.

Novack, David E., and Richard Perlman. "The Structure of Wages in the American Iron and Steel Industry, 1860–1890." *JEH* 22 (1962): 334–47.

Nuwer, Michael. "From Batch to Flow: Production Technology and Work Force Skills: The Steel Industry, 1880–1920." *Technology and Culture* 29 (October 1988): 808–35.

O'Brien, Anthony Patrick. "Factory Size, Economies of Scale, and the Great Merger Wave of 1898–1902." *JEH* 48 (September 1988): 560–66.

O'Connor, Harvey. *Mellon's Millions.* New York: John Day Co., 1933.

———. *Steel-Dictator.* New York: John Day Co., 1935.

Oakmont Country Club: Constitution and By-Laws. Pittsburgh: privately printed, 1919.

Oestreicher, Richard. "Working Class Formation, Development, and Consciousness in Pittsburgh, 1790–1960." In *City at the Point: Essays on the Social History of Pittsburgh,* edited by Samuel P. Hays, 111–50. Pittsburgh: University of Pittsburgh Press, 1989.

Ostrogorski, Moisei. *Democracy and the Organization of Political Parties.* New York: Macmillan, 1902.

Pailthorpe, Michelle. "The German-Jewish Elite of Pittsburgh: Its Beginnings and Background." Seminar paper, History Department, University of Pittsburgh, 1967.

Parsons, Donald O., and Edward John Ray. "The United States Steel Consolidation: The Creation of Market Control." *Journal of Law and Economics* 20 (April 1975): 181–219.

Parton, James. "Pittsburg." *Atlantic Monthly* 36 (January 1868): 17–36.

Payne, Peter L. "Industrial Entrepreneurship and Management in Britain." In *Cambridge Economic History of Europe.* Vol. VII, pt. 1, 180–230. Cambridge, England: Cambridge University Press, 1978.

Pearse, John B. "The Manufacture of Iron and Steel Rails." *Mining Engineer* (May 1871–Feb. 1873): 162–69.

Peiffer, Layne. "The German Upper Class of Pittsburgh, 1850–1920." Seminar paper, History Department, University of Pittsburgh, 1964.

Pellegrin, Roland J., and Charles H. Coates. "Absentee-Owned Corporations and Community Power Structure." *American Journal of Sociology* 61 (March 1956): 413–19.

Pennsylvania Society of New York. *Yearbook.* New York: The Pennsylvania Society, 1916.

Perkin, Harold. *Origins of Modern English Society, 1780–1880.* London: Routledge & Kegan Paul, 1969.

Persons, Stow. *The Decline of American Gentility.* New York: Columbia University Press, 1973.

Pessen, Edward. "The Social Configuration of the Ante-Bellum City: An Historical and Theoretical Inquiry." *JUH* 2 (1976): 267–306.

Peters, Thomas J., and Waterman, Robert H., Jr. *In Search of Excellence: Lessons from America's Best-Run Companies.* New York: Harper and Row, 1982.

Pittsburgh, Its Industry and Commerce. 1870.

[The] *Pittsburgh Blue Book.* 1887–1966.

Pittsburgh Bulletin and *Pittsburgh Bulletin-Index.*

Pittsburgh Chamber of Commerce. *The Insurrection among the Railway Employees of the United States and the Losses in Pittsburgh Resulting Therefrom in July, 1877.* Pittsburgh: Stevenson, Foster & Co., 1877.

———. *The Mercantile, Manufacturing and Mining Interests of Pittsburgh, 1884.* Pittsburgh: W. G. Johnston, 1887.

Pittsburgh Chronicle-Telegraph.

Pittsburgh Civic Commission, *Plan and Scope.*

[The] *Pittsburgh Civic Frontage.* Vol. 5 of *The Pittsburgh Survey,* edited by Paul Underwood Kellogg. New York: Charities and Commons Publication Committee, 1914.

[The] *Pittsburgh Club.* Club directory. Pittsburgh: privately printed, 1910–.

Pittsburgh Directory. 1815–1966.

Pittsburgh Directory of Directors. 1906.

Pittsburgh Dispatch.

Pittsburgh Gazette and *Pittsburgh Gazette-Times.*

Pittsburgh Gazette-Times. The Story of Pittsburgh and Vicinity. Pittsburgh: Gazette-Times, 1908.

Pittsburgh Iron City.

Pittsburgh Leader.

Pittsburgh Post and *Pittsburgh Post-Gazette.*

Pittsburgh Press.

Pittsburgh Press Club. *Prominent Men of Pittsburgh and Vicinity.* Pittsburgh: Murdoch, Kerrick & Co., 1912–13.

Pittsburgh Regional Planning Association. *Region in Transition.* Pittsburgh: University of Pittsburgh Press, 1965.

Pittsburgh Social Directory. Privately printed, 1904.

Pittsburgh Sun-Telegraph.

Polsby, Nelson. "Pluralism in the Study of Community Power: Or *Erklärung* before *Verklärung* in *Wissensociologie.*" *American Sociologist* 9 (1969): 118–22.

Porter, Glenn. *Encyclopedia of American Economic History: Studies of the Principal Movements and Ideas.* 3 vols. New York: Charles Scribner's Sons, 1980.

_____. "Oligopoly in Small Manufacturing Industries." *EEH* 7, no. 5 (Spring 1970): 371–79.

_____. *The Rise of Big Business, 1860–1910.* Arlington Heights, Ill.: AHM Press, 1973.

_____, and Harold Livesay. *Merchants and Manufacturers: Studies in the Changing Structure of 19th Century Marketing.* Baltimore: Johns Hopkins University Press, 1971.

Potter, E. C. "Rails, Past and Present." *Iron Age* (17 February 1898): 14.

Potts, Thomas Maxwell. *Our Family Ancestors.* Armstrong, Pa.: author, 1895.

Powelson, Frank W. *Founding Families of Allegheny County.* 4 vols. Pittsburgh: typescript copy at Carnegie Public Library, 1963.

_____. *More Founding Families of Allegheny County.* Pittsburgh: typescript copy at Carnegie Public Library, 1965.

Power 8– (1888–).

Price, Lucien, *Immortal Youth: A Memoir of Fred A. Demmler.* N.p.: privately printed, n.d.

Proceedings of the Pittsburgh Conference for Good City Government and the Fourteenth Annual Meeting of the National Municipal League. Pittsburgh: National Municipal League, 1909.

Prominent Families. Pittsburgh: Index Co., 1911–1915.

Prude, Jonathan. *The Coming of Industrial Order: Town and Factory Life in Rural Massachusetts, 1810–1860.* New York: Cambridge University Press, 1983.

Pusateri, Joseph. *A History of American Business.* Arlington Heights, Ill.: Harlan Davidson, 1984.

Rea, Henry Oliver. *Henry William Oliver, Ancestry and Descendents.* Dungannon, Northern Ireland: Tyrone Printing Co., 1959.

_____. *Samuel Rea . . . Heritage and Descendents.* Dungannon, Northern Ireland: Tyrone Printing Co., 1960.

Redlich, Fritz. *History of American Business: Leaders.* Vol. 1, *Iron and Steel, Iron Ore Mining.* Ann Arbor: Edmunds Brothers, 1940.

Reed, George Irving, ed. *Century Cyclopedia of History and Biography of Pennsylvania.* 2 vols. Chicago: Century Publishing Co., 1904.

Reiser, Catherine Elizabeth. *Pittsburgh's Commercial Development, 1800–1850.* Harrisburg: Pennsylvania Historical Museum Commission, 1951.

Reitman, Renee. "The Elite Community in Shadyside, 1880–1920." Seminar paper, History Department, University of Pittsburgh, 1964.

Renner, Marguerite. "A Study of Women's Participation in Voluntary Organizations." Seminar paper, History Department, University of Pittsburgh, 1971.

Riddle, James. *The Pittsburgh Directory for 1815.* Reprint. Pittsburgh: Duquesne Smelting Co., 1940.

Rikard, Marlene H. "A Case Study of Welfare Capitalism and Industrial Communities: The Tennessee Iron, Coal and Railroad Company of Birmingham, Alabama, 1907–1950." Paper presented to conference on Steel and Coal Communities in Comparative Perspective, 1900–1990. Pittsburgh, 20–22 April 1990.

———. "An Experiment in Welfare Capitalism: The Health Care Services of the Tennessee Coal, Iron and Railroad Company." Unpublished Ph.D. diss., History Department, University of Alabama, 1983.

Rishel, Joseph Francis. "The Founding Families of Allegheny County: An Examination of 19th Century Elite Continuity." Ph.D. diss., University of Pittsburgh, 1975.

Robertson, James O. *America's Business.* New York: Hill & Wang, 1985.

Robinson, Arabelle. *Daniel Yandes and His Family: Pioneers from Pennsylvania to Indiana.* Crawfordsville, Ind.: privately printed, 1936.

Robinson, Jesse S. *The Amalgamated Association of Iron, Steel and Tin Workers.* Baltimore: Johns Hopkins University Press, 1920.

Rolling Rock Club Directory. Ligonier, Pa.: privately printed, 1947.

Rosen, Philip. "Thirty Years at Kingsley House." Seminar paper, History Department, Carnegie Mellon University, n.d.

Rossi, Peter H. "Power and Politics: A Road to Social Reform." *Social Service Review* 35 (December 1961): 359–69.

Rousmanier, John. "Cultural Hybrid in the Slums." *American Quarterly* 20 (1970): 45–66.

Rubinstein, W. D. *Men of Property.* London: Croon Helm, 1981.

———. "Wealth, Elites and the Class Structure of Modern Britain." *Past and Present* 76 (August 1977): 99–126.

Sabadasz, Joel. "Twentieth Century Aliquippa, Duquesne and Other Pittsburgh Area Steel Towns." Seminar paper, History Department, University of Pittsburgh, 1983.

Santos, Michael W. "Brother against Brother: The Amalgamated and the Sons of Vulcan at the A. M. Byers Co., 1907–1913." *WPHM* 111, no. 2 (April 1987): 195–212.

———. "Iron Workers in a Steel Age: The Case of the A. M. Byers Company, 1900–1969." D.A. thesis, History Department, Carnegie-Mellon University, 1984.

———. "Laboring on the Periphery: Managers and Workers at the A. M. Byers Co., 1900–1956." *BHR* 61 (Spring 1987): 113–33.

Schroeder, Gertrude G. *The Growth of Major Steel Companies, 1900–1950.* Baltimore: Johns Hopkins University Press, 1953.

Schuchman, Stephen. "The Elite at Sewickley Heights, 1900–1940." Seminar paper, History Department, University of Pittsburgh, 1964.

Schulze, Robert O. "The Bifurcation of Power in a Satellite City." In *Community Political Systems*, edited by Morris Janowitz, 19–80. New York: Free Press, 1961.

Scranton, Philip. *Figured Tapestry: Production, Markets and Power in Philadelphia Textiles, 1885–1941.* New York: Cambridge University Press, 1989.

———. "Milling About: Paths to Capitalist Development in the Philadelphia Textile Industry, 1840–1865." Paper presented at the Social Science History Association Meetings, Nashville, 22–25 October 1981.

———. *Proprietary Capitalism: Textile Manufacture at Philadelphia, 1800–1885.* Philadelphia: Temple University Press, 1983.

Seilhamer, George O. *Leslie's History of the Republican Party.* 2 vols. New York: L. A. Williams Publishing and Engraving Co., 1899.

Shaw, S. Adele. "Closed Towns: Intimidation as It is Practiced in the Pittsburgh Steel District." *Survey* 43 (8 November 1919): 58–64.

Shefter, Martin. "The Emergence of the Political Machine: An Alternative View." In *Theoretical Perspectives on Community Politics*, edited by Willis D. Hawley, 14–44. Englewood Cliffs, N.J.: Prentice Hall, 1976.

Shinn, Josiah H. *A History of the Shinn Family in America.* Chicago: Genealogical and Historical Publishing Co., 1903.

Shinn, William P. "Pittsburgh—Its Resources and Surroundings." American Society of Mechanical Engineers. *Transactions* (1879–80): 24.

———. "Pittsburgh & Vicinity: A Brief Record of Seven Years Progress." American Society of Mechanical Engineers. *Transactions* (1885–86).

Sketches from the Life and Experiences of J. H. Demmler. Pittsburgh: privately printed, 1893.

Smith, Dennis. *Conflict and Compromise: A Comparative Study of Birmingham and Sheffield.* London: Routledge & Kegan Paul, 1982.

Smith, Percy F. *Notable Men of Pittsburgh and Vicinity.* Pittsburgh: Pittsburgh Printing Co., 1901.

Social Justice Review 35 (October 1942).

Social Register, Pittsburgh. New York: Social Register Association, 1908–66.

Soltow, James. *Origins of Small Business: Metal Fabricators and Machinery Makers in New England, 1890–1957.* Philadelphia: American Philosophical Society, 1965. (Transactions of the American Philosophical Society, new series 55, pt. 10.)

———. "Origins of Small Business and the Relationships between Large and Small Firms: Metal Fabricating and Machinery Making in New England, 1890–1957." In *Small Business in American Life*, edited by Stuart Bruchy, 192–211. New York: Columbia University Press, 1980.

Spencer, Ethel. *The Spencers of Amberson Avenue: A Turn-of-the-Century Memoir.* Pittsburgh: University of Pittsburgh Press, 1983.

Sportsmen's Association of Cheat Mountain. Pittsburgh: privately printed, 1889.

Stave, Bruce M. *The New Deal and the Last Hurrah: Pittsburgh Machine Politics.* Pittsburgh: University of Pittsburgh Press, 1970.

"Steel City Saga: Pittsburgh's Early Years." *U.S. Steel News* 14 (1949): 1–8.

Steffens, Lincoln. "Pittsburgh: A City Ashamed." In *Shame of the Cities,* 147–89. New York: McClure, Phillips, 1904.

Stewman, Shelby, and Joel A. Tarr. "Public-Private Partnerships in Pittsburgh: An Approach to Governance." In *Pittsburgh-Sheffield, Sister Cities,* edited by Joel Tarr. Pittsburgh: Carnegie Mellon University Press, 1986.

Stigler, George J. "The Division of Labor Is Limited by the Extent of the Market." *JPE* 59 (1951): 185–93.

———. "The Economies of Scale." *Journal of Law & Economics* 1 (1958): 54–71.

———. "Monopoly and Oligopoly by Merger." In *Organization of American Industry.* Homewood, Ill.: P. D. Irwin, 1968.

Stone, Katherine. "The Origins of Job Structures in the Steel Industry." *Review of Radical Political Economics* 6 (Summer 1974): 61–97.

[The] *Story of the Childs Family.* Pittsburgh: privately printed, 1967.

Stoughton, Bradley. *The Metallurgy of Iron and Steel.* 3d ed. New York: McGraw-Hill, 1923.

Strassmann, W. Paul. *Risk and Technological Innovation in American Manufacturing during the Nineteenth Century.* Ithaca, N.Y.: Cornell University Press, 1956.

Stromquist, Sheldon. "Working Class Organization and Industrial Change in Pittsburgh, 1860–1890: Some Themes." Seminar paper, History Department, University of Pittsburgh, 1973.

Sullivan, William A. *The Industrial Worker in Pennsylvania, 1800–1840.* Harrisburg: Pennsylvania Historical and Museum Commission, 1955.

Swank, James M. *History of the Manufacture of Iron in All Ages.* Philadelphia: American Iron and Steel Association, 1892.

———. *Iron Manufacturing and Coal Mining in Pennsylvania.* Philadelphia: American Iron and Steel Association, 1878.

Swauger, John. "Pittsburgh's Residential Patterns in 1815." *Annals of the Association of American Geographers* 68, no. 2 (June 1978): 265–77.

Swetnam, George. "Labor-Management Relations in Pennsylvania's Steel Industry, 1800–1959." *WPHM* 62 (October 1979): 321–32.

———, and Chester A. Locke. *Bi-Centennial History of Pittsburgh and Allegheny County.* 3 vols. Pittsburgh: Historical Record Association, 1955.

Taber, Martha. *A History of the Cutlery Industry in the Connecticut Valley.* Northampton, Mass.: Smith College Department of History, 1941. (Smith College Studies in History, No. 41.)

Tarbell, Ida. *The Life of Elbert H. Gary.* New York: D. A. Appleton, 1925.

Tarkington, Booth. *The Magnificent Ambersons.* New York: Doubleday, Page, 1918.

Tarr, Joel A. *A Study in Urban Politics: Boss Lorimer of Chicago.* Urbana: University of Illinois Press, 1971.

_____. "Infrastructure and City Building in the Nineteenth and Twentieth Centuries." In *City at the Point: Essays on the Social History of Pittsburgh,* edited by Samuel P. Hays, 213–64. Pittsburgh: University of Pittsburgh Press, 1989.

_____. *Transportation, Innovation, and Changing Spatial Patterns in Pittsburgh, 1850–1934.* Chicago: Public Works Historical Society, 1978.

_____. "The Urban Politician as Entrepreneur." In *Urban Bosses, Machines, and Progressive Reformers,* edited by Bruce M. Stave, 62–72. Lexington, Mass.: D. C. Heath, 1972.

_____, and Denise Di Pasquale. "The Mill Town in the Industrial City: Pittsburgh's Hazelwood." *Urbanism Past and Present* 7 (Winter/ Spring 1982): 1–14.

Taussig, Frank W. "The Iron Industry in the United States." *Quarterly Journal of Economics* 14 (1900): 143–70.

Taylor, Donald L. "The Woods Run Settlement, 1895–1932." Seminar paper, History Department, Carnegie-Mellon University, n.d.

Temin, Peter. "The Composition of Iron and Steel Products, 1869–1909." *JEH* 23 (December 1963): 447–71.

_____. *Iron and Steel in Nineteenth Century America: An Economic Inquiry.* Cambridge, Mass.: MIT Press, 1964.

Tener: A History of the Family. Pittsburgh: privately printed, 1949.

Thompson, F. L. M. *English Landed Society in the 19th Century.* London: Routledge & Kegan Paul, 1963.

Thurston, George H. *Pittsburgh as It Is.* Pittsburgh: W. S. Haven, 1857.

_____. *Pittsburgh's Progress, Industries and Resources.* Pittsburgh: A. A. Anderson & Co., 1886.

Trasher, Eugene C. "The Magee-Flinn Political Machine, 1895–1903." M.A. thesis, University of Pittsburgh, 1951.

Trusilo, Sharon. "The Iron Workers' Case for Amalgamation." *WPHM* 71, no. 1 (1988): 47–67.

Tweedale, Geoffrey. *Sheffield Steel and America: A Century of Commercial and Technological Interdependence, 1830–1930.* Cambridge, England: Cambridge University Press, 1987.

Twiss, Harold. "The Pittsburgh Business Elite, 1850–1890–1919." Seminar paper, History Department, University of Pittsburgh, 1964.

U.S. Steel News 1 (June 1936): 5.

Vanderblue, H. B., and W. L. Crum. *The Iron Industry in Prosperity and Depression.* Chicago: A. W. Shaw, 1927.

Van Urk, J. Blau. *The Story of Rolling Rock.* New York: Charles Scribner's Sons, 1950.

Vatter, Harold. *Small Enterprise and Oligopoly: A Study of the Butter,*

Flour, Automobile, and Glass Container Industries. Corvallis: Oregon State College Press, 1955.

Virkus, Frederick A., ed. *The Abridged Compendium of American Geneology.* 7 vols. Chicago: A. N. Marquis, 1925– .

Wade, Richard C. *The Urban Frontier: Pioneer Life in Early Pittsburgh, Cincinnati, Louisville, and St. Louis.* Chicago: University of Chicago Press, 1964.

———. *The Urban Frontier: The Rise of Western Cities, 1790–1830.* Cambridge, Mass.: Harvard University Press, 1959.

Walker, Charles R. *Steeltown.* New York: Harper & Row, 1950.

Wall, Joseph F. *Andrew Carnegie.* New York: Oxford University Press, 1970.

Wallace, Anthony F. C. *Rockdale: The Growth of an American Village in the Early Industrial Revolution.* New York: A. A. Knopf, 1978.

Wallhauser, Fred. "The Upper Class Society of Sewickley Valley, 1830–1914." Seminar paper, History Department, University of Pittsburgh, 1964.

Walsh, Victor Anthony. "Across the 'Big Wather': Irish Community Life in Allegheny City, 1850–1855." Unpublished Ph.D. diss., University of Pittsburgh, 1983.

Warner, Sam Bass. *The Private City: Philadelphia in Three Periods of Its Growth.* Philadelphia: University of Pennsylvania Press, 1968.

———. *Streetcar Suburbs: The Process of Growth in Boston, 1870–1900.* Cambridge, Mass.: Harvard University Press, 1962.

Warren, Kenneth. *The American Steel Industry, 1850–1970: A Geographical Interpretation.* Oxford, England: Clarendon Press, 1973.

Warrentee Atlas of Allegheny County, Pennsylvania. Harrisburg, 1907.

Webb, Steven B. "Tariffs, Cartels, Technology and Growth in the German Steel Industry, 1879–1914." *JEH* 40 (June 1980): 309–29.

Weeks, Joseph D. *Labor Differences and Their Settlement.* New York: Society for Political Education, 1886.

Weiss, Leonard W. *Case Studies in American Industry.* New York: John Wiley, 1971.

———. "The Extent of Suboptimal Capacity: A Correction." *JPE* 73 (1965): 300–301.

———. "The Survival Technique—the Extent of Suboptimal Capacity." *JPE* 72 (1964): 246–61.

Wells, Samuel Calvin. *Ancestry and Descendents of Col. Daniel Wells, 1760–1815 of Greenfield, Mass.* N.p., n.d.

Wendt, Lloyd, and Herman Kogan. *Bet A Million: The Story of John W. Gates.* Indianapolis: Bobbs, Merrill, 1943.

Western Pennsylvania Biographical Association. *Western Pennsylvanians.* Pittsburgh: WPBA, 1923.

Wheeler, Albert Gallatine, Jr. *History of the Wheeler Family in America.* Boston: American College of Genealogy, 1914.

Who's Who in America. Chicago: A. N. Marquis, 1899– .

Who's Who in Industry and Commerce.

Who's Who in Pennsylvania. New York: L. R. Hammersly & Co., 1904.

Who Was Who in America, 1899–1942. Chicago: A. N. Marquis, 1963.

Wilhelm, Carl. *History of the City of Allegheny in Pennsylvania, 1740–1890.* Pittsburgh, 1891.

Williamson, Leland M., ed. *Prominent and Progressive Pennsylvanians of the Nineteenth Century.* 3 vols. Philadelphia: Record Publishing Co., 1898.

Willson, Seelye A. "The Growth of Pittsburgh Iron and Steel." *Magazine of Western History* 2 (1885): 540–71.

Wilson, Erasmus, ed. *Standard History of Pittsburgh, Pennsylvania.* Chicago: H. R. Cornell & Co., 1898.

Winkler, John K. *Incredible Carnegie.* New York: Vanguard Press, 1931.

Wolf, Stephanie Grauman. *Urban Village: Population, Community, and Family Structure in Germantown, Pennsylvania, 1683–1800.* Princeton, N.J.: Princeton University Press, 1976.

Woodruff, A. M. and T. G. Alexander. *Success and Failure in Small Manufacturing.* Westport, Conn.: Greenwood Press, 1974. (Rpt., University of Pittsburgh Press, 1958.)

Woods, Robert. "Pittsburgh: An Interpretation." In *The Pittsburgh District: Civic Frontage.* Vol. 5 of *The Pittsburgh Survey,* edited by Paul Underwood Kellogg, 7–43. New York: Charities and Commons Publication Committee, 1914.

Woodworth, R. B. "The Evolution of Structural Steel." *Iron Age* (April 1912): 942–44.

Wright, Carroll D. "The Amalgamated Association of Iron and Steel Workers." *Quarterly Journal of Economics* 7 (July 1893): 400–432.

Young, Mary. "The Pittsburgh Chamber of Commerce and Allied Board of Trade in 1910." Seminar paper, History Department, University of Pittsburgh, 1964.

Zahavi, Gerald. "Negotiated Loyalty: Welfare Capitalism and the Shoeworkers of Endicott Johnson, 1920–1940." *JAH* 70 (December 1983): 102–20.

INDEX

CPSIA information can be obtained
at www.ICGtesting.com
Printed in the USA
FFOW04n0342260216
21752FF